Developing Quality Complex Database Systems: Practices, Techniques and Technologies

Shirley A. Becker
Florida Institute of Technology, USA

IDEA GROUP PUBLISHING
Hershey • London • Melbourne • Singapore

Acquisition Editor:	Mehdi Khosrowpour
Managing Editor:	Jan Travers
Development Editor:	Michele Rossi
Copy Editor:	Amy Poole & Maria Boyer
Typesetter:	Tamara Gillis
Cover Design:	Deb Andree
Printed at:	Sheridan Books

Published in the United States of America by
    Idea Group Publishing
    1331 E. Chocolate Avenue
    Hershey PA 17033-1117
    Tel: 717-533-8845
    Fax: 717-533-8661
    E-mail: cust@idea-group.com
    Web site: http://www.idea-group.com

and in the United Kingdom by
    Idea Group Publishing
    3 Henrietta Street
    Covent Garden
    London WC2E 8LU
    Tel: 44 20 7240 0856
    Fax: 44 20 7379 3313
    Web site: http://www.eurospan.co.uk

Library of Congress Cataloging-in-Publication Data

Becker, Shirley A., 1956-
  Developing quality complex database systems : practices, techniques, and technologies
/ Shirley A. Becker.
    p. cm.
  Includes bibliographical references and index.
  ISBN 1-878289-88-8 (paper)
  1. Database design. I. Title.

QA76.9.D26 B43 2001
005.74--dc21

                              00-054189
British Cataloguing in Publication Data
A Cataloguing in Publication record for this book is available from the British Library.

NEW from Idea Group Publishing

- ❏ **Developing Quality Complex Database Systems: Practices, Techniques and Technologies/** Shirley Becker, Florida Institute of Technology/ 1-878289-88-8
- ❏ **Human Computer Interaction: Issues and Challenges/**Qiyang Chen, Montclair State University/ 1-878289-91-8
- ❏ **Our Virtual World: The Transformation of Work, Play and Life via Technology/**Laku Chidambaram, University of Oklahoma, and Ilze Igurs/1-878289-92-6
- ❏ **Text Databases and Document Management:Theory and Practice/**Amita Goyal Chin, Virginia Commonwealth University/1-878289-93-4
- ❏ **Computer-Aided Method Engineering: Designing CASE Repositories for the 21st Century/**Ajantha Dahanayake, Delft University/ 1-878289-94-2
- ❏ **Managing Internet and Intranet Technologies in Organizations: Challenges and Opportunities/**Subhasish Dasgupta, George Washington University/1-878289-95-0
- ❏ **Information Security Management: Global Challenges in the New Millennium/**Gurpreet Dhillon, University of Nevada Las Vegas/1-878289-78-0
- ❏ **Telecommuting and Virtual Offices: Issues & Opportunities/**Nancy J. Johnson, Capella University/1-878289-79-9
- ❏ **Managing Telecommunications and Networking Technologies in the 21st Century: Issues and Trends/**Gerald Grant, Carleton University/-878289-96-9
- ❏ **Pitfalls and Triumphs of Information Technology Management/**Mehdi Khosrowpour/1-878289-61-6
- ❏ **Data Mining and Business Intelligence: A Guide to Productivity/**Stephan Kudyba and Richard Hoptroff/1-930708-03-3
- ❏ **Internet Marketing Research: Theory and Practice/**Ook Lee, University of Nevada Las Vegas/1-878289-97-7
- ❏ **Knowledge Management & Business Model Innovation/**Yogesh Malhotra/1-878289-98-5
- ❏ **Strategic Information Technology: Opportunities for Competitive Advantage/**Raymond Papp, Quinnipiac University/1-878289-87-X
- ❏ **Design and Management of Multimedia Information Systems: Opportunities and Challenges/** Syed Mahbubur Rahman, Minnesota State University/1-930708-00-9
- ❏ **Internet Commerce and Software Agents: Cases, Technologies and Opportunities/**Syed Mahbubur Rahman, Minnesota State University, and Robert J. Bignall, Monash University/ 1-930708-01-7
- ❏ **Environmental Information Systems in Industry and Public Administration/** Claus Rautenstrauch and Susanne Patig, Otto-von-Guericke University Magdeburg/ 1-930708-02-5
- ❏ **Strategies for Managing Computer Software Upgrades/**Neal G. Shaw, University of Texas Arlington/1-930708-04-1
- ❏ **Unified Modeling Language: Systems Analysis, Design and Development Issues/** Keng Siau, University of Nebraska-Lincoln and Terry Halpin, Microsoft Corporation/ 1-930708-05-X
- ❏ **Information Modeling in the New Millennium/**Keng Siau, University of Nebraska-Lincoln and Matti Rossi, Helsinki School of Economics/ 1-878289-77-2
- ❏ **Strategies for Healthcare Information Systems/**Robert Stegwee and Ton Spil, University of Twente/ 1-878289-89-6
- ❏ **Qualitative Research in IS: Issues and Trends/** Eileen M. Trauth, Northeastern University/ 1-930708-06-8
- ❏ **Information Technology Evaluation Methods and Management/**Wim Van Grembergen, University of Antwerp/1-878289-90-X
- ❏ **Managing Information Technology in a Global Economy** (2001 Proceedings)/Mehdi Khosrowpour/1-930708-07-6

Excellent additions to your library!

Developing Quality Complex Database Systems: Practices, Techniques and Technologies

Table of Contents

Preface

Database practices, techniques and technologies continue to play a significant role in riding the increasingly turbulent wave of technological advances. The Internet is having a major impact on information sharing in a global marketplace. Advances in science and engineering fields have resulted in an explosion of information that must be effectively modeled and managed. Legacy software systems have vast amounts of data ready for analysis and interpretation. These are just a few examples of the opportunities and challenges associated with today's database systems.

Effective mechanisms for collection, storage, retrieval, analysis and dissemination of information are needed to take advantage of technological breakthroughs. Data complexity issues need to be addressed such as, security, maintainability, completeness and correctness, in order to minimize the risks associated with these new technologies. Innovations in database practices, techniques and technology are needed to meet the increasing challenges of this new decade.

The objective of this book is to share innovative and groundbreaking database concepts as proposed by the contributing authors. The concepts proposed in these chapters provide a foundation for continuous improvements in the database field. The diversity of coverage includes quality and organizational issues, measurement systems, design and implementation methods, data warehousing and mining techniques, data modeling and reengineering techniques, security and enhanced query capabilities. Each of these chapters is briefly described.

In the chapter entitled, "Organizational Concepts and Measures for the Evaluation of Data Modeling," Ronald Maier presents an organizational perspective on data modeling. His discussion of the evaluation of data modeling is based on existing theoretical approaches and his empirical studies. The chapter proposes that data modeling should include both project-driven activities and enterprise-wide activities inclusive of long-term goals. It also points out the need for focusing on organizational issues associated with data modeling inclusive of process and product perspectives of quality.

In "Dimensions of Database Quality," John Hoxmeier reminds us that data quality is a critical issue because databases are part of virtually all conventional and e-business applications. He points out the need for a comprehensive set of quality dimensions in order to be successful in the development of high-quality database systems. In addition to process and data factors, it is proposed that quality dimensions include model and behavioral factors, as these are not typically part of data quality assessment. A framework is presented, which allows for an assessment of process, data, model and behavior quality dimensions. A test case is used to illustrate the application of the proposed framework.

Coral Calero, Mario Piattini and Marcela Genero address an important but mostly overlooked issue of metrics for assessing database complexity. They propose internal measures in their chapter, "Metrics for Controlling Database Complexity," for assessing the quality of database systems. These measures characterize the complexity of a database in order to promote data quality. The focus of the chapter is on the measurement of complexity that affects the maintainability of the relational, object-relational and active database schemas. The authors are expanding upon their work in collaboration with industry and public organizations.

In "Integrating Hypermedia Functionality into Database Applications," Bhaumik et al. describe their research efforts at exploring all aspects of hypermedia support for database applications. They propose that a dynamic hypermedia engine (DHE) be used to automate features associated with database systems inclusive of Web technology. One such feature is the automatic generation of links based on the database's conceptual schema with its original specification. This technology allows for the developer to specify which kinds of database elements are related to diverse elements in the same application, other database applications or other software systems. It is proposed that data warehousing and data mining be incorporated into this technology.

Many of today's database systems require the processing of large volumes of data in order to support the discovery of new knowledge. In "Optimization of the Knowledge Discovery Process in Very Large Databases," Mehdi Owrang discusses how today's vast amount of data makes the discovery process computationally expensive. It is proposed that domain knowledge be used to reduce the size of the database and to optimize the hypothesis, thus eliminating implied, unnecessary and redundant conditions. The resulting benefits include greater efficiency and the discovery of meaningful, non-redundant and consistent rules.

Data warehousing is the focus of Ladjel Bellatreche, Kamalakar Karlapalem and Mukesh Mohania's chapter on, "Some Issues in Design of Data Warehousing Systems." The authors tell us that data warehousing can assist intelligent decision-making in order to improve the functioning of an organization. Several trade-offs associated with data warehousing designs are discussed inclusive of materialized views, partitioning a data warehouse and index selection to efficiently execute queries. A study is described which addresses these issues, and the findings are shared.

"Data Mining for Supply Chain Management in Complex Networks: Concepts, Methodology and Applications" describes data mining concepts, its methodology and its application in the context of supply chain management of complex networks. Manoj Singh and Mahesh Raisinghani help us make sense of data mining as a set of techniques used to uncover previously obscure or unknown patterns and relationships in very large databases. The authors describe supply chain management with its data complexity, which can be facilitated by data mining.

Relational databases and the current SQL standard are poorly suited to support hierarchical data. Ido Millet, in "Accommodating Hierarchies in Relational Databases," describes techniques to address the data retrieval and maintenance problems posed by hierarchical data structures. Data denormalization is proposed as a means of addressing these problems. But there are costs associated with this approach. The chapter describes how these costs can be avoided using processing logic in the form of triggers.

The chapter by Esperanza Marcos and Paloma Caceres is appropriately entitled, "Object-Oriented Database Design," because it reviews the state-of-the-art in database design for object-relational and object database technologies. The SQL: 1999 and Object Database Management Group (ODMG) object models are summarized in terms of their advantages and disadvantages. An example illustrates the difficulty of using the relational model to represent complex objects and relationships. It is also used to show the how the object-relational and object databases address this complexity.

In "INTECoM: An Integrated Approach to the Specification and Design of Information Requirements," a framework is presented, which was developed to utilize the strength of existing data modeling approaches while compensating for their weaknesses. Clare Atkins presents this framework as a means of using existing techniques as matched by specific requirements of analysis and design. Though it needs further study in an organizational setting, it encompasses an already-recognized framework for database development, doesn't require much in the way of new skills, methods and techniques, and may prove extremely useful for less experienced practitioners, Atkins points out.

The chapter entitled, "Inclusion Dependencies," offers insight into reengineering techniques for quality improvement of existing database systems. Laura Rivero, Jorge Doorn and Viviana Ferragine point out that many of today's database systems have been poorly designed or may have become flawed when physical objects are removed. As a result, database quality suffers until it is re-engineered. The authors provide heuristics to redesign the conceptual schema, which are based on the identification of hidden business rules and the conversion of non-key inclusion dependencies into key-based ones.

Cheryl Dunn and Severin Grabski present a normative semantic model for enterprise information systems in their chapter on "Semantically Modeled Databases in Integrated Enterprise Information Systems." This work focuses on the fact that huge investments have been made in enterprise resource planning (ERP) systems, and more value could be realized if databases semantically reflected the underlying reality of organizations. They review empirical research on semantically modeled information systems and then provide an example of a semantic model as proof of concept. They expand this discussion to include the model's application to ERP and inter-organizational systems.

Mohammad Dadashzadeh presents a generalized approach to formulating set comparison queries in SQL, in "Set Comparison Queries in SQL." This generalized approach can be used to teach advanced users how to formulate complex set comparison queries in on-line analytical processing scenarios.

In "Toward a Framework for Advanced Query Processing," Suk-Chung Yoon presents a method for advanced query processing. The author's approach provides a simple and reasonable way of incorporating user's needs and preferences into query processing. Instead of relying on conventional queries, Yoon proposes that flexible and intensional query processing techniques be used in order include concepts at different levels of abstraction.

In the chapter, "Security in Database Systems: A State of the Art," Eduardo Fernandez-Medina and Mario Piattini address the very important security issue associated with today's technological advances. The Internet, electronic business and data warehousing are a few of the technologies that have shown the need for security considerations early in the development lifecycle. The authors provide a synthesis of the principal aspects that affect confidentiality in the design of databases: control of access, modeling of security requirements and a retrospective view of the important generations of methods for the development of security techniques. They introduce a methodology through which multilevel databases can be designed, while taking into consideration confidentiality requisites and risk management factors.

"A Case Study of the Military Utility of Telemedicine" focuses on the need for implementation of telemedicine at a strategic level in the military. This success of telemedicine efforts requires systematic analysis and effective technology management inclusive of database systems. This chapter differs from the others in that it summarizes a case study with insights into the complexities associated with telemedicine and supporting technologies. David Paper, James Rodger and Parag Pendharkar present methodologies for investigating military utility of telemedicine, and summarize initial lessons learned.

In summary, this book offers an exciting opportunity to find out about current practices, techniques and technologies to meet the needs of today's software and information systems.

Acknowledgment

The editor would like to acknowledge the help of all persons involved in the collation and review process of this book. The authors not only did a remarkable job of ensuring that high quality chapters were created, but many served as referees for chapters written by other authors. Thanks to all of you who have provided constructive and comprehensive reviews. A note of thanks to Mehdi Khosrowpour, who saw a need for this book, and to the staff at Idea Group Publishing for their guidance and professional support. A special thanks goes to David and Marissa Fassino for their unfailing encouragement and patience.

Chapter I

Organizational Concepts and Measures for the Evaluation of Data Modeling

Ronald Maier
University of Regensburg, Germany

ABSTRACT

This chapter presents a concept for the evaluation of data modeling which is based on existing theoretical approaches and three empirical studies conducted or supervised by the author. The main results of these studies with respect to evaluation suggest to extend existing approaches for the evaluation of data models. It is necessary to focus more on organizational issues of data modeling, more on process instead of product quality, to consider different application scenarios of data modeling as well as to distinguish the enterprise-wide evaluation of data modeling from the evaluation of single projects using data modeling. The evaluation concept presented here focuses on the evaluation of single data modeling projects and consists of recommendations for the evaluation procedure, persons involved, instruments, the design of important organizational dimensions as well as some concrete measures of process and product quality.

INTRODUCTION

In a time where the amount of data managed in organizations explodes at an ever-increasing speed, issues of data management become more and more important.

With the advent of advanced database and data warehouse technologies, the evaluation of models and architectures that are built as blueprints for the solutions to be developed, administrated and/or maintained becomes a critical issue. Unfortunately, both in the literature and practice, the state-of-the-art concerning the evaluation of data modeling, as the most established method used in this field, is up to now restricted to a more or less extensive list of desirable attributes of a data model. It remains uncertain which attributes should be focused on in case of conflicts, to which part a single attribute contributes to goals and in particular how these attributes can be embedded into a comprehensive model for the evaluation of data modeling.

Empirical Studies on Data Modeling and Data Management

Despite the large number of papers in the field of data modeling, there is hardly an author who went to the trouble of conducting an empirical field analysis of the subject. Most empirical studies are laboratory studies, with students acting as surrogates for expert or novice data modelers, testing different notations used to display data structures or different data modeling methods. Empirical field studies were conducted mainly in the '80s in the U.S. and the early '90s in Europe, and neither investigated broadly data administration and data management or dealt exclusively with methods and tools (refer to Maier 1996b, for a list of empirical studies on the subject). The starting point for the author's empirical and theoretical work was the fact that there was little documented knowledge about the use of data modeling within companies and organizations. Thus, the author carried out or supervised three empirical studies on data modeling and related areas which are described briefly in the following. These studies, together with the author's own experiences in concrete data modeling projects, were the main sources of knowledge which were used to design the evaluation concept laid out in this chapter.

Study 1: Quality of data modeling

In 1995-96 the author carried out an empirical study on "benefits and quality of data modeling" (see Maier, 1996b for an overview of the results, see also Maier, 1996a for the detailed results in German). This study consisted of a broad questionnaire and of personal interviews with experienced practitioners. The main part of the study was a broad questionnaire. Before the questionnaire, a series of interviews was used to improve the questionnaire and to clarify the research problem. Another series of interviews was conducted after the questionnaire in order to gain more knowledge about the state-of-the-art of data modeling. The sample consisted of 324 German companies with over 5,000 employees, and 261 German software houses and consulting companies with over 50 employees. Eighty-nine respondents filled out the questionnaire resulting in a response rate of 15.2%.

Study 2: Organization of data management

In 1998 the author (see Grupppp, 1998) supervised a follow-up empirical study, which focused on the organizational design of data management, its tasks, roles and processes. The main goal of this study was to evaluate the state-of-the-art of data management in German enterprises in the late '90s. The study consisted of a series of personal interviews with data managers in big German companies which had indicated the application of extensive data modeling in Study 1. We got a comprehensive list of data management tasks and related them to the goals of data management.

Study 3: Benchmarking in data management

In 1999 the author (see Holzhammer, 1999) supervised and participated in a second follow-up study, which aimed at exploring factors and values for a comprehensive benchmarking in data management. The study employed a questionnaire (in English) which was distributed at the European conference of an international user group in the database area. Seven-hundred database administrators and data managers received the questionnaire as part of the information material for the conference. Twenty-two respondents filled out the questionnaire resulting in a response rate of 3.1%. This is a very low rate, however; we estimated that only approximately 250 organizations participated with multiple employees per organization. As we asked for only one questionnaire per organization, the "real" response rate was somewhere near 10%.

The latter two studies were mainly intended to gain further insight into the organizational part of the evaluation or assessment of data modeling. The results of these studies imply that problems in the quality of data modeling become serious only in more complex environments, especially when employees from different organizational units are involved and various projects using data models have to be integrated. All three studies showed the importance of organizational issues in data modeling as opposed to the relative unimportance of technical issues of how to use data modeling tools or which data modeling constructs or notation to use, e.g., the academic discussion about whether to use the original ER approach or an extension thereof. As data modeling efforts in the organization varied widely, the studies revealed the importance of considering the context in the form of application scenarios when evaluating data models (see next section).

Goals and Procedure

The goals of this chapter are:
- to give a brief survey of approaches for the evaluation of quality in data modeling,
- to motivate an extension of existing approaches for the evaluation to consider application scenarios and the organizational context of data modeling, and
- to present a concept for the evaluation of data modeling based on the results of the empirical studies described above.

The next section briefly surveys existing approaches of the evaluation of data modeling. It also provides a motivation for a change in the focus of data model quality from product quality to the quality of the process of development and application of data models. Moreover, a classification of enterprise-wide data modeling efforts is proposed based on a matrix model. Then we focus on the evaluation of process quality of an individual project using data modeling. Next, the section presents a set of measures for process and product quality which can be used to guide an evaluation. The final section summarizes the main findings and presents a brief outlook at future development opportunities.

EXTENDING THE EVALUATION
OF DATA MODELING

The term data model represents different concepts in the relevant literature (for a review of definitions of the terms "model" and "data," see Lehner et al., 1995). In general, the term data model denotes either a method for describing data structures (instrument for modeling) or the results of the application of this method (result of modeling, see Heinrich and Roithmayr, 1992, 148). In this chapter the latter term is used: a data model describes the data items of a certain part of the perceived reality, the business domain, relevant for a specific application or a specific group of users in a structured way. This model includes the relationships between the data items. Referring to Juran's general definition of quality (Juran and Gryna, 1988, 2.3ff), we consider the quality of data models as the match between the data model and the requirements of its users with regard to the defined application areas of data models. The definition of quality criteria for data models always has to consider the requirements defined by the application context.

The approaches on quality of data models in the literature can be categorized into the following groups:

Group 1–Quality Frameworks: The authors of the first group attempt to develop a comprehensive frame for quality of data modeling (e.g., Lindland et al., 1994; Krogstie et al., 1995). Reinruber and Gregory, 1994; Moody and Shanks, 1994).

Group 2–Quality Characteristics: This group develops concrete proposals for the assessment and improvement of individual aspects of data models defining desirable characteristics and criteria for data models (e.g., Batini et al., 1992; Hars, 1994; Heilandt et al., 1993; Marche, 1993; Zamperoni and Löhr-Richter, 1994).

Group 3–Quality Approaches: The third group does not affect the quality of data models directly. This group either develops approaches or methods to support the process of data modeling, the application of which should result in better models.

These approaches to the quality of data modeling lack integration and agreement among one another as well as with related concepts, such as software engineering or project management. For example, the quality frameworks are altogether at a very high level of abstraction and only define quality areas. They do not take into account single quality characteristics, nor do they provide help to integrate quality measures and variables into their areas. However, integrating the very high-level quality frameworks with single characteristics would be a complex undertaking which would need extensive empirical data to define desirable values for each measure.

As for the integration with software engineering and project management, I suppose that the main reason why these approaches are not integrated is that both the corresponding researchers and practitioners belong to different communities--the database community and the software engineering or software development community. Study 1 even revealed that in many organizations, data management and application development are two completely separate organizational units with different, often conflicting goals. These were most often long term and focused on the whole organization in the case of data management, and short term and focused on a single project in the case of application development.

Furthermore these concepts do not take into account the following three points, which were found highly important with respect to their influence on the quality of data models in the empirical studies mentioned above:
- different application scenarios of data modeling within organizations,
- organizational design of data modeling and the organizational units involved in data modeling,
- quality of data modeling is not the same as quality of data models.

The author uses these starting points for the definition of his quality concept of data modeling (for a detailed analysis of the related literature and the results of the empirical study, see Ma [1996a; 1996b]).

Consideration of Application Scenarios

In the questionnaire of Study 1, "Quality of Data Modeling," the participants had to scale 64 application fields in two ways: firstly, the (hypothetic) importance of a certain application field for the person answering (target value) had to be estimated using a five-point scale with 5="very important" and 1="not important." Secondly, the "real" benefit for the organization the person works for (actual value) had to be estimated using a five-point scale with 5="benefits are realized very strongly" and 1="benefits are not realized in our organization." The averages of the respondents' estimations for the 64 application fields in the questionnaire were aggregated to 12 application areas which are shown in Table 1. The aggregation was done by averaging the averages of the single application fields for each application area. Table 1 shows the means of the target values (target means) and the actual values (actual means) per application area, as well as the differences between these two figures. Generally, the differences between the respondents' estimations of actual values were significantly lower than the estimations of the target values (statistical test: t-test, level of significance for the differences between target and actual mean for all application fields < 0,001, number of valid cases between 36 and 43). For detailed results refer to Maier (1996a).

Note that data modeling turns out to be more important as an organization instrument outside the IT department than within it. The value of "means for improving communication" is quite low, even though one of the major advantages usually attributed to this method is its good applicability for communicating data structures. When reviewing the application fields in detail, it turns out that the value for "communication within the project team" is very high (4.12) whereas the value for "communication to managers, to external persons and to other organizations" is low (3.22).

The low actual value for "basis for the use of standard software" is not surprising if we take into account that the study was conducted in 1995-96. Not surprisingly in the follow-up studies this area showed increased importance. Generally, the actual mean shows that in the view of the persons answering significant benefits are gained in several different application areas by the use of data modeling. However, the standard deviations for all application areas are quite high, showing that different organizations use data modeling for different application areas. This result was supported by the personal interviews which revealed several application scenarios for data modeling (see below). The column "differences between means" gives an indication of the potentials of data modeling as perceived by the respondents: the higher the value, the higher the potentials of data modeling.

To summarize, the situations in which data modeling is used within organizations fall into several distinct categories. It is not possible to determine one single scenario for the application of data modeling. The term data modeling has a different meaning in nearly every organization, and often the meaning changes even between different organizational units within the same organization. The following ideal application scenarios of data modeling were extracted by means of building clusters

Table 1. Means of target and actual values per application area and differences between the means (ordered by target means)

application area	target means	actual means	differences between means
basis for database design or physical data organization respectively	4.17	3.19	0.98
instrument for standardization	4.17	2.94	1.23
basis for management information systems (MIS)	4.05	2.67	1.38
basis for the integration within the IT department	3.98	2.69	1.29
basis for the development of application systems	3.96	3.02	0.94
organization instrument outside the IT department	3.83	2.42	1.41
means for reduction of maintenance costs	3.79	2.70	1.09
basis for the use of standard software	3.69	2.25	1.44
means for improving communication	3.68	2.56	1.12
basis for the use of application systems in functional departments	3.62	2.39	1.23
means for improving motivation/acceptance	3.39	2.53	0.86
organization instrument in the IT department	3.18	2.20	0.98

of organizations engaged in different application areas. For each application scenario, the application areas which are focused most are given:

- *Data modeling within projects for the development of application systems*: basis for the development of application systems, basis for database design or physical data organization respectively, means for reduction of maintenance costs.
- *Support of integration within the IT department*: basis for the integration within the IT department, basis for the use of standard software, organization instrument in the IT department, instrument for standardization in the IT department.
- *Improvement of communication between functional departments and the IT department*: means for improving communication, means for improving motivation/acceptance, basis for the use of application systems in functional departments, instrument for standardization in the functional departments.
- *Data modeling as an organizational instrument*: organizational instrument in the IT department, basis for management information systems – MIS.

Consideration of the Organizational Design

Data modeling methods and instruments are well known and accepted in many of the organizations, at least by data modelers and database designers. Even though functional specialists and application designers often do not know the method as well, the technical application of methods and instruments does not cause a lot of difficulties, as data modeling personnel usually train or help them, or participate in the respective projects. In all the organizations visited by the author, the technical expertise of data management personnel was high. However, organizations face serious problems regarding the design of an organizational context suitable for data modeling. In the following an example of the difficulties organizations have concerning the organizational design of data modeling is discussed.

Figure 1 shows a set of responsibility areas for data modeling. The questionnaire of Study 1, "Quality of Data Modeling," required the naming of the organizational unit in charge of each responsibility area. Apart from the option "no responsibility defined," the questions were open. Figure 1 shows the share of responsibility of data administration, application development, functional departments as well as other units (number of respondents between 41 and 43 per question).

Note the very small share of responsibility attributed to the functional departments. Even regarding the contents of data models, it is the department responsible for the development of applications which is responsible in far more cases than the functional departments. In none of the companies in this sample were the functional departments responsible for norms--both norms specific to the organization and external norms--education and training as well as problems with methods and tools. Most of the time the main task of data administration is the integration process with respect to the contents of the data models and the resolving of conflicts about contents, for example between different functional departments. The main areas of

Figure 1. Responsibility for data modeling tasks according to selected organizational units

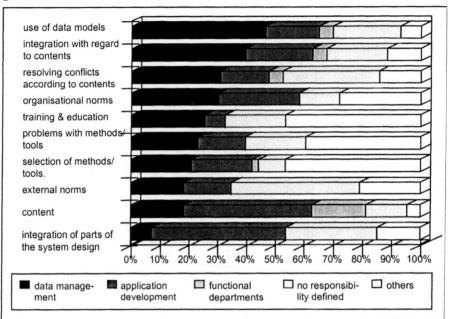

responsibility attributed to the application development team are the content of the data models and the integration of the individual parts of the system design, for example the functional decomposition, the data flow diagram and the entity relationship model. Note that a substantial share of companies have not defined responsibilities for such central areas as content of data models or the selection of methods and tools to be used.

The application of data modeling, and therefore its quality, is highly dependent on the organizational context. Thus, it is very important that an evaluation of data modeling takes into account the organizational design of the data modeling effort.

Quality of Data Modeling is More Than Quality of Data Models

Quality of data modeling is not the same as quality of data models. In former approaches to assure and assess quality of data models, the product quality–quality of data models–was considered almost exclusively. Data modeling as it is used in most organizations is a method which supports the process of adaptation, standardization and integration in the development of application systems (see Maier, 1996a). During this process the individual perceptions and understandings of the members of the organization involved are brought together, discussed and integrated.

Figure 2 shows the classification of the evaluation into the two dimensions *focus of analysis* and *organizational scope,* and gives some examples of areas to be evaluated. The focus of analysis of organizational data modeling is divided into process quality and product quality. Process quality is the quality of the development

Figure 2. Examples of areas of data modeling to be evaluated according to focus of analysis and organizational scope

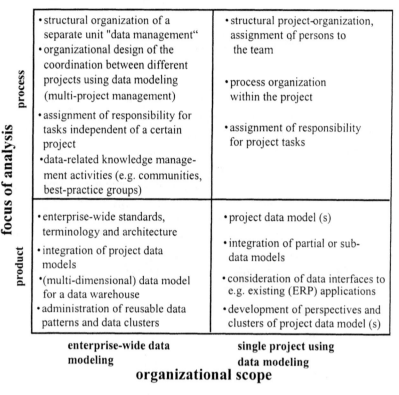

	enterprise-wide data modeling	**single project using data modeling**
process	• structural organization of a separate unit "data management" • organizational design of the coordination between different projects using data modeling (multi-project management) • assignment of responsibility for tasks independent of a certain project • data-related knowledge management activities (e.g. communities, best-practice groups)	• structural project-organization, assignment of persons to the team • process organization within the project • assignment of responsibility for project tasks
product	• enterprise-wide standards, terminology and architecture • integration of project data models • (multi-dimensional) data model for a data warehouse • administration of reusable data patterns and data clusters	• project data model (s) • integration of partial or sub-data models • consideration of data interfaces to e.g. existing (ERP) applications • development of perspectives and clusters of project data model (s)

focus of analysis (vertical axis), **organizational scope** (horizontal axis)

and application of data models. Product quality is considered the quality of the results of the modeling process. Moreover, along the dimension organizational scope, we have to distinguish between an enterprise-wide assessment of data modeling and the assessment of an individual project using data modeling.

Due to the assumed high importance of the processes of developing and applying data models in projects, this chapter is limited to the evaluation of the process and product quality of single data modeling projects. One might refer to Maier (1996a), Holzhammer (1999) and Schwinn et al. (1998) for an assessment of the other two matrix areas.

ORGANIZATIONAL CONCEPTS FOR THE EVALUATION OF THE PROCESS QUALITY OF DATA MODELING

Six organizational dimensions can be identified as key factors influencing data management in general and the quality of data modeling. Data management is represented by a set of data management tasks which were found in the empirical studies–data architecture, data modeling, data administration, database administration, data analysis, data warehousing, Web data management and data security. The organizational design of these tasks influences the quality of data modeling which in turn influences the quality of the resulting models (refer to Figure 3).

The "dimensions" represent perspectives on the organizational context of data modeling. There are also interdependencies between the perspectives, which have to be considered.

In the following, we discuss how to proceed in an evaluation of data modeling and what persons should be involved. The next sections discuss the evaluation of the process quality for a single data modeling project with the help of the six dimensions mentioned above (see Maier,1999).

The following groups of employees can be involved in the evaluation of data modeling projects:
- members of the project team: e.g., application developers, employees of the functional departments involved, data administrators or experienced data modelers involved in the project such as "consultants," database developers;
- members of other project teams who also perform tasks of data modeling;
- data administrators and experienced data modelers who are not involved in the individual project but who are responsible for assuring quality of data modeling;

Figure 3. Dimensions of the organizational design of the data modeling environment and their effects on the quality of data modeling and the quality of data models

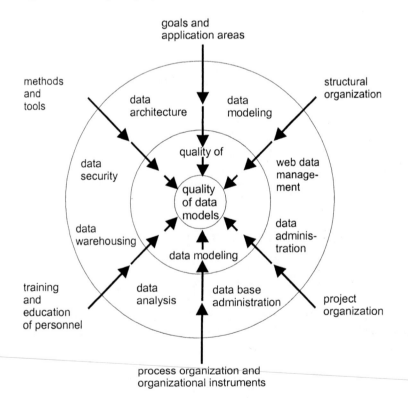

- employees involved in quality control;
- externals: data modeling experts external to the organization.

The assessment by each of these groups has advantages and disadvantages. The advantage of the assessment by *project members* is that they have the best knowledge of the area to be modeled as well as of the process of modeling. A disadvantage is the missing objectivity concerning the project to be assessed.

In the second case employees of different projects assess each other's data models (a kind of peer review). This results in potential advantages concerning the integration of data modeling projects. The data modelers become attentive to the problems of other teams. If the models that have to be assessed are selected appropriately, the data modelers gain knowledge about models that are related to their own models. Also they are best suited to evaluate the interfaces and overlaps between their own models and the models that have to be assessed. On the other hand, conflicts between the teams may arise that may lead to inefficiencies.

Data administrators and experienced data modelers can assess the integration and consistency with already existing models very well. This is due to their independent, organization-wide perspective. Moreover, data administrators usually have good knowledge about the rules, regulations and guidelines, the methods and the standards to be considered. A comparably restricted knowledge about the details of the business domain to be modeled can take effect disadvantageously. On the one hand this causes the problem that data administrators do not make any or make only a few comments about the content of the data models. On the other hand the data modelers in the project team may reject their comments and suggestions, pointing to the lack of domain knowledge of the data administrators.

Employees involved in quality control know best about the implementation into an integrated organizational or IT-wide quality control system for application development. A disadvantage could be that employees involved in quality control do not have enough knowledge about the business domain represented in the data model and are usually not familiar with data modeling.

The assessment by externals bears the advantage of their assumed total independence. In addition there is low risk that the assessment causes conflicts with the assessed employees or groups of employees. On the other hand, it can be a disadvantage that the know-how won in the assessment leaves the organization and could be made available to competitors.

Table 2 shows recommended areas of evaluation for each of these groups. It is recommended to conduct the evaluation, not only by one group, but to include several groups in the evaluation procedure. The evaluations done by each of these groups are to be compiled and should be explained to the modelers in a meeting. Modelers and evaluators can decide on measures for improvement together.

Concerning the procedure of the assessment, we basically have to distinguish between tool-based (automated) quality assessment, reviews and subjective assessment by employees involved in data modeling or by non-members of the project team, for example by experienced data modelers. In general we will find a combination of all three types. As the availability of tool-based assessment increases the manual inspection concentrates more and more on the content-related criteria and the processes of development and use of data models.

When reviews are used the following guidelines regarding the schedule are suggested (see Reingruber and Gregory, 1994, 28f): at least two reviews should be done independent of the size of the modeling effort. After the final review is done, the team should have sufficient time to consider the suggestions for improvement. In more complex modeling projects, there should be one review per month. Additionally we suggest support of an analysis of the grade to which the goals are reached. Table 3 shows an estimation of the expected duration of the first review, depending on the size of the data model to be assessed. Note that only conceptual, not "technical," entity types are considered.

The duration of the review is influenced by several factors like goals and application areas of modeling, number and heterogeneity of the persons involved, importance of the model, size of the model, degree of completion, complexity of the business domain, type of the model (strategic or operational), number and experience of the reviewer and the tools used for the review (see Maier [1996a], 308f).

Goals and Application Areas of Data Modeling

Data modeling is used in several application areas in organizations. The organizational setup has to be chosen depending on the goals to be reached in a certain project using data modeling. If the goals and the application areas of data modeling are clearly defined, we expect an improvement of the motivation and the acceptance of all employees involved in the data modeling project, a precise and unambiguous design of the surrounding organizational dimensions as well as the avoidance of unproductive conflicts between the employees involved.

Table 2. Examples for evaluating groups with recommended areas to be evaluated

evaluating group	area to be evaluated
members of the project	representation of the business domain correct and complete, project goals reachable and sensible; project organization useful, cooperation with non-project members involved
members of other projects	interfaces (e.g., consistency, understandability); overlappings with other project data models correct and useful; coordination and cooperation with other teams
data administrators	re-use and re-usability; ease of integration and consistency, e.g., with enterprise-wide or departmental data models; standards, rules and regulations, descriptions complete and understandable
(software) quality assurance	integration of data modeling in the context of application development; comparing the quality of the resulting application system(s) to the quality of the data model(s)
externals (e.g., consultants)	application of methods and tools for data modeling; structural and process organization

Table 3. Estimated duration of the first review dependent on the size of the model (Reingruber & Gregory 1994)

size of the model	estimated duration of the review
50 entity types	ž 1 day
100 entity types	2-3 days
200 entity types	5-7 days
300 entity types	9-12 days

Goals, importance and application areas of data modeling can be stated in data modeling guidelines which have been derived from the results of Study 1, "Quality of Data Modeling," and Study 3, "Benchmarking in Data Management." Data modeling has to be directly related to modeling other views of the organization (e.g., function or process modeling). The guidelines could provide information about these areas:

- *Goals of data modeling*: IT-related goals (e.g., integration of application systems, support in the selection of standard software), goals related to functional departments (e.g., support of the understanding of data structures, extension of the data volume that can be requested autonomously by functional departments), goals of senior management (e.g., improvement of the decision support by management information systems and on-line analytical processing);
- *Persons and person groups who are involved in data modeling*: clear definition, restriction and coordination of roles of different groups involved (e.g., functional departments, application development, data administration) both during the development and use of data models;
- *Interdependence to IT strategy or to business strategy*: significance of the data in the organization and the contribution to the achievement of IT-related goals expected from data modeling (e.g., improvement of the time needed to answer requests of business partners by integration of application systems which is supported by data modeling);
- *Related areas*: to the modeling of other views, to integration of data modeling into a data life-cycle and to application system development;
- *Assurance of the support of the project*: by senior management, by defining the "ata modeling concept" obligatorily.

It is important that all participants and the representatives of all involved groups know about the guidelines. The ideal application scenarios identified in Study 1 can be used during the definition of the application areas.

Structural Organization

First we need to determine areas of responsibility regarding data modeling and then we need to assign these responsibilities to the employees and groups involved in data modeling. Responsibility for data modeling can be assigned to functional departments, application areas, projects to develop application systems or data modeling tasks. Most times a combination is reasonable.

Problems with the assignment of responsibility can occur especially if employees from different organizational departments co-develop a data model or if data models must be integrated. Table 4 proposes an assignment of responsibility to selected groups of employees. An evaluation can be based on this proposal.

A decision about the establishment of a separate organizational unit for data-related tasks (e.g., data management) depends on the role of data within the organization. Basically we can say that: The more varying and the more extensive the application areas of data modeling are,

- the more data modeling is used for integration and standardization, not only within the IT department;
- the more employees are involved in data modeling;
- the more employees with different professional experience are involved in data modeling;
- the more data models are used;
- the more reasonable it is to create a separate organizational unit for data-related tasks.

Table 4. Recommendation for assigning responsibility for data modeling to groups of employees (legend: C=consulting, Ca=carrying out, D=decision, E=examination)

area of responsibility	functional dept.	application development	data manage-ment	methods/ tools
selection of methods/tools	C	C	C	D/Ca
support for problems with methods/tools			Ca	Ca
observation of organizational norms		Ca, E	D, E	
observation of external norms		Ca, E	D, E	
(functional) content	D/Ca, E	C	C, E	
(structural) content		D/Ca, E	C, E	
resolving conflicts according to contents			D/Ca	
integration of partial data models with regard to contents	C	C	D/Ca	
integration with other parts of the systems design		D/Ca	C	
training and education			D/Ca	
use of data models	Ca	Ca	Ca, E	

Project Organization

Due to length constraints it is not possible to discuss general findings about project organization within this chapter. Here are some characteristics of the organization and suggestions particularly for the management of data modeling projects:

(1) Team formation and team composition

As shown earlier, there should be project-independent rules or guidelines available regarding how to form a data modeling team. The team members are to be recruited and their roles in the team are to be determined. The need for training has to be analyzed. The qualifications of potential team members can be compared to a standardized profile for data modelers. It seems to be important to determine all employees involved in data modeling who are not members of the data modeling team ("stakeholders"). This could be the heads of the departments from which employees are sent into the project team or specialists who will work with an application system to be implemented. The project-related goals and the relation to their work are to be pointed out to them in order to achieve acceptance and support for the project. Furthermore, regular information can keep the stakeholders up to date about project status and allow for feedback.

(2) Integration of the functional departments

There are several possibilities to involve functional departments in the development of data models. Up to now we discussed the role of certain employees from functional departments as regular members of the project team. Further possibilities are in the order of the frequency they appear in the organizations I surveyed: meetings, interviews, feedback sessions, document analyses, workshops, prototyping and questionnaires.

A general statement, about which form of involvement of the functional departments is the best, seems impossible. In the case of projects to develop application systems in limited areas with unambiguous requirements, and after consultation of the functional departments, application developers can do data modeling without involvement of other members of the organization. This does not necessarily cause quality problems and it results in lower costs.

In those cases in which data modeling focuses on standardization across departmental or even organizational borders, harmonization of interfaces, and is used to reach agreements between the project members involved, a combination of workshops with altering members, feedback sessions and–if application systems are to be developed–prototyping is considered the best solution.

Process Organization and Organizational Tools

The design of processes should be based on the methods used for data modeling. In some methods, a phase-oriented procedure is proposed (see, e.g., Ortner and Sollner, 1989, 34; Szidzek,1993, 164). However, most "methods" for data modeling are limited to structuring data and the graphic representation of data and data requirements (a notation). The description of an ideal process, which a project using data modeling should follow, is necessary in order to coordinate the work of employees involved in projects.

In order to guarantee the subsequent use of data models during implementation and in order to ensure the actuality of data models in a changing organizational environment the adjustment of parts of the data models (e.g., individual data elements) might be necessary. A central data dictionary or repository ensures the actuality of data definitions. Changes in the repository should be made only by certain persons at specified times (unfreezing-freezing). Tests should guarantee that no unwanted side effects occur.

Organizational instruments are used to state and document the decisions taken concerning organizational design of data modeling. The decisions are institutionalized in method manuals, tool manuals, guidelines for enterprise-wide standardization of data elements, organization-specific rules for data modeling (e.g., for the definition of names, for the use of elements of data modeling that are not provided in the methods used, for the integration and merging with other partial models and for the definition of the process), guidelines concerning the documentation of the history and the implementation of elements of data models, and guidelines for quality control.

In organizations in which several data modeling projects with different goals occur at the same time, a multi-level design of the organizational instruments--e.g., in organization-wide guidelines, guidelines for specific application areas and guidelines specific for user groups--are recommended. In addition to rules, guidelines and manuals, a part of coordination of data modeling can be covered by consistent application of the functions provided by data modeling tools.

Personnel Training and Education

There is limited information about the necessary education and professional experience of data modelers in the literature. The description of functions developed by the Swiss Union for Data Processing can be used as a source for the generation of job profiles (see SVD, 1993), in particular the job description of data administrator, database expert I-III as well as data architect I-II).

During the initial education, an introduction to the goals and application of data modeling has to be taught. Then a sense for data modeling should be communicated by means of easy examples. These examples should show that different data models, for example concerning the name selection, the structuring and the necessary degree of detail, can represent an optimal solution depending on the context of modeling.

After initial training, negotiation and agreement between several groups of employees should be simulated in case studies or role-plays. This demonstrates the most important challenges of data modeling and which approaches can be used to solve related problems.

Training and education should be designed with respect to the different groups of employees. Table 5 shows the knowledge assumed to be necessary for data modelers according to the employees' position in the organization. It has to be considered that different kinds of knowledge are important depending on the application scenario. The responsibilities could be distributed as shown in Table 5. Data management plays the role of a coordinator in the development of data models.

Methods and Tools

Methods and tools support the tasks of data modeling. They define a framework for the process of data modeling and for the participation of employees. They force them to stick to the rules and guidelines. Thus, they standardize the development of data models. Methods and tools have a significant impact on process and product quality of data modeling (see Szidzek, 1993,163).

Information about requirements for methods and instruments of data modeling can be found in Maier (1996a). The selection of methods and tools should not be done before the application context has been determined and the organizational framework of data modeling has been designed.

Groupware and knowledge management systems can be used to support communication, coordination and cooperation during the process of data modeling. Teamwork in data modeling projects is characterized by workshops or sessions, which can be supported by these technologies. Furthermore, it is conceivable to have virtual teams working synchronously and asynchronously on problem solutions in different locations.

The use of reference data models should have positive effects on the costs for development and maintenance of organization-specific data models. We expect

Table 5. Content of education and training and their priority according to groups of employees (5 = highest, 1 = lowest)

content of education and training	functional dept.	application developmt.	data mgmt.
DM methods	4	5	5
DM tools	3	5	5
DB systems	1	5	3
DB theory	1	5	3
communication	4	4	5
systems analysis & development	1	5	3
project management	1	3	5
business domain	5	3	3
quality management	5	5	5
didactics	1	1	5
organizational design	3	3	5
security	5	5	5

potential benefits for training and education, development and maintenance of data models from the application of reference data models (see Hars ,1994, 32ff).

When deciding about the use of a reference data model, the costs of the model have to be compared to the benefits. Due to strong regulations by law or by other requirements, many organizations use similar data structures (e.g., financial accounting, wage processing). In these organizations the use of reference data models can have great advantages. In areas in which organizations try to differentiate from their competition, the application of reference data models is not recommended. In particular it has to be considered that not only the resulting data models, but in particular the process of development and use of the data models generate benefits. This can be supported by the use of reference data models, but not replaced.

MEASURES FOR THE EVALUATION OF DATA MODELING

In the following sections, some measures that can be used to evaluate data modeling are presented. The measures can be categorized into measures of process quality and measures of product quality. These measures are still quite immature. Thus, a concrete evaluation of a data modeling effort always has to rely on a review done by knowledgeable experts, both in the field of data modeling and in the business domain which the data model represents. This review can be supported by checklists (see, e.g., Maier, 1996a). However, the following measures can be used to draw the attention of reviewers to specific areas in complex data modeling efforts where it is not economically feasible to review every detail of a model.

Measures of Process Quality

The assessment of development and application of data models up to now has not been supported by measures. It is important, however, to gain experiences about the effect of different configurations of the organizational dimensions in order to be able to estimate the quality of data modeling in a better way.

(1) Expenses/productivity

To give an estimation of productivity, the expenses of the development, the number of developers and the number of persons involved in a data modeling project have to be recorded. This has to be done separately for the different groups of employees, functional departments, application development, data administration and the group responsible for methods and tools. The costs of data modeling have to be assessed according to the following areas:

- expenses for employees who are responsible exclusively for data modeling (e.g., data administrators);
- expenses for team members per group of employees (e.g., functional departments, application development);

- expenses for external experts (e.g., experts who support the introduction of data modeling in the organization);
- expenses for hardware and software: (e.g., data modeling tools, workstations, communication system, printers);
- current expenses for the operation of the data modeling environment: (e.g., repair costs, costs for support by developers of the tools, paper, transfer costs, costs for the use of computers (mainframes);
- expenses for initial education and on-going training.

The costs determined can be compared with the expenses for the overall software or system design:

The number of elements developed per unit of time measures the productivity of data modeling. These elements can be entity types, relationship types or attributes depending on the type of data model (e.g., architecture or detailed model). We have to differentiate between productivity of the development of data models (PNEW) and productivity of the modification and extension of data models (PCHANGE). Additionally the number of conflicts about the meaning of terms solved and the number of standardized terms per unit of time can be used as dimensions of productivity.

(2) Variability

$$Variability(m) = \frac{Number\ of\ changed\ elements}{Number\ of\ elements\ *\ Time}$$

(3) Modeling environment

This examines the relationship between the data model and an implementation into an application system or a database system.

$$PNEW(m) = \frac{Number\ of\ newly\ developed\ entity\ types\ (or\ relationship\ types,\ attributes)\ (m)}{Number\ of\ person\ hours\ (m)}$$

$$PCHANGE(m) = \frac{Number\ of\ changed\ entity\ types\ (or\ relationship\ types,\ attributes)\ (m)}{Number\ of\ person\ hours\ (m)}$$

$$Implementation1(m) = \frac{Number\ of\ entity\ types(m)\ +\ Number\ of\ relationship\ types(m)}{Number\ of\ data\ base\ tables(db[m])}$$

$$Implementation2(m) = \frac{Number\ of\ attributes\ (m)}{Number\ of\ data\ base\ attributes(db[m])}$$

(4) Complexity of the application situation

The complexity is affected by:

- *person-oriented factors*: the number, the variation and the hierarchical classification of the groups of employees involved;
- *application-oriented factors*: the type, the number and the variation of the application areas, and the estimated grade of newness of the project (ratio of parts reused from other data models to newly modeled parts);
- *type of the model*: strategic versus functional data model.

The complexity of the modeling project can be related to the expenses.

Measures of Product Quality

In the literature, a number of measures of data model (product) quality can be found (see, e.g., Batini et al.,1992; Heilandt and Kruck,1993; Marche, 1993; Zamperoni and Löhr-Richter,1994). Unfortunately, so far these measures are not tied to application areas of data modeling which are supposed to influence the notion of product quality intensively, if not quite as much as was stated for process quality. Moreover, up to now these measures have not been empirically assessed as to their value for decision makers in concrete organizational settings. There are, however, a number of checklists, which can be used to evaluate project data models. An example for an amalgamated checklist for data models can be found in Maier (1996a). As opposed to these checklists the measures of product quality are quite immature at this moment. The following categories for measures can be distinguished:

- size of the data model;
- granularity and context of the model;
- complexity;
- method-oriented structure;
- content-oriented structure.

Some of the measures, especially concerning size, complexity and method-oriented structure, are well-described in the literature (see, e.g., Heilandt and Kruck,1993; Zamperoni and Löhr-Richter, 1994]). In the following some additional measures for product quality are suggested which were obtained on the basis of the empirical studies conducted and supervised by the author. As stated above these measures lack generality in the sense that they have to be adapted according to the concrete application situation of an organization that wishes to adapt the measures.

This is especially true for the definition of the variables used (e.g., entity type, relationship type, business object) and for the interpretation of values as good and bad.

(5) Size of a data model

The size can be judged using the number of elements in a data model, e.g., the number of entity types, relationship types, attributes, integrity constraints. These numbers can be weighed according to their relative importance/added complexity which varies depending on the data modeling method used and the application situation (see, e.g., Hars,1994).

(6) Granularity and context of the model

Scope represented in the model:
1: (part of an) application system/sub-project
2: application system/project
3: business process/department
4: (whole) organization
Granularity
1: detailed model
2: architecture

The dimension "granularity" can be measured using the ratio of attributes to entity types. Additionally, the existence of artificial elements which are used in some modeling methods on a detailed level (e.g., m:n-relationships have to be split into 1:m relationships) and the level of abstraction can be used to describe this continuum (see Figure 4).

In the following four measures for granularity are shown:

$$G\ 2(m) = \frac{number\ of\ attributes}{number\ of\ entity\ types} \qquad G\ 1(m) = \frac{number\ of\ relationship\ types}{number\ of\ entity\ types}$$

According to the definitions used for the terms "entity type" and "relationship

Figure 4. Granularity as a continuum

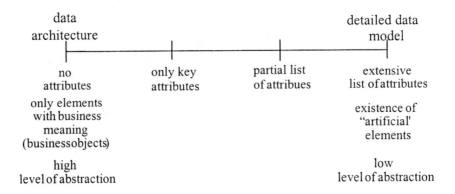

type," in some cases those relationship types that contain separate attributes have to be counted as entity types (see Hars, 1994, 224f).

$$G_4(m) = \frac{number\ of\ business\ objects}{number\ of\ entity\ types} \qquad G_3(m) = \frac{number\ of\ sub\text{-}entity\ types}{number\ of\ entity\ types}$$

Generality with respect to the business domain

The level of generality with respect to the business domain denotes the ratio of (specific) business-related terms used in the model as compared to the total number of terms used. The more specific terms are used, the lower the level of generality.

Context

$$Relative\ breadth\ of\ context\ (m) = \frac{number\ of\ entity\ types\ (or\ relationship\ types,\ attributes)}{number\ of\ organizational\ roles/positions\ involved}$$

The organizational roles or positions involved refer to those employees whose work processes or parts of their work processes are modeled. The same role (e.g., nurse) is counted only once.

The relative breadth of context shows how many elements of a data model are used to describe one single role or position. The lower this measure, the broader the context of modeling in relation to the size of the data model. The measure can also be applied to the number of business processes, organizational departments or divisions involved. The more different business processes, involved, the more important it is to standardize the terms used in the model throughout the domain (and the people) it represents.

$$Relative\ breadth\ of\ context\ (m) = \frac{number\ of\ entity\ types\ (or\ relationship\ types,\ attributes)}{number\ of\ business\ processes\ involved}$$

Harmony of detailing of the data model

In order to determine the harmony of the detailing of a data model, the number of generalization/specialization hierarchies is compared to the number of business objects. First we determine the average number of generalization/specialization hierarchies (AGH):

$$AGH(m) = \frac{\sum_{for\ all\ business\ objects\ BO} number\ of\ generalization\ hierarchies\ BO}{number\ of\ business\ objects}$$

Using this formula we can now determine the harmony of detailing of the data model (HoD):

$$HoD(m) = \sqrt{\frac{\sum\limits_{\text{for all business objects BO}} [(\text{number of generalization hierarchies}BO - AGH(m)]^2}{\text{number of business objects}}}$$

Using this measure special emphasis should be put on the analysis of those business objects of which the number of generalization hierarchies deviates most from the average.

(7) Method-oriented measures of structure

Heilandt and Kruck suggest the two measures "specialization" and "quality of structure" for a data model (see Heilandt and Kruck,1993). In the following some additional measures are suggested:

Quality of generalization

The measure "quality of generalization" can be used to evaluate recommendations for the modeling of generalizations. According to some recommendations as stated by participants of the empirical studies conducted and supervised by the author, good generalizations are those in which the specialized entity types contain many common and only a few different attributes and/or that the specialized entity types are processed by the same application functions and processes. In the following evaluation, a measure for the quality of generalization is presented which is based on these recommendations for modeling:

- the number of attributes in the generalized entity type should be greater than or equal to the average number of attributes in the specialized entity type, or
- the average number of attributes in the specialized entity types should be less than or equal to 3.

$$QoG(m) = \frac{card\{g \in G(m) \mid card\{attributes(g)\} \geq \varnothing \, card\{attributes(sp(g))\} \vee \varnothing \, card\{attributes(sp(g))\} \leq 3\}}{card\{G(m)\}}$$

QoG   quality of generalization
m   data model to be evaluated
g   generalized entity type (father entity type)
G(m)   set of generalized entity types in the model m
sp(g) set of specialized entity types to the entity type g
SP(G) set of specialized entity types to G(m)

The following measure uses the corresponding process model (stated in, e.g., event-driven process chain notation, see Scheer, 1998) in order to determine the quality of generalization:

$$QoG(m) = \frac{card\{g \in G(m) \mid \exists p \in P(m) \mid \forall e \in sp(g) \mid \exists p(e)\}}{card\{G(m)\}}$$

QoG   quality of generalization
m   data model to be evaluated
g   generalized entity type (father entity type)
G (m)   set of generalized entity types in the model m
sp (g)   set of specialized entity types to the entity type g
p (e)   process that uses entity type e
P (m)   set of processes in the process model corresponding to the data model m

Cohesion and coupling of areas in the data model

Cohesion and coupling are measures per area of the data model to be evaluated. The unit of analysis is an area. The breaking down of a data model into areas depends on the application situation. These measures can be used to find so-called "hot" areas with a high measure of coupling and also areas that are quite independent of the rest of the data model.

$$Cohesion(a) = \frac{number\ of\ relationship\ types\ within\ (a)}{number\ of\ entity\ types\ (a)}$$

a   area of a data model to be evaluated

$$Coupling(a) = \frac{number\ of\ relationship\ types\ between\ (a)}{number\ of\ connected\ areas\ (a)}$$

a   area of a data model to be evaluated

Degree of isolation

Entity types are termed isolated if they are not connected to any other element of the data model (relationship type or entity type).

$$DOI_1(m) = \frac{number\ of\ isolated\ entity\ types\ *\ 100}{number\ of\ entity\ types}$$

Entity types are termed "dangling" (see Batini, Ceri & Navathe, 1992) if they are only connected with one single other element of the data model (relationship type or entity type).

$$DOI_2(m) = \frac{number\ of\ "dangling"\ entity\ types\ *\ 100}{number\ of\ entity\ types}$$

The degree of isolation of a data model can then be written as follows:

$$DOI\,(m) = DOI_1(m) + DOI_2(m)$$

(8) Content-oriented measures of structure

These measures consider the semantics, the meaning of the elements of the data model. As opposed to the method-oriented measures of structure, this area is in large part still subject to the subjective assessment of a person evaluating the data model. This person has to have profound knowledge about the domain modeled.

Level of abstraction

The level of abstraction represents the relation between the number of business terms in the requirements definition as outcome of requirements analysis, and the number of entity types and relationship types in the resulting data model. Business term in this sense corresponds to a term as used in the work processes analyzed. Examples are customer, product, order, contract, account and the like.

$$LoA\,(m) = \frac{number\ of\ entity\ types\,(m) + number\ of\ relationship\ types\,(m)}{number\ of\ business\ terms\ (RA(m))}$$

$RA(m)$ documentation of the requirements analysis phase of a software development project

It is supposed that the higher the level of abstraction, the more difficult it is for functional experts who are not experts in data modeling to understand the model.

Relationship to business objects

The following measures show how detailed a data model is with respect to business objects. It is especially interesting to compute the standard deviation for these measures. Those business objects should be analyzed, specifically the measures of which deviate most from the average.

$$Structure2(m) = \frac{number\ of\ attributes}{number\ of\ business\ objects} \qquad Structure1(m) = \frac{number\ of\ entity\ types}{number\ of\ business\ objects}$$

CONCLUSION

What is quality of data modeling? How can quality be assessed and assured? These questions cannot be answered easily. Due to the varying nature of data modeling, no general concept for the evaluation of data models can be given. This chapter presents recommendations for the evaluation of important organizational dimensions, which influence the quality of data modeling. These recommendations have to be related to certain application situations and to the goals of data modeling. Ideal application scenarios were used to show the varying nature of the application of data modeling.

Moreover, it is not the quality of data models but the quality of data modeling that has to be focused on. The chapter suggests a categorization into process and product quality for the assessment of data modeling, as well as into single data modeling projects and enterprise-wide data modeling. A portion of data modeling activities is not directly related to projects to develop application systems, but is a part of the enterprise-wide data management and its long-term goals. In other words, it is part of the IT infrastructure and has to be separated from other expenses used for data modeling. Schwinn, et al. suggest a general checklist for the assessment of enterprise-wide data management efforts (see Schwinn et al., 1998, 176ff).

Additionally, it is important to note the massive changes happening to data management with the exploding growth of semi-structured data in organizations. These changes are regularly connected with the implementation of an organization-wide intranet, groupware platform or sophisticated document and knowledge management solutions (see, e.g., Abiteboul et al., 2000 for a comprehensive analysis of implications of the Web to data management; see Dogac et al., 1999 for general trends in data management; see also Lehner, 2000 or Maier and Lehner, 2000 for an overview of issues and approaches of knowledge management).

The author believes that the importance of issues of data modeling and data management does not decline in the age of the Web and electronic business as the amount and complexity of organizational data is still growing. However, the tasks related to data management are extended to comprise not only relational data, but semi-structured data as well. Additionally, the focus of data management will more and more move from organizing the storage of data to organizing the access to data. This will change not only the methods and tools used, but also the roles of data management in general.

REFERENCES

Abiteboul, S., Buneman, P., Suciu, D. (2000). *Data on the Web – From Relations to Semistructured Data and XML*, San Francisco (USA).

Batini, C., Ceri, S., Navathe, S. B. (1992). Conceptual Database Design: An Entity-Relationship Approach. Redwood City.

Dogac, A., Özsu, M. T., Ulusoy, O. (1999). Current Trends in Data Management Technology, Hershey (USA) .

Grupp, D. (1998). State-of-the-Art des Datenmanagements in Theorie und Praxis – Aufgaben, Abläufe, Aufgabenträger und Instrumente, Diploma Thesis at the Department of Business Informatics III, University of Regensburg.

Hars, A. (1994). Referenzdatenmodelle. Grundlagen effizienter Datenmodellierung. Wiesbaden.

Heilandt, T., Kruck, P. (1993). Ein algorithmisches verfahren zur bewertung und Verdichtung von Entity-Relationship-Modellen. *Informatik-Forschung und Entwicklung* 8, S. 197-206.

Heinrich, L.J., Roithmayr F. (1992). Wirtschaftsinformatik-Lexikon. 4th ed., Munich, Vienna.

Holzhammer, U. (1999). Benchmarking im Datenmanagement, Diploma Thesis at the Department of Business Informatics III, Unversity of Regensburg.

Juran, J. M., Gryna, F. M. (Eds.)(1988). *Juran's Quality Control Handbook*. 4th ed., New York.

Krogstie, J., Lindland, O.I., Sindre, G. (1995). Defining quality aspects for conceptual models. In *ISCO 3-Proceedings of the International Conference on Information System Concepts-Towards a Consolidation of Views*, Marburg.

Lehner, F., Hildebrand, K., Maier, R. (1995). Wirtschaftsinformatik-Theoretische Grundlagen, Munich, Vienna.

Lehner, F. (2000). Organisational Memory. Konzepte und Systeme für das organisatorische Lernen und das Wissensmanagement, Munich, Vienna.

Lindland, O.I., Sindre, G., Sølvberg, A. (1994). Understanding Quality in Conceptual Modeling. In: *IEEE Software 11* (1994) 2, 42-49.

Maier, R. (1996a). Qualität von Datenmodellen. Wiesbaden 1996.

Maier, R. (1996b). Benefits and quality of data modeling-Results of an empirical analysis and definition of a framework for quality management, in: Thalheim, B. (Ed.): *Conceptual Modeling-ER '96-Proceedings der 15th International Conference on Conceptual Modeling ER '96 in Cottbus* (Germany), 245-260.

Maier, R. (1999). Evaluation of Data Modeling, in: Eder, J., Rozman, I., Welzer, T. (Eds.): Advances in Databases and Information Systems, *Proceedings of the 3rd East European Conference on Advances in Databases and Information Systems – ADBIS '99*, Maribor (Slovenia), September 1999, Berlin et al. 1999, 232-246.

Maier, R., Lehner, F. (2000). Perspectives on Knowledge Management Systems – Theoretical Framework and Design of an Empirical Study, accepted at the European Conference on Information Systems–ECIS 2000, Vienna (Austria).

Marche, S. (1993). Measuring the Stability of Data Models. In: *European Journal of Information Systems*, 2(1), 37-47.

Moody, D.L., Shanks, G. G. (1994). What Makes a Good Data Model? Evaluating the Quality of Entity Relationship Models. In: Loucopoulos, P. (Ed.): ER '94-Business Modeling and Re-Engineering, *Proceedings of the 13th International Conference on the Entity-Relationship Approach*, Manchester, GB, Berlin et al. 1994, 94-111.

Ortner, E., Söllner, B. (1989). Semantische Datenmodellierung nach der Objekttypen-methode. In: Informatik-Spektrum 12, 1, 31-42.

Reingruber, M. C., Gregory, W. W. (1994). The Data Modeling Handbook. A Best-Practice Approach to Building Quality Data Models. New York.

Scheer, A. W. (1998). ARIS-Business Process Modeling, 2nd edition, Berlin.

Schwinn, K., Dippold, R., Ringgenberg, A., Schnider, W. (1998). Unternehmensweites Datenmanagement–Von der Datenbankadministration bis zum modernen Informationsmanagement, Braunschweig/Wiesbaden.

SVD-Schweizerische Vereinigung für Datenverarbeitung, VDF-Verband der Wirtschaftsinformatik-Fachleute (Ed.) (1993). Berufe der Wirtschaftsinformatik in der Schweiz. Zürich.

Szidzek, A. (1993). Datenmodellierung-Vorgehensmodell zur Konstruktion und Ein-führung einer unternehmensweiten, konzeptionellen Datenstruktur. Würzburg 1993.

Zamperoni, A., Löhr-Richter, P. (1994). Enhancing the Quality of Conceptual Database Specifications through Validation. In: Elmasri, R., Kouramajian, V., Thalheim, B. (Ed.): Entity-Relationship Approach-ER '93, *Proceedings of the 12th International Conference on the Entity-Relationship Approach in Dallas-Arlington (USA)*, Berlin., 96-111.

Chapter II

Dimensions of Database Quality

John A. Hoxmeier
Colorado State University, USA

ABSTRACT

Databases are a critical element of virtually all conventional and e-business applications. How does an organization know if the information derived from the database is any good? To ensure a quality database application, should the emphasis during model development be on the application of quality assurance metrics (designing it right)? A large number of database applications fail or are unusable. It is evident that a quality process does not necessarily lead to a usable database product. A database application can also be well-formed with high data quality but lack semantic or cognitive fidelity (the right design). This chapter expands on the growing body of literature in the area of data quality by proposing additions to a hierarchy of database quality dimensions that include model and behavioral factors in addition to process and data factors.

INTRODUCTION

The ultimate objective of database analysis, design and implementation is to establish an electronic repository that faithfully represents the conceptual and logical model of the manageable aspects of a user's information domain. Enterprise and Web-enabled databases must satisfy a wide set of demands and constituents. Software engineering in general and database development in particular can be a complex, complicated process. There is probably no other product development process that faces the same amount of uncertainty, which may account for the high failure rate of software projects.

For the purposes of this discussion, a database is defined as a self-describing collection of data that represents a model of an information domain. The database server manages the data, and the application presents the information to the consumer in some form of programmed behavior. Many internal and external factors must be considered during the development lifecycle, including, but not limited to, historical and future information requirements, the diversity of the data consumer community, organizational integration requirements, security, cost, value, ownership, performance, interface issues and data integrity. These factors contribute to the success of a database application in both quantitative and qualitative ways, and determine the real or perceived quality of the database application. *Process* and *data* quality are quantitative database management factors that are fairly well documented and understood, albeit underutilized. However, data *model* and *behavioral* considerations include important qualitative factors that contribute to overall database quality. A database is more than the collection of instances of the data managed by the server. Data quality, while important, is just one element of assessing overall database quality.

This chapter expands on the growing body of literature in the area of data quality by proposing additions to a hierarchy of database quality dimensions that include model and behavioral factors in addition to the process and data factors. While data quality has been the focus of a substantial amount of research, a standard definition does not exist in the literature (Wang and Madnick, 2000). The International Organization for Standardization (ISO) supplies an acceptable definition of data quality using accepted terminology from the quality field. These standards are documented agreements containing technical specifications or other precise criteria to be used consistently as rules, guidelines or definitions of characteristics, to ensure that materials, products, processes and services are fit for their purpose. Applying the term "database quality" in this context would build on the ISO definition of quality, i.e., *conformance to requirements* and *fitness for use* (1993). ISO 8402 as a quality management and quality assurance metric provides a formal definition of quality: the characteristics of an entity that represent its ability to satisfy stated and implied needs. This definition is consistent with the notion of "customer satisfaction" prevalent in the quality literature (Juran, 1989; Crosby, 1995). Thus, a database can be defined to be of the required quality if it satisfies the requirements stated in a specification, and the specification reflects the implied needs of the user. Therefore, an acceptable level of quality has been achieved if the database conforms to a defined specification, and the specification correctly reflects the intended use. Unfortunately, neither of these definitions is adequate for the purposes of assessing database quality. Because there are so many functions that are transparent to the user, user satisfaction itself is not a sufficient condition for assessing database quality. Applying quality techniques to the development process is also a frequently prescribed method of ensuring software quality. While the requirement definition phase of the system development lifecycle is critical to the success of an application, doing a good job of defining requirements is not sufficient in the implementation of a successful database application. A database must also be judged by how closely it represents the world of the data consumer (the model), its ability to respond to both routine and unanticipated requests within the domain it is expected to manage (the behavior), and maintain this representation over time. The framework presented herein expands on work previously proposed (Hoxmeier, 1997; Hoxmeier and Monarchi, 1996) and incorporates data quality dimensions put forth by several prominent data quality researchers (Ballou and Pazar, 1995; Krogstie et al., 1995; Lindland et al., 1994; Storey and Wang, 1994; Strong et al., 1997; Orr, 1998; Wand and Wang, 1996; Wang, 1998; Wang et al., 1993, 1995, 1999).

THE PROBLEM/SOLUTION CYCLE

The database design process is largely driven by the requirements and needs of the consumer, who establishes the boundaries and properties of the problem domain and the requirements of the information. As organizations seek to preserve organizational memory and manage richer forms of information over broader networks, this task has become increasingly more difficult.

Figure 1 illustrates the process that is currently used in the problem-to-solution database development cycle. This is consistent with the process-centered approach being used to develop database applications today. It is not difficult to see why so

Figure 1. Problem-to-Solution Cycle

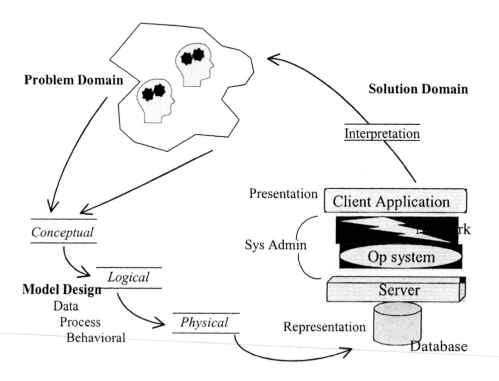

many database applications are ultimately unsuitable to the consumer. The process must incorporate three conceptually distinguishable domains: the modeling, the performance and the enactment domains (Pohl et al., 1999). Designers attempt to conceptualize the problem domain into a suitable physical model. The proposed physical model is subject to many performance constraints, including the physical representation, the network topology, system configuration and system administration. Finally, and what may be the most difficult to administer, the information is presented to the consumer for interpretation and enactment. The representation of the database after each of these domain layers all contribute to the perceived quality of the solution by the information consumer. Figure 1 also shows the critical elements in the problem-to-solution cycle that are the bases for the discussion on database quality dimensions:

- The cycle *process* must be managed toward a successful outcome.
- The *model* itself must represent a usually diverse and fuzzy problem domain.
- The quality of the *data* in the database must be of sufficient grade.
- The application must *behave* or have the ability to behave in a way the consumer understands.

The last step depicted in the illustration, interpretation by the consumer, is probably outside of the direct control of the design and development team. However, the consumer's ability to interpret the information is also critical to the success of a database application and, therefore, to the perceived quality of the database.

To ensure a quality database application, should the emphasis during model development be on the application of quality assurance metrics (designing it right)? It's hard to argue against this point, but there are a significant number of studies and anecdotal evidence that suggest that a large number of database applications fail, are unusable or contribute to negative organizational consequences (Abate et al., 1998; Standish Group, 1997; Redman, 1998; Wand and Wang, 1996). A quality process does not necessarily lead to a usable database product (Arthur, 1997; Hoxmeier, 1995; Redman, 1995). A database should be evaluated in production based on certain quantitative and information-preserving transformation measures, such as data quality, data integrity, normalization and performance. However, there are also many examples of database applications that are in most ways well-formed with high data quality but lack semantic or cognitive fidelity (the right design) (Motro and Rakov, 1999). Additionally, determining and implementing the proper set of database behaviors can be an elusive task. Depending on the risk factors affecting the application, there may be certain aspects of the quality assessment that deserve heavier weights. Contrary to the popular notion of product quality discussed below, whether the database meets the expectations of its end-users is only one aspect of overall database quality.

SIGNIFICANT PRIOR RESEARCH

Quality metrics have been used for years in the design, development and marketing for consumer goods and services. Quality engineering methods, such as Total Quality Management (TQM) and Quality Function Deployment (QFD), are commonly used by many product design and manufacturing disciplines, and are rapidly entering the service disciplines. In the area of information quality, however, the use of these techniques in practice is virtually non-existent. Recently, researchers have begun to evaluate and study the characteristics of information as they would any other product or service (Kahn and Strong, 1998; Kaplan et al., 1998; Wang et al., 1996).

A set of characteristics or data quality attributes are appropriate for the objective and measurable assessment of database quality. Researchers and practitioners alike have tried to establish a set of factors, attributes, rules or guidelines in order to evaluate system quality (Abate et al., 1998). More than two decades ago, Zmud concluded that a set of four dimensions divided into 25 factors represented the dimensions of information quality (Zmud 1978). The dimensions included data quality, relevancy, format quality and meaning quality. Referring to information systems, Martin stated (1976) that the collection of data has little value unless the data are used to understand the world and prescribe action to improve it. He proposed 12 qualities that computer-provided information should possess. The information should be:

- accurate
- tailored to the needs of the user
- relevant
- timely
- immediately understandable
- recognizable
- attractively presented
- brief
- up-to-date
- trustworthy
- complete
- easily accessible

Cap Gemini Pandata, a Dutch company, uses a framework that decomposes the entire information quality notion into four dimensions, 21 aspects and 40 attributes (Delen and Rijsenbrij, 1992). Cap Gemini has adopted this framework on the company procedures covering software package auditing. AT&T is researching data quality and has identified four primary factors, including accuracy, currentness, completeness and consistency (Fox et al., 1994). Another group, the Southern California On-line Users Group (SCOUG), defined characteristics of a quality library on-line database (Tenopir, 1990). The purpose of the set of characteristics was to allow professional searchers to rate each library on-line database system. The result of the retreat produced the following list of components that a professional searcher can use to evaluate a database:

- consistency
- coverage/scope
- timeliness
- value in terms of cost
- accuracy/error rate
- accessibility
- system performance/ease of use
- integration with other databases
- output
- documentation
- customer support

Marketing research has identified approaches used to assess product quality attributes that are important to consumers (Churchill, 1991; Menon, 1997). Wang, et al. (1996) applied this concept toward a data consumer. They performed a comprehensive survey that identified four high-level categories of data quality after evaluating 118 variables from the data quality literature, from researchers and from consumers. They used factor analysis to collapse their list of attributes into 15 data quality dimensions. Table 1 shows the dimensions, with a brief description of each.

Whereas attributes represent the lowest level at which data quality problems can be identified and understood, dimensions represent a higher level of granularity. That is, attributes represent the lowest level mechanism by which data problems become apparent and dimensions represent conditions that would not occur if data quality problems became apparent at the attribute level. Although data may have quality problems in one dimension while being satisfactory in others, it is possible that a single root cause could precipitate problems in multiple dimensions (Abate, et al., 1998). As with attributes, it appears that an inherent grouping of factors may exist that would further help researchers recognize patterns of data quality problems (Firth and Wang, 1993; Kon et al., 1993). Wang, (et al. 1999) observed that attributes seem to form several natural categories, or factors. The factors include intrinsic data quality, contextual data quality, representation data quality and accessibility data quality. A recent study applied the model to a series of field studies that focused on the concerns of the data consumer (Strong et al., 1997). These field studies confirmed the dimensions of data quality set forth in the Wang study, although consumers have found it difficult to distinguish the difference between many of the attributes. One recent study in the health care field collapsed the attribute framework to the following: accessibility, believability, completeness, conciseness, easy to understand, free of error, timeliness and value-added (Chun and Davidson, 1999). In the study survey of "information users," three attributes were consistently rated as most important by all respondents; believability, free of errors and timeliness. All respondents also consistently chose the three attributes most needing improvement: accessibility, completeness and timeliness.

There appear to be many similarities in the factors identified in these studies based on the perspective of the evaluators. Both developers and data consumers are concerned with data quality metrics like accuracy, timeliness, consistency, etc. Most of the research, while focused on data or information quality, indicates that there is a diverse set of factors influencing data quality. Any individual variable however, such as accuracy, is difficult to quantify. As can be seen from the studies above, commonly used attributes to measure data quality include accuracy, completeness, consistency, reliability, timeliness, uniqueness and validity. Assessing database quality by using just these specific attributes suffers from a number of deficiencies. Clearly, depending on user requirements, the appropriate set of attributes and properties may differ. But even if an appropriate set can be defined, it is likely that interdependencies will exist among attributes and a single cause can manifest itself

Table 1. Data quality dimensions and descriptions

Dimension	Description
Access Security	Access to data must be restricted and secure.
Accessibility	Data must be available or easily and quickly retrievable.
Accuracy	Data must be correct, reliable and certified free of error.
Amount of Data	The quantity or volume of available data must be appropriate.
Believability	Data must be accepted or regarded as true, real and credible.
Completeness	Data must be of sufficient breadth, depth and scope for the task at hand.
Concise Representation	Data must be compactly represented without being overwhelming.
Ease of Understanding	Data must be clear, without ambiguity and easily comprehended.
Interpretability	Data must be in appropriate format, and definitions must be clear.
Objectivity	Data must be unbiased and impartial.
Relevancy	Data must be applicable and helpful for the task at hand.
Representation	Data presentation must be compatible with previous data.
Reputation	Data must be trusted in terms of their source or content.
Timeliness	The age of the data must be appropriate for the task at hand.
Value-Added	Data must be beneficial and provide advantages from their use.

in multiple variables. Nonetheless, researchers have developed a fairly consistent view of data quality. There is little available in the literature on the evaluation of overall database quality including other considerations such as semantic fidelity (model), behavioral and value factors.

THE PROPOSED FRAMEWORK

A set of characteristics or data quality attributes grouped into dimensions is appropriate for the objective and measurable assessment of database quality. As can be seen from the studies above, commonly used attributes to measure data quality include accuracy, completeness, consistency, reliability, timeliness, uniqueness and validity. Assessing database quality by using just these specific attributes suffers from a number of deficiencies. Clearly, depending on user requirements, the appropriate set of attributes and attribute levels may differ. But even if an appropriate set can be defined, it is likely that interdependencies will exist among attributes and a single cause can manifest itself in multiple variables.

It is proposed that through the hierarchical framework presented below, one can consider overall database quality by assessing four primary dimensions: process, data, model and behavior. Portions of the hierarchy draw heavily from previous studies on data and information quality, and documented process quality standards (Arthur, 1997; Wang, 1998). A dimension is a set of database quality attributes or components that most data consumers react to in a fairly consistent way (Wang et al., 1996). Wang et al. (1994) define "data quality dimension" as a set of data quality attributes that represent a single data quality abstract or construct. The use of a set of dimensions to represent a quality typology is consistent with previous quality research (Dvir and Evans, 1996; Kon et al., 1993; Wang et al., 1996; Strong et al., 1997). The framework presents the four dimensions in a dimension-attribute-property hierarchy.

PROCESS QUALITY

Much attention has been given over the years to process quality improvement. ISO-9000-3, Total Quality Management (TQM), Quality Function Deployment (QFD) and Capability Maturity Model (CMM) are approaches that are concerned primarily with the incorporation of quality management within the process of systems development (Costin, 1994; Dvir and Evans, 1996; Herbsleb, 1997; Schmauch, 1994). Quality control is a process of ensuring that the database conforms to predefined standards and guidelines using statistical quality measures (Dyer, 1992). It compares variations of identified activities with the results of predetermined standards and assesses the variation between the two. When deviations from the problem domain are found, they are resolved and the process is modified as needed. This is an effective, yet reactive form of quality management. Quality assurance attempts to maintain the quality standards in a proactive way. In addition to using quality control measures, quality assurance goals go further by surveying the customer to determine their level of satisfaction with the product. Conceivably, potential problems can be detected early in the process.

The philosophy of ISO-9000-3 and CMM are to build quality into a software system on a continuous basis, from conception through implementation. ISO-9000-3 as a process quality standard does not offer any particular metrics to be utilized during the process. In addition, as a general software standard, ISO-9000-3 does not deal specifically with database issues. CMM is best regarded as a tool to be used to pursue an organization's business goals. The time and cost of a CMM-based software process improvement often exceeds the expectations of those involved.

Figure 2. Database quality dimensions

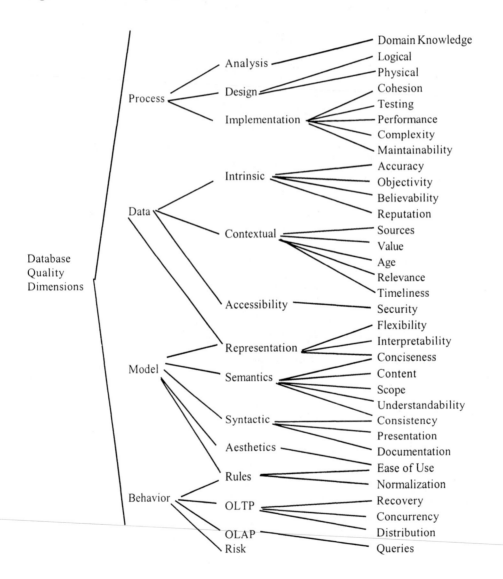

A specific property addition to the framework within the dimension of process implementation quality is performance. All too often, specific performance requirements are either ignored during the design process or evaluated after implementation. While performance may be viewed by some as an implementation issue, it should be considered an important factor in overall database quality, even in the conceptual phase. Both relational and object databases can contain rather serious problems in terms of data redundancy, relationships, integrity and structure. The objective is to design a normalized, high-fidelity database while minimizing complexity. When evaluating performance there are times when de-normalization may represent an optimal solution. However, anytime a general-purpose database is optimized for a given situation, other requirements inevitably arise that negate the advantage. The measures used to assess the trade-off may include query and update performance, storage and the avoidance of data anomalies. Similar to the contrast between data and semantic quality, a database that is otherwise well designed but does not perform well is useless.

DATABASE DATA QUALITY

Data integrity is one of the keys to developing a quality database. Without accurate data, users will lose confidence in the database or make uninformed decisions (Redman, 1992). While data integrity can become a problem over time, there are relatively straightforward ways to enforce constraints and domains, and to ascertain when problems exist (Moriarty, 1996). The identification, interpretation and application of business rules, however, present a more difficult challenge for the developer. Rules and policies must be communicated and translated, and much of the meaning and intent can be lost in this process. In addition to the data quality attributes discussed earlier and used as a basis for the data dimension presented here, the individual attributes will not be discussed. However, a couple of additional properties are worth noting.

A frequently overlooked metric in the evaluation of data integrity is the age of the data, database and model. Data or model age is different than the timeliness property. Timeliness refers to the delay between availability and accessibility. Age refers to the time that has passed since the data was entered into the database or when the data model was developed. The data should only be as old as the problem domain and information sources will allow, and maintained only as long as the situation requires. This can be a few seconds or several years. At some point, the data needs to be refreshed in order to maintain its currency. Over time, the age of the model may degrade in its ability to depict the problem domain. The model must be updated so that as the problem domain changes, the model of the database changes as well.

Additionally, the assessment of data quality must include value considerations. Time and financial constraints are real concerns. As IT departments are expected to do more with less, and as cycle times continue to decrease for database applications, developers must make decisions about the extent to which they are going to implement and evaluate quality considerations. Shorter cycle times present a good argument for modularity and reusability, so quality factors must be addressed on a micro basis.

DATA MODEL QUALITY

As has been presented, data quality is usually associated with the quality of the data values. However, even data that meets all other quality criteria is of little use if it is based on a deficient data model (Levitin and Redman, 1995). Data model quality is the third of the four high level dimensions presented above. Information and an application that represent a high proportional match between the problem and solution domains should be the goal of a database with high semantic quality. Representation, semantics, syntax and aesthetics are all attributes of model quality (Hoxmeier and Monarchi, 1996; Levitin and Redman, 1995; Lindland et al., 1994).

The database design process is largely driven by the requirements and needs of the data consumer, who establishes the boundaries and properties of the problem domain and the requirements of the task. The first step in the process, information discovery, is one of the most difficult, important and labor-intensive stages of database development (Chignell and Parsaye, 1993; Sankar and Marshall, 1993). It is in this stage where the semantic requirements are identified, prioritized and visualized. Requirements can rarely be defined in a serial fashion. Generally, there is significant uncertainty over what these requirements are, and they only become clearer after considerable analysis, discussions with users and experimentation with prototypes. This means previous work may be revisited. Additionally, while many studies point to the importance of user involvement in the discovery and design phase, many information consumers are uncertain about their requirements or have insufficient database knowledge to provide much insight.

Concentric design is an approach that is appropriate in database design. This cyclical process emulates the philosophy of continuous quality improvement used in TQM and CMM (Braithwaite, 1994; Dvir and Evans, 1994; Herbsleb, 1997). Similar to other products and services, the costs associated with developing quality into the application from design to implementation are much lower than the costs of correcting problems that occur later due to poor design (Crosby, 1995). However, the learning curve within the domain for the designer may be steep and the demand for the application may force rapid delivery. So, how do designers arrive at high semantic quality in a very short period of time?

Qualitative techniques address the ambiguous and subjective dimensions of conceptual database design. The interaction between people and information is one where human preference and constraints have a huge impact on the effectiveness of database design. The use of techniques such as affinity and Pareto diagrams, semantic object models, group decision support systems, nominal group and interrelationship diagraphs help to improve the process of problem and solution domain definition. Well-studied quantitative techniques, such as entity-relationship diagrams, object models, data flow diagrams and performance benchmarks, on the other hand, allow the results of the qualitative techniques to be described in a visual format and measured in a meaningful way (Kesh, 1995). Other object attributes that explicitly express quality can be included in the model as well. Storey and Wang present an innovative extension to the traditional ER approach for incorporating quality requirements (database quality data and product quality data) into conceptual database design (1994). The underlying premise of the approach is that quality requirements should be distinct from other database properties (Motro and Rakov, 1999).

Qualitative and quantitative techniques can be used to assist the developer to extract a strong semantic model. However, it is difficult to design a database with high semantic value without significant domain knowledge and experience (Moody and Shanks, 1998; Navathe, 1997). These may be the two most important considerations in databases of high semantic quality. In addition, conceptual database design remains more of an art than a science. It takes a high amount of creativity and vision to design a solution that is robust, usable and can stand the test of time.

DATABASE BEHAVIOR QUALITY

Many databases are perceived to be of low quality simply because they are difficult to use. In a survey in the UK, managers and professionals from various disciplines were asked to evaluate the quality of information they were using (Rolph and Bartram, 1994). Using eight factors, "accuracy" rated the highest, "usable format" the lowest. Developers tend to focus on aspects of data quality at the expense of behavioral quality. Granted, the behaviors associated with a general-purpose database used for decision and analytical support are varied and complex.

What constitutes a database of high behavioral quality? Are the criteria different than those used for software applications in general? Clearly the behaviors for a database that is used to support transaction processing (OLTP) are different than those of a database used to support analytical processing (OLAP). Software development, in general, is very procedure- or function-driven. The objective is to build a system that works (and do it quickly). Database development, on the other hand, should be more focused on the content, context, behavior, semantics and persistence of the data. Rapid application development and prototyping techniques contribute to arriving at a close match between the problem and solution domains. There may be no substitute for experience and proficiency with the software and tools used in the entire development process. It is one thing to discuss how a database should behave and even document these behaviors completely. Implementation and modification of these behaviors is an altogether different issue. The process of behavior implementation consists of the design and construction of a solution following the identification of the problem domain and the data model.

Because of the difficulties associated with the definition of a fixed set of current requirements and the determination of future utilization, the database problem domain is typically a moving target represented by the polygon in Figure 3. The size and shape are constantly changing. In addition, insufficient identification of appropriate database behaviors, poor communication and inexperience in the problem domain leads to inferior solutions. As a result, the solution domain rarely approaches the optimal solution presented in Figure 3C. The database developer must attempt to develop a database model that closely matches the perceptions of the consumer, and deliver a design that can be implemented, maintained and modified in a cost-effective way. A partial solution, such as that indicated in 3B, is more likely. The consumer will then dictate whether 1) there is enough of a solution to use, 2) the solution is of sufficient quality and 3) they trust the database. Additionally, databases to be used in on-line analytical processing, data warehousing or data mining applications present difficult challenges. The information consumer in these areas generally does not know what may be asked of the database. The database must behave in a fashion to respond to the most difficult requirement of all, that which the consumer has not yet thought of.

And finally, an additional important contributor to database quality that is difficult to categorize is that of information risk. Risk is addressed in the project management literature, but not discussed in the information quality literature. Risk may determine the grade of acceptable information quality. Consumers of on-line critical care database information that monitors hospital patients require a very high grade of information quality because the risk is very high. A database that tracks responses to a customer satisfaction survey, on the other hand, may be of lower grade because the overall information risk is low.

Figure 3. Solution domain to problem mapping

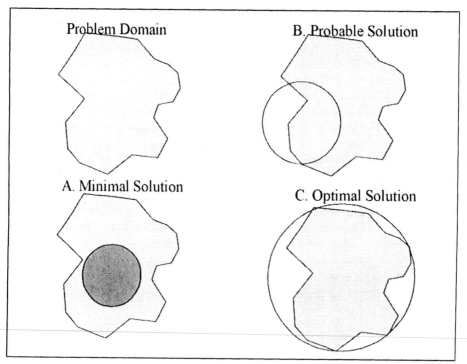

Problem Domain

B. Probable Solution

A. Minimal Solution

C. Optimal Solution

CASE STUDY

The framework was used as a basis to assess the overall quality of a production database for a manufacturer of computer hardcopy devices. The database is classified as an on-line analytical processing application in that it is used for decision support and is not part of the organization's mission critical OLTP applications. The database maintains information accumulated from the typical product warranty registration process. It includes product, demographic, purchase process and customer profile information. The data was captured via an OCR scan and electronically loaded into the database. The data comes from all over the world and at the time of the review, represented well over 200,000 customers and more than 2 million warranty card responses. The marketing department originally articulated several objectives for the database:

- Capture important sales statistics for the product line as a basis for positioning future products.
- Track the purchase location for each of the products to quantify channel decisions.
- Establish a profile of customer information for future customer segmentation and product positioning.
- Report units sold by geographic region, product line, segment, period and card question.

The system users within the marketing department became dissatisfied with the database based on several shortcomings that were contributing to a perceived lack of quality. Their concerns included:

- The information reported in the cross-tab type reports was not accurate and difficult to verify.
- The process for updating the database with new registrations was cumbersome and time-consuming.
- The department was unable to select a subset of the data for further analysis, e.g., list all customers who purchased their scanner through a particular retail store in the United States.
- The reports that were generated by the database took more than 24 hours to produce. If the process was unsuccessful, the entire report had to be run again.

These were just a few of the concerns that led the company to initiate a review and potential redesign of the database. The company had invested a significant amount of time and resources on the system and was on the verge of dropping the project. The framework presented herein was used as a methodology for evaluating the database application and making suggestions for possible improvement. The four primary dimensions of process, data, model and behavior quality were evaluated. Each will be briefly discussed in the following sections.

Process Quality

The process that was deployed to develop the database was probably inadequate. The company had used a developer from outside the company because their internal

IT group could not respond to their request for service. The consultant had developed the system based on very little interaction with the company. The contractor had significant experience in the hardware and software architecture used by the company and database management system targeted for the application. However, the contractor had never designed and implemented a marketing application and the lead designer had limited formal relational training. While the implementation had gone smoothly, the contractor had not tested the database under loaded conditions and left the company with limited technical or design specifications. After interviewing company personnel about the process, they indicated that the contractor had never gone through a conceptual data model with them.

Data Quality

There were several problems with the quality of the data in the database. Data quality was assessed using the information quality assessment (IQA) designed by Wang et al. (1999). This instrument uses 65 data quality assessment items to measure 15 different data quality variables. The scale for each item ranges from zero to 10, where zero is labeled "not at all" and 10 is labeled "completely." Questions measured the data quality variables of believability, accessibility, completeness, etc. This analysis indicated many data quality problems:

- The domain concept had not been implemented, so there were many inconsistencies within the attributes. For example, a query against the state attribute for the customer's address led to 61 distinct values. This type of variance was found in virtually every attribute. As a result, the reports produced combinations of crosstabs that were impossible to interpret.
- Because of the OCR process, many records had unrecognized characters and, as a result, were rejected during the acquisition process and not even included in the importation.
- Because of an inadequate design, many columns were duplicated, leading to erroneous totals.
- The time between initial data acquisition and final report aged the data to a point where it was unreliable.
- The consumers of the information had lost confidence in the data and overall believability was low.

Model Quality

The contractor had not produced a conceptual data model of the application so it was difficult to assess the semantic match between the model produced by the contractor and the problem domain. However, an assessment of the logical and physical models revealed an impedance mismatch. The basic relationship that existed between the customer and the product they purchased was not represented in the database. The database should have shown-a one to many to many-between customers, products and warranty responses. Rather, the physical implementation of the database repeated information on the customer for each product that the customer purchased. The individual survey questions were stored as attributes in a very long row. There were many null values, and it was difficult to analyze the questions that were marked, "Please check all that apply." This led to many data integrity and duplication problems that SQL simply cannot account for.

Application Behavior Quality

The application presented a user interface that was graphically appealing and relatively easy to use, but lacked certain behaviors that were necessary to capture a smooth workflow. For example, it was possible to run the analytical reports for a particular period of time without having the data loaded in the database for that time period. In addition, because the primary key was automatically sequenced, it was possible to load the same data twice without knowing it. The physical indices that should have prevented such an occurrence were not present. Other application behaviors that were not present or insufficient included:

- The data was electronically loaded so there was no manual data entry. The forms for manually editing the data did not utilize any technique to enforce domain controls.
- The dates and times of reports and data changes were not recorded making audits difficult.
- The database had insufficient concurrency controls.
- The reports took several hours to produce and there was no status indicator.

Prescriptions

This database application suffered from several real and perceived deficiencies that contributed to its poor quality. The problems went beyond those associated with data quality alone. The process could have been improved and the project could have been better managed. Process improvement alone may not have been sufficient to improve the quality of the database itself. After all four areas of database quality were evaluated, and considering the original objectives of the database, this customer registration application ranked very low for overall quality. Simply addressing the data quality problems would not have improved its utility. Several suggestions were made, all with varying associated costs. The following modifications were recommended with the applicable framework factor shown in parentheses:

- Redesign the basic data model to accurately reflect the problem domain. (model)
- Conform to data normalization strategies for relational tables. (model)
- Perform a series of data cleansing queries on each attribute after identifying the domain set. (data)
- Construct and implement domain enforcement within the database. (data)
- Add additional attributes for date and time stamping the rows. (data)
- Modify the user interface to encourage the user to follow a workflow. (behavior)
- Modify the application to protect against concurrency and update issues. (behavior)

- Add features to the forms to make it easy for the user to modify data using pre-approved domains. (behavior and data)
- Add physical indices to the database to prevent redundant information and improve performance. (process)
- Redesign the reports to represent the problem domain specified by the consumers. (behavior)
- Deploy the reports on the company intranet to reduce time and paper. (process)
- Summarize the results and highlight extraordinary or exceptional areas for the consumer. (data)
- Add a new layer to the user interface that makes it possible for the consumer to select certain areas for further analysis. (behavior)

CONCLUSION AND RESEARCH DIRECTIONS

How does one ensure a final database product that is of high quality? Database quality must be measured in terms of a combination of dimensions including process and behavior quality, data quality and model fidelity. By organizing attributes into database quality dimensions, many difficulties encountered when dealing with singular attributes can be effectively addressed. So, not only are dimensions more comprehensive, but organizing attributes into dimensions both organizes and minimizes the material that must be comprehended. Moreover, by analyzing dimensions a data quality researcher may discover systemic root causes of data errors. The framework presented above offers a typology for assessing these dimensions. The purpose of this chapter was to expand on the existing research on data and process quality in an attempt to provide a more comprehensive view of database quality. The area is of great concern as information is viewed as a critical organizational asset and preserving organizational memory becomes a high priority (Saviano, 1997). A test case was shown as an example of an application of the framework, but further research is required to continue to validate the framework, to identify additional quality dimensions and develop metrics to quantify the properties, and to develop and deploy techniques to improve the fidelity of the data model.

REFERENCES

Abate, M., Diegert, K. and Allen, H. (1998). A hierarchical approach to improving data quality. *Data Quality*, 4(1), [On-line] http://www.dataquality.com/998abate.htm [2000, October].

Arthur, L. (1997). Quantum improvements in software system quality. *Communications of the ACM*, 40(6), 47-52.

Ballou, D. and Pazer, H. (1995). Designing information systems to optimize the accuracy timeliness tradeoff. *Information Systems Research*, 6(1), 51-72.

Braithwaite, T. (1994). *Information Service Excellence Through TQM, Building Partnerships for Business Process Reengineering and Continuous Improvement*. ASQC Quality Press.

Chignell, M. and Parsaye, K. (1993). *Intelligent Database Tools and Applications*. California: Wiley.

Chun, A., and Davidson, B. (1999). Baseline vs. follow-Up results of an IQ survey for Cedars-Sinai Health System, *Proceedings of the 1999 Conference on Information Quality*, Lee, Y. and Tayi, G., Eds., 266-284.

Churchill, G. A. (1991). *Marketing Research: Methodological Foundations*. United States: Dryden Press.

Costin, H. (1994). *Total Quality Management*. United States: Dryden.

Crosby, Philip. (1995). *Quality Is Still Free*. New York: McGraw-Hill.

Delen, G. and Rijsenbrij, D. (1992). A Specification, Engineering and Measurement of Information Systems Quality. *Journal of Systems Software*, 17(3), 205-217.

Dvir, R., and Evans, S. (1996). *A TQM Approach to the Improvement of Information Quality*. [On-line], http://Web.mit.edu/tdqm/www/wpaper.htm [2000, October].

Dyer, M. (1992). *The Cleanroom Approach to Quality Software Development*. Wiley.

Firth, C. and Wang, R. (1993). Closing the Data Quality Gap: Using ISO 9000 to study data quality. Working paper TDQM-93-03, [On-line], http://Web.mit.edu/tdqm/www/wpaper.html, [2000, October].

Fox, C., Levitin, A. and Redman, T. (1994). The notion of data and its quality dimensions. *Information Processing and Management*, 30(1), 9-19.

Herbsleb, J., Zubrow, D., Goldenson, D., Hayes, W. and Paulk, M. (1997). Software quality and capability maturity model. *Communications of the ACM*, 40(6), 30-40.

Hoxmeier, J. (1997). A framework for assessing database quality. *Proceedings of the Workshop on Behavioral Models and Design Transformations: Issues and Opportunities in Conceptual Modeling, ACM Sixteenth International Conference on Conceptual Modeling*, Los Angeles, CA, November.

Hoxmeier, J. (1995). Managing the legacy systems reengineering process: Lessons learned and prescriptive advice. *Proceedings of the Seventh Annual Software Technology Conference*, Ogden ALC/TISE, Salt Lake City, April.

Hoxmeier, J. and Monachi, D. (1996). An assessment of database quality: Design it right or the right design? *Proceedings of the Association for Information Systems Annual Meeting*, Phoenix, AZ, August.

ISO, International Organization for Standardization. (1993). *Quality-Vocabulary (Draft International Standard 8402)*. Geneva, Switzerland: ISO Press.

Juran, J. M. (1989). *Juran on Leadership for Quality: An Executive Handbook*. New York: The Free Press.

Kahn, B. and Strong, D. (1998). Product and Service Performance Model for Information Quality, *Proceedings of the 1998 Conference on Information Quality*, Cambridge, MA., 102-115.

Kaplan, D., Krishnan, R., Padman, R. and Peters, J. (1998). Assessing data quality in accounting information systems. *Communications of the ACM*, 41(2), 72-78.

Kesh, S. (1995). Evaluating the quality of entity relationship models. *Information and Software Technology*, 37(12), 681-689.

Kon, H., Lee, J. and Wang, R. (1993). A process view of data quality. Working paper TDQM-93-01, MIT TDQM Research Program, E53-320, 50.[On-line] http://Web.mit.edu/tdqm/www/wpaper.html [2000, October].

Krogstie, J., Lindland, O. and Sindre, G. (1995). Towards a deeper understanding of quality in requirements engineering, *Proceedings of the 7th CaiSE*, Finland, (932), 82-95.

Levitin, A. and Redman, T. (1995). Quality dimensions of a conceptual view. *Information Processing and Management*, 31(1).

Lindland, O., Sindre, G. and Solvberg, A. (1994). Understanding quality in conceptual Modeling. *IEEE Software*, 11(2), 42-49.

Martin, J. (1976). *Principles of Database Management*. New Jersey: Prentice-Hall, Inc.

Menon, A., Jaworski, B. and Kohli, A.(1997). Product quality: Impact of interdepartmental interactions. *Journal of the Academy of Marketing Science*, 25(3).

Moody, D. and Shanks, G. (1998). What makes a good data model? A framework for evaluating and improving the quality of entity relationship models, *The Australian Computer Journal*, 30(4), 97-110.

Moriarty, T. (1996). Barriers to data quality. *Database Programming and Design*, 61, (May).

Motro, A. and Rakov, I. (1999). Estimating the quality of databases. *Lecture Notes in Computer Science*, Heidelberg:Springer Verlag, (1495).

Navathe, S. (1997). Conceptual modeling in biomedical science. *Proceedings of the ACM Entity Relationship '97 Modeling Preconference Symposium,* Los Angeles, CA.

Orr, K. (1998). Data quality and systems theory. *Communications of the ACM*, 41(2), 66-71.

Pohl, K. and Weidenhaupt, K., Domges, R., Haumer, P., Jarke, M. and Klamma, R. (1999). PRIME- Toward Process-Integrated Modeling Environments. *ACM Transactions on Software Engineering and Methodology*, 8(4), October, 343-410.

Redman, T.C. (1992). *Data Quality: Management and Technology*. New York: Bantam Books.

Redman, T.C. (1995). Improve data quality for competitive advantage. *Sloan Management Review*, 36(2), 99-107.

Redman, T.C. (1998). The impact of poor data quality on the typical enterprise. *Communications of the ACM,* 41(2), 79-82.

Rolph, P. and Bartram, P. (1994). *The Information Agenda: Harnessing Relevant Information in a Changing Business Environment*. London: Management Books 2000, 65-87.

Sankar, C., and Marshall, T. (1993). Database design support: An empirical investigation of perceptions and performance. *Journal of Database Management*, 4(3), 4-14.

Saviano, J. (1997). Are we there yet? *CIO*, 87-96, June 1.

Schmauch, C. (1994). *ISO-9000 for Software Developers*. ASQC Quality Press.

Standish Group. (1997). *The Chaos Report.* [On-line], http://standishgroup.com/visitor/chaos.htm [2000, October].

Storey, V. and Wang, R. (1994). Modeling quality requirements in conceptual database design. *Total Data Quality Management, Working Paper Series*: TDQM-02-94 [On-line] http://Web.mit.edu/tdqm/www/wp94.html [2000, October].

Strong, D., Lee, Y., and Wang, R. (1997). Data Quality in Context. *Communications of the ACM*, 40(5), 103-110.

Tenopir, C. (1990). Database quality revisited. *Library Journal*, Pctpber 1, 64-67.

Wang, R. (1998). A product perspective on total data quality management. *Communications of the ACM*, 41(2), 58-65.

Wand, Y. and Wang, R. (1996). Anchoring data quality dimensions in ontological foundations. *Communications of the ACM.* November.

Wang, R., Kon, H. and Madnick, S. (1993). Data quality requirements analysis and modeling. *9th International Conference on Data Engineering*, 670-677.

Wang, R. and Madnick, S. (2000). *Introduction to the TDQM Program, MIT Data Quality Program*, [on-line], http://Web.mit.edu/tdqm/www/intro.html [2000, October].

Wang, R., Strong, D. and Guarascio, L. (1996). Beyond accuracy: What data quality means to data consumers. *Journal of Management Information Systems*, 12(4), 5-34.

Wang, R., Strong, D., Kahn, B., and Lee, Y. (1999). An information quality assessment methodology: Extended abstract. *Proceedings of the 1999 Conference on Information Quality,* Yang Lee and Giri Tayi, Eds., Cambridge, MA., 258-263.

Wang, R., Storey, V. and Firth, C. (1995). A framework for analysis of data quality research. *IEEE Transactions on Knowledge and Data Engineering*, 7(4), 349-372.

Zmud, R. (1978). Concepts, theories and techniques: An empirical investigation of the dimensionability of the concept of information. *Decision Design*, 9(2), 187-195.

Chapter III

Metrics for Controlling Database Complexity

Coral Calero, Mario Piattini and Marcela Genero
Universidad de Castilla-La Mancha, Spain

INTRODUCTION

Software engineers have been proposing large quantities of metrics for software products, processes and resources (Fenton and Pfleeger, 1997; Melton, 1996; Zuse, 1998). Metrics are useful mechanisms in improving the quality of software products and also for determining the best ways to help practitioners and researchers (Pfleeger, 1997). Unfortunately, almost all the metrics put forward focus on program characteristics (e.g., McCabe, 1976, cyclomatic number) disregarding databases (Sneed and Foshag, 1998). As far as databases are concerned, metrics have been used for comparing data models rather than the schemata itself. Several authors (Batra et al., 1990; Jarvenpaa and Machesky, 1986; Juhn and Naumann, 1985; Kim and March, 1995; Rossi and Brinkemper, 1996; Shoval and Even-Chaime, 1987) have compared the most well-known models--such as E/R, NIAM and relational--using different metrics. Although we think this work is interesting, metrics for comparing schemata are needed most for practical purposes, like choosing between different design alternatives or giving designers limit values for certain characteristics (analogously to value 10 for McCabe complexity of programs). Some recent proposals have been published for conceptual schemata (MacDonell et al., 1997; Moody, 1998; Piattini et al., 2001), but for conventional databases, such as relational ones, nothing has been proposed, excepting normalization theory.

This lack of metrics support could be explained, as databases have been until recently just simple files/tables with minor contributions to the complexity of the overall system. However, this is no longer the case because databases now play a new role with information systems being their core, and a new database generation is necessary for supporting all the new applications. This new generation is the "third database generation" (Carey et al., 1990; Cattell, 1991), where new data types, rules, generalizations, complex objects and functions (Stonebraker and Brown, 1999) are being supported within the database realm.

Databases are becoming more complex, and it is necessary to measure schemata complexity in order to understand, monitor, control, predict and improve database development and maintenance projects. In modern information systems (IS), the database has become a crucial component, so there is a need to propose and study some measures to assess its quality.

Database quality depends on several factors: functionality, reliability, usability, efficiency, maintainability and portability (ISO, 1999). Our focus is on maintainability, because maintenance accounts for 60 to 90% of lifecycle costs, and it is considered the most important concern for modern IS departments (Frazer, 1992; McClure, 1992; Pigoski, 1997).

The International Standard, ISO/IEC 9126, distinguishes five subcharacteristics for maintainability: analysability, changeability, stability, testability and compliance (see Figure 1). Analysability, changeability and testability are in turn influenced by complexity (Li and Cheng, 1987). However, a general complexity measure is *the impossible holy grail* (Fenton, 1994), i.e., it is impossible to get one value that captures all the complexity factors of a database. Henderson-Sellers (1996) distinguishes three types of complexity: computational, psychological and representa-

Figure 1. Relation between software quality and product complexity

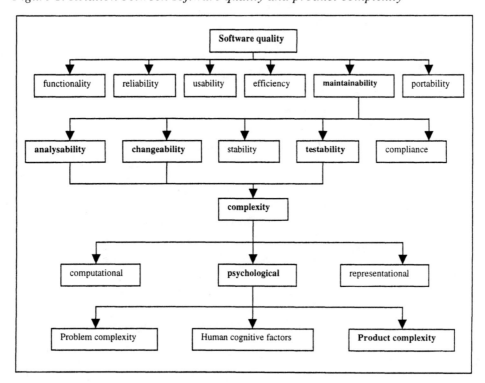

tional, and for psychological complexity he considers three components: problem complexity, human cognitive factors and product complexity. The last one is our focus, and for our purposes the product will be databases.

In this chapter, we will propose internal measures for databases, which can characterize their complexity by helping to assess database maintainability (the external quality characteristic). In the next section we will present the framework followed to define and validate database metrics. Next we summarize the proposed metrics for relational, object-relational and active databases; then the formal validation of some of these metrics is described. Some empirical validations are presented in the next section, and conclusions and future work will be presented at the end.

A FRAMEWORK FOR DEVELOPING AND VALIDATING DATABASE METRICS

As we have said previously, our goal is to define metrics for controlling database maintainability. But because metrics definition must be done in a methodological way, it is necessary to follow a number of steps to ensure the reliability of the proposed metrics. Figure 2 presents the method we apply for the metrics proposal.

In this figure we have four main activities:

- **Metrics definition.** The first step is the proposal of metrics. Although it looks simple, it is an important step in ensuring metrics are correctly defined. This definition is made by taking into account the specific characteristics of the database we want to measure and the experience of database designers and administrators of these databases.

Figure 2. Steps followed in the definition and validation of the database metrics

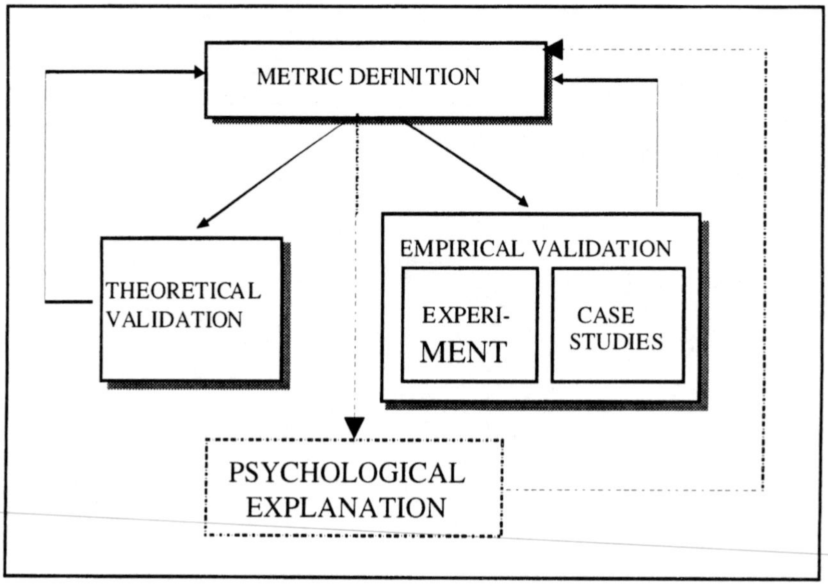

- **Theoretical validation.** The second step is the formal validation of the metrics. The formal validation helps us to know when and how to apply the metrics. There are two main tendencies in metrics validation: the frameworks based on axiomatic approaches and the ones based on the measurement theory. The goal of the first ones is merely definitional. On this kind of formal framework, a set of formal properties is defined for a given software attribute, and it is possible to use this property set for classifying the proposed measures. The most well-known frameworks of this type are those proposed by Weyuker (1988), Briand et al. (1996) and Morasca and Briand (1997).

  The main goal of axiomatisation in software metrics research is the clarification of concepts to ensure that new metrics are in some sense valid. However, if we cannot ensure the validity of the set of axioms defined for a given software attribute, we cannot use it to validate metrics. It cannot be determined whether a measure that does not satisfy the axioms has failed because it is not a measure of the class defined by the set of axioms (e.g., complexity, length...) or because the axiom set is inappropriate. Since the goal of axiomatisation in software metrics research is primarily definitional, with the aim of providing a standard against which to validate software metrics, it is not so obvious that the risks outweigh the benefits (Kitchenham and Stell, 1997).

  The measurement theory-based frameworks (such as Zuse, 1998; Withmire, 1998) specify a general framework in which measures should be defined. The strength of measurement theory is the formulation of empirical conditions from which we can derive a hypothesis of reality. Measurement theory gives clear definitions of terminology, a sound basis of software measures, criteria for experimentation, conditions for validation of software measures, foundations of prediction models, empirical properties of software measures and criteria for measurement scales. However, most research in the software measurement area does not address measurement scales. Much of it argues that scales are not so important. These arguments do not take into account that empirical properties of software measures are hidden behind scales. Units are also closely connected to measurement scales. The discussion of scale types is important for statistical operations. Because many empirical and numerical conditions are not covered by a certain scale type, the consideration of the empirical and numerical conditions is necessary and very important, too.
- **Empirical validation.** The goal of this step is to prove the practical utility of the proposed metrics. Although there are various ways of performing this step, basically we can divide the empirical validation into experimentation and case studies. Experimentation is usually made using controlled experiments and the case studies usually work with real data. Both of them are necessary, the controlled experiments for having a first approach and the case studies for making the results stronger. In both cases, the results are analyzed using either statistics tests or advanced techniques as C4.5 (a machine learning algorithm), RoC (a robust Bayesian classifier) and so on. Replication of the experiment is necessary because it is difficult to understand the applicability of isolated

results from one study and, thus, to assess the true contribution to the field (Basili, 1999).

- **Psychological explanation**. Ideally we will be able to explain the influence of the values of the metrics from a psychological point of view. Some authors, such as Siau (1999), propose the use of cognitive psychology as a reference discipline in the engineering of methods and the studying of information modeling. In this sense, cognitive psychology theories such as the Adaptive Control of Thought (ACT, Anderson, 1983) could justify the influence of certain metrics in database understandability. The knowledge of the limitation of human information processing capacity could also be helpful in establishing a threshold in the metrics for assuring the database quality.

As shown in Figure 2, the process of defining and validating database metrics is evolutionary and iterative. As a result of the feedback, metrics could be redefined based on discarded theoretical, empirical or psychological validations.

PROPOSED METRICS

In this section, we present the different metrics that we have proposed for relational, object-relational and active databases. For each kind of database, a brief summary of its main characteristics is given and an example using ANSI/ISO SQL:1999 code is used to illustrate the calculation of the proposed metrics.

Metrics for Relational Databases

A relational database is perceived by the user as tables, and the database operators at the user's disposal generate new tables from old tables, e.g., the SQL "Select" statement (Date, 1995). Tables have primary keys, which serve to identify the rows of the table, and foreign keys, which link the tables of the relational database. Related to the foreign key concept, a relational model may include the referential integrity rule: the database must not contain any unmatched foreign key values (Date, 1995).

Traditionally, the only indicator used to measure the "quality" of relational databases has been the normalization theory, upon which Gray, et al. (1991) propose to obtain a normalization ratio. But we think that normalization is not enough to measure complexity in relational databases, so we propose the following four metrics in addition to normalization (Calero, et al., 2000):

Number of attributes (NA)

NA is the number of attributes in all the tables of the schema.

Depth referential tree (DRT)

DRT is defined as the length of the longest referential path in the database schema. Cycles are only considered once.

Number of foreign keys (NFK)

The NFK metric is defined as the number of foreign keys in the schema.

Cohesion of the schema (COS)

COS is defined as the sum of the square of the number of tables in each unrelated subgraph of the database schemata, that is:

We apply the previous metrics to the following example (suppliers-and-parts database) taken from Date (1995):

$$COS = \sum_{i=1}^{|US|} NTUSi^2$$

US| number of unrelated subgraphs

$NTUS_i$ number of tables in the related subgraph "i"

This relational database schema can be represented as a relational graph (see figure 3).

CREATE TABLE $_S$		**CREATE TABLE** $_P$		**CREATE TABLE** $_{SP}$	
(S#	S#,	(P#	P#	(S#	S#,
SNAME	NAME,	PNAME	NAME,	P#	P#,
STATUS	STATUS,	COLOR	COLOR,	QTY	QTY,
CITY	CITY,	WEIGHT	WEIGHT,	PRIMARY KEY (S#, P#),	
PRIMARY KEY (S#));		CITY	CITY,	FOREIGN KEY (S#) REFERENCES S,	
		PRIMARY KEY (P#));		FOREIGN KEY (P#) REFERENCES P);	

In this schema the value of the metrics are: NA = 12, DRT = 1, NFK = 2, COS = 9.

Metrics for Object-Relational Databases

Object-relational databases combine the characteristics of relational databases with object-oriented principles. These database products provide the capability to define classes or abstract data types in addition to relational theory. An object-relational database schema is composed of a number of tables related by referential integrity, which have columns that can be defined over simple or complex (user-defined) data types. Simple data types may be one of the classic data types such as

Figure 3. Relational graph for the example

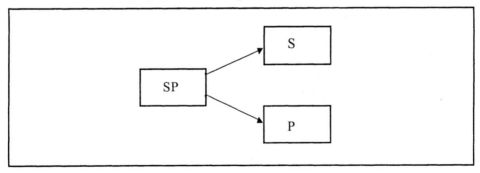

integer, number or character. Complex or user-defined data types, also called classes, can be related with other data types by generalisation associations.

We define the next metrics for object-relational databases (Calero et al., 1999):

Schema size (SS)

We define the size of a system as the sum of the size of every table in the schema:

$$SS = \sum_{i=1}^{NT} TSi$$

And, we can define the table size (TS) as the sum of the total size of the simple columns (TSSC) and the total size of the complex columns (TSCC) in the table:

$$TS_i = TSSC + TSCC$$

We consider that all simple columns have a size equal to one, then the TSSC metric is equal to the number of simple columns in the table (NSC).

$$TSSC = NSC$$

And the TSCC is defined as the sum of each complex column size (CCS):

$$TSCC = \sum_{i=1}^{NCC} CCS_i$$

Being NCC the number of complex columns in the table.
The value for CCS is obtained as:

$$CCS = \frac{SHC}{NCU}$$

SHC is the "size of the hierarchy" (formed by the user-defined data types and their antecessors)" above which the column is defined and NCU is the number of columns defined above this hierarchy. This expression reflects the fact that the effort to understand two complex columns decreases if both are defined over the same class.

The SHC may be defined as the sum of each data type size in the hierarchy (DTS):

$$SHC = \sum_{i=1}^{NDTH} DTS_i$$

NDTH being the number of data types in the hierarchy.
The size of a data type is defined as:

$$DTS = \frac{SADT + SMDT}{NHDT}$$

SADT being the sum of the size attributes of the data type, SMDT the size methods of the data type and NHDT the number of hierarchies to which the data type pertain.

The attributes of a data type may be simple or complex. The SADT is defined as the sum of the simple attributes size (SAS, that have size equal to one like simple attributes) and the complex attributes size (CAS, that can be calculated using the same expression as DTS) in the data type.

$$SADT = SAS + CAS$$

And the SMDT is calculated with the version of the cyclomatic complexity of McCabe given by Li and Henry (1993):

$$SMDT = \sum_{i=1}^{NMDT} V_i(G)$$ NMDT being the number of methods in the data type

Complexity of references between tables (DRT, NFK)

In object-relational databases, other characteristics of relational databases are preserved. Metrics related with the referential integrity, such as NFK and DRT proposed in the previous section, can also be used.

We can apply these metrics to the following example:

```
CREATE TYPE project AS      CREATE TYPE employee AS (     CREATE TABLE works (
(                           emp_num      INTEGER,         key         CHAR(10),
        name                level        INTEGER,         emp         employee,
        CHAR(10),           salary_base  FLOAT,           adm_date    DATE,
        budget FLOAT);      proj         project)         manager     employee);
                            method calc_salary()
                                RETURNS DECIMAL(7,2));
```

Let us assume that all methods have a cyclomatic complexity equal to 1. In Table 1, we present the value of the size of each data type.

Then, the value for the other metrics are: SHC = 6, CCS = 3, TSCC = 6, TSSC = 2, TS = 8, SS = 8.

Metrics for Active Databases

Active databases provide a way to describe events and their associated reactions (the knowledge model) as well as the runtime strategy to process and combine this active behaviour (the execution model) (Paton and Díaz, 1999).

A common approach to the knowledge model uses event-condition-action rules (ECA rules) that have an event which describes a happening to which the rule may be able to respond, a condition that examines the context in which the event has taken place and an action which describes the task to be carried out by the rule if the relevant event has taken place and the condition has been evaluated to be true. The event part can be a primitive event (e.g., a database operation) or a composite event (e.g., a combination of primitive or composite events using a range of operators that constitute the event algebra as conjunction, disjunction, sequence, etc.). For the purpose of the metrics presented here, the *cardinality* of the rule event corresponds

Table 1. Size values of the data types

Name data type	SMDT	SADT SAS + CAS	DTS
PROJECT	0	2 + 0	2
EMPLOYEE	1	3 + 2	6

to the number of primitive events that are (either directly or indirectly) referred to in the event part of the rule, regardless of the composite operator used.

When measuring active databases, we can make use of the notion of a triggering graph as defined in Aiken, et al. (1995). A triggering graph is a pair <S, L> where S represents the set of ECA rules, and L is a set of directed arcs where an arc is drawn from Si to Sj if Si's action causes the happening of an event occurrence that participates in Sj's events. This notion of triggering graph is modified by Diaz and Piattini (1999) in two aspects. First, arcs are weighted by the number of potential event occurrences produced by the triggering rule (i.e., Si) that could affect the rule (i.e., Sj's event). Second, the nodes S are extended with the set of transactions T. A transaction is an atomic set of (database) actions where any of these actions could correspond to an event triggering one or more rules. Therefore, T nodes will have outgoing links but never incoming links, as we assume that a transaction can never be fired from within a rule's action or another transaction.

An example of an extended triggering graph is shown in Figure 4, where T0 can produce three significant events for S4 and one for S1. The figure also illustrates the fact that S4's events can arise from T0, S2 and S3, which potentially produce 3, 1 and 2 significant events, respectively.

The active database could be characterized by the following triggering graph measures (Díaz et al., 2000):

Figure 4. Measures for assessing the rule's circumstance

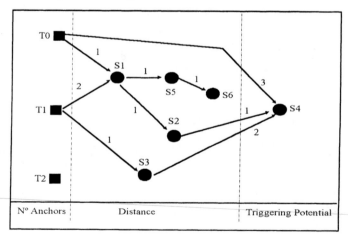

- *NA, the minimum number of anchors required to encompass the whole set of potential causes of Si.* An anchor is a transaction node of the triggering graph, which has a link (either direct or transitive) with at least one cause of Si.
- *D, the distance.* This measure corresponds to the length of the longest path that connects Si with any of its anchors.
- *TP, the triggering potential.* Given a triggering graph <S, L> and a node of the graph, rule Si (the number of causes of Si), is the sum of weights of the incoming arcs arriving to Si. The triggering potential for a rule R is the quotient between the number of potential causes of Si, and Si's event cardinality.

These metrics have to be adapted to particular DBMSs, which differ in the actual support of ECA rules (see for example Widom and Ceri, 1996). In the following example, we will calculate this metric for two SQL:1999 triggers.

CREATE TRIGGER ONE	**CREATE TRIGGER** TWO
AFTER DELETE ON TABLE 3	AFTER DELETE ON TABLE 4
FOR EACH ROW	FOR EACH ROW
WHEN (OLD.NUMBER=3)	WHEN (OLD.NAME='SMITH')
BEGIN	BEGIN
DELETE FROM TABLE 4 WHERE	DELETE FROM TABLE 5 WHERE
DELETE FROM TABLE 5 WHERE	TABLE 4.S#=:OLD.S#;
TABLE4.S#=:TABLE3.J#;	END TWO;
END ONE;	

For trigger ONE: NA = 1, TP = 1 and D = 1; for trigger TWO: NA = 1, TP = 1 and D = 2.

METRICS FORMAL VALIDATION

There are two basic tendencies in formal metrics validation: axiomatic approaches and measurement theory.

In this section, we will present both validation techniques with an example of a formal framework. The formal framework proposed by Briand, et al. (1996) is an example of axiomatic approach, and Zuse's formal framework is based on measurement theory.

Briand's Formal Framework

The Briand, et al. (1996) mathematical framework presents a series of properties that must be fulfilled by certain types of metrics. The different kinds of metrics, and the properties which identify every one, are applicable to modules and modular systems. The main elements of this framework are:

- A *System* is defined as a pair *(E,R)*, where *E* is the set of elements of *S*, and *R* is a binary relation among the elements of *E* $(R \subseteq ExE)$. From this point, we say that *m* is a *Module* of S if and only if $E_m \subseteq E$, $R_m \subseteq E_m x E_m$ and $R_m \subseteq R$.

- The elements of a module are connected with elements of other modules of the system with input and output relations. So, the following two sets are defined:
  $InputR(m)=\{(e_1,e_2)\in R \mathbin{/} e_2\in E_m \wedge e_1\in E\text{-}E_m\}$
  $OutputR(m)=\{(e_1,e_2)\in R \mathbin{/} e_1\in E_m \wedge e_2\in E\text{-}E_m\}$
- $MS=(E,R,M)$ is a *Modular System* if $S=(E,R)$ is a system according to the previous definition and M is a collection of modules of S with no common elements (they are disjoint).
- IR is the union of all the relations, which relate the entities of a concrete module (intramodule relationship). According to this definition, $R\text{-}IR$ is the set of relations among elements of different modules (intermodule relationship).

This framework provides a set of mathematical properties that characterize and formalize several important measurement concepts: size, length, complexity, cohesion and coupling (see Table 2).

Zuse's Formal Framework

This framework is based on an extension of the classical measurement theory. People are interested in establishing "empirical relations" between objects, such as "higher than" or "equally high or higher than." These empirical relations will be indicated by the symbols "• >" and "• >=" respectively. We called Empirical

Table 2. Measurement concepts and their properties (Briand et al., 1996)

	SIZE	LENGTH	COMPLEXITY	COHESION	COUPLING
Nonnegativity	X	X	X	X	X
Null value	X	X	X	X	X
(Disjoint) Module additivity	X		X		X
Nonincreasing monotonicity for nonconnected components		X			
Nondecreasing monotonicity for nonconnected components		X			
Disjoint modules		X			
Symmetry			X		
Module Monotonicity			X		
Normalization				X	
Monotonicity				X	X
Cohesive modules				X	
Merging of modules					X

Relational System a triple: A = (A, • >=, o), where A is a non-empty set of objects, • >= is an empirical relation to A and o is a closed binary (concatenation) operation on A.

Zuse (1998) defines a set of properties for measures, which characterize different measurement structures. The most important ones are shown in Table 3. In this table the mathematical structures proposed by the author are presented. Based on these structures, it is possible to know to which scale a metric pertains (see Zuse, 1998, for more information).

When a measure accomplishes the modified extensive structure, it can be used on the ratio scale. If a measure does not satisfy the modified extensive structure, the combination rule (which describes the properties of the software measure clearly) will exist or not exist depending on the independence conditions. When a measure assumes the independence conditions but not the modified extensive structure, the scale type is the ordinal scale. Finally, if a metric accomplishes the modified relation of belief, it can be characterized above the ordinal scale (the characterization of measures above the ordinal scale level is very important because we cannot do very much with ordinal numbers).

Example

We present the formal validation made with the NFK metric on both formal frameworks:

Table 3. Zuse's formal framework properties

MODIFIED EXTENSIVE STRUCTURE	INDEPENDENCE CONDITIONS	MODIFIED RELATION OF BELIEF
Axiom1: (A, • >=) (weak order) **Axiom2**: A1 o A2 • >= A1 (positivity) **Axiom3**: A1 o (A2 o A3) ≈ (A1 o A2) o A3 (weak associativity) **Axiom4**: A1 o A2 ≈ A2 o A1 (weak commutativity) **Axiom5**: A1 • >= A2 ⇒ A1 o A • >= A2 o A (weak monotonicity) **Axiom6**: If A3 • > A4 then for any A1, A2, there exists a natural number n, such that A1o nA3 • >A2 o nA4 (Archimedean axiom)	**C1**: A1 ≈ A2 ⇒ A1 o A ≈ A2 o A and A1 ≈ A2 ⇒ A o A1 ≈ A o A2 **C2**: A1 ≈ A2 ⇔ A1 o A ≈ A2 o A and A1 ≈ A2 ⇔A o A1 ≈ A o A2 **C3**: A1 • >= A2 ⇒ A1 o A • >= A2 o A, and A1 • >= A2 ⇒ A o A1 • >= A o A2 **C4**: A1 • >= A2 ⇔ A1 o A • >= A2 o A, and A1 • >= A2 ⇔A o A1 • >= A o A2 Where A1 ≈ A2 if and only if A1 • >= A2 and A2 • >= A1, and A1 • > A2 if and only if A1 • >= A2 and not (A2 • >= A1).	**MRB1**: ∀ A, B ∈ ℑ: A • >= B or B • >= A (completeness) **MRB2**: ∀ A, B, C ∈ ℑ: A • >= B and B • >= C ⇒ A • >= C (transitivity) **MRB3**: ∀ A B ⇒ A • >= B (dominance axiom) **MRB4**: ∀ (A ... B, A ∩ C = f) ⇒ (A • >= B ⇒ A U C • > B U C) (partial monotonicity) **MRB5**: ∀ A ∈ ℑ: A • >= 0 (positivity)

Briand's formal framework

To demonstrate that NFK is a complexity metric, we prove the properties given by Briand, et al. (1996) for this kind of metrics:

1. *Non-negativity*. The complexity of a system $S=<E,R>$ is non-negative. Complexity$(S) \geq 0$
2. *Null value*. The complexity of a schema is null if it has no referential integrity relations.
   $(R=\varnothing)$ fi (Complexity$(S)=0$)
3. *Symmetry*. The complexity of a schema does not depend on the convention chosen to represent the referential integrity relations between its elements.
   ($S=<E,R>$ and $S^{-1}=<E,R^{-1}>$) fi Complexity(S) = Complexity(S^{-1})
   The definition of NFK is the same disregarding the direction of the reference.
4. *Module Monotonicity*. The complexity of a schema $S=<E,R>$ is no less than the sum of the complexities of any two of its modules with no referential integrity relationships in common.
   ($S=<E,R>$ and $m_1=<E_{m1},R_{m1}>$ and
   $m_2=<E_{m2},R_{m2}>$ and $m_1 \cup m_2 \subseteq S$ and
   $R_{m1} \cap R_{m2}=\varnothing$) fi Complexity$(S) \geq$ Complexity(m_1)+Complexity(m_2)
   If the modules are not disjointed, this means that between elements of both modules, there is a relation of referential integrity, so NFK never decreases.
5. *Disjoint Module Additivity*. The complexity of a schema composed of two disjointed modules is equal to the sum of the complexities of the two modules.
   ($S=<E,R>$ and $S= m_1 \cup m_2$ and $m_1 \cap m_2=\varnothing$)
   $\Rightarrow$ Complexity$(S) \geq$ Complexity(m_1) + Complexity(m_2)
   Every module will have a value for NFK. When modules are disjointed, neither a foreign key nor a table will be common to both modules. Therefore, the result of NFK of the system will be the sum of the NFK of the two modules.

Zuse's formal framework

In order to obtain the combination rule for NFK, we can observe that the number of foreign keys when we made a concatenation by a natural join decreases when this join is made by foreign keys and candidate keys, and remains the same when the join is made in other ways.

So, we can characterize the combination rule for NFK as:
NFK$(R_i o R_j)$ = NFK(R_i) + NFK(R_j) -v

NFK and the modified extensive structure

- *Axiom 1.* Weak order is fulfilled because it fulfills transitivity: NFK(R1)>=NFK(R2) or NFK(R2)>=NFK(R1) and completeness: NFK(R1)>=NFK(R2) and NFK(R2)>=NFK(R3) $\Rightarrow$ NFK(R1)>=NFK(R3).
- *Axiom 2. Positivity.* It is not fulfilled because if R1 has one foreign key (which connects R1 with R2) and R2 hasn't foreign keys, the result of the R1oR2 is zero.
- *Axiom 3. Weak associativity.* It is fulfilled because the natural join operation is associative.

- *Axiom 4. Weak commutativity.* It is fulfilled because the natural join operation is commutative.
- *Axiom 5. Weak monotonicity.* It is not fulfilled as we can see in Figure 5:
- *Axiom 6. Archimedean axiom.* It is necessary to prove every axiom because when we combine a table with itself, the number of foreign keys vary, then the metric is not idempotent. In order to prove that the Archimedean axiom is not fulfilled, see Figure 6, where an example that does not fulfill the axiom is shown.

NFK and the independence condition structure

- C1. is not fulfilled. If we observe Figure 11, R2 and R4 have NFK=1; if we combine both tables with R5, we obtain NFK(R2oR5)=1 and NFK(R4oR5)=0.
- C2. If the first is not fulfilled, the second is not fulfilled.
- C3. The third is not fulfilled because the weak monotonicity is not fulfilled.
- C4. If the third is not fulfilled, the fourth cannot be fulfilled.

NFK and the modified structure of belief

- As NFK fulfills weak order, it also fulfills conditions one and two.
- The third condition is also fulfilled because if all the foreign keys of B are in A, then it is clear that NFK(A)>=NFK(B).
- Fourth condition, if A□B, then NFK(A)>NFK(B), if there are neither common foreign keys between A and C, nor can be common foreign keys between B and C, then the condition is fulfilled.
- The last conditions are also fulfilled because if A does not have foreign keys, NFK(A)=0 but it cannot be less than zero.

To summarize, we can characterize NFK as a measure above the level of the ordinal scale, assuming the modified relation of belief.

Figure 5. NFK does not fulfill weak monotonicity

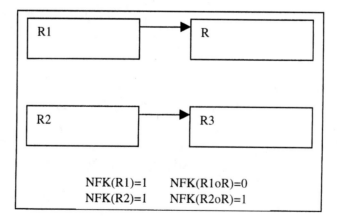

Figure 6. NFK does not fulfill the Archimedean axiom

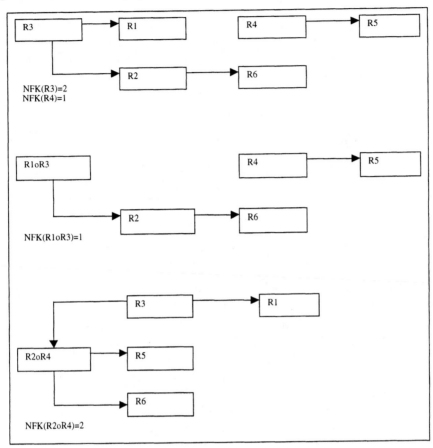

Summary of the Metrics Formal Validation

In Table 4, we present the results obtained for all the presented metrics on both formal frameworks.

With the axiomatic approach results, we can know, for example for relational databases, that we need some metrics for capturing cohesion and coupling and covering all the characteristics defined by the framework. From the measurement theory results, we can know what kind of operations it is possible to make with the defined metrics and the statistics that it is possible to apply to them.

METRICS EMPIRICAL VALIDATION

In the past, empirical validation has been an informal process relying on the credibility of the proposer. Often times, when a measure was identified theoretically as an effective measure of complexity, then practitioners and researchers began to use the metric without questioning its validity. Today, many researchers and practitioners assume that validation of a measure (from a theoretical point of view) is not sufficient for widespread acceptance. They expect the empirical validation to demonstrate that the measure itself can be validated. Useful results of an experiment depend on careful, rigorous and complete experimental design. A claim that a measure is valid because

Table 4. Summary of metrics formal validation

		BRIAND ET AL(1996)	**ZUSE(1998)**
Relational	**NFK**	COMPLEXITY	ABOVE THE ORDINAL
	DRT	LENGTH	ABOVE THE ORDINAL
	NA	SIZE	ABOVE THE ORDINAL
	COS	SIZE	RATIO
Orel	**SS**	SIZE	ABOVE THE ORDINAL
	TS	SIZE	ABOVE THE ORDINAL
Active	**NA**	COMPLEXITY	ABOVE THE ORDINAL
	TP	NOT CLASSIFIABLE	ABOVE THE ORDINAL
	D	LENGTH	ABOVE THE ORDINAL

it is a good predictor of some interesting attribute can be justified only by formulating a hypothesis about the relationship and then testing the hypothesis (Fenton and Pfleeger, 1997).

In the rest of this section, we summarize different experiments that we have done with some of the metrics discussed in this chapter. All of these initial experiments require further experimentation in order to validate the findings. However, these results can be useful as a starting point for future research.

A complete description of the experiments can be found in Calero, et al. (2000) for relational database metrics, in Piattini, et al. (2000) for object-relational ones and in Díaz, et al. (2000) for active ones.

Relational Experiment

Our objective was to demonstrate that the metrics related with referential integrity (DRT and NFK) can be used for measuring the complexity of the relational database schema, which influences the relational database understandability. The formal hypotheses were:

- *Null hypothesis*: Different values of metrics do not affect the comprehension of the database schema.
- *Alternative hypothesis 1*: The value of the DRT metric affects the comprehension of the database schema.
- *Alternative hypothesis 2*: The value of the NFK metric affects the comprehension of the database schema.
- *Alternative hypothesis 3*: The combination of the DRT and NFK metrics affects the comprehension of the database schema.

The participants of this study were computer science students at the University of Castilla-La Mancha (Spain), who were enrolled in a two-semester databases course. To test the hypotheses, four separate software designs were required. In each design, the values of the two metrics were different. There were two possible values for both the NFK metric (eight or five) and for the DRT metric (two or five). As each level of one factor appears with each level of the other one, we have selected the crossing design. The documentation accompanying each test was approximately seven pages long and includes the schema database, the tables with their rows and the question/answer paper. For each of the four designs, the database schema had six tables. The subjects were asked to perform three tasks with the values of the database schema: insert, delete and update.

Based on the results of this experiment, we concluded that the number of foreign keys in a relational database schema is a more solid indicator of its understandability than the length of the referential tree. This metric is not relevant by itself, but can modulate the effect of the number of foreign keys in a database system

Object-Relational Experiment

Five object-relational databases were used in this experiment with an average of 10 relations per database. Five subjects participated in the experiment. All of them were experienced in both relational databases and object-oriented programming.

The subjects were given a form, which includes for each table a triplet of values to compute using the corresponding schema. These values are those of three measures: TS, DRT and NFK. Our idea is that to compute these measures, we needed to understand the subschema (objects and relations) defined by a particular table. A table (and the corresponding subschema) is easy to understand if (almost) all the subjects find the right values in a limited time (two minutes per table). Formally, a value "1" is assignefd to the understandability of a table if at least 10 of 12 measures are computed correctly in the specified time (four subjects and three measures). A value "0" is assigned otherwise. The tables are given to the subjects in a random order and not by the database.

After compiling the results, 28 tables were classified as difficult to understand (0) and 22 easy to understand (1). To analyze the usefulness of the metrics, we used two techniques: C4.5 (Quinlan, 1993), a machine learning algorithms, and RoC (Ramoni, 1999), a robust Bayesian classifier.

In conclusion, both techniques demonstrate that the table size is a good indicator for the understandability of a table. The depth of the referential tree is also presented as an indicator by C4.5 but not clearly by RoC. The number of foreign keys does not seem to have a real impact on the understandability of a table.

Active Experiment

Our objective was to assess the influence of D and TP in rule interaction understandability. However, such understanding could be influenced by how the reasoning is conducted. As rules can be seen as cause-and-effect links, two questions can be posed by the user: "What effects can a rule produce (forward reasoning)?" and

"How can an effect be produced (backward reasoning)?" The former question begins with an operation (event), which determines its effects in the database. This process is more common during trigger definition. By contrast, backward reasoning begins with a database state and strives to ascertain the causing operation. This process is more common during trigger maintenance.

The participants of the experiment were final-year computer science students at the University of the Basque Country, who were enrolled in an advance database course. The students were already familiar with relational database, and some laboratories were previously conducted on the definition of triggers. Three documents were prepared: 1) a document with a database schema together with the corresponding entity/relationship diagram and an extension (set of tuples) for each of the four tables, 2) the forward-reasoning document with four tests and 3) the backward-reasoning document with four tests.

For the forward experiment, we concluded that the triggering potential in a database schema is a solid indicator of its understandability, and that the distance is not relevant by itself and cannot modulate the effect of the triggering potential. For the backward experiment, we concluded that both metrics are solid indicators of its understandability.

All the presented experiments need to be replicated to have more consistent results. However, controlled experiments made in the laboratory are useful as a starting point but present some problems, such as the large number of variables that can cause differences. So, it is convenient also to run case studies working with real data.

CONCLUSIONS AND FUTURE WORK

Databases are becoming more complex, and it is necessary to measure schemata complexity in order to understand, monitor, control, predict and improve database development and maintenance projects. Database metrics could help designers, to choose between alternative semantically equivalent schemata, and to understand their contribution to the overall IS maintainability.

We have put forward different measures (for internal attributes) in order to measure the complexity that affects the maintainability (an external attribute) of the relational, object-relational and active database schemas.

It is not enough to propose the metrics; a formal validation is also needed for knowing their mathematical characteristics. We have presented the two main tendencies in metrics formal validation, axiomatic approaches and measurement theory. Although the information obtained from both techniques are different, the final objective is the same--to obtain objective mathematical information of the metrics we are working on. As an example of axiomatic approach, we have presented here the formal framework proposed by Briand, et al. (1996), and as an example of measurement theory, the formal framework proposed by Zuse (1998). For both frameworks we have presented an example of formal validation.

However, research into software measurement is needed from a theoretical, but also from a practical point of view (Glass, 1993). We have presented some experiments we developed for the different kinds of databases. But controlled experiments have problems (like the large number of variables that cause differences) and limits (they do not scale up, are done in a class in training situations, are made in vitro and face a variety of threats of validity). Then, is convenient to run multiple studies, mixing controlled experiments and case studies. For these reasons, a more deep empirical evaluation is under way in collaboration with industrial and public organizations in real situations.

ACKNOWLEDGMENT

This research is part of the MANTICA project, partially supported by the CICYT and the European Union (CICYT-1FD97-0168) and by the CALIDAT project carried out by Cronos Ibérica (supported by the Consejería de Educación de la Comunidad de Madrid, Nr. 09/0013/1999).

REFERENCES

Aiken, A., Hellerstein, J.M. and Widom, J. (1995). Static analysis techniques for predicting the behaviour of active database rules. *ACM Transactions on Databases*, 20(1), 3-41.

Anderson, J.R. (1983). *The Architecture of Cognition*. Cambridge, MA: Harvard Universitiy Press.

Basili, V.R., Shull, F. and Lanubille, F. (1999). Building knowledge through families of experiments, *IEEE Transactions on Software Engineering*, July/August, 4, 456-473.

Batra, D., Hoffer, J.A. and Bostrom, R.P. (1990). A comparison of user performance between the relational and the extended entity relationship models in the discovery phase of database design. *CACM*, 33(2), 126-139.

Briand, L.C., Morasca, S. And Basili, V. (1996). Property-based software engineering measurement. *IEEE Transactions on Software Engineering*, 22(1), 68-85.

Calero, C., Piattini, M., Ruiz, F. and Polo, M. (1999). Validation of metrics for object-relational databases, *International Workshop on Quantitative Approaches in Object-Oriented Software Engineering (ECOOP99)*, Lisbon (Portugal), June 14-18.

Calero, C., Pascual, C., Serrano, M.A. and Piattini, M. (1999). Measuring Oracle database schemas, *3rd IMACS International Multiconference on Circuits, Systems, Communications and Computers (CSCC99)*, July 5-8.

Calero, C., Piattini, M., Genero, M., Serrano, M. and Caballero, I. (2000). Metrics for relational databases maintainability, *UKAIS2000*, Cardiff, UK.

Carey et al. (1990). Thir-generation database system manifesto. Committee for Advanced DBMS Function. *SIGMOD Record*, 19(3), 31-44.

Cattell, R.G.G. (1991). What are next-generation database systems? *Communications of the ACM*, 34(10), 31-33.

Churcher, N.J. and Shepperd, M.J. (1995). Comments on "A Metrics Suite for Object-Oriented Design." *IEEE Transactions on Software Engineering*, 21(3), 263-265.

Date, C.J. (1995). *An Introduction to Database Systems*. 6th edition. Addison-Reading: MA.

Díaz, O. and Piattini, M. (1999). Metrics for active databases maintainability. *CAISE '99*. Heidelberg, June 16-18.

Díaz, O., Piattini. M. and Calero, C. (2000). Measuring active databases maintainability. Accepted for publication in *Information Systems Journal.*

Fenton, N. (1994). Software measurement: A necessary scientific basis. *IEEE Transactions on Software Engineering*, 20(3), 199-206.

Fenton, N. and Pfleeger, S. L. (1997). *Software Metrics: A Rigorous Approach.* 2nd edition. London: Chapman & Hall.

Frazer, A. (1992). Reverse engineering-hype, hope or here? In Hall, P.A.V. *Software Reuse and Reverse Engineering in Practice.* Chapman & Hall.

Glass, R. (1996). The Relationship between theory and practice in software engineering. *IEEE Software*, 39(11), 11-13.

Gray R.H.M., Carey B.N., McGlynn N.A. and Pengelly A.D. (1991). Design metrics for database systems. *BT Technology J.* 9(4), 69-79.

Henderson-Sellers, B. (1996*). Object-oriented metrics - Measures of Complexity.* Stet L.C. Upper Saddle River, NJ: Prentice-Hall.

ISO. (1994). Software product evaluation-quality characteristics and guidelines for their use. *ISO/IEC Standard 9126*, Geneva.

Jarvenpaa, S. and Machesky, J. (1986). End-user learning behavior in data analysis and data modeling tools. Proceedings of the *7th International Conference on Information Systems*, San Diego, 152-167.

Juhn, S. and Naumann, J. (1985). The effectiveness of data representation characteristics on user validation. Proceedings of the *6th International Conference on Information Systems*, Indianapolis, 212-226.

Kim, Y.G. and March, S.T. (1995). Comparing Data Modeling Formalisms. *CACM* 38(6), 103-115.

Kitchenham, B. and Stell, J.G. (1997). The danger of using axioms in software metrics. *IEEE Proceedings on Software Engineering.* 144(5-6), 279-285.

Li, H.F. and Cheng, W.K. (1987). An empirical study of software metrics. *IEEE Transactions on Software Engineering*, 13(6), 679-708.

Li, W. and Henry, S. (1993). Object-oriented metrics that predict maintainability. *J. Sys. Software*, 23, 111-122.

MacDonell, S.G., Shepperd, M.J. and Sallis, P.J. (1997). Metrics for database systems: An empirical study. *Proceedings of the Fourth International Software Metrics Symposium – Metrics '97*, Albuquerque. IEEE Computer Society, 99-107.

McCabe, T.J. (1976). A complexity measure. *IEEE Transactions Software Engineering,* 2(5), 308-320.

McClure, C. (1992). *The Three Rs of software automation: Re-engineering, Repository, Reusability.* Englewood Cliffs, NJ: Prentice-Hall.

Melton, A. (Ed.). (1996). *Software Measurement.* London: International Thomson Computer Press.

Moody, D. L. (1998). Metrics for evaluating the quality of entity relationship models. *Proceedings of the Seventeenth International Conference on Conceptual Modeling (ER '98),* Singapore.

Morasca, S. and Briand, L.C. (1997). Towards a theoretical framework for measuring software attributes. *Proceedings of the Fourth International, Software Metrics Symposium*, 119-126.

Paton, M. and Díaz, O. (1998). Active Databases Systems. *ACM Computer Surveys*, 31(1), 63-103.

Pfleeger, S. L. (1997). Assessing software measurement. *IEEE Software*. March/April, 25-26.

Piattini, M., Calero, C., Sahraoui, H. and Lounis, H. (2000). An empirical study with object-relational database metrics, *ECOOP'2000*, Cannes, June 13.

Piattini, M., Genero, M., Calero, C., Polo, M. and Ruiz, F. (2001). Metrics for managing quality in information modeling. In M. Rossie and K. Siau (Eds.) *Information Modeling in the New Millennium*. Hershey, PA: Idea Group Publishing.

Pigoski, T.M. (1997). *Practical Software Maintenance*. Wiley Computer Publishing: New York.

Quinlan, J.R. (1993). C4.5: Programs for machine learning,, *Morgan Kaufmann Publishers.*

Ramoni, M. and Sebastiani, P. (1999). Bayesian methods for intelligent data analysis. In M. Berthold and D.J. Hand, (Eds.). *An Introduction to Intelligent Data Analysis,* New York: Springer.

Rossi, M. and Brinkkemper, S. (1996). Complexity Metrics for Systems Development Methods and Techniques. *Information Systems,* 21(2), 209-227.

Shoval, P. and Even-Chaime, M. (1987). Database schema design: An experimental comparison between normalization and information analysis. *Database*, 18(3), 30-39.

Siau, K. (1999). Information modeling and method engineering: A psychological perspective. *Journal of Database Management* 10 (4), 44-50.

Sneed, H.M. and Foshag, O. (1998). Measuring Legacy Database Structures. Van Huysduynen and Peeters (Eds.). *Proceedings of the European Software Measurement Conference FESMA 98*, Antwerp, May 6-8, Coombes, 199-211.

Stevens, S. (1946). On the theory of scales and measurements. *Science,* 103, 677-680.

Stonebraker, M. and Brown, P. (1999*). Object-Relational DBMSs: Tracking the Next Great Wave.* Morgan Kauffman Publishers: CA.

Weyuker, E.J. (1988). Evaluating software complexity measures. *IEEE Transactions on Software Engineering.* 14(9), 1357-1365.

Whitmire, S.A. (1997). Object-oriented design measurement. Wiley.

Widom, J. and Ceri, S. (Eds.). (1996). *Active Database Systems*. Morgan-Kaufmann.

Zuse, H. (1998). *A Framework of Software Measurement.* Berlin: Walter de Gruyter.

Chapter IV

Integrating Hypermedia Functionality into Database Applications

Anirban Bhaumik, Deepti Dixit, Roberto Galnares, Aparna Krishna,
Michael Bieber, Vincent Oria, Firas Alljalad and Li Zhang
New Jersey Institute of Technology, USA

Michalis Vaitis and Manolis Tzagarakis
University of Patras, Greece

Qiang Lu
New Jersey Institute of Technology, USA and
Suzhou University, Peoples Republic of China

ABSTRACT

The general goal of our research is to automatically generate links and other hypermedia-related services to analytical applications, such as geographic information systems and decision support systems. Using a dynamic hypermedia engine (DHE), we propose to automate the following features for database systems, both on and off the Web. First, we automatically generate links based on the database's relational (conceptual) schema and its original (non-normalized) entity-relationship specification. Second, the application developer can specify which kinds of database elements are related to diverse elements in the same or different database application, or even another software system. Our current DHE prototype illustrates these for a relational database management system. We propose integrating data warehousing applications into the DHE. We also propose incorporating data mining as a new kind of automated link generation. Passing the application element selected by a user, a data mining system would discover interesting relationships for that element. DHE would then map each relationship to a link. DHE's linking is based on the structure of the application, not keyword search or lexical analysis based on the display values within its screens and documents. DHE aims to provide hypermedia functionality without altering applications by building "application wrappers" as an intermediary between the applications and the engine.

INTRODUCTION AND MOTIVATION

Database queries typically return results in a plain text format. Some applications on the World Wide Web generate link anchors for database elements, but these anchors normally hold a single link to the most obvious destination for the dominant type of user.

We could consider each element within a database application as a potential starting point for information exploration. Each element could have multiple links, each representing a different relationship (schema-based or otherwise). The ability to explore a piece of information in more detail could help users resolve doubts about or simply better understand that item, as well as the analysis or display of which it is a part. Users may wish to dig deeper around data values and symbols, labels on graphs or user input forms, options in pop-up lists or even on the menu commands they can invoke.

To complicate the developer's job, users often have different mental models of an application and its underlying domain than the developer. Even when developers work closely with users, the end result might not be intuitive for all users or serve each user's individual tasks equally well. Many people visit a given application's screen aside from the most dominant type of user(s) for which it was developed. These include other users of the application, customer service representatives, company analysts, managers, trainees, people inside the company designing new databases or applications based on the current one, external analysts and stockholders, among others. Each may be interested in different aspects of application elements, according to their current task-at-hand. Customization is one solution, but even so, users might often wish to explore several different relationships from a given anchor, and therefore should have several links available.

The purpose of this chapter is to explore all aspects of hypermedia support for database applications. We base much of our discussion on our experience designing the Dynamic Hypermedia Engine (DHE). DHE automatically generates anchors, sets of links and metadata within database applications, as well as supporting users with other types of hypermedia structuring, navigation and annotation functionality, including guided tours and annotation. As we explain later, the links provide direct access to a broad range of relationships among application elements, including those outside a database schema. Metadata, defined as data about data, shows users parameters and other characteristics about any given element.

This work makes many contributions to both the database and hypermedia fields. Many database applications do not take as much advantage of hypermedia as they could. This chapter puts forth a series of opportunities for integrating hypermedia and database systems. As we shall describe in the next section, DHE is the only tool that provides automated linking and hypermedia services based on the application structure (as opposed to search or lexical analysis), without altering applications. Thus it is uniquely suited to support databases and other analytical applications on the Web that generate the contents of their displays dynamically in response to user queries.

This chapter proceeds as follows. After introducing the Dynamic Hypermedia Engine, we describe hypermedia support for databases. We show how DHE can support existing relational database management systems, then we describe how DHE uses databases internally to support hypermedia. Next we look at integrating data warehousing and applications that use database support. Then we consider generating links through data mining. After this we present a literature review of hypermedia and database integration, followed by a short conclusion. Table 1 gives the set of acronyms we use in this chapter.

THE DYNAMIC HYPERMEDIA ENGINE

We have just developed the very first cut of a Web-based prototype of the Dynamic Hypermedia Engine (DHE), which redesigns an older PC-based prototype (Bieber, 1999). Figure 1 shows a screenshot of a database query result in the top frame. DHE has added anchors to all parts of the query result, including the field names at the column heads. The user has clicked on "Counseling Center-department,"

Table 1. Acronyms in this chapter

Acronym	Full Name
DHE	Dynamic Hypermedia Engine
DSM	Database Schema Mapper
JDBC	Java Database Connectivity
OLAP	On-Line Analytical Processing
RDBMS	Relational Database Management System
RDF	Resource Description Framework
RDWM	Relational Database Wrapper Module
RMI	Remote Method Invocation
SQL	Structured Query Language
UI	User Interface
URI	Uniform Resource Identifier
XML	Extended Markup Language

resulting in metadata for the element in the bottom center frame and a list of links in the bottom right-hand frame. Selecting any link will generate a standard Structured Query Language statement (SQL query) to create the appropriate result. Currently the list of links includes only database structural links, such as finding the primary keys for this element. As we later describe, however, we are developing a module to add links automatically based on a database's original (non-normalized) entity-relationship schema. The bottom left-hand frame contains menus for any integrated application or DHE internal module. Links represent relationships, and relationships have meta-information as well. Selecting an asterisk next to any link will provide metadata and a list of links for it. DHE's next release will provide these for menu items as well. The metadata frame currently displays the full Resource Description Framework record. DHE's next release will format the metadata nicely. Future

Figure 1: Screen from our preliminary DHE Web prototype

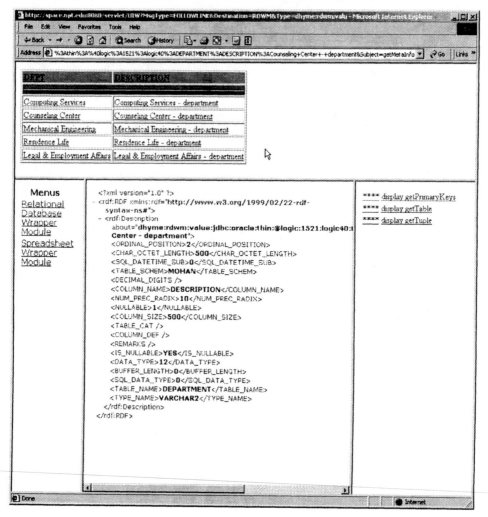

versions will filter and rank order the links and metadata based on the user task and preferences.

As this demonstrates, DHE link generation does not result from any type of lexical analysis. Our focus is not on the display content of the link anchor, but rather on the application elements underlying each anchor. A mapping rule encodes each relationship found between two elements of interest at the class level. For example, suppose an application display shows the name of a university department. Departments generally have professors and courses taught (based on the standard entity-relationship diagram within a database system), as well as a Web page, an annual budget (within the accounting system), hires-in-progress (within the personnel system), a location on a map (within a geographic information system), etc. Individual mapping rules contain an algorithm or computation (set of commands) leading to the appropriate component in these respective systems. When the user selects a particular department, DHE constructs these commands with the actual department instance selected and sends them to the appropriate destination system, which then retrieves—or more often generates—the resulting page. For example, one mapping rule could state that an element of type "department" would be related to an element of type "annual budget" through a relationship with the semantic type "annual budget for" and with a parameterized command to retrieve annual budgets from the accounting system. Developers may take advantage of this to integrate database applications with other applications without altering their contents; they only have to add new mapping rules for the relevant element types.

DHE executes concurrently with database management systems, database applications and other applications such as the accounting system, providing automated link generation and other hypermedia functionality without altering them. Developers write an independent application wrapper and a set of mapping rules. Note that once a wrapper is written and the mapping rules are specified for each type of application (geographic information system, relational database management system, accounting package, etc.), DHE will support all instances of that application in the future (new maps, database contents, budget sheets, etc.).

DHE executes as follows. Applications or their wrappers connect to DHE through World Wide Web components, such as servlets and JavaServer pages. DHE intercepts all messages passing between the application and its user interface, and uses the mapping rules to map each appropriate element of the message to a hypermedia anchor. Our Web browser wrapper merges these anchors into the document being displayed and passes the resulting HTML document through the Web component servlet to the user's Web browser. When the user selects an anchor, the browser wrapper passes it to DHE, which returns a list of possible links (one for each appropriate relationship as determined by the mapping rules) and metadata. If the user selects a DHE link (e.g., to add an annotation or stage in a guided tour), DHE processes it entirely. If the user selects a relationship with a destination in a known application, DHE infers and instantiates the appropriate SQL queries or other application commands from the relationship's mapping rule and passes them to the target application for processing. If the user selects a user-created annotation or tour, etc., DHE retrieves it. Thus DHE automatically provides all hypermedia linking (as well as navigation) to applications, which remain hypermedia-unaware and in fact often entirely unchanged.

Figure 2 shows DHE's logical engine architecture. We shall describe some of the major components here. The others are described on our project Web site (http://dhe.njit.edu). For our current Web prototype, we have programmed all modules in Java. We use XML as our message format. While the browser wrapper currently produces HTML documents for display, we intend to migrate to XML documents, which take advantage of the Web's new XLink, and XPointer standards to handle anchors and links. We use RMI for inter-module communications. We intend to keep up with Web standards as they become available, whenever practical for our environment.

User Interface Wrappers serve three important functions: first, they translate DHE's internal messages from DHE's standard format to a format the browser (or other user interface or UI) can process, and vice versa. Second, they handle communication between the engine and the UI. Third, they implement any functionality DHE requires from the UI (e.g., maintaining parameters), which the UI cannot provide itself.

The Message Manager Module enables the communication between all DHE modules, routing all DHE internal messages.

The Mapping Rules Module maps the application data and relationships to hypermedia objects at run-time. The Mapping Rules Module maps the element instances in the virtual document to global element types (classes), and infers all relevant relationships (links) and metadata for the given element classes. These links and metadata are passed in messages to the UI Wrapper for display.

Figure 2. DHE's logical architecture

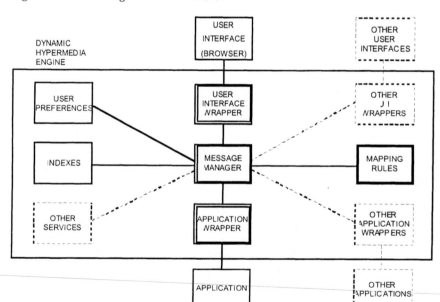

Application Wrappers, like user interface wrappers, manage the communication between DHE and their application systems, such as database applications and DBMS. They translate user requests from DHE's internal format to the application's programming interface (if any). They receive output from the application, convert it to the DHE format, mark the elements for the mapping rules module and send it to DHE for eventual display on the UI.

Other Hypermedia Services: We are planning to implement a series of other service modules over the next few years. Most will implement various kinds of hypermedia structuring, navigation and annotation functionality (Bieber, et al., 1997; Conklin, 1987; Nielsen, 1995). Hypermedia structuring functionality includes local and global information overviews; node, link and anchor typing; as well as keywords, attributes and metadata on all of these. Navigation functionality includes structure-based query, sophisticated history-based navigation and bi-directional linking. Annotation functionality includes adding user-declared links, comments and bookmarks to dynamically generated documents and displays.

What distinguishes these DHE modules from similar modules in other Web applications and other non-Web hypermedia systems is the dynamic nature of the applications we are considering. Our target applications generate documents and screens in response to user queries and other dynamic prompts. Therefore the screens and documents are not static, but "virtual"; they must be generated every time they are needed, and regenerated upon demand within each of these modules. Thus documents on a guided tour, pointed to by a bookmark or link, or found during structural search, may not exist until the user actually selects the anchor representing it (Bieber & Kacmar, 1995). We do this by maintaining sufficient parameters about each document or screen to create the SQL queries or other commands to regenerate them. These commands are not always the same as the original command that generated the document in the first place. (Bieber [1990, 1995] discusses this regeneration in more detail.)

DHE should be able to streamline a company's software development efforts in several ways. It automatically supplements the organization's applications with hypermedia links, structuring, navigation and annotative functionality, and metadata. It also implements inter-application linking, as the university department example shows. Mapping rules can point to any accessible application. DHE also can speed the development of applications. Developers can offload link management, navigational structures (such as guided tours), user preference management and other features to DHE.

Several approaches exist for integrating hypermedia functionality into primarily non-hypermedia information systems. These include employing hypermedia data models (Campbell & Goodman, 1988; Halasz & Schwartz, 1994), hypermedia toolkits (Anderson, 1996), link services (Pearl, 1989; Davis, et al., 1992; Anderson, 1997), hyperbases (Leggett & Schnase 1994), hypermedia development environments (Nanard & Nanard, 1995a; Marshall & Shipman, 1995; Akscyn et al. 1988), open hypermedia systems (Whitehead 1997; Wiil, 1997; Grønbæk & Trigg, 1999) and independently executing hypermedia engines, such as DHE.

Hypermedia engines execute independently of an application with minimal modifications to it, and provide the application's users with hypermedia support. Few approaches provide transparent hypermedia integration as our engine does. Notable projects include Microcosm's Universal Viewer, Freckles and the OO-Navigator and SFX.

Microcosm's Universal Viewer (Davis et al., 1994) and Freckles (Kacmar, 1993, 1995) seamlessly support an application's other functionality but provide only manual linking. OO-Navigator comes the closest to our approach, providing a seamless hypermedia support for computational systems that execute within a single Smalltalk environment (Garrido & Rossi 1996; Rossi et al., 1996). This approach meets our goal of supplementing Smalltalk applications with hypermedia support without altering them. Our approach, however, applies to both object-oriented and non-object-oriented applications.

SFX's engine is very similar to DHE, but it only serves one specific environment. SFX dynamically generates anchors within the reference section of academic papers being displayed on the Web. Selecting these will lead to the original work within bibliographic databases (Van der Stemple, 1999a,b,c). DHE, in contrast, provides a generalized approach for linking and additional hypermedia functionality for most analytical applications.

In the sections that follow, we describe various ways that we can support database management systems and applications, and the ways that databases support our implementation of hypermedia.

HYPERMEDIA SUPPORT
FOR EXISTING DATABASE SYSTEMS

Developers can retrofit existing database applications to work with DHE. This section begins by describing such an integration. Then we describe the different kinds of links and metadata that DHE provides, and conclude with a brief description of a system we have integrated with the DHE.

Integrating Database Applications with DHE

One of the first tasks in providing hypermedia support is to intercept messages between the computational and user interface (UI) portions of the application (Bieber & Kacmar, 1995). In the case of a Relational Database Management System (RDBMS), the application comprises only a computational portion. The RDBMS provides a standard way of requesting computational services (i.e., store, retrieve and analyze data) by means of Structured Query Language (SQL) statements. The Relational Database Wrapper Module we describe below does this and provides its own interface for entering SQL queries and displaying their results.

Database applications build a customized interface and possibly a larger set of functionality around a RDBMS. Database applications, therefore, are responsible for their own UI. Database applications send SQL statements to their RDBMS. The

RDBMS then executes these statements and returns the results of these statements to the application, which then customizes and displays them.

If the UI displays are easy to parse, i.e., a developer could easily figure out which elements are in each display screen and how to pass back database and application commands to the application, then one could write an application wrapper that intercepts all displays and redirects them to DHE. This would satisfy our goal of providing automated hypermedia functionality with minimal change to the application. DHE's UI could display the enhanced screens with hypermedia anchors as shown in Figure 1.

In general, Web-based database applications (Internet storefronts, catalogs, etc.) have a clear distinction between their UI and the database; usually the UI uses a middleware to communicate with the database. The DHE may supplement or replace this middleware. However, most legacy database applications (client server or mainframe based) usually don't have such a clear distinction between their UI and the underlying database; most often the data presentation is commingled. Integration with DHE could be much more difficult in this case.

We have developed a service module, the Relational Database Wrapper Module (RDWM), which accepts requests to execute SQL statements on the underlying

Figure 3. States of the Relational Database Wrapper Module

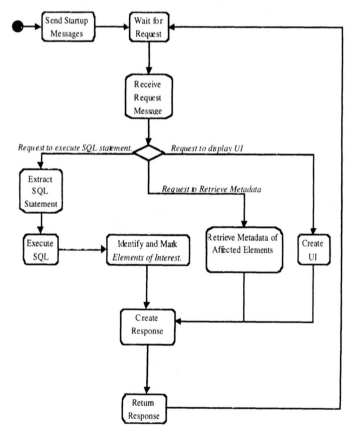

database, and retrieves metadata for a database element. It also provides a UI allowing users to execute SQL statements and view results, metadata and all the relationships among the data affected by the SQL statement. This UI provides a view of the data stored in the database enhanced by metadata, hyperlinks and additional hypermedia functionality.

The RDWM passes through states shown in Figure 3. We next briefly describe each of these.

Sending startup messages

Because of DHE's distributed nature, all modules must register themselves with the DHE Message Manager at startup time, so that the Message Manager knows which modules are currently active and able to receive and process requests.

Receiving request messages

A module waits until it receives a request to perform a service. The RDWM either interacts with the RDBMS, retrieves metadata for an element or generates an input form for users to enter SQL statements.

Extracting and executing SQL statements

The RDWM uses an XML parser to extract the action to be performed and the SQL statement (if any) from the request message. If the request is to execute an SQL statement, then the UI wrapper will have embedded the actual SQL in a request message. (This is its default procedure for user input forms.) The RDWM then uses a persistent pool of JDBC (Java Database Connectivity) Connection Objects, to execute an SQL statement on, or retrieve metadata from the RDBMS.

Identifying an element of interest

Once the result of the SQL statement has been passed to the RDWM for display, the RDWM parses the results. It uses the SQL query itself to determine what elements are in the results. The following 12 types of elements exist in the RDBMS context:

Any instance of the above types can be uniquely identified, have metadata and have one or more relationships associated with it. If any user might be interested in exploring that type of object in terms of its metadata or relationships, the RDWM would mark each of its instances as an "element of interest," and therefore a potential anchor. Marking an item involves providing its unique identifier and its element type. (Later, the Mapping Rules Module will use the element type to find relationships and metadata for a given element. If an element has at least one relationship [link] or piece

Columns	Tables	Indices
Stored Procedures	Catalogs	Schema
Drivers	Users	User Rights
Table and Column Privileges	JDBC Types	The RDBMS Product Instance Itself

of metadata, then the Mapping Rules Module will specify that the UI Wrapper make it into an anchor.)

Using the Uniform Resource Identifier (URI) syntax (Berners-Lee et. al., 1998):

<scheme name>:<scheme-specific-part>

the RDWM defines its element identification scheme as follows:

dhe:rdwm:<element type>:<RDBMS Name>:<Database Name>:<element specific part>

For example, the column named "student_id" in the table "student" in the "Oracle" database on the host "logic.njit.edu" would have the following URI:

dhe:rdwm:column:oracle:logic.njit.edu:student:student_id

Figure 4. Marked up message

```
<OutDoc>

<![CDATA[<table border="0">

    <tr><td><b><#id1>DEPT</#id1></b></td><td><b><#id2>DESCRIPTION</#id2></b></td></tr>

    <tr><td colspan="2"><hr></tr>

    <tr><td><#id3>Computing Services</#id3></td><td><#id4>Computing Services
    department</#id4></td></tr>

    </table>]]>

</OutDoc>

<List_Of_Elements>

<Element>

<Locator>#id3</Locator>

<Type>dhyme:rdwm:value</Type>

<URI>dhyme:rdwm:value:jdbc:oracle:thin:@logic:1521:logic40:DEPARTMENT:DEPT:Computing
Services</URI>

    <Action></Action>

</Element>

<Element>

<Locator>#id2</Locator>

<Type>dhyme:rdwm:column</Type>

<URI>dhyme:rdwm:column:jdbc:oracle:thin:@logic:1521:logic40:DEPARTMENT:DESCRIPTION</URI>

<Action></Action>

</Element>

<Element>

<Locator>#id1</Locator>
```

Marked Up Element

Type of Marked Up Element

URI of Marked Up Element

Because of the case insensitive nature of SQL statements, this scheme, too, is case insensitive.

Figure 4 shows an example marked-up query result.

Structural Links and Metadata for Database Applications

Continuing on with the RDBW states described in Figure 3, we look at the basic structural links and metadata DHE provides database applications.

Relationships between elements

DHE specifies relationships based on the element type. The 12 types of relationships noted above are each interrelated. Figure 5 shows these structural interrelationships. DHE could write a mapping rule for each, which DHE could then use to generate a link for each of its instances containing the appropriate SQL command to generate the contents of the link's endpoint. Figure 1 shows some of these links. Wan (1996; Wan & Bieber 1997) gives several mapping rules (called "bridge laws") for relational databases.

Each relationship depicted in Figure 5 is reflexive, e.g., if a column has an "in table" relationship with a table, then the table has a relationship called "has columns" with the column.

Retrieving metadata

The RDWM retrieves metadata on demand. It is passed the URI of the element whose metadata is being asked for. It then uses the Java Database Connectivity

Figure 5. Relationships between element types

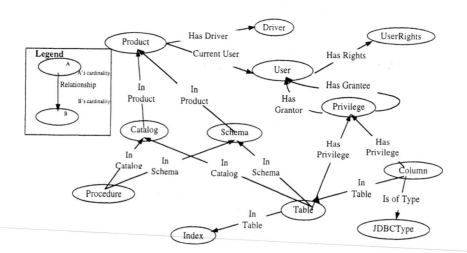

(JDBC) API to retrieve information relevant to the element. The current version of the DHE uses the relational schema to retrieve metadata. Future versions of the DHE will use dedicated metadata repositories and data dictionaries to retrieve additional metadata as well.

The RDWM uses the Resource Description Framework (RDF) to model database metadata. RDF defines metadata in terms of resources, where each resource is any entity that can be uniquely identified, i.e., has a URI (Lassila et. al., 1999). Hence all elements of interest are resources and have associated metadata. Resources and elements are thus interchangeable in the RDWM context, and the element identifier corresponds to its URI.

For example the following segment in RDF/XML serialization syntax represents metadata about a column called "Description" in the table "Department" on the Oracle instance on "logic":

```
<rdf:RDF xmlns:rdf="http://www.w3.org/1999/02/22-rdf-syntax-ns#">
<rdf:Description
about="dhe:rdwm:column:jdbc:oracle:thin:@logic:1521:logic40:DEPARTMENT:DESCRIPTION">
<ORDINAL_POSITION>2</ORDINAL_POSITION>
<CHAR_OCTET_LENGTH>500</CHAR_OCTET_LENGTH>
<SQL_DATETIME_SUB>0</SQL_DATETIME_SUB>
<TABLE_SCHEM>MOHAN</TABLE_SCHEM>
<DECIMAL_DIGITS></DECIMAL_DIGITS>
<COLUMN_NAME>DESCRIPTION</COLUMN_NAME>
<NUM_PREC_RADIX>10</NUM_PREC_RADIX>
<NULLABLE>1</NULLABLE>
<COLUMN_SIZE>500</COLUMN_SIZE>
<TABLE_CAT></TABLE_CAT>
<COLUMN_DEF></COLUMN_DEF>
<REMARKS></REMARKS>
<IS_NULLABLE>YES</IS_NULLABLE>
<DATA_TYPE>12</DATA_TYPE>
<BUFFER_LENGTH>0</BUFFER_LENGTH>
<SQL_DATA_TYPE>0</SQL_DATA_TYPE>
<TABLE_NAME>DEPARTMENT</TABLE_NAME>
<TYPE_NAME>VARCHAR2</TYPE_NAME>
</rdf:Description>
</rdf:RDF>
```

Enhanced Links Through a Database Schema Mapper

Most database applications provide no contextual information about the underlying schema of the database from which query results were retrieved. The DHE utilizes a dedicated Database Schema Mapper Module to add value to database applications by making this information explicit.

Figure 6 shows a preliminary snapshot of our Database Schema Mapper

(DSM). When complete, its three frames will subdivide the top, main frame of our system shown in Figure 1. The leftmost division of the main frame contains the database query results as before. The middle division shows the relational (conceptual) schema behind the query results. The rightmost division shows the original, non-normalized entity-relationship schema corresponding to the query results.

The DSM runs in conjunction with the Relational Database Wrapper Module (DSM). As mentioned earlier the RDWM provides metadata by examining the relational schema and returns attributes such as names of columns, data types, etc. To this metadata the DSM adds schematic information for the values retrieved from a database query.

The entity-relationship schematic information about a particular database has to be entered one time through a user interface by a system developer or administrator at the time the system is being designed or integrated with DHE. At runtime when a query has been issued, the DSM checks its internal database to see if the schematic information is available. If it is, then it allows the user the ability to view the underlying E-R schema, as well as the relational schema of the database from which the query result was retrieved.

The DSM receives messages either from the RDWM or from the User Interface Wrapper. The RDWM passes query result sets through the DSM to add schematic information. The DSM parses the original query to get the table name. It then queries

Figure 6. A sample relational database schema mapper showing the E-R schema, physical schema and database query results in three frames

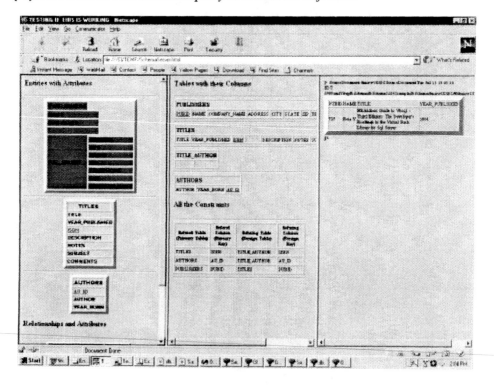

its own internal database to see if it contains schema information for that table. If so, the DSM generates the E-R and relational schemas, marks whichever elements of interest each contains, and sends a message to the UI Wrapper to display these together with the regular query results.

The UI Wrapper sends the DSM messages when a user follows a DSM-related link. Assume, for example, that the user selects a table and chooses a link to highlight that table in the relational schema. The mapping rule corresponding to that link sends the appropriate command to the DSM. The DSM must follow its internal mapping from the RDWM URI scheme to the DSM URI scheme to identify the corresponding table element in the relational schema. Then the DSM creates a new display where it indicates that the UI Wrapper should highlight certain elements.

When parsing the RDWM's query results, the DSM marks the following as elements of interest in the corresponding E-R schema, and includes the properties shown as parameters:

1. E-R Database Schema
   - Name (of the database in the DSM internal database)
2. Entities
   - Name
   - Type (weak entity or normal entity)
3. Relationship
   - Name
   - Type (identifying relationship or weak entity relationship)
4. Attributes
   - Name
   - Type:
     - Composite or simple
     - Multi-valued or single-valued
     - Stored or derived
     - Key or not

The mapping rules capture the relationships among each of these elements. Given any particular database, entity, relationship or attribute in the E-R schema, the DSM will find the corresponding database, entities, relationships and attributes related to it in the E-R schema. Additional mapping rules will find the corresponding elements in the relational schema and query result currently displayed, and vice-versa.

When parsing the RDWM's query results, the DSM marks the following as elements of interest in the corresponding relational schema, and includes the properties shown as parameters, with corresponding relationships:

1. Relational Database Schema
   - Name
2. Relation
   - Name
3. Attribute

- Primary key
- Foreign key
4. Referential Integrity Constraint
   - Relation name where the foreign key resides
   - Relation name where the foreign key references
   - Attribute name of the foreign key in the residing relation
   - Attribute name of the primary key of the referenced table

NJ DOT Freight Database Application

The New Jersey Department of Transportation has an extensive database that contains commodity (coal, vegetable oil etc.) flow information between various counties in New Jersey and various zones in the northeastern United States. A rudimentary Web interface to this database exists; we have created a DHE module that supplements this system, provides enhanced metadata, exposes the various interrelationships between the "elements of interest" in the system and provides additional functionality.

Architecture

The Freight Database Wrapper is a DHE module that acts as the wrapper to the freight application. Like other application wrappers described in previous sections, the Freight Database Wrapper provides a gateway to application-specific commands. Users may view the system through the DHE's user interface and view reports on commodity flows between counties and zones, via a set of menu items and mapping rules.

The Freight Database Wrapper may also use the RDWM to completely bypass the existing Web-based freight system and access the underlying database directly. This serves a twofold purpose:

- Metadata that is currently not provided by the system can be extracted directly from the database by means of SQL statements executed by the RDWM.
- New mapping rules may be formulated; these mapping rules would correspond to SQL statements that would be executed on the freight database, thus providing additional functionality not available in the existing system.

The Freight Database Wrapper may also be used in conjunction with the Database Schema Module, providing users with a view of the internal schema of the freight system's database, which would benefit analysts wishing for a deeper understanding of the freight application's structure.

TIGHTLY INTEGRATING
DATABASE APPLICATIONS

Prior sections discussed integrating database applications created independently of DHE. In this section we describe how database applications could be developed more quickly if designed to take advantage of DHE's infrastructure. We conclude by analyzing a system we are building using the DHE and describing the benefits the DHE provides to this system.

In this role the DHE will provide access to a relational database for applications that need it. All requests to a database, i.e., SQL statements that need to be executed on a database, will be routed to the RDWM, which will execute the statement and return the hypermedia-enriched results to the application.

To integrate with DHE, an application normally routes all database access requests to its application wrapper. In this case, because the application is being developed from the ground up, this wrapper maybe a part of the application itself. The wrapper (or wrapper portion of the application) would pass a DHE-formatted XML message to the RDWM to perform any database services requested by the application—usually the execution of an SQL statement or retrieval of metadata from the RDBMS being wrapped by the RDWM.

RDWM would still be responsible for marking up any query results; passing the hypermedia-enriched document is then routed back to the application wrapper. Figure 7 sketches this architecture. Figure 8 provides a state diagram for the

Figure 7. Architecture for database application in the Dynamic Hypermedia Engine[1]

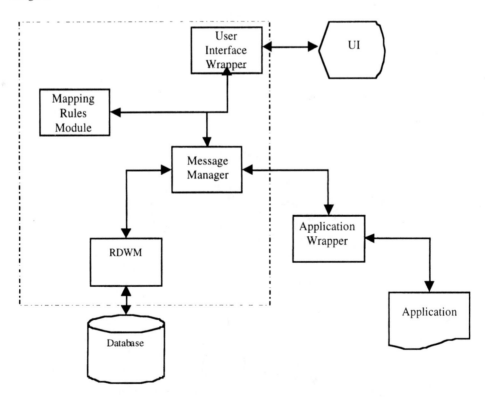

Note: The double-headed arrows denote bi-directional message flow between modules/ subsystems.

information flow.

At this point the application wrapper may take the enriched document, translate it to the application's native user interface and display it there. However, should the application developer decide to use DHE's user interface instead of writing its own, then the Application Wrapper could add any additional content and pass the final display document to the Mapping Rules Module via the Message Manager. If it adds additional, non-database elements, then the application wrapper should mark these up too, as previously described, so they also may be made into anchors. Each of these additional element types will require its own mapping rules for determining links

Figure 8. State diagram for application using the DHE

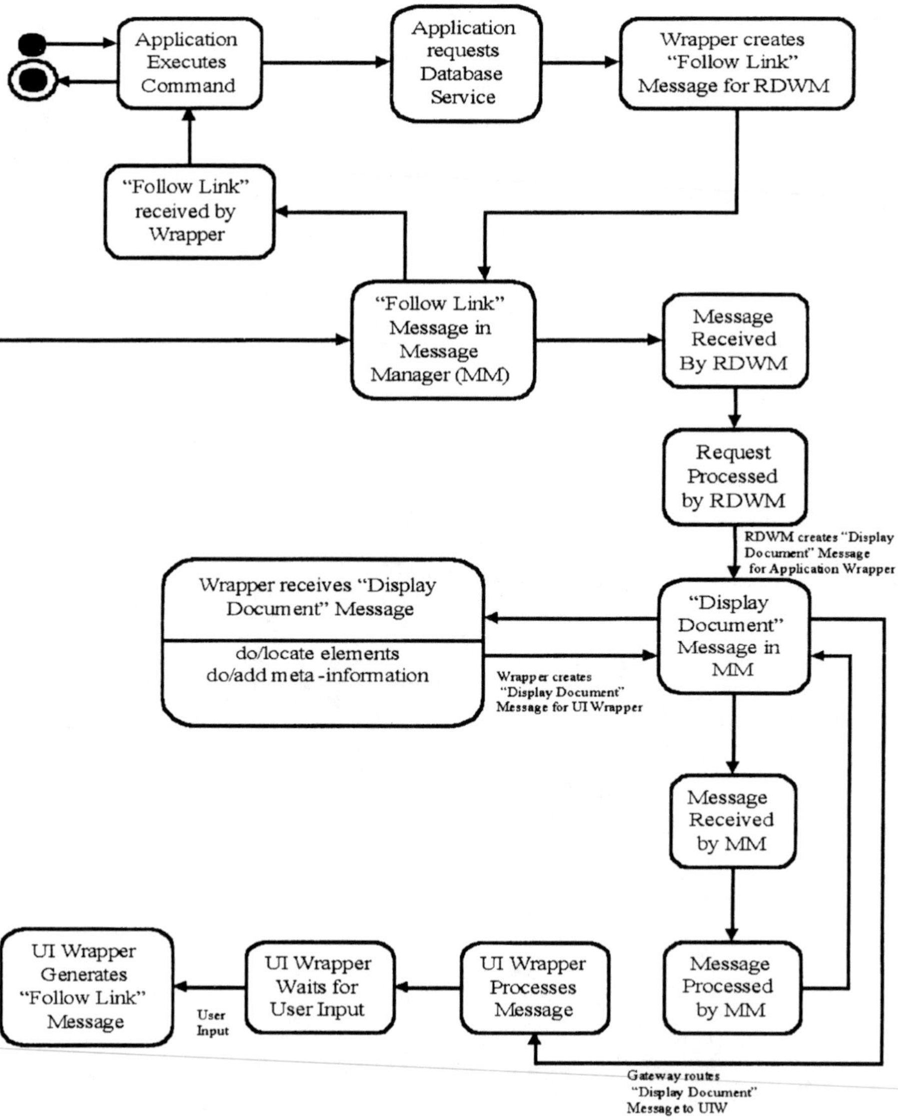

and metadata. Many application commands can be moved into the link's mapping rules.

The application could also take advantage of other DHE services, such as the menu manager for displaying application-specific menus and the user preference manager for managing users' sessions, login, profiles, etc., not to mention the other hypermedia functionality that all applications receive.

Case Study

This section describes a proposal to develop a student paper review information system using the DHE.

Problem description

As part of their coursework for the introductory IS Principles Class at the New Jersey Institute of Technology, students must review a published paper. In part students would email the instructor the bibliographic reference to the article they would like to review, and the instructor would approve or reject the request. If rejected, the student would have to resubmit his/her request with a new article. If approved the student would review the article and email it to the instructor. The instructor would then grade the review. Because of the volume of email an instructor receives, it became difficult for him or her to quickly approve or reject a request, because he or she must go through previously approved requests and make sure that this article has not been approved for review by another student.

To ameliorate this situation we propose to develop a DHE module that would allow a student to check the articles already approved to ensure his or hers was not already chosen, request approval, check the approval status, post a link to the review once completed and check his or her grade. The instructor would be able to view pending requests, approve a request, view submitted reviews, assign grades, view reports on approved articles, submitted reviews, etc. The instructor would also be able to perform administrative tasks such as registering students and deleting old reviews.

Architecture

The paper review application module itself does not have to manage customized menus or user authentication issues; the DHE provides this service. Once a user has logged in and been authenticated, any subsequent requests (view grades, approve a review request, etc.) will always contain the username and the group the user belongs to. The application can thus perform or reject the action based on the privileges the user may have. The application developer may also register customized menus with DHE's menu manager module based on user groups; thus users belonging to the student group will not see menus for administrative tasks.

The DHE provides database access to this application. For example when the instructor wishes to view a report on all approved articles not yet submitted, he or she would click on the appropriate menu item and a message would be issued to the application module with a request to generate this report. The application module would then issue a message to the RDWM containing the appropriate SQL statement, the RDWM would execute the statement and return a document containing the results of the statement, with the "elements of interest" marked up. At this point the application module may simply forward this message to the user interface wrapper, and it will be displayed in the instructor's browser with link anchors automatically embedded within them. The instructor may click on this anchor to get more metadata for this element, and view a list of links, generated from the set of mapping rules for its element type. For example, if the element is an article, the metadata may be the complete bibliographic reference to the article. One mapping rule might generate a list of students who have requested this article. A second could provide a link to the article itself.

The DHE thus speeds up the development process by freeing the developer from having to program user management, menu management, database access and above all hyperlink creation. All the developer would have to do is:

- Create a set of display screens (without links) with any elements marked up with their element types and internal identifiers.
- Register a set of mapping rules corresponding to the additional functionality desired (i.e., view a list of students who have requested a specific article, view a list of pending approval requests for a given section, etc.).
- Formulate a set of SQL statements corresponding to each of the main commands underlying the mapping rules (i.e., retrieve grades for a student, display submitted reviews, etc.)
- Write a DHE-compatible module that receives requests for each of the main commands and sends the appropriate SQL statement to the RDWM.

INTEGRATING DATA WAREHOUSING

This section proposes integrating a data warehousing application within the DHE infrastructure, one of our future research topics. This would provide hypermedia support to data warehousing applications, as well as facilitate linking among data warehouses and other applications.

A data warehouse is a subject-oriented, integrated, time-variant and non-volatile collection of data in support of management decision making (Inmon, 1996). A data warehouse comprises a repository of information built using data from diverse, and often departmentally isolated, application systems within an organization so this data can be modeled and analyzed by managers (Johnson, 1999; Inmon, 1996). Data warehouses usually are customized for a particular enterprise. Most vendors offer platforms on which enterprise data warehouses (or smaller datamarts) may be built.

A data warehouse architecture integrates a metadata repository that contains:

- *Administrative metadata*: source databases and their contents; gateway description; warehouse schema, view and derived data definitions; dimensions and hierarchies; predefined queries and reports; datamart locations and contents; data partitions; data extraction, cleaning, transformation rules, default values; data refresh and purge rules; user profiles, user groups; security.

- *Business metadata*: business terms and definitions; ownership of data; charging policies.
- *Operational metadata*: data lineage (history of migrated data and sequence of transformation applied); currency of data: active, archived, purged; monitoring information: warehouse usage statistics, error reports, audit trails.

The DHE maybe used to offer a complete end-to-end solution with the added benefit of obtaining hypertext functionality without any additional effort.

The data warehouse has two broad functions:

- Accessing the data from the data warehouse.
- Loading the data from the operational systems into the data warehouse.

Data warehouses are typically used for on-line analytical processing (OLAP). The key structure of a data warehouse always contains some element of time and some dimension hierarchies. OLAP queries are complex. They involve grouping and aggregation. A single OLAP query can lead to several closely related queries (Chaudhuri et al., 1997). The visualization of an OLAP query result using DHE will involve links between data from one hierarchy level to the other, and links SQL subqueries contained in the OLAP query. In addition, an OLAP query can result in a large collection of data with several dimensions. In the rest of this section, we concentrate on the loader module.

To load data into the data warehouse, a loader module will have to be designed and developed. The Loader Module will be like any other DHE module, and will perform the following functions.

Map Data from operational systems to the data warehouse

Operational systems store data in their own structure, encoding, etc. This has to be mapped to the data warehouse's format which is consistent across all operational systems.

Extract metadata from operational systems

Metadata is the road map or blueprint to the data in the data warehouse and needs to be operational. Also, metadata needs to be preserved for analysis once it has been loaded (Gardner, 1998). Metadata may include:

- The structure of the operational data
- Relationships in the operational data
- Other user-defined metadata

Eliminate noise

Operational data may contain data irrelevant to the warehouse (i.e., noise), which needs to be eliminated before loading.

The Loader Module is supplied a template (an Extended Stylesheet Language or XSL stylesheet) that maps data from the operational system's format to the data warehouse's format. It processes the template and maps data from the operational system to the data warehouse.

Any data not specified in the template is noise and will be eliminated.

Once the extraction process is complete, the Loader Module sends a message to the RDWM containing the data to be loaded as well as the metadata. The RDWM then loads this into the data warehouse. Figure 9 describes the extraction process.

An argument could be made that a Loader Module is not required and the DHE is simply used to access data from the warehouse. However, this approach would not allow the DHE to retrieve metadata from the operational systems. Moreover a complete end-to-end solution requires that we provide a Loader Module.

RESEARCH IN HYPERMEDIA AND DATABASES

Several techniques have been proposed recently for the integration of hypertext and databases. Some of them address the issue of building hypertext structures over existing databases to provide more direct navigation through hyperlinks.

Hara and Botafogo (1994) use an SQL-like data definition language to map single relations or relational views to node types. A node type is similar in nature to an entity type, i.e., it models a real-world object or concept in the hypertext relational and ER schemata defined over the database contents. Its specification includes the correspondences between relation attributes and node fields, as well as presentation information. At run time, a node type produces two kinds of nodes: a composite one for the whole relation, and a number of nodes corresponding to the tuples of the

Figure 9. Data warehouse loader module

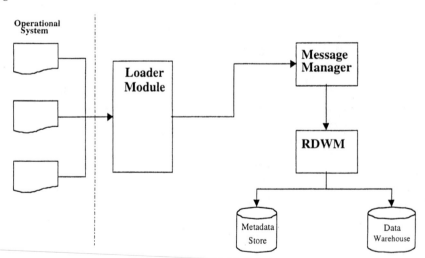

relation. The same language is used to define link types among node types. A WHERE-clause is used to constraint the creation of links during navigation.

In a similar approach, Falquet, et al. (1995, 1998) offer a declarative language to produce database views composed of node and link schemas, accessed through the WWW. Each node schema is based on one object class or a set of inter-related object classes. The content of the node is composed of a subset of the attributes of the class(es). Foreign keys to other classes constitute link types to the corresponding nodes. Two kinds of links are supported: reference links are indented to offer navigation structure within the nodes, while inclusion links are indented to create nested structures (part-of relationships). In addition, the specification of the relational view includes presentation information. The above definitions form the input to a CGI-script that produces HTML pages for the end-user. DHE would enhance the existing views specified through the database application.

The above approaches leave the original client application intact, introducing a new interface that provides hypermedia-based interaction with the database. On the contrary, DHE overlays linking facilities within the original user interface application by means of user interface wrappers.

Domenicus (Constantopoulos, et al., 1996) is a hypermedia engine developed over a repository management system, called Semantic Index System (SIS). Domenicus offers hypermedia functionality (such as alphabetic lists, subject catalogs, guided tours, query cards, hyperlinks, image annotations, bookmarks and history), based on predefined queries over the information objects and their structure, managed by SIS. Presentation Card Specifications are executed at runtime to present objects or classes of objects stored in SIS, while hyperlink classes dynamically produce links during navigation. Different presentation models can coexist for the same repository instance, to fulfill the searching, browsing and updating requirements of different user groups. DHE provides many of these features in a generic way over any application, allowing tours and indexes to contain elements from several systems. Also, DHE queries are only predefined to the extent that mapping rules hold skeleton queries for particular classes of database elements.

Other approaches suggest embedding database queries into HTML pages. For example, a mechanism offering cross-language variable substitution between HTML and SQL is the core of the *DB2 WWW Connection* system (Nguyen, et al., 1996), which enables quick and easy construction of applications accessing relational databases from the Web. The developer creates *macros* that consist of HTML and SQL commands, written in distinct sections. The sections are tied together via variable substitution. Macros are stored at the Web server and are processed by CGI-scripts in order to get user input or produce output reports. DHE does not store single database queries in the pages displayed on the Web. Instead we generate a list of several possible links for any element from specifications in the mapping rules.

Instead of providing hypertext functionality for a specific database, Geldof (1996) uses an abstract page definition language to construct templates embodying presentation guidelines for terms of an ontology--a conceptualization containing objects, concepts and relationships among them, that are presumed to exist in some area of interest. Actual information sources are linked separately with the terms of the ontology, using a definition language as well. CGI-scripts in Perl are computed to dynamically generate the HTML pages returned to the user for browsing. While this approach adds a certain level of automated linking to aid navigation, DHE provides a generally larger set of links based solely on the database structure and entity-relationship schemas, as well as metadata. DHE, however, does not provide customized templates for domain-specific navigational contexts. DHE might integrate well with Geldof's approach to provide an additional level of functionality.

Moreover, many products have been released recently that aim to interface RDBMS and Web servers (Frank, 1995). The solutions employed in these products require huge programming effort in SQL or a scripting language. The ease of integration with DHE depends on how easy it is to parse application displays to identify the elements of interest, and to specify the commands to return to the application in the mapping rules. If the application has an API or marks the elements in the displays (as should become the custom as XML becomes more prevalent), building the application wrapper should be relatively easy.

The approaches presented above presuppose the hypertext designer's insight into the intrinsic semantics of the relational structure. A different approach was proposed by Papadopoulos, et al. (1996). Instead of relying on the relational schema of the database, a more semantically enriched extended entity-relationship (EER) schema is semi-automatically produced, by incorporating a reverse engineering methodology. Hypertext views, consisting of node and link types, can be defined over the EER schema, while the SQL queries to instantiate them at run-time were automatically created, based on mapping information gathered during the reverse engineering process. Currently DHE requires people to enter the entity-relationship schemas manually into the Database Schema Mapper. This application could help to automate this process, and perhaps provide additional relationships, which DHE could provide for database applications.

While the hypermedia paradigm embodies an approach to structure and navigate information, it has several shortcomings. In particular, few hypermedia systems have focused on methodologies for information storage and retrieval. Database systems, on the contrary, are only concerned with storage and retrieval of information based on a formal model. They exhibit powerful methodologies for information storage, and effective indexing and querying. Furthermore they provide facilities such as transaction management, concurrency and access control as well as locking mechanisms.

Early hypermedia systems used proprietary data formats for storage (Fountain, et al., 1990). Over the years, hypertext researchers, trying to satisfy the requirements of new application domains, have studied various techniques for integrating hypertext and database facilities. Depending on the purpose of such an integration, these approaches can be categorized as: managing internal hypermedia data, supporting hypermedia application design and assisting information retrieval.

Managing Hypermedia Data

Several hypermedia systems employ databases internally to hold hypermedia content and structure. Hyperbase management systems make heavy use of database facilities to provide persistent storage of hypermedia data (Leggett, 1993). HyperDisco (Wiil, et al., 1996), HyperStorM (Bapat, et al., 1996) and DHM (Grønbæk, et al., 1994) use database facilities to store, update and retrieve hypermedia constructs such as node, link and anchor data. Chimera (Anderson, 1999) enhanced its ad hoc storage management capabilities with a relational database management system in order to handle data scalability issues. In a similar manner, DHE modules use relational databases to manage internal data such as the message log, menus and mapping rules.

Hypermedia Application Design

Many systems use database concepts in order to enable hypermedia application design. Hypermedia design methodologies (Christodoulou, et al., 1998) not only help designers with the standard conceptual structuring of application designs, but also focus on designing the navigational structures (links, indexes, guided tours, etc.), and thus are especially well suited to designing Web applications. RMM (Isakowitz et al., 1995; Balasubramanian, et al., 2000) is the hypermedia design methodology based most strongly on the relational database paradigm. It was developed specifically to design hypermedia interfaces for relational database applications. It has an accompanying tool, RMCase, that then generates the application based on the RMM design (Diás, et al., 1995). RMM has seven steps:

1) *Entity-Relationship Design*: models the information domain and its relationships.
2) *Slice Design*: how information units are sub-divided for display.
3) *Navigational Design*: how users will access information.
4) *User-Interface Design*: how information will be presented.
5) *Conversion Protocol Design*: how abstract constructs are to be transformed into physical-level constructs, e.g., what kind of WWW page corresponds to an index or a guided tour.
6) *Run-Time Behavior Design*: how to populate the application with data and how to provide interaction behavior.
7) *Construction and Testing*: actual development of programs and testing.

OOHDM (Schwabe et al., 1995, 1996) currently is the most popular hypermedia design methodology. While OOHDM does not follow the relational database paradigm as strongly as RMM, it still could be quite useful in designing the navigation over Web-based database applications.

Assisting Information Retrieval

Some systems utilize hypermedia as well as information retrieval facilities resulting in Hypermedia Information Retrieval Systems. Such systems provide users with the possibility of storing large amounts of textual and multimedia elements, as well as building networks of semantic relationships among these elements within the database for use in retrieval (Agosti, et al., 1996). Although querying and browsing are considered as complementary paradigms (Chiramella, 1997), the particular difficulty in creating such systems lies in the fundamental distinction between structure and content. Hypermedia Information Retrieval Systems concentrate on providing automatic and semi-automatic conversion of text into hypertext (Salton, et al., 1994; Furner, et al., 1996; Golovchinsky, 1997) aiming at "interactive retrieval" as well as applying information retrieval capabilities to hypermedia structures (Savoy, 1996; Chiramella, et al., 1996).

FUTURE RESEARCH PLANS

Given our basic DHE infrastructure, we can begin to research many interesting ways to take advantage of and enhance database systems and technologies.

Integrating Data Mining

Currently DHE determines links from the mapping rules. Because the person who develops the application wrapper also writes the mapping rules at the same time, the types of relationships DHE finds are known ahead of time. Data mining brings the opportunity of a new kind of dynamic linking. Data mining searches large databases for relationships and global patterns, and relationships that are not immediately obvious, such as a relationship between patient data and their medical diagnosis (Holsheimer, 1994).

Data mining tools discover these relationships or models at runtime as opposed to design time. Thus, DHE must request the Data Mining Tool to discover the relationships for an element of interest at run-time, and then use these discovered relationships to create hyperlinks.

Of course, in addition, the DHE could provide hypertext functionality to commercial data mining tools. A commercial data mining tool could have a wrapper written for it, just as with any other application.

Relationship-Based Design of Database

We currently are developing a relationship-based systems analysis methodology, Relationship-Navigation Analysis (RNA), to help analysts determine the interrelationships within their applications (Bieber & Yoo, 2000; Yoo & Bieber, 2000a, b; Yoo, 2000). Once identified, each relationship could be designed and implemented as a link in the application. We have developed RNA to help in any application domain, not just databases. In future research we intend to compare RNA with a traditional database analysis technique. We believe RNA could be used as a tool to help designers make the "hidden" relationships explicit in an application, as well as identify relationships in application components outside the database contents.

CONCLUSION

While the main purpose of this chapter has been to describe our hypermedia and database research, we hope that it also sets forth a research agenda for joint research in these two fields. Database applications need to interact with their users. Hypermedia can supplement database applications in many ways, making them more effective. The Dynamic Hypermedia Engine enriches the user's experience with the power of hypermedia by automatically providing it to applications with supplemental links, metadata, navigation and other hypermedia functionality. It also eases the development of complex database systems by automatically providing these metadata and hypermedia services.

ACKNOWLEDGMENTS

We gratefully acknowledge funding by the United Parcel Service, the NASA JOVE faculty fellowship program, the New Jersey Center for Multimedia Research, the National Center for Transportation and Industrial Productivity at the New Jersey Institute of Technology (NJIT), the New Jersey Department of Transportation, the New Jersey Commission of Science and Technology, and by NJIT's SBR program.

REFERENCES

Agosti, M. and Smeaton A. (1996). Information retrieval and hypertext, Kluwer Academic Publishers, Boston.

Akscyn, R. M., McCracken, D. L. and Yoder, E. A. (1988). KMS: A distributed hypermedia system for managing knowledge in organizations, *Communications of the ACM*, 31(7), 820-835.

Anderson, K. (1996). Providing automatic support for extra-application functionality," In Ashman, H.L., Balasubramanian, V., Bieber, M. and Oinas-Kukkonen, H. (Eds.). *Proceedings of the Second International Workshop on Incorporating Hypertext Functionality into Software Systems (HTF II)*, Hypertext '96 Conference, Bethesda, MD, March.

Anderson, K. (1997). Integrating open hypermedia systems with the world wide Web, Hypertext'97 *Proceedings, ACM Press*, New York: NY, 157-166.

Anderson, M. K. (1999). Data scalability in open hypermedia systems, *Proceedings of the ACM Hypertext '99 Conference*, Darmstadt, Germany, February 21-25, 27-36.

Balasubramanian, V., Bieber, M. and Isakowitz, T. (2000). A case study in systematic hypermedia design, *Information Systems Journal*.

Bapat, A., Waesch, J., Aberer, K. and Haake, J. (1996). HyperStorM: An extensible object-oriented hypermedia engine, *Proceedings of the ACM Hypertext '96 Conference*, Washington, DC, 203-214.

Berners-Lee, T., Fielding, R. and Masinter, L. (1998). Uniform Resource Identifiers (URI): Generic Syntax, Internet Engineering Task Force Request for Comments 2396, August 1998.

Bieber, M. (1990). *Generalized Hypertext in a Knowledge-Based DSS Shell Environment*, PhD Dissertation, University of Pennsylvania, Philadelphia, PA.

Bieber, M. (1995). On Integrating Hypermedia into Decision Support and Other Information Systems, Decision Support Systems 14, 251-267.

Bieber, M. (1999). *Supplementing Applications with Hypermedia*, Technical Report, New Jersey Institute of Technology, Information Systems Department.

Bieber, M. and Kacmar, C. (1995). Designing hypertext support for computational applications, *Communications of the ACM*, 38(8), 99-107.

Bieber, M., Vitali, F., Ashman, H., Balasubramanian V. and Oinas-Kukkonen, H. (1997). Fourth generation hypermedia: some missing links for the World Wide Web, *International Journal of Human Computer Studies.* 47, 31-65.

Bieber, M. and Joonheee, Y. (2000). Hypermedia: A design philosophy, *ACM Computing Surveys.*

Campbell, B. and Goodman, J. M. (1988). HAM: A general purpose hypertext abstract machine," *Communications of the ACM*, 31(7), 856-861.

Chaudhuri, S. and Dayal, U. (1997). An overview of data warehousing and OLAP technology, *ACM SIGMOD Record*, 26(1), 65-74.

Chiramella, Y. and Kheirbek, A. (1996). An Integrated Model for Hypermedia and Information Retrieval, Information Retrieval and Hypertext, M. Agosti, A. Smeaton (Eds.), Kluwer, Amsterdam, NL, 139-176.

Chiramella, Y. (1997). Browsing and querying: Two complementary approaches for multimedia information retrieval, *Proceedings of Hypertext – Information Retrieval – Multimedia (HIM '97)*, Dortmund, Germany, 9-26.

Chiu, C. and Bieber, M. (1997). A generic dynamic-mapping wrapper for open hypertext system support of analytical applications, *Proceedings of the ACM Hypertext '97*, Souhtampton, UK, April, 218-219. (http://www.cis.njit.edu/~bieber/pub/ht97/ht97-mac.html).

Christodoulou, S., Styliaras, G. and Papatheodorou, T. (1998). Evaluation of hypermedia application development and management systems, *Proceedings of the ACM Hypertext '98 Conference*, Pittsburgh, PA, 1-10.

Conklin, J. (1987). Hypertext: A survey and introduction, *IEEE Computer*, 20(9), 17-41.

Constantopoulos, P., Theodorakis, M. and Tzitzikas, Y. (1996). Developing hypermedia over an information repository, *Proceedings of the 2nd Workshop on Open Hypermedia Systems*, ACM Hypertext '96 Conference, Washington, DC.

Davis, H., Hall, W., Heath, I., Hill, G. and Wilkins, R. (1992). Towards an integrated information environment with open hypermedia systems, *Proceedings of the ACM Conference on Hypertext Milan*, 181-190.

Davis, H., Knight, S. and Hall, W. (1994). Light hypermedia link services: A study of third-party application integration, *Proceedings of the Fifth ACM Conference on Hypermedia Technologies*, Edinburgh, Scotland, 158-166.

Diáz, A., Isakowitz, T., Maiorana, V. and Gilabert, G. (1995). RMC: A tool to design WWW applications, *Proceedings of the Fourth International World Wide Web Conference*, Boston, December 1995.

Falquet, G., Guyot, J. and Prince, I. (1995). Generating hypertext views on databases, *CUI Technical Report No 101*, University of Geneva.

Falquet, G., Guyot, J. and Nerima, L. (1998). Languages and tools to specify hypertext views on databases, selected papers of the *International Workshop on the WWW and Databases* (WebDB '98), Valencia, Spain, March 27-28, Springer-Verlag LNCS 1590, 1999.

Frank, M. (1995). Database and the Internet, *DBMS Magazine*, December, 8(13).

Fountain, A., Hall, W., Health, I. and Davis, H. C. (1990). Microcosm: An open model for hypermedia with dynamic linking, *Proceedings of the European Conference on Hypertext*, Paris, France, 298-311.

Furner, J., Ellis, D., Willett, P. (1996). The Representation and Comparsion of Hypertext structures using Graphs, Information Retrieval and Hypertext, M. Agosti, A. Smeaton (Eds.), Kluwer, Amsterdam, NL, 75-96.

Gardner, S. R. (1998). Building the data warehouse, *Communications of the ACM*, September, 41(9), 52-60.

Garrido, A. and G. Rossi (1996). A framework for extending object-oriented applications with hypermedia functionality, *The New Review of Hypermedia and Multimedia*, 2, 25-41.

Geldof, S. (1996). Hyper-text generation from databases on the Internet, *Proceedings of the 2nd Intl. Workshop on Applications of Natural Language to Information Systems (NLDB '96)*, Amsterdam, IOS Press, 102-114.

Golovchinsky, G. (1997). What the query told the link: The integration of hypertext and information retrieval, *Proceedings of ACM Hypertext'97 Conference*, Southampton, UK, April, 67-74.

Grønbæk, K., Hem, J., Madsen, O. and Sloth, L. (1994). Cooperative hypermedia systems: A dexter-based architecture, *Communications of the ACM*, 37(2), 64-74.

Grønbæk, K. and Trigg, R. (1994). Design issues for a dexter-based hypermedia system. *Communications of the ACM*, 37(2), 40-49.

Grønbæk, K. and Trigg, R. (1999). From Web to workplace: Designing open hypermedia Systems, MIT Press.

Halasz, F. and Schwartz, M. (1994). Grønbæk, K. and Trigg, R. (Eds.) The dexter hypertext reference model, *Communications of the ACM* 37(2), 30-39.

Hara, Y. and Botafogo, R. A. (1994). Hypermedia databases: A specification and formal language, *Proceeding of the Databases and Expert Systems Applications Conference (DEXA '94)*, Springer-Verlag LCNS 856, 520-530.

Holsheimer, M. and Siebes, A. (1994). Data mining, The search for knowledge in databases (Report CS-R9406), CWI, Amsterdam. (ftp://ftp.cwi.nl/pub/CWIreports/AA/CS-R9406.ps.Z).

Inmon, W. H. (1996). Building the Data Warehouse, Second Edition, Wiley Comp., ISBN 0471-14161-5, USA, 1996.

Johnson, A. H. (1999). Data warehousing, *Computerworld*, December, 33(49), 74-75.

Kacmar, C. (1993). Supporting hypermedia services in the user interface, *Hypermedia* 5(2), 85-101.

Kacmar, C. (1995). A process approach for providing hypermedia services to existing, non-hypermedia applications, *Journal of Electronic Publishing: Organization, Dissemination and Design*.

Isakowitz, T., Stohr, E. and Balasubramanian, P. (1995). RMM: A methodology for structuring hypermedia design, *Communications of the ACM*, August, 38(8), 34-44.

Lassila, O. and Swick R. R. (Eds.) (1999). Resource description framework (RDF) model and syntax specification, *W3C Recommendation* 22 February 1999.

Leggett, J. J. (Ed.). (1993). Workshop on hyperbase systems, *ACM Hypertext '93 Conference, Technical Report TAMU-HRL 93-009*, Texas A&M University.

Leggett, J. and Schnase, J. (1994). Viewing dexter with open eyes, *Communications of the ACM* 37(2), 77-86.

Marshall, C. and Shipman III, F. (1995). Spatial hypertext: Designing for change, *Communications of the ACM* 38(8), 88-97.

Nanard, J. and Nanard, M. (1995). Hypertext design environments and the hypertext design process, *Communications of the ACM,* 38(8), 49-56.

Nguyen, T. and Srinivasan, V. (1996). Accessing relational databases from the world wide Web, *Proceedings of the ACM SIGMOD '96 Conference,* 529-540.

Nielsen, J. (1995). Multimedia and hypertext: The Internet and beyond, *AP Professional.*

Papadopoulos, A., Vaitis, M. and Christodoulakis, D. (1996). Building hypertext interfaces to existing relational databases, *Proceeding of the 7th Intl. Conference on Database and Expert Systems Applications (DEXA '96),* Springer-Verlag LCNS 1134, Zürich, Switzerland, 276-288.

Pearl, A. (1989). Sun's link service: A protocol for open linking, *Hypertext'89 Proceedings,* Pittsburg, November 5, 137-146.

Rossi, G., Garrido, A. and Carvalho, S. (1996). Vlissides, J, Coplien, J. and Kerth, N. (Eds.) Design Patterns for Object-Oriented Hypermedia Applications. *Pattern Languages of Programs II.* Addison-Wesley, 177-191.

Schwabe, D., Rossi, G. (1995). The object-oriented hypermedia design model, *Communications of the ACM,* August, 38(8), 45-46.

Schwabe, D., Rossi, G. and Barbosa, S. D. J. (1996). Systematic hypermedia application design with OOHDM, *Proceedings of the ACM Hypertext '96 Conference,* Washington, DC, March 16-20, 116-128.

Salton, G. (1989). Automatic text processing: the transformation, analysis, and retrieval of Information, Reading, Addison-Wesley, MA.

Salton, G., Allan, J., Buckley, C. and Singhal, A. (1994). Automatic analysis, theme generation, and summarization of machine-readable texts, *Science,* 264, 1421-1426.

Savoy, J. (1996). Agosti, M. and Smeaton, A. (Eds.) Citation schemes in hypertext information retrieval, *Information Retrieval and Hypertext,* Kluwer, Amsterdam, NL, 99-120.

Van de Sompel, H. and Hochstenbach, P. (1999). Reference linking in a hybrid library environment, Part 1: Frameworks for linking, *D-lib Magazine* 5(4).

Van de Sompel, H. and Hochstenbach, P. (1999). Reference linking in a hybrid library environment, Part 2: SFX, A generic linking solution, *D-lib Magazine* 5(4).

Van de Sompel, Herbert and Hochstenbach, P. (1999) Reference linking in a hybrid library environment, Part 3: Generalizing the SFX solution in the "SFX@Ghent & SFX@LANL" experiment, *D-lib Magazine* 5(10).

Wan, J. (1996). Integrating hypertext into information systems through dynamic linking. PhD Dissertation, New Jersey Institute of Technology, Institute for Integrated Systems Research, Newark: NJ.

Wan, J. and Bieber, M. (1997). Providing relational database management systems with hypertext, *Proceedings of the Thirtieth Annual Hawaii International Conference on System Sciences (Wailea, Maui; January 1997), IEEE Press,* Washington, D.C., 6, 160-166.

Whitehead, E. J. (1997). An architectural model for application integration in open hypermedia environments, *Hypertext'97 Proceedings, ACM Press,* New York, 1-12.

Wiil, U. K. (Ed.). (1999). *Proceedings of the 3rd Workshop on Open Hypermedia Systems, CIT Scientific Report #SR-97-01,* 1997, The Danish National Centre for IT Research, Forskerparken, Gustav Wieds Vej 10, 8000 Aarhus C, Denmark [on-line] http://www.cit.dk/.

Wiil, U. K. and Leggett, J. J. (1996). The hyperdisco approach to open hypermedia systems, *Proceedings of the ACM Hypertext '96 Conference,* Washington, DC, 140-148.

Yoo, J. (2000). Relationship analysis. PhD Dissertation, New Jersey Institute of Technology, CIS Department, 2000.

Yoo, J. and Bieber, M. (2000). Towards a relationship navigation analysis, *Proceedings of the 33rd Hawaii International Conference on System Sciences, IEEE Press*, Washington, DC, January.

Yoo, Joonhee, and Bieber, M. (2000). Finding linking opportunities through relationship-based analysis, *Proceedings of the ACM Hypertext '00 Conference*, San Antonio, TX, ACM Press, June.

Chapter V

Optimization of the Knowledge Discovery Process in Very Large Databases

M. Mehdi Owrang
American University, USA

Current database technology involves processing a large volume of data in order to discover new knowledge. The high volume of data makes the discovery process computationally expensive. In addition, real-world databases tend to be incomplete, redundant and inconsistent which could lead to discovery of redundant and inconsistent knowledge. We propose use of domain knowledge to reduce the size of the database being considered for discovery and to optimize the hypothesis (representing the pattern to be discovered) by eliminating implied, unnecessary and redundant conditions from the hypothesis. The benefits can be greater efficiency and the discovery of more meaningful, non-redundant, non-trivial and consistent rules. Experimental results are provided and analyzed.

INTRODUCTION

Modern database technology involves processing a large volume of data in databases in order to discover new knowledge. Knowledge discovery is defined as the nontrivial extraction of implicit, previously unknown and potentially useful information from data (Adriaans et al., 1996; Fayyad, 1996; Fayyad et al., 1996; Ganti et al., 1999; Groth, 1998). While promising, the available discovery schemes and tools are limited in many ways. Some databases are so large that they make the discovery process computationally expensive. Databases containing on the order of $N=10^9$ records are becoming increasingly common, for example, in the astronomical sciences. Similarly, the number of fields can easily be on the order of 10^2 or 10^3, for example, in medical diagnostic applications (Fayyad, 1996).

If we apply discovery algorithms to discover all the correlations between concepts in a real database, we will generally observe the production of a set of results whose size is just too large to be handled in a useful manner. Another major concern in knowledge discovery, in addition to the large size of the databases, is data redundancy in the databases. Databases include data redundancies that could lead to discovering redundant knowledge. A common form of redundancy is a functional dependency in which a field is defined as a function of other fields, for example, profit = sales - expenses. The discovered knowledge may contain redundancy when two pieces of knowledge are exactly the same (rules having the same premises and conclusions) or semantically equivalent. In addition, the discovered knowledge may indeed be a previously known fact (i.e., a domain knowledge) rather than a new discovery. In addition to data redundancy, data inconsistency in databases is another issue in knowledge discovery. Databases are normally incomplete; thus, discovered knowledge may be inconsistent and inaccurate. It may be impossible to discover significant knowledge about a given domain (i.e., medicine) if some attributes essential to knowledge about the application domain are not present in the data. For example, we cannot diagnose Malaria from a patient database if the data does not contain the patient's red blood cell counts.

A major challenge in knowledge discovery is computational efficiency. The vastness of the data and the data redundancy that exists in databases force us to use techniques for optimizing the discovery of consistent and accurate patterns. A pattern represents the useful knowledge to be discovered from the database.

There are several approaches to knowledge discovery for handling the large volume of data and minimizing search efforts. These techniques include: parallel processor architecture, providing some measure of "interestingness of patterns," elimination of irrelevant attributes, data sampling, data segmentation, and data summarization. These techniques are used to reduce the size of the databases for discovery and to define a bias in searching for interesting patterns. These techniques are described in greater detail later in the chapter.

The human user almost always has some previous concepts or knowledge about the domain represented by the database. This information, known as domain or background knowledge, can be defined as any information that is not explicitly presented in the data (Adriaans et al., 1996; Fayyad, 1996; Owrang, 1997), including the relationship (or lack of it) that exists among attributes, constraints imposed on data and redundant data definition. The domain knowledge reduces search time by optimizing the hypothesis associated with knowledge discovery. A hypothesis represents the pattern to be discovered.

Once the concept of domain knowledge is defined, it can be incorporated into a Knowledge Discovery System (KDS). A KDS is a system that finds knowledge that it previously did not have, i.e., it was not implicit in its algorithms or explicit in its representation of domain knowledge (Silberschatz, 1995). A KDS system uses knowledge of the database domain to autonomously select relevant fields, to guide the application of different pattern-extraction algorithms, and to identify and filter the most meaningful results for presentation. We recognize that in knowledge discovery, a discovery system can generate a lot of patterns, most of which are not interesting to the user. A hypothesis refinement engine (Figure 1) can be placed inside the KDS so that it can focus the search only on the consistent/nontrivial patterns. This approach avoids generating many non-interesting patterns, thus speeding the discovery process. This is the approach that we are taking. We show that domain knowledge can be used to reduce the size of the database by eliminating the records that are irrelevant to the specific discovery case. In addition, we discuss the use of domain knowledge to optimize the hypothesis that represents the interesting knowledge to be discovered.

The effort put into the data selection and hypothesis optimization process is justified considering today's very large databases have millions of records and a lot of attributes. The end result will lead to an improvement in the speed of the knowledge discovery process and in the quality of the discovered knowledge by generating more meaningful rules.

The work that we present here has the same goal as the existing techniques in that we too are interested in avoiding the generation of uninteresting patterns. Our work complements the existing schemes by preventing the discovery of known and redundant patterns. Other research efforts try to filter out the uninteresting patterns after they have been generated. Our approach optimizes the knowledge discovery process as is demonstrated in this chapter. We provide our experimental results and analysis of the knowledge discovery on different databases using IDIS (1994) knowledge discovery tool. (See section "Optimized Hypothesis to Eliminate

Figure 1. General view of the knowledge discovery process

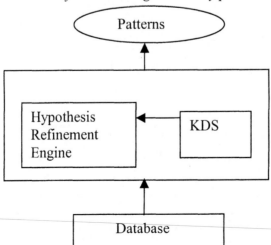

Implies Conditions" for more information on IDIS). The results indicate an improvement in knowledge discovery using domain knowledge, both in terms of the quality of the discovered rules and the time to discover rules.

KNOWLEDGE DISCOVERY PROCESS

The KDD (Knowledge Discovery in Databases) process is outlined in Figure 2. The KDD process is interactive and iterative (with many decisions made by the user), involving numerous steps, summarized as (Adriaans et al., 1996; Fayyad, 1996; Fayyad et al., 1996):

1. *Learning the application domain*: includes relevant prior knowledge and the goals of the application.
2. *Creating a target dataset*: includes selecting a dataset or focusing on a subset of variables or data samples on which discovery is to be performed.
3. *Performing data cleaning and preprocessing*: includes basic operations such as removing noise or outliers if appropriate, collecting the necessary information to model or account for noise, deciding on strategies for handling missing data fields and accounting for time sequence information and known changes. It also includes resolving DBMS issues such as appropriate data types, schema and mapping of missing and unknown values.
4. *Performing data reduction and projection*: includes finding useful features to represent the data, depending on the goal of the task. It also uses dimensionality reduction or transformation methods to reduce the effective number of variables under consideration or to find invariant representations for the data.
5. *Choosing the function of data mining*: includes deciding the purpose of the model derived by the data mining algorithm (e.g., summarization, classification, regression and clustering).
6. *Choosing the data mining algorithm(s)*: includes selecting method(s) to be used for searching for patterns in the data, such as deciding which models and parameters may be appropriate (e.g., models for categorical data are different from models on vectors over numbers) and matching a particular data mining method with the overall criteria of the KDD process (e.g., the user may be more interested in understanding the model than in its predictive capabilities).
7. *Performing data mining*: includes searching for patterns of interest in a particular representational form or a set of such representations, including classification rules or trees, regression, clustering, sequence modeling, dependency and line analysis.
8. *Interpreting discovered knowledge*: includes interpreting the discovered patterns and possibly returning to any of the previous steps, as well as possible visualization of the extracted patterns removing redundant or irrelevant patterns, and translating the useful ones into terms understandable by users.
9. *Using discovered knowledge*: includes incorporating this knowledge into the performance system, taking actions based on the knowledge or simply docu-

Figure 2. Overview of the steps constituting the KDD process

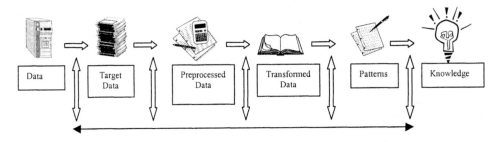

menting it and reporting it to interested parties. It also includes checking for and resolving potential conflicts with previously believed (or extracted) knowledge (Fayyad et al., 1996).

INHERENT PROBLEMS IN VERY LARGE DATABASES

Knowledge discovery systems rely on databases to supply the raw data for input, and this raises problems in that databases tend to be dynamic, incomplete, noisy and large. The problems associated with the large volume of data includes (Adriaans et al., 1996; Fayyad, 1996; Fayyad et al., 1996; Owrang, 1997):

Large Databases

Databases with hundreds of fields and tables, millions of records and multi-gigabyte size are quite common, and terabyte databases are starting to appear (Adriaans et al., 1996; Fayyad et al., 1996; Groth, 1998; Parsaye et al., 1993).

High Dimensionality

There are often a very large number of records in the database. In addition, there can be a very large number of fields (attributes, variables) so that the dimensionality of the problem is high. A high dimensional database creates problems in terms of increasing the size of the search space for discovering rules in a combinatorially explosive manner (Fayyad et al., 1996). In addition, it increases the chances that a data-mining algorithm will find spurious patterns that are not valid. Approaches to this problem include methods to reduce the effective dimensionality of the problem and the use of prior knowledge to identify irrelevant variables (Fayyad et al., 1996).

Irrelevant Attributes

Another issue is the relevance or irrelevance of the attributes involved in the current focus of discovery (Adriaans et al., 1996; Fayyad et al., 1996). For example, height and diagnosis may not be causally related if the discovery focus deals with liver disease, but they may be causally related for physiotherapy.

Overabundance of Patterns

When search for patterns has a wide scope, a very large number of patterns can be discovered. Proper statistical controls are needed to avoid discoveries due to change, while domain knowledge can help to focus on the interesting finding (Fayyad et al., 1996). In knowledge discovery, the concepts of large databases and useful patterns often interact in a seemingly paradoxical way (Parsay, 1995, 1996). On one hand, the larger a database, the richer its pattern content and as the database grows, the more patterns it includes. On the other hand, if we analyze too large a portion of a database, patterns from different data segments begin to dilute each other, and the number of useful patterns begins to decrease.

Discovering Non-Trivial and Consistent Rules

In knowledge discovery, it is all too easy to discover a large number of patterns (or rules) from a database and most of these patterns are actually redundant, inconsistent, useless and uninteresting to the user. However, due to the large number of patterns, it is difficult for the user to manually process them to identify those patterns that are redundant, inconsistent and those that are interesting.

EXISTING APPROACHES TO THE OPTIMIZATION OF THE KNOWLEDGE DISCOVERY PROCESS

The goals for the optimization of the KDD process can be identified as:
1. To reduce the size of the database being considered for discovery, which leads to faster response.
2. To minimize the search efforts by avoiding the discovery of inconsistent, redundant, trivial knowledge.

In the following, we provide an overview of the existing approaches to the optimization of the KDD process. The main concern in the optimization of the KDD is the performance versus the accuracy of the KDD process. That is, any of the following optimization techniques (or combination of techniques) can improve the performance. However, the final discovery results may suffer when the chance of blocking unexpected discovery increases. For example, when we do data sampling, we throw away data, not knowing what we discard, and the discarded data may indeed contains the unexpected discovery.

Optimizing the Data Selection Process

A database contains a variety of data, not all of which is needed to achieve each knowledge discovery goal. The data selection step of the KDD process involves creating a target data set, selecting a data set or focusing on a subset of variables or data samples, on which discovery is to be performed. In the following, we overview the approaches for reducing the size of the databases being considered for knowledge discovery.

Elimination of Irrelevant Attributes. Eliminating the attributes that do not participate in the discovery can reduce the size of the database. Ziarko (1991) uses the theory of rough set for the identification and the analysis of data dependencies or cause-effect relationships in databases. He demonstrates how to evaluate the degree of the relationship and identify the most critical factors contributing to the relationship. Identification of the most critical factors allows for the elimination of irrelevant attributes prior to the generation of rules describing the dependency.

Subramanian (1990) proposes an irrelevance principle to minimize a formulation by removing all facts that are either logically or computationally irrelevant to the specified discovery case. However, in attempting to discover, facts cannot be removed on the basis of such an irrelevance principle because the concepts to be discovered might precisely involve knowledge initially considered as irrelevant.

Data Sampling. Limiting the number of fields alone may not sufficiently reduce the size of the data set, in which case a subset of records must be selected (Adriaans et al., 1996; Parsaye, 1996, 1999). Instead of using a complicated discovery process on all the data, one first takes a small sample, finds the regularities in it and then possibly validates these on the whole data. Sampling is sometimes recommended to get a general feeling for the data, and in such cases, one would recommend taking several samples and comparing them.

Proper sampling techniques must be used to obtain the data sets to avoid bias in the samples. For example, we should not select the sample data from the top of the data set (e.g., first 1,000 records) or bottom of the data set. Random sampling is the most important characteristic of proper sampling. Obviously a sample should be significantly smaller than the original data set, but if the sample is too small, it contains many spurious regularities, and much additional work is needed in the validation. In Kivinen et al., (1994), the authors address the question of sufficient sample size.

We can apply the discovery algorithms to a random sample of data. However, the resulting discoveries in these cases are necessarily uncertain. When we sample data, we lose information, because we throw away data without knowing what we keep and what we ignore. Sampling will almost always result in a loss of information, in particular with respect to data fields with a large number of non-numeric values (Parsaye, 1999). The rules discovered in sample data can be invalid on the full data set. Statistical techniques, however, can measure the degree of uncertainty. Piatetsky (1991) presents a formal statistical analysis for estimating the accuracy of sample-derived rules when applied to a full data set.

Data Summarization. Summarization techniques can be used to reduce database size (Adriaans et al., 1996; Fayyad, 1996; Fayyad et al., 1996; Parsaye, 1996, , 1999). Data summarization greatly enhances the performance of data retrieval in a very large database environment. In general, summary tables hold pre-aggregated and pre-joined data. Basically, for any given detailed data, there are numerous ways to summarize it. Each summarization or aggregation can be along one or more dimensions. For the general case, given N items (or columns), there are $2^N - 1$ possible ways of combining the items. The number of aggregate rows required depends on the number of valid combinations of item values, and the situation is complicated further when the items are in multi-level hierarchies (e.g., with month rolling up to quarter and year).

It is easy to say summary tables are required to improve performance against large volumes of data. But it is much more difficult to provide the correct pre-aggregated summary tables to users, explain to them exactly what they are, when to use them and how to maintain them. In addition, processing the summary tables may not discover accurate knowledge. The problem is that the summarization of the same data set with two summarization methods may produce either the same or different results.

Information loss and information distortion can occur when summarization is used (Parsaye, 1996, 1999). Consider a retail database where Monday to Friday sales are exceptionally low for some stores, and weekend sales are exceptionally high for others. The weekly summarization of daily sales data will hide the fact that weekdays are money loser, while weekends are money makers for some stores. In other words, key pieces of information may be lost through summarization, and there is no way to recover them by further analysis.

Data Segmentation. Segmentation is defined as the process or process results that create a mutually exclusive collection of records, which share similar attributes in either unsupervised learning (such as clustering) or supervised learning for a particular prediction field. It is also known as database clustering, which is finding the clusters in the data that contain similar subsets of records (Adriaans et al., 1996; Fayyad, 1996; Fayyad et al., 1996; Parsaye, 1996).

Most of the time, it does not make sense to analyze all the data in a large database because patterns are lost through dilution. To find useful patterns in a large database, we usually have to select a segment (not a sample) of data that fits a business objective. Then we perform data mining on the selected data. Patterns may be hidden when the data is viewed in an aggregated form because factors that apply to distinct business objectives often dilute each other. As we segment, we deliberately focus on a subset of the data (e.g., select one model year for a car, or select one marketing campaign), thus sharpening the focus of the analysis.

Consider a vehicle warranty database. In order to find patterns for customer claims, it is essential to store details of each claim in a large database. The question is whether it makes sense to analyze all of the data at the same time. The answer is no. In practice, cars are built at different plants and different models of cars use different parts, and some parts are discontinued. In addition, the parts used in cars change over the course of years. As a result, analyzing the entire database may tell us less than analyzing part of it. In practice, it works best to analyze the claims for a given model year for cars built at a given plant, a segmentation task.

The need for segmentation is even clearer when we consider predictive modeling (Parsaye, 1996). When we try to predict the response to a new campaign, it simply does not make sense to base the predictions on all previous campaigns that have ever taken place, but on those that are most similar to the one being considered. For instance, responses to campaigns for a new checking account may have little bearing on responses to campaigns for a new credit card or refinancing a home. By considering more data, we lose accuracy since some of the data will not be relevant to the task we are considering.

The main concern in segmentation is what happens if there are one or two key indicators that are common to all of the campaigns and whether they will be lost if we just analyze the campaigns a few at a time. The answer is no in some cases, because if a pattern holds strongly enough in the entire database, it will also hold in the segment. For example, if the people with more than five children never respond to campaigns, this fact will also be true in each individual campaign.

Optimizing the Data Mining Process

The data-mining step of the KDD process involves searching for patterns of interest in a particular form or a set of such representation, including classification rules or trees, regression and clustering. The performance and quality of the mined information is a function of the effectiveness of the data-mining technique used, the quality and often the size of the data being mined. In the following, we provide an overview of the approaches to optimizing the data-mining step.

Interestingness of Patterns. Databases contain a variety of patterns, but few of them are of much interest. Thus, some techniques are needed in order to prevent the discovery system from generating trivial / uninteresting rules. One approach to solve the problem of searching the large databases is to provide some measure of interestingness of patterns and then search only for these patterns (Piatetsky, 1991; Piatetsky et al., 1994; Silberschatz, 1995).

A pattern is interesting to the degree that it is not only accurate, but that it is also useful with respect to the end-user's knowledge and objectives (Adriaans et al., 1996; Fayyad et al., 1996; Piatetsky et al., 1994). Interestingness is driven by factors such as novelty, utility, relevance and statistical significance (Silberschatz et al., 1995). An automated discovery system requires specific interestingness factors which it can measure, as well as a way of combining these factors into a metric that accurately reflects how domain experts judge key patterns.

Parallel Processing. Mining a database of even a few gigabytes is a very difficult and time-consuming task, and requires advanced parallel hardware and parallelized data-mining algorithms to reduce the size of the database (Fayyad et al., 1996; Parsaye, 1995). Numerous algorithms have been developed for data mining (Adriaans et al., 1996; Fayyad, 1996; Savasere et al., 1995). Inherent parallelism exist in these algorithms, which provide us some flexibility in choosing a particular parallelisms scheme most suited for a specific parallel machine.

In Chattratichat et al. (1997), the authors identify two major schemes for exploiting parallelism within data mining algorithms--as task parallelism and data parallelism. In the task parallelism approach, the computation is partitioned among the processors of a particular machine. Each processor is computing a distinct part of a learning model before coordinating with the other processors to form the global model. In the data parallelism approach, the training set is partitioned amongst the processors, with all processors synchronously constructing the same model, each operating on a different portion of the data set. For example, in a classification tree algorithm, each branch of the tree is formed into a task (task parallelism). For data parallelism, the training set is partitioned across the processors, and each processor evaluates a node of tree in parallel.

The experimental results in Chattratichat et al., (1997) indicate that while the parallelization of certain data-mining algorithms shows a consistent performance behavior when applied to different data sets, this is not necessarily true for all algorithms. For example, induction-based classification algorithms appear to have no ideal scheme for their parallelization. The performance of the different parallelisation scheme varies greatly with the characteristics of the data set to which the algorithm is applied.

Another problem in using parallel processing is the administrative complexity of a system with any number of parallel processors. A major issue associated with parallel processing is how to distribute the data among different processors and to integrate the results produced by different processors.

Optimization of the Data-Mining Algorithm. Recent work has focused on optimizing data-mining algorithms that are applied to very large databases (Adriaans et al., 1996; Ganti et al., 1999; Savasere et al., 1995). In particular, apriori algorithm (Adriaans et al., 1996; Ganti et al., 1999) has been defined for the optimization of the algorithms for market-basket analysis, clustering and classification. The basic concept in apriori algorithm is to run analysis against transaction databases in order to find sets of items, or itemsets, that appear together in many transactions. Each pattern extracted through the analysis consists of an itemset and the number of transactions that contain it.

The a priori algorithm computes the frequent itemsets in several rounds. Round i computes all frequent i-itemsets. A round has two steps: candidate generation and candidate counting. In the first round, the generated set of candidate itemsets contains all 1-itemsets. The algorithm counts their support during the candidate counting step. Thus, after the first round, all frequent 1-itemsets are known. In round two, naively, all pairs of items are candidates. Apriori algorithm reduces the set of candidate itemsets by pruning-a priori-those candidate itemsets that cannot be frequent, based on knowledge about infrequent itemsets obtained from previous rounds. The pruning is based on the observation that if an itemset is frequent, all its subsets must be frequent as well. Therefore, before entering the candidate counting step, the algorithm can discard every candidate itemset with a subset that is infrequent.

A major problem with the apriori algorithm is that it scans the database several times, depending on the size of the longest frequent itemset. Several refinements have been proposed that focus on reducing the number of database scans, the number of candidate itemsets counted in each scan or both (Brin, 1997; Savasere et al., 1995).

USING DOMAIN KNOWLEDGE
TO OPTIMIZE THE KDD PROCESS

A major problem with some of the above techniques (i.e., sampling, and segmentation) is that they reduce the size of the database by throwing away records/attributes without knowing exactly what they are throwing away. The consequence is the increased chance of missing the discovery of some of the hidden patterns when these records/attributes are eliminated. In addition, the existing schemes may generate uninteresting, trivial and redundant knowledge.

Although a database stores a large amount of data, usually only a portion of it is relevant to the discovery task. For example, to find the factors causing ovarian Cancer, in a medical database system, we can eliminate male patients from discovery consideration since male patients cannot get ovarian cancer (a medical fact, considered as a domain knowledge).

Domain or background knowledge can be defined as any information that is not explicitly presented in the database (Fayyad et al., 1996; Owrang, 1997). In a medical database, for example, the knowledge "male patients cannot be pregnant" or "male patients do not get ovarian cancer" is considered to be domain knowledge since it is not contained in the database directly. Similarly, in a business database, the domain knowledge "customers with high-income are good credit risks" may be useful even though it is not always true.

Domain knowledge originates from many sources. A data dictionary is the most basic form of domain knowledge (Adriaans et al., 1996; Date, 1990; Owrang, 1997). Typical information in the data dictionary includes the types of attributes, size of attributes, name of attributes, meaning of each attribute, format, constraints, domain of attribute, usage statistics, access control, mapping definitions, etc. (Date, 1990). Additional information about the specific analysis objectives may come from the domain expert (although it may be generated automatically from the database (Adriaans et al., 1996) and can assume many forms. A few examples include: lists of relevant fields on which to focus for the discovery purposes; definition of new fields (e.g., age = current_date - birth_date); lists of useful classes or categories of fields or records (e.g., revenue fields: profits, expenses,...); generalization hierarchies (e.g., A is-a B is-a C); and functional or causal dependencies. Formally, domain knowledge can be represented as $X \Rightarrow Y$ (meaning X implies Y), where X and Y are simple or conjunctive predicates over some attributes in the database.

In the following sections, we discuss our approach of using domain knowledge in reducing the size of the database for discovery cases; as well as in defining more consistent, accurate and efficient hypotheses in order to optimize the knowledge discovery process. In using domain knowledge, we knowingly throw away data, records, attributes and the conditions used in the hypotheses to discover patterns, which do not participate in the specific discovery cases.

Reducing Database Size

Domain knowledge can be used to reduce the size of the database that is being searched for discovery by eliminating data records that are irrelevant to a discovery case. The following examples show how domain knowledge can be used to focus a proper subset of the database for the discovery case.

Example 1:

Careful understanding of the domain can guide the KDD analyst in developing a hypothesis to discover valuable knowledge. Take for example a large department store in Minnesota which wants to discover ways to improve sales. The analyst asks questions to understand the store's client base and their lifestyle. The store's representative notes that the surrounding area is very rural and many of the people of the region enjoy hunting and fishing. The analyst asks when hunting and fishing seasons start. Based on this information, the analyst can focus the discovery process to search for high sales products during the year, looking at the year in terms of the hunting and fishing seasons. As a result, the analyst can find a correlation such as "chain saw and beds sell well together in Minnesota in October, possibly due to people getting their vacation homes ready for the hunting season." When the analyst looks for product correlation in the store sales for the year or by quarter, this correlation may not have been strong enough to be discovered." Subsequently, the domain knowledge about the appropriate time for hunting and fishing can help us focus on the right data (in this case, data related to October) for discovery.

Example 2:

Consider a medical database in which we are interested in finding out the factors affecting an individual in developing ovarian cancer (or what type of medication is effective for ovarian treatment). Through medical research we know that only women can develop ovarian cancer. We can use this as domain knowledge to select female patients into the data set for KDD and then search for clusters of characteristics that are highly correlated (positively or negatively) with the presence of ovarian cancer in the patient. To formalize the process, assume the set of domain knowledge is represented as:

DK={(cancer_type=ovarian) $\Rightarrow$ (sex=female), (cancer_type=ovarian) $\Rightarrow$ (age > 20), ... }.

The initial hypothesis (note that the actual hypothesis for discovery may include other attributes of the patients, e.g., race, weight, etc.) can be represented as a rule as follows:

IF Using_Birth_Control_Pills = No AND Using_Fertility_Drugs=Yes AND
Family_Member="had ovarian cancer" AND age > ... AND .....
THEN cancer_type=ovarian.

The database reduction process can apply the domain knowledge to the initial hypothesis to create a set of constraints. Basically, for each condition (or goal) in the hypothesis, the reduction process searches the set of domain knowledge. If the condition is found to be in the Y (or X) part of a domain knowledge, then the X (or Y) part of the domain knowledge is selected as a constraint. The set of constraints can then be used to create an SQL statement to be executed in order to produce the reduced database. For the above hypothesis, the following SQL statement can be created and executed to produce the reduced database.

Select *   Into Reduced-Patient-Relation
FROM Patient-Relation
Where sex = 'female' AND age > 20

Hypothesis Optimization

The basis for knowledge discovery is the hypothesis that represents the pattern to be discovered. Most of the problems previously mentioned for very large databases can be avoided by a well-defined hypothesis; that is, one that does not include any redundant and/or inconsistent conditions relating the attributes in the patterns. Knowledge discovery can be perceived as a search problem in which we have to find the correct hypothesis (pattern to be discovered). The basic form of representing a hypothesis is the rule representation as:

IF $P_1, P_2, P_3, ..., P_n$ THEN C, where "," means "and," and P_i is a proposition of the form : *attr* OP *value,* where *attr* is the name of an attribute in the data set, *value* is a possible value for *attr* and OP 0 $\{ =, \leq, \geq, \neq, <, > \}$ is the operation. C is the consequent of the form *attr* OP *value.*

An important element in search problems is the establishment of the complexity of the search space. That is, how many hypotheses there are and how they are related. When there are only a few different hypotheses, it is possible to find and test the correct hypothesis simply by enumeration. In the case of several thousands or even an infinite number of hypotheses, enumeration would not be such a good strategy (Adriaans et al., 1996). The only way to cope with the search problem in such a case is to develop some kind of refinement theory for hypotheses. We can use that measure to select potentially good hypotheses leading to consistent/nontrivial discovery. In most discovery situations, even if it is not strictly necessary, domain or background knowledge will speed up the discovery process. Domain knowledge is a form of bias that helps us constrain the search of a hypothesis (or to prove a hypothesis). Our approach to hypothesis optimization is to use domain knowledge to eliminate implied, unnecessary and redundant conditions from the hypothesis.

Figure 3 shows the overall view of the discovery process optimization using domain knowledge.

A discovery process can be guided by specifying the criteria to focus on, although the process may allow for moving randomly through the database to find any pattern or relationship. For each pattern or relationship to be discovered, one would (Parsaye, 1996):

1) Form hypotheses.
2) Make some queries to the database.

Figure 3. Overall view of the discovery process optimization using domain knowledge

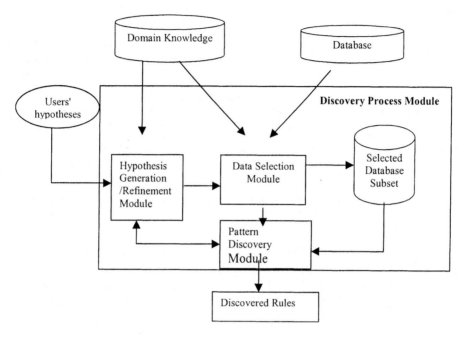

3) View the result and modify the hypotheses if needed.

4) Continue this cycle until a pattern merges.

This task can be automated with a discovery module that can repeatedly query the database until knowledge is discovered. Initially, hypotheses can be formed by domain experts (or by the discovery system automatically). The objective for initial hypothesis development is to aim for one specific concept.

To discover consistent and accurate knowledge, we[1] need to define the hypothesis accurately and efficiently. The propositions in the hypothesis involve attributes that are normally related to each other, implied by each other or not related at all. The information regarding the relationship among the attributes (known as domain knowledge) can be used to eliminate unnecessary, implied and redundant propositions from the hypothesis, thereby producing less but more accurate and consistent rules. In general, for knowledge discovery on any database, an appropriate set of domain knowledge (relevant to the database being processed for discovery) can be identified and utilized by the Hypothesis Generation/Refinement and Data Selection modules of the Discovery Process Module (Figure 3). In the next section, we discuss how to define a more accurate and efficient hypothesis using domain knowledge.

Optimized Hypothesis to Eliminate Implied Conditions. Domain knowledge can be used to define an optimal hypothesis by eliminating unnecessary conditions in the hypothesis, thereby reducing the search time for discovering interesting knowledge from the database. In general, there may be some interdependency between or among conditions (or propositions) in a hypothesis, indicating that some conditions imply others. Of course, these dependencies can be identified by domain knowledge. Subsequently, those conditions that can be implied by others may be removed from the hypothesis (since they provide no additional information in knowledge discovery) resulting in a faster discovery process.

To show how the hypothesis optimization process works, consider the CAR1 data relation in Figure 4. A collection of cars is described in terms of such attributes as overall length (SIZE), number of cylinders (CYL), presence of a turbocharger (TURBO), type of fuel system (FUELSYS), engine displacement (DISPLACE), compression ratio (COMP), POWER, type of transmission (TRANS), WEIGHT and mileage (MILEAGE) (Ziarko, 1991). Suppose we are interested in factors affecting high car mileage. The full functional dependency means that the mileage of a car is affected by interactions of all or some possible causes represented by attributes contained in the CAR1 relation. We[1] may start with the following hypothesis represented as a rule:

IF SIZE = subcompact AND CYL = 4 AND TURBO = no AND
FUELSYS = efi AND   DISPLACE = small AND COMP = high AND
POWER = medium AND   TRANS = manual AND WEIGHT = light
THEN MILEAGE = high

The set of domain knowledge may include :
(SIZE = subcompact) $\Rightarrow$ (WEIGHT = light) ; (TURBO = no) $\Rightarrow$ (POWER = medium)
By applying domain knowledge to the initial hypothesis, conditions 7 (POWER = medium) and 9 (WEIGHT = light) can be removed from the hypothesis. The discovery system will evaluate the hypothesis with respect to actual data and may remove additional irrelevant conditions from the hypothesis in discovering knowledge.

We have performed several runs on the CAR1 relation using a microcomputer-based knowledge discovery tool called IDIS (1994). IDIS, the *Information Discovery System* (IDIS, 1994) generates possible rules for explaining relationships among attributes in a database. It uncovers information based on questions no one thought to ask by posing a hypothesis and then testing it for accuracy and relevancy. It concludes with a list of rules in two- and three-dimensional, hypermedia graphs. IDIS uses induction, guided by the user, to assign weights to attributes used in the rules. It finds suspicious entries and unusual patterns automatically, including data items that violate correlations, extreme boundary items and items which are beyond normal standard deviations. IDIS has been used in areas as diverse as financial analysis, marketing, scientific discovery, quality control, medical discovery and manufacturing. IDIS induces classification rules, generalized rules with intervals and inexact rules. A generated rule can be saved as a constraint and then used along with an anomaly detection facility in order to find the values and exceptions that violate a specific rule. In addition, ad hoc queries can be used to verify simple, human-generated hypotheses. In effect, ad hoc queries are a method of knowledge verification.

Figure 4. A sample CAR1 data relation

SIZE	CYL	TURBO	FUELSYS	DISPLACE	COMP	POWER	TRANS	WEIGHT	MILEAGE
Compact	6	yes	Efi	Medium	High	High	Auto	Medium	Medium
Compact	6	no	Efi	Medium	Medium	High	Manual	Medium	Medium
Compact	4	yes	Efi	Medium	High	High	Manual	Light	High
Compact	6	no	Efi	Medium	Medium	Medium	Manual	Medium	Medium
Compact	6	no	2-bbl	Medium	Medium	Medium	Auto	Heavy	Low
Compact	6	no	Efi	Medium	Medium	High	Manual	Heavy	Low
Subcompact	4	no	2-bbl	Small	High	Low	Manual	Light	High
Compact	4	no	2-bbl	Small	High	Low	Manual	Medium	Medium
Compact	4	no	2-bbl	Small	High	Medium	Auto	Medium	Medium
Subcompact	4	no	Efi	SmallL	High	Low	Manual	Light	High
Subcompact	4	no	Efi	Medium	Medium	Medium	Manual	Medium	High
Compact	4	no	2-bbl	Medium	Medium	Medium	Manual	Medium	Medium
Subcompact	4	yes	Efi	Small	High	High	Manual	Medium	High
Subcompact	4	no	2-bbl	Small	Medium	Low	Manual	Medium	High
Compact	4	yes	Efi	Medium	Medium	High	Manual	Medium	Medium
Compact	6	no	Efi	Medium	Medium	High	Auto	Medium	Medium
Compact	4	no	Efi	Medium	Medium	High	Auto	Medium	Medium
Subcompact	4	no	Efi	Small	High	Medium	Manual	Medium	High
Compact	4	no	Efi	Small	High	Medium	Manual	Medium	High
Compact	4	no	2-bbl	Small	High	Medium	Manual	Medium	Medium
Compact	6	no	Efi	Medium	High	High	Manual	Medium	Medium

Figure 5. Rules generated by IDIS tool based on the CAR1 relation in Figure 4, with mileage as the goal and the rest of attributes as conditions

```
Rule 1: CF = 100.00 %     Rule 2: CF = 100.00 %     Rule 3: CF = 100.00 %
        MILEAGE = "high"          MILEAGE = "high"          MILEAGE = "high"
        IF SIZE = "subcompact"    IF WEIGHT = "light"       IF FUELSYS ="efi"
                                                            and DISPLACE =
                                                            "small"

Rule 4: CF = 100.00 %     Rule 5: CF = 100.00 %     Rule 6: CF = 100.00 %
        MILEAGE = "high"          MILEAGE ="high"           MILEAGE = "high"
        IF CYL = "4"              IF CYL ="4"               IF CYL ="4"
        and TURBO = "yes"         and FUELSYS ="efi"        and TURBO ="no"
        and COMP = "high"         and POWER ="medium"       and FUELSYS ="efi"
                                                            and TRANS =
                                                            "manual"
```

Figure 5 shows the rules generated by IDIS when all conditions are applied. In the second run, we eliminated the WEIGHT condition because of the existence of domain knowledge (e.g., SIZE implies WEIGHT). Except for Rule 2 in Figure 5, the rest of the rules were generated in the second run. We note that Rule 2 seems to be another domain knowledge and not a new discovery. In the third run, the POWER condition was removed using the domain knowledge (e.g., TURBO implies POWER). Except for Rule 5 in Figure 5, the rest of the rules were generated in the third run. Note again that if we replace the POWER condition with the TURBO condition, then Rule 5 becomes a subsumption of Rule 6 (a redundant discovery). Therefore, the absence of Rule 5 in the third run is not an indication of blocking the unexpected discovery. Finally, in the fourth run, the WEIGHT and POWER conditions have both been removed from the initial hypothesis. Except for Rules 2 and 5, the rest of the rules in Figure 5 were generated. The absence of Rules 2 and 5 do not mean the blocking of unexpected discovery as explained in the second and third runs as above.

More Accurate Hypothesis to Avoid Possible Contradictory Rule Discovery. Rules are contradictory when they have the same conditions and different mutually exclusive conclusions. The following rules are contradictory:

Rule 1:   If Car Model=Honda AND Cylinders=4 Then Mileage = High

Rule 2:   If Car Model=Honda AND Cylinders=4 Then Mileage = Low

Domain knowledge can be used to avoid generating contradictory rules. Consider our CAR1 relation in Figure 4 (with the added attributes Car Model and Car Year). Suppose one is interested in finding out whether Car Model and Cylinders have any relationships with highway mileage. Without using domain knowledge, our discovery system could discover the above rules. Assume we have the available domain knowledge that cars produced after 1980 have special features that result in a better performance and better mileage. We could use the domain knowledge to define a more accurate hypothesis in order to avoid generating rules that seem to be contradictory. The basic idea is to expand the hypothesis by adding more conditions based on the available domain knowledge. The process is to examine the set of available domain knowledge and find any set that involves the goal defined for the discovery. In the above example, let's assume we have the following domain knowledge:

(Car Year > 1980) $\Rightarrow$ (Mileage = High).

Subsequently, we[1] should include the Car Year attribute into the hypothesis. Then, we may get the following rules that do not seem to be contradictory.

Rule 1: If Car Model=Honda AND Cylinders=4 AND Car Year > 1980 Then Mileage = High

Rule 2: If Car Model=Honda AND Cylinders=4 AND Car Year <= 1980 Then Mileage = Low

Optimized Hypothesis to Avoid Possible Redundant Rule Discovery. Databases normally contain redundant data and definitions that could lead to discovering redundant rules. The redundant data/definitions are generally different syntactically. For instance, consider the CAR relation in Figure 6. The relation contains the attribute Engine_Size, Bore, Stroke and Cylinder among other attributes. The redundant attribute Engine_Size is defined as: Engine_Size = Bore * Stroke * Cylinder. The problem with redundant information is that it can be mistakenly discovered as knowledge even though it is usually uninteresting to the end-user.

Discovered knowledge may contain redundancy when two pieces of knowledge are exactly the same (rules having the same premises and conclusions) or semantically equivalent (Owrang et al., 1990; Piatetsky, 1991). In our discovery experiment, we defined the High_MPG as the goal and the rest of the attributes as premise. The discovery tool IDIS discovered rules relating the Engine_Size to High_MPG as well as rules relating (Bore,Stroke,Cylinder) to High_MPG. Obviously, the discovered rules based on Engine_Size and (Bore, Stroke, Cylinder) are syntactically different, but they are semantically identical.

We can define the redundant information in the database as domain knowledge and apply this domain knowledge in the discovery process in order to avoid generating rules that are syntactically different but semantically equivalent. Before knowledge discovery, we[1] should check the available domain knowledge to find one that has attributes involved in the discovery hypothesis. If there is such domain knowledge, then the attributes in one side of the domain knowledge should be included in the discovery process (in the hypothesis). For the CAR relation, we could use the Engine_Size attribute or the (Bore, Stroke, Cylinder) attributes in the

Figure 6. The CAR relation

CAR *(Symboling, Losses, Make, Fuel-Type, Aspiration, Doors, Body, Drive, Engine-Loc, Wheel-Base, Length, Width, Height, Weight, Engine-Type, Cylinders, Engine-Size, Fuel-Sys, Bore, Stroke, Compress, Horse-Power, Peak-RPM, City-MPG, High-MPG, Price)*

discovery process. The choice depends on whether we are looking to generate more general rules or more detailed rules. The advantage of using this process is not only an avoidance of redundant rules, but also the generation of rules that are more meaningful.

Optimized Hypothesis to Avoid Possible Uninteresting Rule Discovery. As we noted previously, databases contain a variety of patterns, but only a few of them are of much interest. A pattern is interesting to the degree that it is useful with respect to the user's knowledge and objectives. In our knowledge discovery from the CAR relation in Figure 6, some of the generated rules were uninteresting and/or known facts. For example, the tool discovered that "the smaller the Weight, the better High-MPG," which is a trivial discovery since it is a known fact (or a domain knowledge). Similarly, the discovered rule "the more expensive the car, the better High-MPG" seems to be uninteresting since there is no relationship between the price of the car and highway mileage (based on domain expert's information).

Statistical significance is usually a key factor in determining interestingness (Piatetsky, 1991, 1994; Silberschatz, 1995). The specific factors that influence the interestingness of a pattern will vary for different databases and tasks, thus requiring outside domain knowledge (Piatetsky, 1991). For example, height and diagnosis may not be causally related if the database deals with liver disease; however, they may be causally related for physiotherapy. Such domain knowledge should be used in constructing the hypothesis in order to discover a more meaningful rule. So, if the database has data about patients with liver disease, and the generated hypothesis involves height and diagnosis, we should use the domain knowledge (that height and diagnosis have no relationship) in order to avoid including attributes in the hypothesis that have no significance in the knowledge being discovered.

Optimized Query Used to Prove Hypothesis. To discover patterns, a discovery system forms the hypotheses, makes queries to the database, views the result and modifies the hypotheses if needed. This process continues until a pattern merges.

A major component of a discovery system is the database interface. Raw data is selected from the DBMS (using queries) and then processed by the extraction algorithms that produce the discovered patterns. The queries can be posed in SQL, a standard query language for many relational databases (Date, 1990). The DBMS interface is where database queries are generated.

Domain knowledge can be used to optimize a query used to prove a hypothesis. For example, consider the following data relations in a database:

    employee(E#,Ename,title,experience,seniority)

    money(title,seniority,salary,responsibilities)

Assume the knowledge to be discovered is "What are the criteria for an employee to earn more than $50,000?." An expert may suggest that experience and seniority are the two criteria contributing to having a salary more than $50,000. The hypothesis may be represented as the following rule:

IF has experience   AND has seniority   THEN earn more than 50000 .

To prove (or disprove) the hypothesis, a discovery system may execute the following SQL statement:

Select experience,seniority   From employee E,money M
Where salary >= 50000   AND E.title=M.title   AND E.seniority=M.seniority.

Now, assume that we have the following domain knowledge:

Only level-1 and level-2 managers have a salary more than 50000, represented as
(title = level-1) $\Rightarrow$ (salary >= 50000)
(title = level-2) $\Rightarrow$ (salary >= 50000)

We can use this domain knowledge to minimize our search by eliminating the unnecessary join operation. Basically, for each condition in the hypothesis, the query optimization algorithm searches the set of domain knowledge. If the condition is found to be in the Y part of a domain knowledge, then the X part of the domain knowledge will replace the condition and the unnecessary join operation will be removed from the query. The optimized SQL statement for the above example would be:

Select experience,seniority From employee
Where title=level-1   or title=level-2.

Evaluation of Using Domain Knowledge

In this section, we evaluate the benefits of utilizing domain-specific knowledge in the discovery process. In particular, the performance of the discovery system is measured with and without domain-specific knowledge along the time to discover knowledge, and the consistency and non-triviality of the discovered knowledge.

Experimental Results of Using Domain Knowledge. As we noted before, the hypothesis represents the pattern to be discovered. A hypothesis can be provided by a user or generated automatically by the discovery tool/system. As it was illustrated in Figure 3, our extended view of the knowledge discovery process utilizes the domain knowledge in order to define and process the hypothesis more efficiently. To evaluate the usefulness of domain knowledge in discovering rules from databases, the knowledge discovery tool IDIS (1994) has been used on different databases.

The following experiments used data that was downloaded from the National Highway Traffic Administration Web site at www.fars.nhtsa.dot.gov/fars/fars.cfm. The data was gathered from the Fatality Analysis Reporting System (FARS), which contains data on all vehicle crashes in the United States that occur on a public roadway and involve a fatality. The data was downloaded to a table containing 4,037 records. The table contains all the crash data from Washington DC, Maryland and Virginia for 1997 and includes 120 fields. Because of the operating constraints on the discovery knowledge tool used (IDIS), for each experiment the number of attributes was reduced. The one master FARS data table could logically be broken up into four different tables: persons, crashes, vehicles and drivers. Each of these table types was created as needed for each experiment.

The experiments involve creating two new tables using data from one of the four newly created tables, one without using any domain knowledge and one applying domain knowledge. The table using domain knowledge would have fewer fields and/or records, applying the methods mentioned before (Using Domain Knowledge to Reduce Database Size and Using Domain Knowledge to Optimize Hypotheses). The discovery process would then be run using each table separately, analyzing results and logging information.

Domain knowledge analysis charts were created to track the number of rules generated, time to generate rules, subsuming, trivial and interesting rules. A trivial rule was defined as a one that was obvious or if any of the fields contained in the rule had values that spanned the entire spectrum for that field. For example, if a rule includes "where the blood-alcohol test was between 0 and .94+ (every possible value)," then that rule would be labeled as trivial. An interesting rule was defined as one where it is not obvious and the "IF" portion of the rule has either a small range or one value. This experiment used the IDIS Version 3.0 by Information Discovery Inc. knowledge discovery tool running on a Pentium II 350 Mhz PC.

With this experiment, data relating to crash information was used. Table 1 shows the attributes for this table.

The goal of "manner of collision" (MCOL) was used for all three tests. This field can contain values of: Not Collision; Rear-End; Head-On; Rear-to-Rear;

Table 1. Attributes in Crash Table

	Related Factors (ARF1)
Crash Month (ACCMON)	ARF2
Crash Time (TIME)	ARF3
Atmosphere Condition (ATM)	Relation to Junction (JUNCTION)
Construction/Maintenance Zone (CMZONE)	Relation to Roadway (RRDWY)
	Roadway Function Class (RFUN)
County (COUNTY)	Roadway Alignment (ALIGN)
Arrival Time EMS (ATIME)	Roadway Profile (PROFILE)
Notification Time EMS (NTIME)	Roadway Surface Type (TSURF)
EMS Time at Hospital (EMSHOSP)	Roadway Surface Condition (SCOND)
First Harmful Event (FHE)	Route Signing (CLF)
Hit and Run (HIUN)	School Bus Related (SBUS)
Light Condition (LIGHT)	Special Jurisdiction (SPJUR)
Manner of Collision (MCOL)	Speed Limit (SPLIM)
National Highway System (NHS)	Traffic Control Devices (CTDEV)
Number of Non-Motorist Forms (PEDFORMS)	Traffic Control Device Functioning (TCTRL)
Number of Person Forms (PFORMS)	Trafficway ID (TRFID)
Number of Vehicle Forms (VFORMS)	Trafficway Flow (FLOW)
Number of Travel Lanes (TLANES)	

Angle; Sideswipe - Same Direction; Sideswipe - Opposite Direction; and Unknown. The original premise of the goal before applying domain knowledge uses every other field in the table.

For the domain knowledge (DK), the following were assumed.

• Crash Time implies the Light Condition
• Atmospheric Condition implies the Roadway Surface Condition
• Route Signing implies if it is a National Highway System or not
• Any value where the manner of collision is "Unknown" is not relevant to discovery
• Any Emergency Medical information has no relevance on the manner of collision.

In summary, this domain knowledge will remove the fields: LIGHT (Light Condition), SCOND (Roadway Surface Condition), NHS (National Highway System), TLANES (Number of Travel Lanes), EMSHOSP (EMS Time at Hospital), NTIME (EMS Notification Time) and ATIME (EMS Arrival Time), as well as any record where MCOL (Manner of Collision) = "9."

This experiment was first run with the Maximum Rule Length set to "2" (Test #1). This generated 2,905 rules without domain knowledge and 2,073 with domain knowledge. Because of the large number of rules, the Maximum Rule Length was set to 1, which generated 584 rules without domain knowledge and 276 with domain knowledge (Test #2). To analyze the rules better, the number was reduced again by narrowing the goal to only generate rules where MCOL = "Not Collision". This generated 80 rules without and 52 with domain knowledge (Test #3). The maximum rule length parameter in the IDIS system determines how many "IF" conditions there can be in the generated rules. For example, the rule:

"MCOL" = "Not Collision" IF "PROFILE" = "2" AND "CTDEV" = "0"

has two conditions to satisfy for MCOL to be equal to "Not Collision". Therefore, when this parameter is set to 2, it generates rules with 1 and 2 "IF" conditions.

The following is an example of a redundant rule considering the LIGHT field. If the time the collision occurred was between 1 and 3:33 AM, then the analyst already knows that it was dark when the accident occurred (2 equates to "Dark" in the LIGHT attribute).

1."MCOL" = "Not Collision" IF "LIGHT" = "2"

Table 2. Experiment Results

Test #	Data Set	# of Rules Generated	Time to Generate Rules	# of Redundant Rules	# of Subsuming Rules	# of Trivial Rules	# of Interesting Rules
1	Without DK	2905	25 min.	254	508	1126	1017
1	With DK	2073	12 min.	0	318	678	1076
2	Without DK	584	1.5 min.	51	102	226	204
2	With DK	276	< 1 min.	0	42	90	143
3	Without DK	80	<1 min.	7	14	31	28
3	With DK	52	<1 min.	0	8	17	27

2."MCOL" = "Not Collision" IF "1" <= "TIME" <= "333"

Below, Rule 2 was considered subsuming because Rule 1 already states that there were no collisions if the number of travel lanes was between 1 and 4, inclusively. Rule 2 restates that if the number of travel lanes was 4, there were no collisions. Therefore, this knowledge is already known from Rule 1.

1."MCOL" = "Not Collision" IF "1" <= "TLANES" <= "4"

2."MCOL" = "Not Collision" IF "TLANES" = "4"

This next rule is considered trivial because it is obvious that there would be no collision if a hit and run did not occur. (If HITRUN="0" then no hit and run occurred.)

"MCOL" = "Not Collision" IF "HITRUN" = "0"

The following rule is considered an interesting rule. It is stating that if there was no junction, then there was no collision. (If Junction = 1, then there was no junction.)

"MCOL" = "Not Collision" IF "JUNCTION" = "1"

In this experiment, fewer trivial rules were generated, which shows the benefit of using domain knowledge. This can greatly reduce the amount of time an analyst will spend evaluating trivial rules. The only concern with this test result is that without DK, there was one more interesting rule generated. That rule is related to the number of lanes, which in the stated domain knowledge was implied by the roadway function class. This particular rule may also be considered redundant.

Also worth noting in this experiment is the time to generate the rules. In tests 2 and 3, the amount of time to generate the rules was trivial and the difference was difficult to measure. In the first test with DK applied, the generation took less than half of the time it took when applying DK.

Avoid Blocking Unexpected Discovery. The main purpose of using domain knowledge is to bias the search for interesting patterns. This can be achieved by focusing the discovery on portions of the data. The benefits are greater efficiency and more relevant discoveries. Too much reliance on domain knowledge, however, may unduly constrain the knowledge discovery and may block unexpected discovery by leaving portions of the database unexplored.

There is one possible scheme to improve the effective use of domain knowledge in knowledge discovery and to avoid blocking the unexpected discovery. This scheme assigns a confidence factor to each domain knowledge and uses it only if the confidence factor is greater than a specified threshold. The assignment of a confidence factor to a domain knowledge depends on how close the domain knowledge is to the established facts.

We should note that our discovery experiments on the Crash table did not show any blocking of unexpected discovery when domain knowledge is used.

CONCLUSION AND FUTURE DIRECTION

Databases are becoming larger, with potential for more incomplete and inaccurate data, making knowledge discovery more difficult. Domain knowledge can be used to provide some assistance in different aspects of knowledge discovery. We have discussed the benefits of using domain knowledge to constrain the search when discovering knowledge from databases. Domain knowledge can be used to reduce the search by reducing the size of the hypotheses by eliminating unnecessary conditions from the hypotheses. Currently, we are studying mechanisms for gathering domain knowledge. Domain knowledge can be obtained from domain experts or extracted automatically from databases.

Using too much domain knowledge can produce a specialized discovery scheme that can be more efficient than any general scheme in its domain, but will not be useful outside its domain. To effectively use domain knowledge, we can develop a general scheme for knowledge discovery and then augment it with the specific domain knowledge. The interface, integration of the general-purpose discovery scheme and domain knowledge, may require developing a set of rules that can recommend when and how much of the domain knowledge to be used in different phases of the general-purpose discovery scheme. These phases include creation of the hypothesis, querying the database and modifying the hypothesis. The hypothesis optimization process defined in this chapter, for example, can be part of such an interface and can automatically be applied to every hypothesis generated by the general-purpose discovery scheme. The interface should have a mechanism for reducing the size of the database of possible, by using all the available domain knowledge efficiently. We can use the criteria explained in this section. The reduced database should be provided to the general-purpose discovery scheme for knowledge discovery.

The optimization scheme based on domain knowledge can be used to optimize the concepts discovered from object-oriented databases by representing the domain knowledge as concepts (hierarchical concepts) rather than rules. Similarly, we could use fuzzy terms in defining domain knowledge, with appropriate fuzzy sets describing the fuzzy terms, to optimize and validate the set of rules discovered from the fuzzy relational databases.

In the future, the techniques for the optimization of the knowledge discovery process need to be expanded in order to handle the following problem:

Although a relational database stores a large amount of data, usually only a portion of it is relevant to a specific discovery task. Obviously, preprocessing must be performed to extract and group the task-relevant data from a database before generalization. The preprocessing can be viewed as a relational query which takes a discovery request as a retrieval command to search for the necessary sets of data from the database and group them according to the discovery task. Future discovery tools should be able to look at the nature of data and available domain knowledge in order to automatically produce the retrieval command to search for the relevant data to be processed by the discovery tool.

ENDNOTE

[1] In the context of this chapter, "we" refers to users of the discovery system.

REFERENCES

Adriaans, P. and Zantinge, D. (1996). *Data Mining*, Addison-Wesley.

Brin, S. (1997). Dynamic itemset counting and implication rules for market-basket data, *Proceedings ACM SIGMOD International Conf. Management of Data*, New York: ACM Press, 255-264.

Chattratichat, J., Darlington, J. and Ghahem, M. (1997). Large scale data mining: Challenges and responses, *Proceedings of the 3rd Inter. Conf. on Knowledge Discovery and Data Mining*, 143-146.

Date, C.J. (1990). *An Introduction to Database Systems*, Vol. 1, 5th Edition, Addison-Wesley, Reading, Mass.

Fayyad, U. (1996). Data mining and knowledge discovery: Making sense out of data, *IEEE Expert*, 11(5), 20-25.

Fayyad, U., Piatetsky-Shapiro, G. and Symth, P. (1996). Knowledge discovery and data mining: Towards a unifying framework, *Proceedings of the Second International Conference on Knowledge Discovery and Data Mining*, August, 82-88.

Ganti, V., Johannes, G. and Ramakrishnan, R. (1999). Mining very large databases, *IEEE Computer*, August, 32(8), 38-45.

Groth, R. (1998). *Data Mining: A Hands-On Approach for Business Professionals*, Prentice Hall.

IDIS: The Information Discovery System, (1994). *User's Manual*. L.A.: IntelligenceWare.

Kivinen, J. and Heikki Mannila, H. (1994). The power of sampling in knowledge discovery, *Proceedings of the 1994 ACM SIGACT-SIGMOD-SIGACT Symp. on Principles of Database Theory (PODS'94)*, 77-85.

Owrang, M. M., Frame, M.C., Larry R. and Medsker, L.R. (1990). Testing for inconsistencies in rule-based knowledge bases. *Expert Systems Applications*, EXPERSYS-90, 281-286.

Owrang O. M. M. (1997). The role of domain knowledge in knowledge discovery in databases, *Microcomputers Applications*, 16(1), 11-18.

Parsaye, K. (1995). Large scale data mining in parallel, *DBMS Magazine*, March.

Parsaye, K. (1996). Data mines for data warehouses, *Database Programming & Design*, September.

Parsaye, K. (1999). Small data, small knowledge-The pitfalls of sampling and summarization, *Information Discovery Inc.*, http:\\www.datamining.com/datamine/ds-start1.htm.

Piatetsky-Shapiro, G. (1991). Discovery, analysis, and presentation of strong rules, knowledge discovery in databases, AAAI Press/MIT Press, 229-247.

Piatetsky-Shapiro, G. and Matheus, C. J. (1994). The interestingness of deviations, *Proceedings of the AAAI-94 Workshop on KDD*, 25-36.

Savasere, A., Omiecinski, E. and Navathe, S. (1995). An efficient algorithm for mining association rules in large databases, *Proceedings of the 21st International Conference Very Large Data Bases*, Morgan Kaufmann, San Francisco, 432-444.

Silberschatz, A. and Tuzhilin, A. (1995). On subjective measures of interestingness in knowledge discovery, *Proceedings of the First International Conf. On Knowledge Discovery and Data Mining*.

Subramanian, D. (1990). A Theory of Justified Reformulation, Change of Representation and Inductive Bias, Benjamin, D. (Ed.) Kluwer Academic Publishing, Boston, 147-167.

Ziarko, W. (1991). The Discovery, Analysis and Presentation of Data Dependencies in Databases, Knowledge Discovery in Databases, AAAI/MIT Press, 195-209.

Chapter VI

Some Issues
in Design
of Data Warehousing
Systems

Ladjel Bellatreche and Kamalakar Karlapalem
University of Science Technology, Hong Kong

Mukesh Mohania
Western Michigan University, USA

INTRODUCTION

Information is one of the most valuable assets of an organization, and when used properly can assist intelligent decision-making that can significantly improve the functioning of an organization. Data warehousing is a recent technology that allows information to be easily and efficiently accessed for decision-making activities. On-line analytical processing (OLAP) tools are well studied for complex data analysis. A data warehouse is a *set of subject-oriented, integrated, time varying and non-volatile databases used to support the decision-making activities* (Inmon, 1992).

The conceptual architecture of a data warehousing system is shown in Figure 1. The data warehouse creation and management component includes software tools for selecting data from information sources (which could be operational, legacy, external, etc., and may be distributed, autonomous and heterogeneous), cleaning, transforming, integrating and propagating data into the data warehouse. It also refreshes the warehouse data and meta-data when source data is updated. This component is also responsible for managing the warehouse data, creating indices on

Figure 1. A Conceptual data warehousing architecture

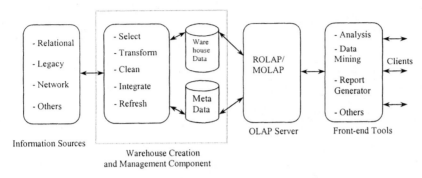

data tables, data partitioning and updating meta-data. The warehouse data contains the detail data, summary data, consolidated data and/or multidimensional data.

The meta-data is generally held in a separate repository. The meta-data contains the informational data about the creation, management and usage of the data warehouse. It serves as a bridge between the users of the warehouse and the data contained in it. The warehouse data is also accessed by the OLAP server to present the data in a multidimensional way to the front-end tools (such as analytical tools, report writers, spreadsheets and data-mining tools) for analysis and informational purposes. Basically, the OLAP server interprets client queries (the client interacts with front-end tools and passes these queries to the OLAP server) and converts them into complex SQL queries required to access the warehouse data. It might also access the data from the primary sources if the client's queries need operational data. Finally, the OLAP server passes the multidimensional views of data to the front-end tools, and these tools format the data according to the client's requirements.

There are two approaches to creating the warehouse data - bottom-up and top-down. In a bottom-up approach, the data is obtained from the primary sources based on the data warehouse applications and a profile of the likely queries which is typically known in advance. The data is then selected, transformed, and integrated by data acquisition tools. In a top-down approach, the data is obtained from the primary sources whenever a query is posed. In this case, the warehouse system determines the primary data sources in order to answer the query. These two approaches are similar to eager and lazy approaches discussed in Widom (1995). The bottom-up approach is used in data warehousing because user queries can be answered immediately and data analysis can be done efficiently, since data will always be available in the warehouse. Hence, this approach is feasible and improves the performance of the system. Another approach is a hybrid approach, which combines aspects of the bottom-up and top-down approaches. In this approach, some data is stored in a warehouse, and other data can be obtained from the primary sources on demand (Hull and Zhou, 1999).

The warehouse data is typically modeled *multi-dimensionally*. The multidimensional data model (Agrawal et al., 1997; Mohania et al., forthcoming) has proved to be the most suitable for OLAP applications. OLAP tools provide an environment for decision-making and business modeling activities by supporting ad-hoc queries. There are two ways to implement a multidimensional data model:

- by using the underlying relational architecture to project a pseudo-multidimensional model and
- by using true multidimensional data structures such as, arrays.

We discuss the multidimensional model and the implementation schemes in the next section.

The data fragmentation is a very well-known method used in the relational databases and aims to reduce the cost of processing queries. This technique can be adapted to the data warehouse environments, where the size of the fact tables is very large and there are many join operations. In the third section, we describe the fragmentation technique and show how it can be applied to data warehouse star/ snowflake schemas.

Warehouse data can be seen as a set of materialized views, which are derived from the source data. OLAP queries can be executed efficiently over materialized views, but the number of views that should be materialized at the warehouse needs to be controlled, or else this can result to materialize all possible queries (this is known as *data explosion*).We then discuss the design issues related to warehouse views.

The technique of view materialization is hampered by the fact that one needs to anticipate the queries to materialize at the warehouse. The queries issued at the data warehouse are mostly *ad-hoc* and cannot be effectively anticipated at all times. Thus, answering these queries requires effective indexing methods since queries involve joins on multiple tables. The traditional indexing methods in relational databases do not work well in the data-warehousing environment. New access structures have been proposed for data warehousing environments. We investigate different types of indexing schemes in the next section.

The view and index selection problems are two problems mostly studied independently in data warehouses. This causes an inefficient distribution of resources (space, computation time, maintenance time, etc.) between views and indexes. In the final section, we discuss the problem of distributing space between views and indices in order to select two sets of materialized views and indexes to guarantee a performance.

DATA MODELS FOR A DATA WAREHOUSE

The data models for designing traditional OLTP systems are not well suited for modeling complex queries in data warehousing environment. The transactions in OLTP systems are made up of simple, pre-defined queries. In the data warehousing environments, the queries tend to use joins on more tables, have a larger computation time and are ad-hoc in nature. This kind of processing environment warrants a new perspective to data modeling. The *multidimensional* data model, i.e., the *data cube,* turned out to be an adequate model that provides a way to aggregate facts along multiple attributes, called dimensions. Data is stored as *facts* and *dimensions,* instead of rows and columns, as in relational data model. Facts are numeric or factual data that represents a specific business activity, and the dimension represents a single perspective on the data. Each dimension is described by a set of attributes.

A multidimensional data model (MDDM) supports complex decision queries on huge amounts of enterprise and temporal data. It provides us with an integrated environment for summarizing (using aggregate functions or by applying some formulae) information across multiple dimensions. MDDM has now become the preferred choice of many vendors as the platform for building new On-Line Analytical Processing (OLAP) tools. The user has the leverage to and the dimensions, thereby allowing him/her to use different dimensions during an interactive query session. The data cube allows the user to visualize aggregated facts multidimensionally. The level of detail retrieved depends on the number of dimensions used in the data cube. When the data cube has got more than three dimensions, it is called the *hypercube*. The dimensions form the axes of the hypercube, and the solution space represents the facts as aggregates on measure attributes (see Figure 2).

Implementation Schemes

The conceptual multidimensional data model can be physically realized in two ways: (1) by using traditional relational databases, called ROLAP *architecture* (Relational On-Line Analytical Processing) (example includes Informix Red Brick Warehouse (Informix Inc., 1997); or (2) by making use of specialized multidimensional databases, called MOLAP architecture (Multidimensional On-Line Analyti-

Figure 2. A data cube.

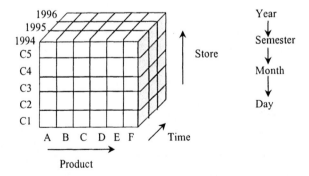

cal Processing) (example includes Hyperion Essbase OLAP Server). The advantage of MOLAP architecture is that it provides a direct multidimensional view of the data, whereas the ROLAP architecture is just a multidimensional interface to relational data. On the other hand, the ROLAP architecture has two major advantages: (1) it can be used and easily integrated into other existing relational database systems, and (2) relational data can be stored more efficiently than multidimensional data (Vasiliadis and Sellis, 1999).

We will briefly describe in detail each approach.

Relational Scheme

This scheme stores the data in specialized relational tables, called fact and dimension tables. It provides a multidimensional view of the data by using relational technology as an underlying data model. Facts are stored in the fact table, and dimensions are stored in the dimension table. Facts in the fact table are linked through their dimensions. The attributes that are stored in the dimension table may exhibit attribute hierarchy.

Example 1: Let us consider a star schema from Informix corporation (1997). It models the sales activities for a given company. The schema consists of three

Figure 3. An example of a star schema

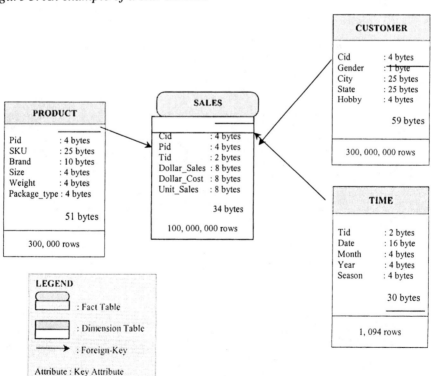

dimension tables CUSTOMER, PRODUCT and TIME, and one fact table, SALES. The tables and attributes of the schema are shown in Figure 3.

Star schema/snowflake schema is used to support multidimensional data representation. It offers flexibility, but often at the cost of performance because of more joins for each query required. A star/snowflake schema models a consistent set of facts (aggregated) in a fact table, and the descriptive attributes about the facts are stored in multiple dimension tables. This schema makes heavy use of de-normalization to optimize complex aggregate query processing. In a star schema, a single fact table is related to each dimension table in a many-to-one (M:1) relationship. Each dimension tuple is pointed to many fact tuples. Dimension tables are joined to fact tables through foreign key reference; there is a referential integrity constraint between fact table and dimension table. The primary key of the fact table is a combination of the primary keys of dimension tables. Note that multiple fact tables can be related to the same dimension table, and the size of dimension table is very small as compared to the fact table.

As we can see in Figure 3, the dimension table TIME is de-normalized and, therefore, the star schema does not capture hierarchies (i.e., dependencies among

Figure 4: Snowflake Schema Example

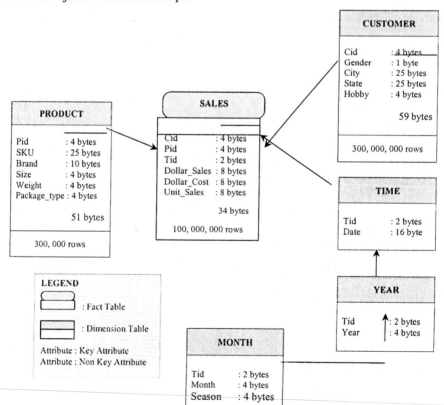

attributes) directly. This is captured in snowflake schema. Here, the dimension tables are normalized for simplifying the data selecting operations related to the dimensions, and thereby capture attribute hierarchies. In this schema, the multiple fact tables are created for different aggregate levels by pre-computing aggregate values. This schema projects better semantic representation of business dimensions. Figure 4 shows an example of snowflake schema after *TIME* dimension table in Figure 3 has been normalized.

A star schema/snowflake schema is usually a query-centric design as opposed to a conventional update-centric schema design employed in OLTP applications. The typical queries on the star schema are commonly referred to as star-join queries, and exhibit the following characteristics:

1) there is a multi-table join among the large fact table and multiple smaller dimension tables, and
2) each of the dimension tables involved in the join has multiple selection predicates on its descriptive attributes.

Multidimensional scheme

This scheme stores data in a matrix using an array-based storage structure. Each cell in the array is formed by the intersection of all the dimensions, therefore, not all cells have a value. The multidimensional data set requires smaller data storage since the data is clustered compactly in the multidimensional array. The values of the dimensions need not be explicitly stored. The n-dimensional table schema is used to support multidimensional data representation, which is described next.

n-*dimensional table schema*

An n-dimensional table schema is the fundamental structure of a multidimensional database, which draws the terminology of the statistical databases. The attribute set associated with this schema is of two kinds: parameters and measures. An n-dimensional table has a set of attributes R and a set of dimensions D associated with it. Each dimension is characterized by a distinct subset of attributes from R, called the parameters of that dimension. The attributes in R, which are not parameters of any dimension, are called the measure attributes. This approach is a very unique way of flattening the data cube since the table structure is inherently multidimensional. The actual contents of the table are essentially orthogonal to the associated structure. Each data cube can be represented in an n-dimensional table as table entries. These table entries have to be extended by certain dimensions to interpret their meaning. The current literature on an n-dimensional table, however, does not give an implementation of the MDDB, which is different from the implementation suggested by the already existing schemas. This implementation breaks up the dimensional table into dimension tables and fact tables, which snowballs into snowflake schema and traditional ROLAP. The challenge with the research community is to find mechanisms that translate this multidimensional table into a true multidimensional implementation. This would require us to look at new data structures for the implementation of multiple dimensions in one table. The relation in relational data model is a classic example of an 0-dimensional table.

Constraints on the Cube Model

In a relational schema, we can define a number of integrity constraints in the conceptual design. These constraints can be broadly classified as key constraints, referential integrity constraints, not null constraint, relation-based check constraints, attribute-based check constraints and general assertions (business rules). These constraints can be easily translated into triggers that keep the relational database consistent at all times. This concept of defining constraints based on dependencies can be mapped to a multidimensional scenario.

The current literature on modeling multidimensional databases has not discussed the constraints on the data cube. In a relational model, the integrity and business constraints that are defined in the conceptual schema provide for efficient design, implementation and maintenance of the database. Taking a cue from the relational model, we need to identify and enumerate the constraints that exist in the multidimensional model. An exploratory research area would be to categorize the cube constraints into classes and compare them with the relational constraints. The constraints can be broadly classified into two categories: *intra-cube* constraints and *inter-cube* constraints. The intra-cube constraints define constraints within a cube by exploiting the relationships that exist between the various attributes of a cube. The relationship between the various dimensions in a cube, the relationships between the dimensions and measure attributes in a cube, dimension attribute hierarchy and other cell characteristics are some of the key cube features that need to be formalized as a set of intra-cube constraints. The inter-cube constraints define relationships between two or more cubes. There are various considerations in defining inter-cube constraints. Such constraints can be defined by considering the relationships between dimensions in different cubes, the relationships between measures in different cubes, the relationships between measures in one cube and dimensions in the other cube and the overall relationship between two cubes, i.e., two cubes might merge into one, one cube might be a subset of the other cube, etc.

Operations in Multidimensional Data Models

Data warehousing query operations include standard SQL operations, such as selection, projection and join. In addition, it supports various extensions to aggregate functions, for example, percentile functions (e.g., top 20 percentile of all products), rank functions (e.g., top 10 products), mean, mode and median. One of the important extensions to the existing query language is to support multiple 'group-by' by defining *roll-up*, *drill-down* and *cube* operators. Roll-up corresponds to doing further group-by on the same data object. Note that the roll-up operator is order sensitive, that is, when it is defined in the extended SQL, the order of columns (attributes) matters. The function of drill-down operation is the opposite of roll-up.

The hypercube, which involves joining of multiple tables to represent facts, needs a new set of algebraic operations. A new algebra needs to be proposed for the multidimensional environment. The idea of faster query processing requires an extension to existing SQL in the existing environment. New operators like *cube*, push, pull, restrict, star join and merge have been proposed in literature but all these operators are very specific to the schema for which they are designed (Agrawal, Gupta and Sarawagi, 1997; Lehner, Ruf and Teschke, 1996; Li and Wang, 1996; Bauer and Lehner, 1997).

DATA PARTITIONING
IN DATA WAREHOUSES

The data-partitioning concept in the context of distributed databases aims to reduce query execution tile and facilitates the parallel execution of queries. In this chapter, we use partitioning and fragmentation interchangeably. Partitioning is an important technique for implementing very large tables in data warehouse environments (Oracle Corp., 1999). The idea is to make a large table more manageable by dividing it in multiple tables. Oracle first introduced a limited form of partitioning with partition views in Oracle7 (Release 7.3). Fully functional table partitioning is available in Oracle8 (Oracle Corp., 1999).

Motivation

The main reasons that motivate us to use the partitioning in data warehouse environments are:

1. Building indices like join indices on the whole data warehouse schema can cause a problem of maintaining them, because whenever we need to execute a query, the whole indices should be loaded from the disk to the main memory. The sizes of this type of indices can be very huge (Bellatreche et al., 1999). But if we have a partitioned data warehouse with N sub-star schemas, we can build for each sub-star schema join indices that can be easier to maintain and to load. On the other hand, even though indexing can help in providing good access support at the physical level, the number of irrelevant data retrieved during the query processing can still be very high. The partitioning aims to reduce irrelevant data accesses (Bellatreche et al., 2000; O'Neil and Quass, 1997).

2. Since the OLAP queries use joins of multiple dimension tables and a fact table, the derived horizontal partitioning developed in the relational databases can be used to efficiently process joins across multiple relations (Ceri et al., 1982).

3. Designing a warehouse database for an integrated enterprise is a very complicated and iterative process since it involves collection of data from many departments/units and data cleaning, and requires extensive business modeling. Therefore, some organizations have preferred to develop a datamart to meet requirements specific to a departmental or restricted community of users.

Of course, the development of datamarts entails the lower cost and shorter implementation time. The role of the datamart is to present convenient **subsets of a data warehouse** to consumers having specific functional needs. There can be two approaches for developing the datamart--either it can be designed integrating data from source data (bottom-up approach) or it can be designed deriving the data from the warehouse (top-down approach) (Firestone, 1997) (see Figure 5). By advocating the top-down design for datamart and without partitioning, we need to assign to each datamart the whole data warehouse; even this datamart accesses only a subset of this data warehouse. By analyzing the needs of each datamart, we can partition the centralized data warehouse into several fragments that can be used as allocation units for datamarts.

4. parallelism is a good technique to speed up the OLAP query execution. With a partitioned sub-star schema, we can associate each star schema to one machine and execute queries in parallel. For example, MCI Telecommunications' IT data center in Colorado Springs is running a massive 2TB decision support data warehouse called warehouseMCI on a 104 node IBM RS/6000 SP massively parallel processing system. The database is growing at the rate of 100GB to 200GB per month (Simpson, 1996).

5. the main disadvantage of the horizontal partitioning in databases is that when update operations occur, some tuples may migrate from one fragment to another. The migration operation is sometimes costly. In the data warehouse environments, updates are not common (Karlapalem et al., 1994) compared to the append operations. Even if there are some update operations (Hurtado et al., 1999), the data warehouses are only periodically updated in a batch fashion (O'Neil and Quass, 1997), during the time where the data warehouses are unavailable for querying. This situation makes the utilization of horizontal

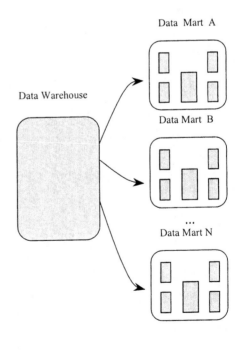

Figure 5. The top-down flow from DWs to datamarts

partitioning feasible, as the reorganization of its fragments can be done off-line.

Partitioning plays an important role in the design of a distributed database system (Özsu and Valduriez, 1991). It enables the definition of appropriate units of distribution, which enhance query performance, by enabling concurrent and parallel execution of queries. Data partitioning involves using the application/query processing characteristics to fragment the database into a set of fragments. Each fragment contains data that is most relevant to one or more applications. Therefore, an application accesses only a subset of fragments (not the complete database) thus reducing the amount of irrelevant data accessed (Öszu and Valduriez, 1991).

Fragmentation Alternatives

Two types of partitioning are possible: vertical and horizontal.

Given a relation $R(K, A_1, A_2, ..., A_n)$, where $A_1, A_2, ..., A_n$ are the attributes and K is the key, each attribute A_i has a domain of values $dom(A_i)$. The vertical partitioning (VP) of R is given by $V^1(K, A^1_1, A^1_2, ..., A^1_{kl})$, $V^2(K, A^2_1, A^2_2, ..., A^2_{kl})$, ... $V^p(K, A^p_1, A^p_2, ..., A^p_{kl})$ where in each $A^i_j \in \{A_1, A_2, ..., A_n\}$. The set of vertical fragments $V_1, V_2, ..., V_p$ is disjointed if each attribute A_i ($1 \leq i \leq n$) of relation R belongs to one and only one vertical fragment. The key K is repeated in each fragment to facilitate the reconstruction of relation R from the vertical fragments. The original relation R is reconstructed by joining the p vertical fragments. The main advantage of vertical partitioning is that it reduces irrelevant attribute accesses of the user queries. The main disadvantage is that it requires the costly join operation to access two or more vertical fragments.

Each horizontal fragment of relation R is a subset of the tuples of R. The tuples of each fragment must satisfy a predicate clause. The horizontal partitioning (HP) of R is given by: $H_1 = \sigma_{cl1}(R) \; H_2 = \sigma_{cl2}(R)$, where cl_i is a predicate clause. The reconstruction of the relation R is obtained by uniting the original fragments with the union operation.

Two versions of HP are cited by the researchers (Ceri et al., 1982): primary HP and derived HP. Primary HP of a relation is performed using predicates that are defined on that relation. On the other hand, derived HP is the partitioning of a relation that results from predicates defined on another relation.

A lot of work has been done on the partitioning in the relational models (Özsu and Valduriez, 1991) and object models (Bellatreche et al., 1997, 1998, 2000; Ezeife and Barker, 1995) compared to the data warehouses. In this chapter, we will concentrate on HP because it is well adapted to data warehouses. Also, the TPC-D benchmark (TPC Home Page) in its implementation allows the utilization of HP, but it discards the utilization of the vertical partitioning.

Horizontal Partitioning Algorithms in Databases

Several algorithms were proposed in performing HP (Ceri and Pelagatti, 1984; Navathe et al., 1984; Navathe et al., 1995; Navathe and Ra, 1989; Bellatreche et al.,

1997; Ezeife and Barker, 1995; Dewitt et al., 1986). These algorithms can be classified into two main categories: (1) query-driven algorithms and (2) data-driven algorithms.

Query-driven algorithms

These algorithms are performed based on a set of most frequently asked queries and their access frequencies for a specific application (Navathe et al., 1995). These queries respect the 80/20 rule, which considers that 20% of user queries account for 80% of the total data access in the database system. This category of algorithms is divided into two types:

- **Affinity based algorithms:** The most proposed algorithms for HP in the relational and object databases are affinity-based (Ceri and Pelagatti, 1984; Özsu and Valduriez, 1991; Navathe and Ra, 1989; Bellatreche et al., 1997; Ezeife and Barker, 1995). The affinities are used between predicates. Predicates having a high affinity are grouped together to form a horizontal fragment. The algorithm of Navathe et al. (1989) starts by performing an analysis on the predicates defined by a set of queries accessing a relation to be horizontally partitioned. From these queries, a predicate usage matrix is built. The rows and the columns of this matrix represent the queries and predicates, respectively. The value of this matrix $use\ (Q_i, p_j)$ is equal to 1, if the predicate p_l is used by the query Q_j, otherwise it is equal to 0. This matrix is used to generate another matrix called predicate affinity matrix, where each value $(p_l, p_{l'})$ represents the sum of the frequencies of queries which access predicates p_l and $p_{l'}$, simultaneously. After that, the authors apply the graph-based algorithm defined in Navathe, Karlapalem and Ra (1995) to group these predicates into a disjointed subset of predicates. (Each subset of predicates can be a potential horizontal fragment.)

In each group, the authors optimize (if it is possible) by using implications between the predicates defined in queries, then they generate the horizontal fragments. Each fragment is defined by a Boolean combination of predicates using the logical connectives $(\wedge, \vee)$.

Özsu et al. (1991) developed a primary algorithm for HP. This algorithm has an input, a set of queries and their frequencies. Its steps are as follows:

1. Determine the set of *complete* and *minimal* predicates $P = \{p_1, p_2, ..., p_n\}$. A complete set of predicates is *minimal* if, and only if, all its elements are relevant.
2. Determine the set of *minterm predicates M* of *P*, which is defined as follow: $M = \{m_i \mid m_i = \wedge_{pj \in p}\ p^*_j\}$, where $p^*_j = p_j$ or $p^*_j = \neg p_j\ (1 \leq j \leq n)$, $(1 \leq i \leq 2^n)$.
3. Eliminate the contradictory minterm predicates using the predicate implications.

This approach can generate 2^n horizontal fragments for n simple predicates.

- **Cost-based algorithms**: The main disadvantage of affinity-based algorithms is that they use affinity as a measure of grouping of predicates. This measure can *only express the affinity between pairs of attributes*, and cannot express the affinity among several (more than two) predicates (Bellatreche et al., 1998). On the other hand, all these algorithms ignore the physical costs corresponding to the savings in the amount of irrelevant data accessed. The utility of the HP can be measured by the amount of savings in disk accesses required for query execution. It is often argued that the advantage of the HP lies in the reduction in the amount of savings in disk accesses required for query execution (Karlapalem et al., 1994; Hevner and Rao, 1988). Although this argument is understandable from an intuitive point of view, not much work has been done to evaluate the impact of this type of partitioning on query evaluation on a quantitative basis. According to Karlapalem et al. (1994), two factors, input/output (IO) operations and data transfer, are the most important for the performance of the applications in distributed database systems. As the goal of partitioning of the classes is to obtain the minimum cost for processing a set of queries, we develop an algorithm based on a cost-driven approach for executing a set of queries that respects the 80/20 rules. In Bellatreche, Karlapalem and Basak (1998) and Bellatreche, Karlapalem and Li,(1998), we have proposed an algorithm for the horizontal partitioning in the object model based on a cost model, but it can be applied to the relational model. The basic idea of this algorithm is that it starts with a set of the most frequently asked queries, and other physical factors (like predicate selectivity, class size, page size, instance length, etc.).

Let C be the class to be horizontally partitioned, and let $P = \{p_1, p_2, ..., p_N\}$ be the set of simple predicates defined on this class using a set of queries. From these simple predicates, we generate all minterm predicates (Ceri, Negri and Pelagatti, 1982) $\{m_1, m_2, ..., m_z\}$. After that, we exhaustively enumerate all possible schemes. A scheme can be represented by a minterm or a combination of several minterms using the logical connector OR. For each scheme, we calculate the cost of executing all these queries. The objective of this cost model is to calculate the cost of executing these queries, each of which accesses a set of objects. The cost of a query is directly proportional to the number of pages it accesses. The total cost is estimated in terms of disk page accesses. Finally, the scheme with minimal cost gives the best HP of the class C.

We note that this algorithm needs an exhaustive enumeration strategy to generate all schemes. For small values of minterms, this procedure is not computationally expensive. However, for large values of number of minterms, the computation is very expensive, for example, for 15 minterms, the number of schemes is 1,382,958,545. For further details about the complexity of enumerating all schemes, see Bellatreche, Karlapalem and Basak (1998).

To reduce the complexity of the cost-driven algorithm, we propose another algorithm called *approximate algorithm*, which is based on a hill-climbing technique (Jain, 1991). The approximate algorithm starts with the set of fragments generated by an algorithm that has a lower complexity (Bellatreche, Karlapalem and Simonet, 1997; Navathe and Ra, 1989). This algorithm gives rise to a set of fragments. Based on the queries accessing these fragments, the approximate algorithm tries to shrink or expand some fragments *in order to reduce the* query *processing cost.*

Data-driven algorithms

This kind of HP was studied in parallel databases and formulated as follows: suppose that we have N disks available, for any given row of a relation R, we must decide on which of the N disks it has to reside (Morse and Isaac, 1998). Three standard approaches are developed: range partitioning, round robin and hashing. With the range partitioning each of the N disks is associated with a range of key values. The main advantage of the range partitioning technique is that it acts as a kind of built-in index if tuples are retrieved based on the key values. But its main disadvantage is the data skew. In the second technique, the tuples are partitioned in a round-robin fashion. This strategy is used as the default strategy in Gamma machine (Dewitt et al., 1986). This technique avoids the load imbalance. Finally, the hash partitioning is performed using a hash function, where identical key values will be hashed to the same disk. It also avoids data skew.

Partitioning Issues in Data Warehouses

All work done on vertical partitioning in the data warehouse context has been applied on the physical design level (index selection problem). The vertical partitioning has been introduced in the definition of projection index proposed by O'Neil et al. (1997). Chaudhuri et al. (1999) developed a technique called index merging to reduce storage and maintenance of an index. Their method is somehow an extension of the vertical partitioning. Recently, Datta et al. (1999) developed a new indexing technique called Curio in data Warehouses, modeled by a star schema. This index speeds up the query processing and it does not require a lot of storage space.

Concerning the HP, a little work has been done. Noaman et al. (1999) proposed architecture for a distributed data warehouse. It is based on the ANSI/SPARC architecture (Tsichritzis and Klug, 1978) that has three levels of schemas: internal, conceptual and external. The distributed data warehouse design proposed by these authors is based on the top-down approach. There are two fundamental issues in this approach: fragmentation and allocation of the fragments to various sites. The authors proposed a horizontal fragmentation algorithm for a fact table of a data warehouse. This algorithm is an adaptation of the work done by Özsu and Valduriez (1991).

In this chapter, we present a methodology for partitioning a data warehouse modeled by a star schema, and we will show the issues and problems related to this problem.

Problems

Partitioning in data warehouses is more challenging compared to that in relational and object databases. This challenge is due to the several choices of partitioning schema of a star or snowflake schema:

1. Partition *only* the dimension tables using the primary partitioning. This scenario is not suitable for OLAP queries, because the sizes of dimension tables are generally small compared to the fact table. Most OLAP queries access the fact table, which is huge. Therefore, any partitioning that does not take into account the fact table is discarded.

2. Partition *only* the fact table using the primary partitioning. In a data warehouse modeled by a star schema, most OLAP queries access dimension tables first, and after that the fact table.

3. Partition *both* fact and dimension tables, but independently. This means that we use the primary partitioning to partition the fact and dimension tables without taking into account the relationship between these tables. Based on the previous choices, this partitioning does not benefit OLAP queries.

4. Partition *some/all* dimension tables using the primary partitioning, and use them to derive a partitioned fact table. This approach is best in applying partitioning in data warehouses, because it takes into consideration the queries requirements and the relationship between the fact table and dimension tables. In our study, we opt for last solution.

Partitioning Algorithm for a Star Schema

In Bellatreche, Karlapalem and Mohania (2000), we have proposed a methodology for fragmenting a star schema with dimension tables $\{D_1, D_2,..., D_d\}$ and one fact table F. This methodology can be easily adapted to snowflake schemas. In this section, we will review the basic ideas of this approach.

Note that any fragmentation algorithm needs application information defined on the tables that have to be partitioned. The information is divided into two categories (Özsu and Valduriez, 1991): quantitative and qualitative. Quantitative information gives the selectivity factors of selection predicates and the frequencies of queries accessing these tables. Qualitative information gives the selection predicates defined on dimension tables.

A simple predicate p is defined by:

$$p : A_i, \theta \text{ Value}$$

where A_i is an attribute, $\theta \in \{=, <, \leq, >, \geq, \neq\}$, Value $\in Dom(A_i)$.

The algorithm we proposed in Bellatreche, Karlapalem and Mohania (2000) has as input a set of most frequently asked OLAP queries $Q = \{ Q_1, Q_2,..., Q_N \}$ with their frequencies. The main steps of this algorithm are:

1. Enumeration of all simple predicates used by the n queries.

2. Attribution to each dimension table D_i ($1 \leq i \leq d$), its set of simple predicates (SSP^{Di}).

3. Each dimension table D_i having $SSP^{Di} = \phi$ cannot be fragmented. Let $D_{canditate}$ be the set of all dimension tables having a non-empty SSP^{Di}. Let g be the cardinality of $D_{canditate}$.

4. Application of COM_MIN algorithm (Özsu and Valduriez, 1991) to each

dimension table D_i of $D_{candidate}$. This algorithm takes a set of simple predicates and then generates a set of complete and minimal.

5. For fragmenting a dimension table D_i, it is possible to use one of the algorithms proposed by Ceri, Negri and Pelagatti (1982) and Özsu and Valduriez (1991) in the relational model. These algorithms generate a set of disjointed fragments, but their complexities are exponential of the number of simple predicates used. As result, we use the algorithm proposed in the object model, which has a polynomial complexity (Bellatreche et al., 2000).

Each dimension table D_i has m_i fragments $\{D_{i1}, D_{i2}..., D_{imi}\}$, where each fragment D_i is defined as follows:

$D_{ij} = \sigma_{cl\,j}^i (D_i)$ where $\sigma_{cl\,j}^i (1 \leq i \leq g, \ 1 \leq j \leq m_i)$ represents a clause of simple predicates.

6. Partition the fact table using the fragmentation schema of the dimension tables.

The number of fragments of the fact table (N) is equal to: $N = \prod_{i=1}^{g} m_i$ (for more details see Bellatreche et al. (2000)).

Therefore, the star schema S is decomposed into N sub-schemas $\{S_1, S_2,..., S_N\}$, where each one satisfies a clause of predicates.

Example 2: *To show how this algorithm works, let us consider the star schema in Figure 3 and the six OLAP queries obtained from Bellatreche, Karlapalem and Mohania (2000). From these queries, we enumerate all selection predicates:*

p_1 : C.Gender = 'M', p_2 : C.Gender = "F", p_3 : P.Packagetype = "Box", p_4 : P.Packagetype = "Paper", p_5 : T.Season = "Summer" and p_6 : T.Season = "Winter."

The set of simple predicates for each table are (Step 2): $SSP^{CUSTOMER} = \{p_1, p_2\}$, $SSP^{PRODUCT} = \{p_3, p_4\}$ and $SSP^{TIME} = \{p_5, p_6\}$.

For each set, we generate the set of complete and minimal simple predicates (Step 4). We obtain the following:

- *$SSP^{CUSTOMER}_{Min\text{-}Com} = \{p_1, p_2\}$,*
- *$SSP^{PRODUCT}_{Min\text{-}Com} = \{p_3, p_4\}$ and*
- *$SSP^{TIME}_{Min\text{-}Com} = \{p_5, p_6\}$*

By applying the fragmentation algorithm (Bellatreche, Karlapalem and Simonet, 2000) for each dimension table, we obtain the following fragments:

- *CUSTOMER : Cust_1 = $s_{Gender = 'M'}$ (CUSTOMER) and Cust_2 = $s_{Gender = 'F'}$ (CUSTOMER),*
- *PRODUCT : Prod_1 = $s_{Package\_type = 'Box'}$ (PRODUCT) and Prod_2 = $s_{Package\_type = 'Paper'}$ (PRODUCT),*
- *TIME : Time_1 = $s_{Saison = 'Winter'}$ (TIME) and Time_2 = $s_{Saison = 'Summer'}$ (PRODUCT),*

Finally, the fact table can be horizontally partitioned into eight ($N = 2 \times 2 \times 2$) fragments.

Our algorithm generates a large number of fragments of the fact table. For example, suppose that the dimension tables are fragmented as follows:

- *CUSTOMER* into 50 fragments using the State attribute case of 50 states in the USA.

- TIME into 12 fragments using the Month attribute.
- PRODUCT into two fragments using the Package_type.

Therefore, the fact table is fragmented into 1,200 (**50** x **12** x **2**) fragments.

Consequently, it will be very hard for the data warehouse administrator (DWA) to maintain these fragments. Therefore, it is important to reduce the number of fragments of the fact table. We focus on this problem in the next sections.

Horizontal partitioning and OLAP queries

When the derived HP is used to fragment a relation R based on the fragmentation schema of a relation S, two potential cases of join exist: simple join and partitioned join.

In the data warehouse context, when the fact table is horizontally partitioned based on the dimension tables, we will never have a partitioned join (i.e., the case wherein a horizontal fragment of the fact table has to be joined with more than one fragment of the dimension table will not occur). As a result, we will have only simple joins as given by the following theorem:

Theorem 1: *Let F and D_i be a fact table and a dimension table of a given star schema, respectively. If the dimension table D_i is horizontally partitioned into set of disjointed horizontal fragments, let say $\{D_{i1}, D_{i2,...}, D_{im}\}$, where each fragment is defined by clause predicate, and the fact table F is derived partitioned based on the HFs of D_i, then, the distributed join between F and D_i is always represented only by a simple join graph.*

*   **Proof 1**: *We prove it by contradiction. Let F_p be a fragment of the fact table F defined by: $F_p = F \chi D_{ij}$. Suppose that F_p can be joined with two fragments $D_{ij,}$ and D_{il} ($l \neq j$) of the dimension table D_i. Consequently, we will have:*

$$F \chi D_{ij} \neq 0 \qquad\qquad (1)$$
$$F \chi D_{il} \neq 0 \qquad\qquad (2)$$

Note that the fragments of D_i are disjointed, and the fragment F_p is obtained using the semi-join operation between the fact table F and a fragment of dimension table D_i. Note that the join attributes are the foreign key of F and the primary key of D_i. Therefore, one semi-join condition among the two above defined in (1) and (2) is satisfied. In this case, $D_{ij} = D_{il}$. Since F_p can be any fragment of, and it is joinable with exactly one fragment of D_i, we conclude that the join graph between F and D_i is always simple. The theorem is true when we have a distributed join between the fact table and several dimension tables.

In a data warehouse modeled by a star schema, any fact table F that is derived from a horizontally partitioned based on HP schema of dimension tables $\{D_1, D_{2,...}, D_d\}$ will result in simple distributed join graph. This has two advantages:

- It avoids costly total distributed join (i.e., every HF F_p ($1 \leq p \leq N$) of the fact table F joins with each and every HF D_{ik} of each and every dimension table D_i ($1 \leq i \leq d$ and $1 \leq k \leq m_i$)).
- It facilitates parallel processing of multiple simple distributed joins.

The Correctness Rules of Our Proposed Algorithm

Any fragmentation algorithm must guarantee the correctness rules of fragmentation: completeness, reconstruction and disjointness.

- The completeness ensures that all tuples of a relation are mapped into at least one fragment without any loss. The completeness of the dimension tables is guaranteed by the use of the COM_MIN algorithm (Özsu and Valduriez, 1991; Ceri et al., 1982). The completeness of the derived horizontal fragmentation of the fact table is guaranteed as long as the referential integrity rule is satisfied among the dimension tables and the fact table.
- The reconstruction ensures that the fragmented relation can be reconstructed from its fragments (Özsu and Valduriez, 1991). In our case, the reconstruction of the fact and the dimension tables are obtained by union operation, i.e., $F = \cup^{N}_{i=1} F_i$ and $D_i = \cup^{mi}_{j=1} D_{ij}$.
- The disjointness ensures that the fragments of a relation are non-overlapping. This rule is satisfied for the dimension table since we used an no-overlap algorithm (Bellatreche et al., 2000). For the fragments of the fact table, the disjointness rule is guaranteed by the theorem 1.

Dimension Table Selection Problem

As we have seen in the previous section, the number of fragments of the fact table can be very large. This is due to the number of dimension tables used in fragmenting the fact table. In this section, we will give some issues on selecting dimension tables that reduce the number of fact table fragments. Any selection algorithm should satisfy the following constraints:

- avoids the explosion of the number of fragments of the fact table, and
- guarantees a good performance for executing a set of OLAP queries.

To reach the first objective, we give the DWA the possibility of choosing the number of fragments (W) that he/she considers is sufficient to maintain. To satisfy the second objective, we need to have the possibility of augmenting the number of fragments of the fact table until the performance is guaranteed. The problem is to

Figure 6: Cost Evolution

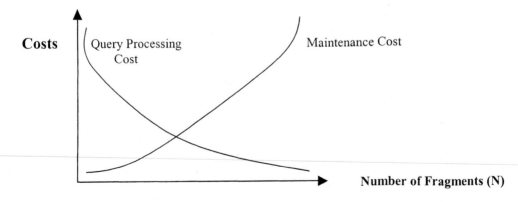

Figure 7. The steps of greedy algorithm

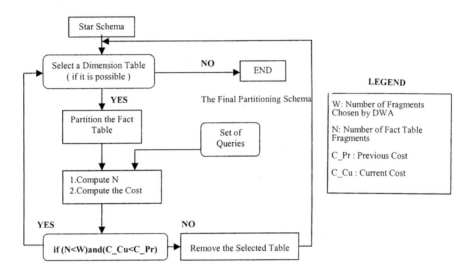

find a compromise between the maintenance cost and query processing cost as shown in Figure 6.

To solve this problem, we developed a greedy algorithm (Bellatreche et al., 2000). From the number of fragments W that the DWA chooses, this algorithm starts by selecting one dimension table randomly. Once the selection is done, we partition the fact table based on the fragmentation schema of the dimension table. We compute the number of fragments of the fact table (N) and then the cost of executing a set of OLAP queries. We suppose we have a cost model for executing a set of queries. If the number of fragments N is less than W and there is an improvement of query processing cost, our algorithm selects another dimension and then it repeats the same process until the two conditions are satisfied. The main steps of this algorithm are shown in Figure 7. At the end of this algorithm, we obtain a partitioned data warehouse ensuring a good query processing cost and a maintenance cost.

Query Execution Strategy in Partitioned Star Schema

Since the dimension tables and fact table are horizontally partitioned, we need to ensure the data access transparency. That is, the user of the data warehouse is purposefully unaware of the distribution of the data. Our goal is to provide to the data warehouse users the unpartitioned star schema, and the query optimizer task is to translate the OLAP queries on the unpartitioned star schema to partitioned star schemas. Before executing a query on a partitioned data warehouse, we need first to identify the sub-schemas satisfying this query as shown in Figure 8.

Table 1. Partitioning specification table

Table	Fragments	Fragmentation Condition
CUSTOMER	Cust_1	Gender = 'M'
	Cust_2	Gender = 'F'
SALES	Sales_1	SALES χ Cuct_1
	Sales_2	SALES χ Cust_2

Definition 1: (**Relevant Predicate Attribute (RPA)**) is an attribute that participates in a predicate that defines an HP. Any attribute that does not participate in defining a predicate that defines an HP is called an irrelevant predicate attribute.

Definition 2: (**Partitioning Specification Table**) Suppose we have an initial star schema S horizontally partitioned into sub-schemas $\{S_1, S_2,..., S_N\}$. The partitioning conditions for each partitioned table can be represented by a table called partitioning specification table of S. This table has three columns: the first one contains the table names, the second provides the fragments of its corresponding table and the last one reports the partitioning condition for each fragment.

Example 3: Suppose the dimension table CUSTOMER is partitioned into two fragments: Cust_1 and Cust_2, and the fact table is fragmented using these two fragments into Sales1 and Sales2. The corresponding partitioning specification table for this example is illustrated in Table 1.

From the partitioning specification table, we can conclude that : each attribute belonging to the partitioning specification table is a RPA. In our example, "Gender"' is the single RPA.

Fragment identification

Let Q be a query with p selection predicates defined on a partitioned star schema $S = \{S_1, S_2,..., S_N\}$. Our aim is to identify the sub-schema(s) that participate in executing Q. Let $SRPA$ be the set of RPA. Based on the selection predicates of the query Q and partitioning specification table, we proceed as follows:

- For each selection predicate SP_i $(1 \leq i \leq p)$, we define the function attr(SP_i), which gives us the name of the attribute used by SP_i. The union of attr(SP_i) gives us the names of all attributes used by Q. We call this set Query Predicate Attributes. Let $SPA(Q)$ be the set of all predicate attributes used by the query Q.
- Using $SPA(Q)$ and $SRPA(S)$, four scenarios are possible:
  1. $SPA(Q) = 0$, (the query does not contain any selection predicate). In this situation, two approaches are possible to execute Q:
     a) Perform the union operations of all sub-schemas and then perform the join operations as in unpartitioned star schema.
     b) Perform the join operations for each sub-schema and then assemble the result using the union operation.

Figure 8. Sub-schemas identification

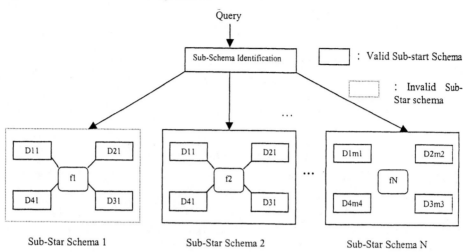

2. $(SPA(Q) \neq 0)$ and $(SPA(Q) \cap SRPA(S) = 0)$ (the query has some selection predicates on non-partitioned dimension tables, or the predicate attribute of Q does not match the relevant predicate attribute). To execute this kind of query, we use the two approaches presented above.

3. $(SPA(Q) \cap SRPA(S) \neq \phi)$ means that some predicate attributes of the query Q match with certain RPA. In this case, we can easily determine the names of dimension tables and the fragments that participate in executing the query Q.

Results

In Bellatreche et al. (2000), we have developed two cost models to evaluate the utility of the HP. The first one is for unpartitioned star schema, and the second one is for partitioned star schema. These cost models are used for executing a set of frequently asked queries in the data warehouse. The objective of these cost models is to calculate the cost of executing these queries in terms of disk page accesses (IO cost) during the selection and join operations (which are the most used and most expensive operations in data warehouses (Lei and Ross, 1998). To characterize the improvement of performance using the horizontal fragmentation technique, we defined a normalized IO metric as follows:

$$Normalized\ IO = \frac{\#\ of\ IOs\ for\ a\ Horizontally\ Partitioned\ Star\ Schema}{\#\ of\ IOs\ for\ a\ Unpartitioned\ Star\ Schema}$$

We note that if the value of normalized IO is less than 1.0, then it implies that HP is beneficial. The main observations are:

- Horizontal fragmentation gives good performance compared to the unpartitioned case.

- Horizontal fragmentation may deteriorate the execution performance of certain queries, for example, the queries that do not have any selection predicates. To evaluate these two queries, we need to access all sub-star schemas.
- The number of partitioned dimension tables has a great impact on reducing the query processing cost. As the number of fragmented dimension tables increases, the performance increases too.

MATERIALIZED VIEWS

One of the techniques employed in data warehouses to improve performance is the creation of sets of materialized views. They are used to pre-compute and store aggregated data such as sum of sales. They can also be used to pre-compute joins with or without aggregations. So materialized views are used to reduce the overhead associated with expensive joins or aggregations for a large or an important class of queries (Oracle Corp., 1989). The data warehouse at the Mervyn's department-store chain, for instance, has a total of 2,400 pre-computed tables to improve query processing (Gupta, 1989). Materialized views can be used in several areas: *distributed computing* and *mobile computing*.

- In distributed environments, they are used to replicate data at distributed sites and synchronize updates done at several sites with conflict-resolution methods.
- In mobile computing, they are used to download a subset of data from central servers to mobile clients, with periodic refreshment from the central servers and propagation of updates by clients back to the central servers.

A materialized view definition can include any number of aggregates, as well as any number of joins. In several ways, a materialized view behaves like an index (Oracle Corp., 1999):

- The purpose of a materialized view is to increase request execution performance.
- The existence of a materialized view is transparent to applications (e.g., SQL applications), so a DWA can create or drop materialized views at any time without affecting the validity of applications.
- A materialized view consumes storage space.
- The contents of the materialized view must be maintained when the underlying tables are updated (modified).

All data warehousing products support materialized views (Oracle Corp., 1999; Sanjay et al., 2000).

Two major problems related to materialized views are: (1) the view selection problem and (2) the view maintenance problem.

View Selection

We initiated a discussion in the beginning of the chapter as to which views should be materialized at the data warehouse. To aid answering the queries efficiently, we materialize a set of views that are closely related to the queries at the data warehouse. We cannot materialize all possible views, as we are constrained by some resources like disk space, computation time or maintenance cost (Gupta, 1999). Hence, we need to select an appropriate set of views to materialize under some resource constraints. The view selection problem (VSP) is defined as: selection of views to materialize minimizes the query response time under some resource constraint. All studies showed that this problem is an NP-hard. The proposed solutions for the VSP can be divided into two categories: the static VSP and the dynamic VSP.

Static VSP: This problem starts with a set of frequently asked queries (apriori known), and then selects a set of materialized views that minimizes the query response time and under some constraint. The selected materialized views will be a benefit only for a query belonging to the set of a priori known queries.

Dynamic VSP: The static selection of views contradicts the dynamic nature of decision support analysis. Especially for ad-hoc queries where the expert user is looking for interesting trends in the data repository, the query pattern is difficult to predict (Kotidis and Roussopoulos, 1999). In addition, as the data and these trends are changing overtime, a static selection of views might very quickly become outdated. This means that the DWA should monitor the query pattern and periodically re-calibrate the materialized views by running theses algorithms. Kotidis and Roussopoulos (1999) present a system called DynaMat that dynamically materializes information at multiple levels of granularity in order to match the demand (workload), but also takes into account the maintenance restrictions for the warehouse, such as down time to update the views and space availability. This system unifies the view selection and view maintenance problems under a single problem. DynaMat constantly monitors incoming queries and materializes the best set of views subject to the space constraint. During updates, DynaMat reconciles the current selected materialized views and refreshes the most beneficial subset of it.

Algorithms for VSP

We have proposed several algorithms for VSP to find the optimal or near-optimal solutions for it. These algorithms can be classified into three categories based on the type of resource: (1) algorithms without resources (Baralis et al., 1997; Yang et al., 1997), (2) algorithms driven by the space constraint (Gupta, 1999) and (3) algorithms driven by maintenance cost (Gupta, 1999).

Algorithms without resource

We now discuss a heuristic (Baralis et al., 1997) in detail which uses the data cube technology and the lattice model. The lattice model feeds on the attribute hierarchy defined earlier. The nodes in the lattice diagram represent views (aggregated on certain dimensions) to be materialized at the data warehouse. If the dimensions of two views a and b exhibit attribute hierarchy such that $dim(a) \rightarrow dim(b)$, then there is an edge from node a to node b. Node a is called the *ancestor* node and node *b* is called the *dependent* or *descendant* node. The lattice diagram allows us to establish relationships between views that need to be materialized. Some queries can be answered by using the already materialized views at the data warehouse. For answering such queries, we need not go to the raw data. The lattice diagram depicts dependencies between the views and a good view selection heuristic exploits this dependency. The view selection algorithm tries to minimize the average time required to evaluate a view and also keeps a constraint on the space requirements. The space requirements that can be expressed as the number of views to be materialized translates this into an optimization problem that is NP-complete. An approximate and acceptable solution for this problem is the *greedy* heuristic. The greedy algorithm selects a view from a set of views depending upon the benefit yielded on selecting that view. A view *a* that is materialized from view *b* incurs a materializing cost that is equal to the number of rows in view *b*. If there is a view *c* (materialized on *b*; number of rows in *c* £ number of rows in *b*) such that the view can be derived from *c*, the cost of materializing *a* reduces to the number of rows in *c*. Thus the benefit of materializing view *c* includes the benefit incurred by view *a* in the form of reduction in its materializing cost (number of rows in *b* - number of rows in *c*). The greedy heuristic selects a view that maximizes the benefit that will be yielded on materializing that view. The benefit of materializing each *dependent* view (a node in the lattice diagram) will change with the selection of an *ancestor* view in the data warehouse. After each selection is made, the benefit at each *dependent* node in the lattice is recalculated and a view with maximum benefit is selected. It has been shown that the greedy algorithm is at least 3/4 of optimal. The greedy algorithm can be extended to restrict on actual space requirements rather than the number of views to be materialized. The frequency with which the views are accessed can be incorporated in this algorithm. Different schema design methods will give a different set of tables at the data warehouse.

Yang et al. (1997) presented a framework to highlight issues of materialized view design. The basic concept the authors used to develop the view selection algorithm is a graph called "multiple view processing plan". This graph specifies the views that the data warehouse will maintain (either materialized or virtual). The MVPP is a directed acyclic graph that represents a query processing strategy of data warehouse views. The leaf nodes correspond to the base relations, and the root nodes represent the queries. We call the layer between root nodes and leaf nodes the potential view layer (PVL). This layer contains all potential materialized views. Each node in the PVL is assigned with two costs: the query processing cost and the maintenance cost (Yang et al., 1997) . Note that there can be more than one MVPP for the same set of queries depending upon the access characteristics of the application and the physical data warehouse parameters. If we have *n*-intermediate nodes, then we need to try 2^n combinations of nodes. Therefore, the authors formulate the VSP as an integer-programming problem.

Algorithms driven by space constraint

In Gupta (1999), the authors present competitive polynomial-time heuristics for selection of views to optimize total query response time, for some important special cases of the general data warehouse scenarios: (i) an OR view graph, in which any view can be computed from any one of its related views, e.g., data cubes; and (ii) an AND view graph, where each query has a unique evaluation. They extend their heuristic to the most general case of AND-OR view graphs.

Algorithms driven by maintenance cost

In Gupta (1999), the authors considered the maintenance-cost-view-selection problem in which it is required to select a set of views to be materialized in order to maximize the query response time under a constraint of maintenance time. This problem is NP-hard. The authors developed a couple of algorithms to solve this problem. For OR view graph, they present a greedy algorithm that selects a set of views. They also present an A^* heuristic for the general case of AND-OR view graphs.

View Maintenance

A *data warehouse* stores integrated information from multiple data sources in *materialized views* (*MV*) over the source data. The data sources (DS) may be heterogeneous, distributed and autonomous. When the data in any source (base data) changes, the MVs at the data warehouse need to be updated accordingly. The process of updating a materialized view in response to the changes in the underlying source data is called view maintenance. The view maintenance problem has evoked great interest in the past few years. This view maintenance in such a distributed environment gives rise to inconsistencies since there is a finite unpredictable amount of time required for (a) propagating changes from the DS to the data warehouse and (b) computing view updates in response to these changes. Data consistency can be maintained at the data warehouse by performing the following steps:

- propagate changes from the data sources (ST_1 - current state of the data sources at the time of propagation of these changes) to the data warehouse to ensure that each view reflects a consistent state of the base data;
- compute view updates in response to these changes using the state ST_1 of the data sources;
- install the view updates at the data warehouse in the same order as the changes have occurred at the data sources.

The inconsistencies at the data warehouse occur since the changes that take place at the data sources are random and dynamic. Before the data warehouse is able to compute the view update for the old changes, the new changes change the state of the data sources from ST_1 to ST_2. This violates the consistency criterion that we have listed. Making the MVs at the data warehouse self-maintainable decimates the problem of inconsistencies by eliminating the finite unpredictable time required to query the data source for computing the view updates. In the next subsection, we describe self-maintenance of materialized views at the data warehouse.

Self-maintenance

Consider a materialized view MV at the data warehouse defined over a set of base relations $R = \{ R_1, R_2, ..., R_d \}$. MV stores a preprocessed query at the data warehouse. The set of base relations R may reside in one data source or in multiple, heterogeneous data sources. A change ΔR_i made to the relation R might affect MV. MV is defined to be self-maintainable if a change ΔMV in MV, in response to the change ΔR_i, can be computed using only the MV and the update ΔR_i. But the data warehouse might need some additional information from other relations in the set R residing in one or more data sources to compute the view update ΔMV. Since the underlying data sources are decoupled from the data warehouse, this requires a finite computation time. Also the random changes at the data sources can give rise to inconsistencies at the data warehouse. Some data sources may not support full database functionalities, and querying such sources to compute the view updates might be a cumbersome, even an impossible task. Because of these problems, the reprocessed query that is materialized at the warehouse needs to be maintained without access to the base relations.

One of the approaches is to replicate all base data in its entirety at the data warehouse so that maintenance of the MV becomes local to the data warehouse (Gupta and Mumick, 1995; Gupta et al., 1993). Although this approach guarantees self-maintainability at the warehouse, it creates new problems. As more and more data is added to the warehouse, it increases the space complexity and gives rise to information redundancy which might lead to inconsistencies. This approach also overlooks the point that the base tuples might be present in the view itself, so the view instance, the base update and a subset of the base relations might be sufficient to achieve self-maintainability in the case of SPJ (Select-Project-Join) views (Huyn, 1997). But how can the subset of the base relations that is needed to compute the view updates be stored at data warehouse? This question was addressed in Quass et al. (1996), which defines a set of minimal auxiliary views (AVs) to materialize that are sufficient to make a view self-maintainable. Although materializing auxiliary views at the Data Warehouse was a novel concept, the minimality of auxiliary views defined was still questionable since the MV instance was never exploited for self-maintenance. Most of the current approaches maintain the MV separately from each other using a separate view manager for each view and such approaches fail to recognize that these views can be maintained together by identifying the set of related materialized views. This issue of multiple-view self-maintenance was addressed for the first time in Huyn, 1997).

In some approaches to multiple-view self-maintenance, a set of auxiliary views (AV) are stored at the data warehouse along with the set of materialized views (MV) such that together MV $\cup$ AV is self-maintainable. The research challenge lies in finding the most economical AV s in terms of space complexity and computational costs. The view self-maintenance is still an active research problem. It is not always feasible to provide self-maintainability of the views at the data warehouse. When the cost of providing self-maintainability exceeds the cost of querying data sources for computing view updates, it is profitable to allow querying of data sources instead.

Consistency maintenance

Current research has also concentrated on ensuring consistency of the data warehouse when the MV s are not self-maintainable since it is not always possible to provide for complete self-maintainability at the data warehouse. The ECA family of algorithms (Zhuge et al., 1995) introduces the problem and solves it partially. The strobe algorithm (Zhuge et al., 1996) introduces the concept of queuing the view updates in the action-list at the data warehouse and installing the updates only when the unanswered query set (UQS) is empty. The algorithm solves the consistency problem but is subject to the potential threat of infinite waiting. There are other mechanisms that are based on time stamping the view updates (Baralis et al., 1996). These methods do not address the consistency problems in their entirety and also assume the notion of global time.

We propose that the self-maintainability of views at the data warehouse should be a dynamic property. We should continuously monitor the cost of providing self-maintainability, and when this cost increases beyond a certain threshold, the maintenance mechanism should be shifted to querying data sources to compute the view updates. This threshold can be computed depending on the cost of querying data sources. An effective algorithm that provides this dynamism and efficient garbage collection is the need of the hour.

Update filtering

The changes that take place in the source data need to be reflected at the data warehouse. Some changes may create view updates that need to be installed at the data warehouse; some changes leave the views at the data warehouse unchanged. If we are able to detect at the data sources that certain changes are guaranteed to leave the views unchanged, we need not propagate these changes to the data warehouse. This would require checking of distributed integrity constraints at a single site. As many changes as possible can be filtered at the sources, and only the changes that result in view updates may be propagated to the warehouse. The update filtering will reduce the size of the maintenance transactions at the data warehouse, thus minimizing the time required to make the data warehouse consistent with the data sources. The side effect of update filtering is that we need to make our data sources (and the wrapper/monitor) components more intelligent. They need to know about their participation in the data warehouse and the data warehouse configuration so that the updates can be checked against the constraint set before propagating them. To be able to realize this, the data sources cannot be decoupled from the data warehouse anymore. This would give rise to new problems like configuration management, i.e., if there is a change in the schema at any data source or at the data warehouse, all the participating entities need to be informed of this change so that they can modify the constraint set to reflect this change. The view maintenance strategies would now be based on the constraint set, and any change to the constraint set would warrant a change in the existing view maintenance transaction.

On-line view maintenance

Warehouse view maintenance can be done either incrementally or by queuing a large number of updates at the data sources to be propagated as a batch update from the data sources to the data warehouse. In current commercial systems, a batch update is periodically sent to the data warehouse, and view updates are computed and installed. This transaction is called the maintenance transaction. A user typically issues read-only queries at the data warehouse and a long-running sequence of user queries is called a reader session. The batch maintenance transaction is typically large and blocks the reader sessions. This makes the data warehouse offline for the duration of the maintenance transaction. The maintenance transaction typically runs at night. With the advent of the Internet and global users, this scheme will have to give way. The 24-hour shop concept is what most companies are striving for, and the data warehouse to be on-line for 24 hours allows the company to be competitive in its strategies. Incremental view maintenance, which updates the data warehouse instantaneously in response to every change at the data source, is expensive and gives rise to inconsistent results during the same reader session. An update from the data source will change the results a user might see over a sequence of queries. We need to get around these problems. Quass and Widom, 1997 discuss a possible approach to this problem by maintaining two versions of each tuple at the data warehouse simultaneously so that the reader sessions and the maintenance transactions do not block each other. A possible solution may need the integration with self-maintenance techniques, where auxiliary views can be used to answer queries during maintenance transactions.

INDEXING IN DATA WAREHOUSES

Indexing has been at the foundation of performance tuning for databases for many years. It is the creation of access structures that provide faster access to the base data relevant to the restriction criteria of queries (Datta et al., 1999). The size of the index structure should be manageable so that benefits can be accrued by traversing such a structure. The traditional indexing strategies used in database systems do not work well in data warehousing environments. Most OLTP transactions typically access a small number of rows; most OLTP queries are point queries. B trees, which are used in most common relational database systems, are geared towards such point queries. They are well suited for accessing a small number of rows. An OLAP query typically accesses a large number of records for summarizing information. For example, an OLTP transaction would typically query for a customer who booked a flight on TWA1234 on say April 25; on the other hand an

OLAP query would be more like "Give me the number of customers who booked a flight on TWA1234 in say one month." The second query would access more records and these are typically range queries. B tree indexing scheme which is so apt for OLTP transactions is not the best suited to answer OLAP queries. An index can be single-column or multi-columns of a table (or a view). An index can be either clustered or non-clustered. An index can be defined on one table (or view) or many tables using a join index (Valduriez, 1987). In data warehouse context, when we talk about index, we refer to two different things: (1) indexing techniques and (2) index selection problem.

Indexing Techniques

A number of indexing strategies have been suggested for data warehouses: Value-List Index, Projection Index (O'Neil and Quass, 1997), Bitmap Index (O'Neil and Quass, 1997), Bit-Sliced Index (O'Neil and Quass, 1997), Data Index (O'Neil and Quass, 1997), Join Index (Valduriez, 1987) and Star Join Index (Red Brick Systems, 1997).

Value-list index

The value-list index consists of two parts. The first part is a balanced tree structure and the second part is a mapping scheme. The mapping scheme is attached to the leaf nodes of the tree structure and points to the tuples in the table being indexed. The tree is generally a B tree with varying percentages of utilization. Oracle provides a B* tree with 100 utilization. Two different types of mapping schemes are in use. First, one consists of a Row ID list, which is associated with each unique search-key value. This list is partitioned into a number of disk blocks chained together. The second scheme uses bitmaps. A bitmap is a vector of bits that store either a 0 or a 1 depending upon the value of a predicate. A bitmap B lists all rows with a given predicate P, such that for each row r with ordinal number j that satisfies

Figure 9 : Example of a Bitmap index on gender

CUSTOMER Table			
Name	Age	...	Gender
Dupond	20		M
Lee	42		F
Jones	21		M
Martin	52		M
Ali	18		F
Qing	17		F
Hung	36		M

BM1
M
1
0
1
1
0
0
1

BM2
F
0
1
0
0
1
1
0

Figure 10: Examples of a Projection Index

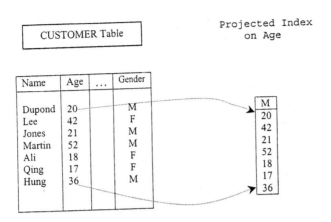

the predicate P, the jth bit in B is set. Bitmaps efficiently represent low-cardinality data, however to make this indexing scheme practical for high-cardinality data, compression techniques must be used. Value-list indexes have been shown in O'Neil and Quass (1997) to outperform other access method in queries involving the MIN or MAX aggregate functions, as well as queries that compute percentile values of a given column. Bitmap indexes can substantially improve performance of queries with the following characteristics (Oracle Corporation, 1999):

- The WHERE clause contains multiple predicates on low-or-medium-cardinality columns (e.g., a predicate on gender that has two possible values: female or male as shown in Figure 9).
- Bitmap indexes have been created on some or all of these low-or-medium-cardinality columns.
- Tables being queried contain many rows.

Projection index

A projection index is equivalent to the column being indexed. If C is the column being indexed, then the projection index on C consists of a stored sequence of column values from C in the same order as the ordinal row number in the table from where the values are extracted (see Figure 10). It has been shown in O'Neil and Quass (1997) that projection indexes outperform other indexing schemes for performing queries that involve computation on two or more column values and appear to perform acceptably well in GROUP-BY like queries.

Bit-sliced index

A bit-sliced index represents the key values of the column to be indexed as binary numbers and projects a set of bitmap slices, which are orthogonal to the data, held in the projection index. This index has been shown in O'Neil and Quass (1997) to particularly perform well for computing sums and averages. Also, it outperforms other indexing approaches for percentile queries if the underlying data are clustered, and for range queries whose range is large.

Join index and bitmap join index

A join index (Valduriez, 1987) is the result of joining two tables on a join attribute and projecting the keys (or tuple IDs) of the two tables. To join the two tables, we can use the join index to fetch the tuples from the tables followed by a join. In relational data warehouse systems, it is of interest to perform a multiple join (a Star Join) on the fact tables and their dimension tables. Therefore, it will be helpful to build join indexes between the keys and the dimension tables, and the corresponding foreign keys of the fact table. If the join indexes are represented in bitmap matrices, a multiple join could be replaced by a sequence of bitwise operations, followed by a relatively small number of fetch and join operations (Wu and Buchmann, 1997).

Data index

A data index, like the projection index, exploits the positional indexing strategy (Datta et al., 1998). The data index avoids duplication of data by storing only the index and not the column being indexed. The data index can be of two specific types: basic data index and join data index (for more information, see Datta et al. (1998).

Index Selection Problem

The index selection problem (ISP) has been studied since the early '70s, and the importance of this problem is well recognized. Like VSP, ISP consists of picking a set of indexes for a given set of OLAP queries under some resources constraints. Most of proposed studies show that ISP is an NP-complete problem. Recently, Microsoft (Chaudhuri and Narasaya, 1999; 1999) developed an index selection tool called AutoAdmin. The goal of our research in the AutoAdmin tool is to make database systems self-tuning and self-administering. This goal is achieved by enabling databases to track the usage of their systems and to gracefully adapt to application requirements. Thus, instead of applications having to track and tune databases, databases actively auto-tune themeselves itself to be responsive to application needs.

Note that indexes require a very huge amount of space. Chaudhuri et al. (1999) (from Microsoft) addressed a problem, called Storage-minimal index merging problem, that takes an existing set of indices, and produces a new set of indices with significantly lower storage and maintenance cost. This is a strong reason to motivate researchers to find novel techniques for better use of storage capacity available for a data warehouse. The merging technique is similar to the reconstruction of vertical fragments of a relation.

Labio et al. (1997) combined the problems of selecting views and indexes into one problem, called the view-index selection problem (VISP). This problem starts with a set of materialized views (primary views) and tries to add a set of supporting views to these primary views. The objective is to minimize total maintenance cost for the data warehouse, but not distribute storage space between materialized views and indices. For that, the authors proposed an algorithm based on A* to find the optimal solution. This algorithm takes as input the set of all possible supporting views and indices to materialize. The space allocation is not taken into consideration by this algorithm, because it supposes that the primary views are already selected (their storage capacity is already assigned). This algorithm is in fact not practical because the number of possible supporting views and indices can be very huge. Heuristic rules (concerning the benefit and cost of supporting views and indices) to reduce the complexity of A* are suggested.

INTERACTION BETWEEN
INDEXES AND VIEWS

Conceptually, both materialized views and indices are physical structures that can significantly accelerate performance (Sanjay et al., 2000). An effective physical database design tool must therefore take into account the interaction between indices and materialized views by considering them together to optimize the physical design for the queries on the system (Bellatreche et al., 2000; Sanjay et al., 2000). An effective physical database design tool must therefore take into account the interaction between indices and materialized views by considering them together to optimize the physical design for the workload on the system. Ignoring this interaction can significantly compromise the quality of the solutions obtained by the physical database design tool.

This interaction gets the great attention of researchers (Bellatreche et al., 2000) and industrials (Sanjay et al., 2000). Recently, architecture and algorithms for selecting views and indexes are presented by Microsoft SQL Server 2000.

Most of the previous work in physical database design has considered the problems of index selection and materialized view selection in isolation. However, both indexes and views are fundamentally similar-both are redundant structures that speed up query execution, compete for the same resource (storage) and incur maintenance overhead in the presence of updates (Sanjay et al., 2000).

When the VSP and ISP are treated independently (i.e., the views and indices are selected in sequential manner), to select them, the DWA does the following tasks:

- The DWA has to run an algorithm to select views to be materialized according to the storage space reserved for views.
- After that, the DWA runs another algorithm to select indices over base relations and materialized views according to storage space reserved for indices.

The combination of VSP and ISP gives rise to two problems that are not addressed by the data warehouse community. The first problem is selecting join index in the presence of materialized views, and the second one is storage space distribution among materialized views and indices.

Join Index Selection with Materialized Views: Once materialized views are selected, all OLAP queries will be rewritten using these materialized views (this process is known as query rewriting (Srivastava et al., 1996). A rewriting of a query Q using views is a query expression Q¢ that refers to these views. In SQL, after the rewriting process of OLAP queries, we can find in the FROM clause a set of materialized views, dimension tables and the fact table. These views can be joined with each other or with other tables. Indexing a single materialized view can be done by using the same indexing techniques for a table (B+-tree). The star join index (SJI) (Red Brick Systems, 1997; O'Neil and Qass, 1997) has been used in data warehouses modeled by a star schema. It denotes a join index between a fact table and multiple dimension tables. The SJI has proven to be an index structure for speeding up joins defined on fact and dimension tables in data warehouses (Red Brick Systems, 1997; O'Neil and Qass, 1997). However, there has not been much research reported in enhancing star join algorithms for efficiently selecting and performing join indices with materialized views.

Space Distribution Between Views & Indices: Since the VSP and ISP are combined, the space distribution becomes a crucial issue. The task of distributing storage space among materialized views and indices in order to improve performance is very difficult for the DWA. This difficulty is due to several factors: (1) metrics are needed to decide on the distribution of the storage space among materialized views and indices, (2) the mutual interdependencies between views and indices need to be considered for an optimal solution and (3) the problem of redistribution of storage space among materialized views and indices after update operations (deletions and insertions), or changes in query sets, needs to be addressed.

Further, when updates are performed over the underlying data warehouse, the corresponding changes should be applied to materialized views and indices (Hurtado, Mendelzon and Vaisman, 1999). Thus, their sizes can increase or decrease. Therefore, it is necessary to re-distribute the storage space among views and indices. Finally, the problem that must be addressed is: how to automatically distribute storage space between materialized views and indices to efficiently execute a set of queries?

In the next sections, we describe the graph join index concept and space distribution among materialized views and indexes.

Graph Join Indexes

The index selection phase is aimed at determining the best set of indices for a given set of OLAP queries. The objective of index selection is to pick a set of indices that is optimal or as close to optimal as possible (Chaudhuri & Narasayya, 1999; Gupta, Harinarayan, Rajaraman & Ullman, 1997; Valduriez, 1987; Lei & Ross, 1998). Like the materialized views, indices require a certain amount of disk space, and only a limited number of indices can be selected for a given set of OLAP queries. Indices can be defined on one table (dimension table, fact table or view) using for example a B^+-tree. They can also be defined on more than two tables to speed up operations such as joins.

In this section, we suggest a new type of join index called a graph join index (GJI), which is used to speed up queries defined on materialized views and on tables (dimension or fact).

Motivating example

Assume that the sales company is interested in determining the total sales for male customers purchasing product of type package "box." The following SQL query Q_1 may be used for this purpose:

```
SELECT          SUM(S.dollar_sales)
FROM            CUSTOMER C, PRODUCT P, SALES S,
WHERE           C.Cid = S.Cid
AND             P.Pid = S.Pid
AND             C.Gender = 'M'
AND             P.Package_type = "Box"
GROUP BY PID
```

We also assume that the company maintains the following view consisting of finding the total sales for each product having "box" as type of package. This view is defined as follows:

```
CREATE          VIEW V_2
SELECT          *
FROM            PRODUCT P, SALES S,
WHERE           P.Pid = S.Pid
AND             C.Package_type = "Box"
GROUP BY PID
```

The materialized view V_2 can be used to evaluate the query Q_1 by joining V_2 with the dimension table CUSTOMER. The rewritten query $Q_1¢$ that uses V_2 is:

```
SELECT          SUM(S.dollar_sales)
FROM            CUSTOMER C, V_2
```

Figure 11. Database schema graph and join graphs

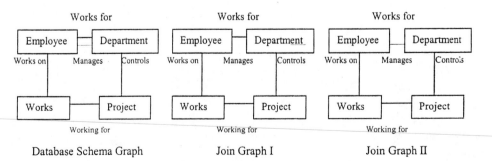

Database Schema Graph   Join Graph I   Join Graph II

WHERE	V_2.Cid = C.Cid
AND	C.Gender = 'M'
GROUP BY PID	

Note that the fact table SALES is huge, and the materialized view V_2 is likely to be orders of magnitude smaller than SALES table. Hence, evaluating Q_1¢ will be much faster than evaluating the query Q_1, because, Q_1 needs two join operations, and Q_1¢ needs only one. There is a solution, to reduce the number of join operations of the query Q_1 which is the SJI (Red Brick Systems, 1997). The suitable SJI for Q_1 is (CUSTOMER, SALES, PRODUCT), but it requires a very high storage capacity (Datta et al., 1999) that can slow down the execution of the query Q_1. We can define a join index between the view V_2 and the dimension table CUSTOMER (V_2, CUSTOMER). This index speeds up the execution of the query Q_1, and its size is much smaller than the SJI (CUSTOMER, SALES, PRODUCT).

Note that the complete SJI (CUSTOMER, SALES, PRODUCT, TIME) would be sufficient to process any query against our star schema in Figure 3. However, without the fact table in its element, this index does not guarantee any performance (Informix corporaiton, 1997). In the presence of materialized views, a join index can be defined on several views; therefore, by removing one view, the join index may still guarantee the performance of some queries. This is because most of materialized views are obtained from joining the fact table with other dimension tables.

Notations definitions

Assume that the OLAP queries are based on the star join: each query is a join between the fact table and dimension tables, filtered by some selection operations and followed by an aggregation. This type of query has the following syntax:

SELECT	*<Projection List> <Aggregation List>*
FROM	<Fact Table> <Dimension Tables>
WHERE	<Selection Predicates Join Predicates>
GROUP BY	<Dimension Table Attributes>

Figure 12. Join graph and graph join indices

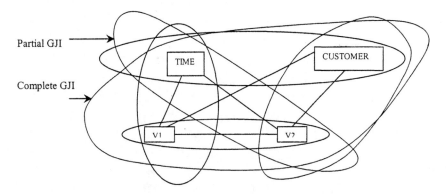

Note that in the syntax of queries without materialized views, the FROM clause contains the fact table and dimension tables. When we consider the materialized views, our queries should be rewritten using these views (Srivastava et al., 1996). Therefore, the FROM clause can contain: fact table, materialized views and dimension tables.

Definition 3: (Database Schema Graph (DBSG) is a connected graph where each node is a relation and an edge between two nodes R_i and R_j implies a possibility of join between relations R_i and R_j.

Definition 4: (Join Graph (JG) is a database schema graph such that there exists exactly one join condition between two relations.

For a given database schema, we can have more than one edge (join) between two nodes as shown in Figure 11, where we have two join operations between tables Employee and Department. One join condition relates employee to the department he/she is working in, and another join condition relates an employee to the department he/she is managing. In this case, we decompose the database schema graph into two join graphs as shown in Figure 11, and then we consider GJIs for each join graph, separately.

Since we are focusing on data warehouse schemas (e.g., star, snowflake), a join graph has only single join condition between tables. Further study on the complexity of GJIs derived from database schema graph with multiple independent join conditions is beyond the scope of this chapter. Therefore, a JG is the same as DBSG.

Claim 1: A JG in a data warehouse with only dimension tables and fact table is always connected. In this case, a JG is called total join graph.

Claim 2: In a data warehouse context with dimension tables, fact table and materialized views, a JG can be disconnected, i.e., it contains more than one subgraph. In this case, it is called partitioned join graph.

The partitioned join graph occurs when:

1. Views do not have common join attributes. For example, a view defined on CUSTOMER and another in PRODUCT.

2. Views have common join attributes, but they can never be joined. For example, suppose we have two views V_1 and V_2 defining the sales activities of female customers and male customers, respectively. The result of joining these two views is always empty.

Definition 5: (Graph Join Index (GJI) A GJI is a subset of nodes of a join graph.

In case of distributed join graph, a GJI is a subset of nodes of each sub-graph.
Claim 3: *A SJI is a particular case of GJI.*

A data warehouse schema consists of a star schema (a set of dimension tables and a fact table) with a set of materialized views. Each table T_i being either a dimension table, or a view, or a fact table has a key K_{T_i}. A GJI on m tables is a table having m attributes $(K_{T1}, K_{T2,...}, K_{Tm})$, and which is denoted as :
$$(T_1 \sim T_2 \sim ... \sim T_m).$$

Since the star schema is connected, there is a path connecting the tables $(T_1, T_{2,...}, T_m)$ by including additional tables, if necessary. The GJI supplies the keys of the relations that form the result of joining all the tables along the path. In case there are multiple paths that connect tables $(T_1, T_2, ..., T_m)$, then there can be multiple GJIs, each catering to a different query. A GJI with all tables of a join graph is known as a complete GJI. A GJI with a subset of nodes of a join graph refers to a partial GJI (see Figure 12).

A similar indexing technique to GJI was proposed by Segev et al. (1996) called join pattern index in expert systems. This index exists on all attributes involved in selection and join conditions. It refers to an array of variables that represent the key and join attributes of the data associated with the join.

Note that for a star schema with n tables, the number of possible GJIs grows exponentially, and is given by:

$$\binom{2^n - n - 1}{0} + \binom{2^n - n - 1}{2} + ... + \binom{2^n - n - 1}{2^n - n - 1} = 2^{(2^n - n - 1)}$$

As GJI has at least two nodes, the total number of GJIs possible is $2^n - n - 1$. Therefore, the above equation gives us the total number of ways a set of GJIs can be generated. However, if we want to find only one GJI, the number of GJI possibilities are $2^n - n - 1$. Therefore, the problem of efficiently finding the set of GJIs that provides the minimum total query processing cost while satisfying a storage constraint is very challenging to solve.

GJI Selection (GJI-S) Problem Formulation

All the index selection algorithms select indices to optimize the objective function employed, subject to the constraint that the indices included cannot consume more than the specified amount of storage.

The inputs of the GJI-S problem are as follows:
1. A star schema with the fact table F and dimension tables $\{D_1, D_2, ..., D_d\}$.
2. A set of most frequently asked queries $Q = \{Q_1, Q_2, ..., Q_s\}$ with their frequencies $\{f_1, f_2, ..., f_s\}$. Each query Q_i $(1 \leq i \leq s)$ is represented by a query graph QG_i.
3. A set of materialized views $V = \{V_1, V_2, ..., V_m\}$ selected to support the execution of queries in Q.
4. A storage constraint S.

The GJI-S problem selects a set of GJIs G' among all possible GJIs (G), that minimizes the total cost for executing a set of OLAP queries, under the constraint that the total space occupied by the GJIs in (denoted by $S_{G'}$ is less than S).

More formally, let $C_g(Q_i)$ denote the cost of answering a query Q_i using a GJI g $(g \in G')$. The problem is to select a set of GJIs G' $(G' \subseteq G)$ that minimizes the total query processing cost $(TQPC)$ such as:

$$TQPC = \sum_{i=1}^{s} f_i \times \{min_{\forall g \in G} C_g(Qi)\} \tag{3}$$

under the constraint that: $S_{G'} \leq S$.

GJI-S Algorithms

In Bellatreche, et al. (2000), we have proposed three algorithms to select an optimal or near-optimal GJI for a set of queries: a naive algorithm, a greedy algorithm for selecting one GJI and a greedy algorithm for selecting more than one GJI. These three algorithms are guided by an objective function that calculates the cost of executing a set of queries.

1. The naive algorithm (NA) is used for a comparison purpose. NA enumerates all possible GJIs, and calculates the contribution of each GJI in executing a set of queries. Finally, it picks the GJI having the minimum cost while satisfying the storage constraint.

2. The greedy algorithm for selecting one GJI (GA1) starts with a storage constraint (SC) S, and then selects a GJI with two nodes that corresponds to most frequently executed join among all the queries, and tries to expand it by adding more nodes while checking whether the total processing cost decreases. When no more expand operations can be applied, the algorithm tries to shrink it to check if a better GJI can be derived. When no more expand or shrink operations can be applied, the algorithm ends, generating the best possible GJI. The details of the algorithm are presented in Bellatreche et al. (2000).

3. Note that as a single GJI generated by GA1 can only efficiently execute some but not all of the queries, we need more than one GJI to efficiently execute all the queries. Therefore, we develop a greedy algorithm for selecting more than one GJI (GAK). The GAK starts with the initial solution provided by GA1 as the first index. After that it selects the edge from weight graph that has the highest query access frequency and which is not a GJI generated by GA1. Then it tries to expand (one or more times) and shrink (one or more times) until no further reduction in total cost can be achieved and the storage constraint is satisfied. This generates the second GJI, and it keeps repeating this procedure until the storage constraint is violated.

Space Distribution Among Views and Indices

The problem of space distribution among views and indices should be treated in two cases: static and dynamic. In the static case, all data warehouse parameters are considered fixed. In the dynamic case, we assume that the tables in the data warehouse are updated.

Static space distribution between materialized views and indexes can be formulated as follows:

Given a set of frequently asked retrieval queries $Q = \{Q_1, Q_2, ..., Q_s\}$, a set of frequently asked update queries $U = \{U_1, U_2, ..., U_s\}$ and their frequencies, and a storage space S to store materialized views V and indices I to support the above queries, distribute S among materialized views and indices so as to minimize the global cost. As output, we obtain:

1) the space distribution between materialized views (S^V) and indices (S^I), and
2) a set of materialized views and indices corresponding to (S^V) and indices (S^I).

Static algorithm

In Bellatreche et al. (2000), we developed a methodology that distributes the storage space among views and indices in an iterative manner, so as to minimize the total query processing cost. First, we developed a cost model that calculates the cost of processing a set of OLAP queries with materialized views and indices. Assume that the DWA initially reserves a space (S^V) and (S^I) for materialized views and indices ($S = S^V + S^I$), respectively. First, we apply an algorithm for selecting a set of materialized views to support the set of queries. The selection of views is constrained by the space quota reserved to them, i.e., S^V. After that, indices are built on base relations and materialized views using the storage space S^I.

The basic idea of this approach is to have two greedy algorithms, namely, index spy and view spy, fight for the same resource (that is, storage space). These two spies work as follows:

- An index spy keeps on stealing space used by materialized views to add/ change the set of indices as long as it reduces the total query processing cost. The index spy should have some policies to select materialized views that can be stolen. We define two policies: Least Frequently Used View (LFUV), where the index spy selects the view that has the lowest frequency, and Smallest View First (SVF), where the index spy selects the smallest view.
- After that, a view spy keeps on stealing space from indices to add/change the set of materialized views as long as it reduces the total cost. Similarly, the view spy should have some policies to select indexes that can be stolen. Two policies are defined: Least Frequently Used Index (LFUI) and Largest Index First (LIF).

The algorithm ends when neither the index spy nor the view spy can reduce the total query processing cost. The winner is the spy who accumulated the most storage space from the other spy. The main strategy of this approach is to have two greedy algorithms, namely, index spy and view spy, fight for the same resource (that is, storage space), while trying to reduce the total cost of processing a given set of queries, and maintaining the set of materialized views and indices. The algorithm terminates when the total cost cannot be reduced any more.

This approach gives two results: (1) a set of materialized views and a set of indices with the lowest total cost, and (2) new *storage space allocation* for materialized views and indices $S^V\phi$ and $S^I\phi$ that may differ from the initial space quotas S^V and S^I.

Table 2. Selected materialized views and their sizes

View Name	View Definition	View Size
V_1	$SALES \chi \sigma_{State = 'IL'} CUSTOMER$	178 094 08
V_2	$SALES \chi \sigma_{Package = 'Box'} PRODUCT$	324 435 968
V_3	$\sigma_{Gender = 'M'} CUSTOMER$	089 047 040
Total		591 577 088

Table 3. Cost reduction due to index spy

Without View & Indices	With Views	With View and Indices	Index Spy	View Spy
68514928	*4054825*	*3263405*	*1955305*	*68514928*

Example 4: To illustrate our approach, we consider the following example. We consider the star schema of a data warehouse (Figure 3, in Section 2). This schema contains a fact table SALES and three dimension tables CUSTOMER, TIME and PRODUCT. Assume the five most frequently asked OLAP queries given in Bellateche et al. (2000). We assume that the DWA has an initial allocation of 600 megabytes for materialized views and 200 megabytes for indices.

Our algorithm starts by selecting an initial solution for VSP and ISP. First, we execute the View Select algorithm (Yang, et al., 1997) to select materialized views using the 600 megabytes storage constraint. The views selected are V_1, V_2 and V_3 as shown in Table 2. Using these three materialized views, we get 4054825 disk block accesses as the total cost of processing all queries.

After that, we build indices to speed up the above queries by selecting indices using the 200 megabytes storage constraint. By using the GJI selection algorithms, (section 6) we select a join index between the view V_2 and the dimension table CUSTOMER, called (V_2 ~ CUSTOMER). The storage required for the selected index is 181821440 bytes. This index reduces the query processing cost from 4054825 to 3263405. Now, the index spy tries to steal storage space from materialized views to add one or more indices. Since the view V_3 is small and less used compared to views V_1 and V_2, the index spy steals 89047040 bytes (size of view V_3), and the storage space that can be allocated for indices is now 289047040 bytes. Note that after deleting the view V_3, we will have only two views V_1 and V_2 and two base relations CUSTOMER and TIME to execute all five queries. Now the index spy runs the index selection algorithm (Bellatreche et al., 2000) to find new indices. The new index is (V_1 ~ V_2 ~ TIME ~ CUSTOMER). It reduces the total query processing cost from **3263405** to **1955305** disk block accesses. *No further reduction in query processing cost is possible by executing the index spy or the view spy. Therefore, by allocating 500 megabytes for materialized views and 300 megabytes for indices results in a total query processing cost of 1955305 disk block accesses as shown in Table 3.*

The solution we propose for distributing space can reuse existing algorithms for views selection and index selection. Thus, the best available algorithms can be selected. Further, our methodology is flexible enough for the DWA to use only index spy or only view spy for data warehouse design. In this way, the DWA can either allocate more storage space to indices or to materialized views.

Issues for Dynamic Space Distribution

The data warehouse environments are known by their dynamic changes over the underlying warehouse database. Whenever the base relations are updated at more or less regular intervals, the materialized views and indexes should also be updated. Following these updates, it is necessary to readjust/redefine the views and the indices.

Several methods have been proposed for fast rebuild of materialized views (Mohania and Kambayashi, 2000). A view after this maintenance can indeed occupy more or less space than before the maintenance. The same observation is also valid for the indices. So, the space constraint may not longer be respected. If the total space occupied by the views and the indices is higher (respectively lower) than the required space, it is necessary to determine which views and/or indices must be removed (respectively added). The iterative algorithm for the static case can be easily adapted to handle this problem.

Let S^V_i and S^I_i be the spaces occupied by the views and indices before the updates. These two values are the new space constraints to respect. After updates, the algorithm of the dynamic case goes through following steps:

- First, we compute the new spaces occupied by the views (S^V_c) and the indices (S^I_i).
- In case of deletions, the total space S_c ($S^V_c + S^I_c$) may decrease. Therefore, unused spaces for both materialized views and indices are available. We fill the unused space for materialized views by selecting a new view. Similarly, the unused space for indices is filled incrementally, using the greedy algorithm GAK. It considers each index of the set of selected indices as an initial solution and then generates a new index (not belonging to the current set of indices).
- When insertions occur, the current total space (S_c) occupied by the views and indices may be higher than their initial space (S_i). This augmentation can affect view space, index space or both.

  1. Only the space occupied by the views is higher than their required space. Intuitively, we need to remove view(s) to satisfy the storage constraint. But before removing view(s), we check out if the view-spy can steal index space to keep these views. If it cannot steal space, we remove view(s) using one of the view policies (LFUV or SVF).

  2. Only the space occupied by the indices is higher than their required space. As in the previous situation, we need to remove index(es) to satisfy the storage constraint. But before removing these index(es), we check out if the index-spy can steal view space to keep these indices. If it cannot steal space, we remove index(es) using one of the index policies (LFUI or LIF).

  3. Both spaces are higher than their required spaces. In this case, we remove views and indices using the policies for views and indices till their storage constraints are satisfied. We then apply our static algorithm to verify if the global cost can be reduced.

Discussion

Our evaluation of the iterative algorithm for the VISP problem shows that there is a balance between amount of space allocated to materialized views vis-à-vis indices in data warehousing environments. Blindly allocating space to either materialized views or indices will not guarantee faster execution of queries. This level of interaction can be easily supported in any data warehouse design tool, and can facilitate efficient query processing in data warehouses. As the approach we developed is essentially a greedy algorithm, one cannot guarantee an optimal distribution of space between materialized views and indices. But, as our illustrative examples show, there is a tremendous reduction in query processing cost, which supports the utility of this approach.

DISCUSSION OF PRACTICAL ASPECTS OF THIS CHAPTER

In this chapter, we have treated two major problems in data warehousing environments: (i) the data partitioning, and (ii) the interaction between indexes and materialized views. Each problem gets an important place in data warehouse trends.

Data Partitioning: Oracle8i incorporates the horizontal partitioning to support very large tables, materialized views and indexes by decomposing them into smaller and manageable pieces called partitions. Oracle 8i defines some partitioning methods: the *range partitioning*, the *hash partitioning*, the *composite partitioning* and the *partition-wise joins*.

In the range partitioning, the data in a table (a view or an index) is partitioned according to a range of values. In the hash partitioning, the data is partitioned according to a hash function. In the composite partitioning, data is partitioned by range and further subdivided using a hash function. Finally, in partition-wise joins, a large join operation is broken into smaller joins that are performed sequentially or in parallel. In order to use this partitioning, both tables must be equi-partitioned.

Indexing Materialized Views: Oracle8i provides a new query-rewrite capability, which transforms an SQL statement so that it accesses materialized views that are defined on the detail tables. Coupled with materialized views, Oracle8i's query-rewrite capability can significantly reduce the response time of queries that summarize or join data in the tables of a data warehouse. When a query targets one or more detail tables to calculate a summary or an aggregate (or perform a join) and an available materialized view contains the requested data, Oracle8i optimizer can transparently rewrite the query to target the precomputed results in the materialized view, which returns the results more quickly.

But when a query targets one or more detail tables to calculate a summary or an aggregate (or perform a join) and *more than one materialized view* contains the requested data (for example, joining these materialized views), Oracle8i's should define a join index covering these tables to optimize this query. We are not sure if these kinds of join indexes are defined by industrials.

The Interaction Between Indexes and Views: This problem gets great attention from the industrials and practitioners. Recently, the Data Management, Exploration Mining group at Microsoft Research considered the interaction between indexes and views. The researchers at this group (Sanjay et al., 2000) presented solutions for automatically selecting an appropriate set of materialized views and indexes for SQL databases.

Business Perspective: Data warehousing has become a standard tool used to evaluate the health of a company and it competitiveness in the marketplace. Therefore, a large amount of decision analysis and processing is performed on data warehousing systems. The tools and techniques proposed in this chapter form the core of techniques that can be applied by the data warehouse administrator in not only designing a data warehouse for the organization, but also fine tuning it by taking in to account the changes in user query processing. A well-designed data warehouse will process user queries faster while maintaining the currency of the data. This enhances competitiveness of the company and makes it agile to address changes in their customer behavior or changes in the environment where the company operates. Finally, a data warehouse developer can build a data warehouse design tool that is based on techniques presented in this chapter.

CONCLUSIONS AND FUTURE WORK

Data warehousing design facilitates efficient query processing and maintenance of materialized views. There are few trade-offs that were introduced in data warehousing design. The first trade-off is whether to materialize a view or not. The view selection problem minimizes the total cost of query processing and maintaining materialized views for a given set of queries. There has been lot of work on selecting materialized views for static environments (such as Yang et al., 1997), and under dynamic environments (such as, Kotidis and Roussopoulos, 1999). The second trade-off is whether to partition a data warehouse or not. In our study (Bellatreche et al., 2000; Gopalkrishnan et al., 2000; Gopalkrishnan et al., 2000; Gopalkrishnan et al., 1999) we found that partitioning helps in reducing irrelevant data access and eliminating (some of the) costly joins. Further, too much partitioning can increase the cost for queries that access entire data warehouses. The third trade-off is index selection to efficiently execute queries. We found that judicious index selection does reduce the cost of query processing, but also showed that indices on materialized views improve the performance of queries even more (Bellatreche et al., 2000) . Since indices require storage space, and so do materialized views, the final trade-off presented was the storage distribution among materialized views and indices. We found that it is possible to apply heuristics to distribute the storage space among materialized views and indices so as to efficiently execute queries and maintain materialized views.

Data warehousing design under dynamic environments is still a very open issue of research. The ability to adapt a given set of materialized views and partitions to dynamically changing queries executed over time by users is required to facilitate optimal performance from a data warehousing system. This problem could be addressed by treating materialized views and partitions to be composed of grid cells (Navathe, et al., 1995) and dynamically changing the materialized views and partitions by changing the composition.

Such a methodology is amenable to heuristics based on composition algebra, and efficient hill-climbing algorithms can be designed. The notion of atomic grid cells can facilitate parallel processing of costly OLAP queries on a shared-nothing parallel processing system. Even though a lot of work has been done on view maintenance algorithms and view adaptation algorithms, there is explicit tie-up between these and data warehousing design. In particular, given a particular view maintenance strategy, what kind of data warehousing design strategy has to be employed and vice-versa? Data warehousing design is application specific; for report generation a specific data warehousing design might be needed, where as for data mining a different data warehousing design might be needed. Hence a design methodology that can support multiple data warehouse designs for different types of applications needs to be developed.

REFERENCES

Agrawal, Gupta, A. and Sarawagi, S. (1997). Modeling multidimensional databases. *Technical Report Research*, IBM.

Baralis,E., S. Ceri, and Paraboschi, S. (1996). Conservative timestamp revisited for materialized view maintenance in a data warehouse. In *Proceeding of the Workshop on Materialized Views: Techniques and Applications (VIEW'1996)*, June, 1-9.

Baralis, E., S. Paraboschi, and Teniente, E. (1997). Materialized view selection in a multidimensional database. *Proceedings of the International Conference on Very Large Databases*, August, 156-165.

Bauer, L. and Lehner, W. (1997). The cube-query-languages (CQL) for multidimensional statistical and scientific database systems. In *Proceedings of the Fifth International Conference on Database Systems for Advanced Applications(DASFAA'97)*, April, 263-272.

Bellatreche, L., Karlapalem, K. and Simonet A. (2000). Algorithms and support for horizontal class partitioning. In *Object-Oriented Databases in the Distributed and Parallel Databases Journal*, April, 8(2), 155-179.

Bellatreche, L., Karlapalem, K. and Basak, G. B. (1998). Query-driven horizontal class partitioning. In *Object-Oriented Databases In 9th International Conference on Database and Expert Systems Applications (DEXA'98), Lecture Notes in Computer Science 1460*, August, 692-701.

Bellatreche, L., Karlapalem, K. and Li, Q. (1998). Derived horizontal class partitioning in oodbss: Design strategy, analytical model and evaluation. In *The 17th International Conference on the Entity Relationship Approach (ER'98)*, November, 465-479.

Bellatreche, L., Karlapalem, K. and Li, Q. (1999). Algorithms for graph join index problem in data warehousing environments. *Technical Report HKUST-CS99-07*, Hong Kong University of Science & Technology, March.

Bellatreche, L., Karlapalem, K. and Li, Q. (2000). Evaluation of indexing materialized views in data warehousing environments. *Proceedings of the International Conference on Data Warehousing and Knowledge Discovery (DAWAK'2000)*, September, 57-66.

Bellatreche, L., Karlapalem, K. and M. Mohania, M. (2000). What can partitioning do for your data warehouses and data marts. *Proceedings of the International Database Engineering and Application Symposium (IDEAS'2000)*, September, 437-445.

Bellatreche, L., Karlapalem, K. and Schneider, M. (2000). Interaction between index and view selection in data warehousing environments. *Information Systems Journal.*

Bellatreche, L., Karlapalem, K. and Schneider, M. (2000). On efficient storage space distribution among materialized views and indices in data warehousing environments. In *The International Conference on Information and Knowledge Management (CIKM'2000)*, November.

Bellatreche, L., Karlapalem, K. and Simonet, A. (1997). Horizontal class partitioning. In *Object-Oriented Databases In 8th International Conference on Database and Expert Systems Applications (DEXA'97), Toulouse, Lecture Notes in Computer Science 1308*, September, 58-67.

Ceri, S., Negri, M. and Pelagatti, G. (1982). Horizontal data partitioning in database design. *Proceedings of the ACM SIGMOD International Conference on Management of Data. SIGPLAN Notices*, 128-136.

Ceri, S. and Pelagatti, G. (1984). *Distributed Databases: Principles & Systems*. McGraw-Hill International Editions.

Chaudhuri, S. and Narasayya, V. (1997). An efficient cost-driven index selection tool for microsoft sql server. *Proceedings of the International Conference on Very Large Databases*, August, 146-155.

Chaudhuri, S. and Narasayya, V. (1998). Autoadmin 'what-if' index analysis utility. *Proceedings of the ACM SIGMOD International Conference on Management of Data*, June, 367-378.

Chaudhuri, S. and Narasayya, V. (1999). Index merging. *Proceedings of the International Conference on Data Engineering (ICDE),* March, 296-303.

Datta, A., Moon, B., Ramamritham, K., Thomas, H. and Viguier, I. (1998). Have your data and index it, too: Efficient storage and indexing for datawarehouses. *Techreport Technical Report 98-7, Department of Computer Science, The University of Arizona.*

Datta, A., Ramamritham, K. and Thomas, H. (1999). Curio: A novel solution for efficient storage and indexing in data warehouses. *Proceedings of the International Conference on Very Large Databases*, September, 730-733.

Dewitt, D., Gerber, R. H., Graefe, G., Heytens, M. L., Kumar, K. B. and Muralikrishna, M. (1986). Gamma-A high performance dataflow database machine. *(VLDB}*, 10, 228-237.

Ezeife, C. I. and Barker, K. (1995). A comprehensive approach to horizontal class fragmentation in distributed object based system. *International Journal of Distributed and Parallel Databases*, 3(3), 247-272.

Firestone, J. M. (1997). Data warehouses and data marts: A dynamic view. *White Paper~3, Executive Information Systems, Inc.*, March.

Gopalkrishnan, V., Li, Q. and Karlapalem, K. (1999). Star/snow-flake schema driven object-relational data warehouse-design and query processing strategies. In *Proceedings of the First International Conference on Data Warehousing and Knowledge Discovery*, 11-22.

Gopalkrishnan, V., Li, Q. and Karlapalem, K. (2000). Efficient query processing with associated horizontal class partitioning in an object relational data warehousing environment. In *Proceedings of 2nd International Workshop on Design and Management of Data Warehouses*, June, 1-9.

Gopalkrishnan, V., Li, Q. and Karlapalem, K (2000). Efficient query processing with structural join indexing in an object-relational data warehousing environment. In *Information Resources Management Association International Conference*, 976-979.

Gupta, A. and Mumick, I. S. (1995). Maintenance of materialized views: Problems, techniques and applications. *Data Engineering Bulletin*, June, 18(2), 3-18.

Gupta, A., Mumick, I. S. and Subrahmanian, V. S. (1993). Maintaining views incrementally. *Proceedings of the ACM SIGMOD International Conference on Management of Data*, June, 157-166.

Gupta, H. (1999) Selection and maintenance of views in a data warehouse. *PhD Thesis, Stanford University*, September.

Gupta, H., Harinarayan, V., Rajaraman, A. and Ullman, J. (1997). Index selection for OLAP. *Proceedings of the International Conference on Data Engineering (ICDE)*, April, 208-219.

Hevner, A.R. and Rao, A. (1988). Distributed data allocation strategies. *Advances In Computers*, 12, 121-155.

Hull, R. and Zhou, G. (1996). A framework for supporting data integration using materialized and virtual approaches. *Proceedings of the ACM SIGMOD International Conference on Management of Data*, 481-492.

Hurtado, C.A., Mendelzon, O. A. and Vaisman A. A. (1999). Maintaining data cubes under dimension updates. *Proceedings of the International Conference on Data Engineering (ICDE),* March, 346-355.

Huyn. N. (1997). Multiple-view self-maintenance in data warehousing environments. *Proceedings of the International Conference on Very Large Databases*, August, 26-35.

Hyperion. *Hyperion Essbase* OLAP Server. http://www.hyperion.com/.

Informix Corporation. (1997). Informix-on-line extended parallel server and informix-universal server: A new generation of decision-support indexing for enterprise data warehouses. *White Paper.*

Informix Inc. (1997). *The Informix-MetaCube Product Suite.* http://www.informix.com.

Inmon, W.H. (1992). *Building the Data Warehouse.* John Wiley.

Jain, R. (1991). *The Art of Computer Systems Performance Analysis.* Wiley Professional Computing.

Karlapalem, K., Navathe, S. B. and Morsi, M. M. A. (1994). Issues in distributed design of object-oriented databases. In *Distributed Object Management*, Morgan Kaufman Publishers Inc., 148-165.

Kimball, R. (1996). *The Data Warehouse Toolkit.* John Wiley & Sons.

Kotidis, Y. and Roussopoulos, N. (1999). Dynamat: A dynamic view management system for data warehouses. *Proceedings of the ACM SIGMOD International Conference on Management of Data*, June, 371-382.

Labio, W., Quass, D. and Adelberg, B. (1997). Physical database design for data warehouses. *Proceedings of the International Conference on Data Engineering (ICDE).*

Lehner, W., Ruf, T. and Teschke, M. (1996). Cross-db: A feature-extended multidimensional data model for statistical and scientific databases. In *The 5th International Conference on Information and Knowledge Management (CIKM'96)*, 253-260.

Lei, H. and Ross, K. A. (1998). Faster joins, self-joins and multi-way joins using join indices. *Data and Knowledge Engineering*, November, 28(3), 277-298.

Li, C. and W. S. Wang. (1996). A data model for supporting on-line analytical processing. In *The 5th International Conference on Information and Knowledge Management (CIKM'96)*, 81-88.

Mohania, M. and Kambayashi, Y. (2000). Making aggregate views self-maintainable. *Data and Knowledge Engineering*, January, 32(1), 87-109.

Mohania, M., Samtani, S., Roddick, J. F. and Kambayashi, Y. Advances and research directions in data warehousing technology. In *The Australian Journal of Information Systems*.

Morse, S. and Isaac, D. (1984) Parallel Systems in the Data Warehouse. Prentice Hall PTR.

Navathe, S. B., Ceri, S., Wiederhold, G. and Dou J. (1984). Vertical partitioning algorithms for database design. *ACM Transaction on Database Systems*, December, 9(4), 681-710.

Navathe, S. B., Karlapalem, K. and Ra, M. (1995). A mixed partitioning methodology for distributed database design. *Journal of Computer and Software Engineering*, 3(4) 395-426.

Navathe, S. B. and Ra, M. (1989). Vertical partitioning for database design : A graphical algorithm. *ACM SIGMOD*, 440-450.

Noaman, A.Y. and Barker, K. (1999). A horizontal fragmentation algorithm for the fact relation in a distributed data warehouse. In *the 8th International Conference on Information and Knowledge Management (CIKM'99)*, November, 154-161.

O'Neil, P. and Quass, D. (1997). Improved query performance with variant indexes. *Proceedings of the ACM SIGMOD International Conference on Management of Data*, May, 38-49.

Oracle Corporation. (1992). *Oracle 7 Server Concepts Manual.* Redwood City, CA.

Oracle Corporation (1999). Oracle8i enterprise edition partitioning option. *Technical report, Oracle Corporation*, February.

Oracle Corporation. (1999). *Oracle8i Concepts.* Release 8.1.5.

Özsu, M.T. and Valduriez, P. (1991). *Principles of Distributed Database Systems.* Prentice Hall.

Quass, D., Gupta, A., Mumick, I. S. and Widom, J. (1996). Making views self-maintainable for data warehousing. In *Proceedings of the Fourth International Conference on Parallel and Distributed Information Systems*, December, 158-169.

Quass, D. and Widom, J. (1997). On-line warehouse view maintenance for batch updates. *Proceedings of the ACM SIGMOD International Conference on Management of Data*, May, 393-404.

Red Brick Systems. (1997). Star schema processing for complex queries. *White Paper*, July.

Sanjay, A., Surajit, C. and Narasayya, V. R. (2000). Automated selection of materialized views and indexes in Microsoft SQL server. In *VLDB'2000*, September.

Segev, A. and Zhao, J. L. (1995). A framework for join pattern indexing in intelligent database systems. *IEEE Transactions on Knowledge and Data Engineering*, December, 7(6), 941-947.

Simpson, D. (1996). Build your warehouse on mpp. Available at *http://www.datamation.com/servr/12mpp.html*, December.

Srivastava, D., Dar, S., Jagadish, H. and Levy, A. Y. (1996). Answering queries with aggregation using views. *Proceedings of the International Conference on Very Large Databases*, 318-329.

TPC Home Page. TPC Benchmark™ (decision support). http://www.tpc.org.

Tsichritzis, D. and Klug, A. (1978) *The Ansi/X3/Sparc Framework*. AFIPS Press, Montvale, N.J.

Valduriez, P. (1987). Join indices. *ACM Transactions on Database Systems*, June, 12(2), 218-246.

Vassiliadis, P. and Sellis, T. (1999). A survey of logical models for olap databases. *SIGMOD Record*, December, 28(4), 64-69.

Widom, J. (1995). Newblock research problems in data warehousing. In *The 4th International Conference on Information and Knowledge Management (CIKM'95)*, 25-30.

Wu, M. C. and Buchmann, A. (1997). Research issues in data warehousing. In *Datenbanksysteme In Büro, Technik und Wissenschaft(BTW'97)*, March, 61-82.

Yang, J., Karlapalem, K. and Q. Li, Q. (1997). Algorithms for materialized view design in data warehousing environment. *Proceedings of the International Conference on Very Large Databases*, August, 136-145.

Zhuge, Y., Garcia-Molina, H., Hammer, J. and Widom, J. (1995). View maintenance in a warehousing environment. *Proceedings of the ACM SIGMOD International Conference on Management of Data*, 316-327.

Zhuge, Y., Garcia-Molina, H. and Widom, J. (1996). The strobe algorithms for multi-source warehousing consistency. In *Proceeding of the Fourth International Conference on Parallel and Distributed Information Systems*, December, 146-157.

Chapter VII

Data Mining for Supply Chain Management in Complex Networks: Concepts, Methodology and Application

Manoj K. Singh
i2 Technologies, USA

Mahesh S. Raisinghani
University of Dallas, USA

ABSTRACT

The concept and philosophy behind supply chain management is to integrate and optimize business processes across all partners in the entire production chain. Since these are not simple supply chains but rather complex networks, tuning these complex networks comprising supply chain/s to the needs of the market can be facilitated by data mining. Data mining is a set of techniques used to uncover previously obscure or unknown patterns and relationships in very large databases. It provides better information for achieving competitive advantage, increases operating efficiency, reduces operating costs and provides flexibility in using the data by allowing the users to pull the data they need instead of letting the system push the data. However, making sense of all this data is an enormous technological and logistical challenge. This chapter helps you understand the key concepts of data mining, its methodology and application in the context of supply chain management of complex networks.

INTRODUCTION

Fundamentally, a supply chain comprises the flow of products, information and money. In traditional supply chain management, business processes are disconnected from stock control and as a result, inventory is a direct output of incomplete or inaccurate information. The focus of contemporary supply chain management is on the organization, planning and implementation of these flows. First, at the organizational level, products are manufactured in one or several stages, transported and stored based on the customer's needs. This helps in determining the optimal structure of production sites, warehouses and transport and may involve business process reengineering. Second, the planning and control of component production, storage and transport are managed using central supply management and replenished through centralized procurement. Third, the implementation of the supply chain involves the entire cycle from the order entry process to order fulfillment and delivery. An order can result in new production orders, reiterations of stock reservations or orders placed with ancillary suppliers. Data mining can create a better match between supply and demand, reducing or sometimes even eliminating stocks.

Data mining, a process of discovering ideas in data, has become an indispensable tool in trying to understand the needs, preferences and behaviors of customers. It is used in pricing, promotion and product development. For instance, at Bank of America, the data mining efforts led to the unusual step of reducing required minimum balances in customers' checking accounts for two consecutive years. The bank learned that customers who have difficulty maintaining a minimum balance may take their business to competitors with lower minimum balance requirements. While it was clear that for a certain segment of the customer base, the minimum checking account balance was a key factor in their choice of banks, they needed to know if handling those customers' accounts was profitable for the bank. If the defecting customer did not contribute to the bottom line of the bank, then the smart decision would have been to leave the minimum balance alone (Fabris, 1998). Bank of America found the answer to this question by utilizing the data mining tool. This is a typical example of the application of data mining in the banking industry.

Traditionally data mining techniques have been used in banking, insurance and retail business. This is largely because of the fact that the implementation of these techniques seemed quite obvious and showed quick returns. For instance, data mining is being used for customer profiling where characteristics of good customers are identified with the goals of predicting new customers and helping marketing departments target new prospects. The patterns found in a customer database are applied to a prospect database for customer acquisition and target promotions. The effectiveness of sales promotions/product positioning can be analyzed using market-basket analysis to determine which products are purchased together or by an individual over time, which products to stock in a particular store and where to place products in each store (Weir, 1998; Groth 2000). In addition, data mining is used in a variety of other industries such as stock forecasting, portfolio analysis and credit risk analysis in the financial industry; cross-selling and customer loyalty in the banking industry; neural networks to perform protein analysis, and fraud detection, customized care in the healthcare industry; and data visualization to show problem areas for a wireless telecommunications network and customer retention in the telecommunications industry, among others.

There are a lot of opportunities and applications of data mining even beyond the obvious. One of the potential areas is "Supply Chain Management." The management of supply chain is essentially the management of supply and demand in the value chain from one end (suppliers) to the other end (customers). This is precisely the area where data mining can be of immense use.

One of the realities of the demand and supply in the manufacturing industry is that no matter how well balanced a system is or how correctly the factors that affect the system are known, there is an element of uncertainty that creates a mismatch between demand and supply. This uncertainty is present in almost all aspects of the supply chain. Some software, typically called supply chain management software, attempt to balance this disparity between supply and demand by reducing the uncertainty in the business process. Unfortunately, uncertainty cannot be completely eliminated.

The objective of this chapter is to identify those areas in the supply chain where most of the uncertainty exists (i.e., ascertain where application of data mining may yield good results) and to determine suitable data mining methods to accurately predict uncertainty. The underlying assumption of this chapter is that a data warehouse has been implemented before the data mining techniques can be applied.

A KEY BUSINESS PROBLEM: UNCERTAINTY

There are two issues that plague the supply chain management, variation in demand and supply, and the speed and extent of communication of the variation to the parts of the supply chain. Variation in demand and supply is due to the inherent uncertainty present in the processes that lead to demand and supply. Hence, it it is correct to say that managing a supply chain management system is synonymous to managing the uncertainty in the supply chain, and improving the communication within the supply chain. Managing uncertainty will be the focus of this chapter.

Uncertainty is present in demand, supply and the process that tries to match the two. Predicting accurately the uncertainties in demand, supply and processes, and then formulating action plans around them, is the essence of supply chain management (SCM).

Figure 1. Information and material flows in the supply chain

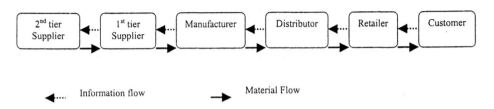

Before we can address the problem of uncertainty in a supply chain and explain the use of data mining techniques to solve them, we need to understand the basic process of SCM where uncertainty exists. In its most simplified form, supply chain can be depicted as the flow of information from a customer's customer to a supplier's supplier and then the flow of material in the reverse direction, as shown in Figure 1.

The whole supply chain can be conceptually broken down into a series of demand and supply with a process in between. Any point in the supply chain can be depicted as:

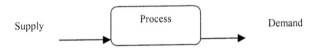

The approach followed in this chapter is to analyze each point in the supply chain as Supply – Process – Demand and then determine specific areas of uncertainty and ways to solve these areas using a data mining tool.

Data mining vs. traditional forecasting planners of supply chains use demand and supply forecasting as a means of controlling uncertainty. There are some inherent limitations in the traditional forecasting methods since a model has to be built based on the known set of parameters before statistical techniques can be applied on the past data to predict the future values as closely as possible.

The three major drawbacks to traditional methods of forecasting are:
1. Incorrect forecasting model
2. Incorrect number of parameters
3. Incorrect coefficients values of these parameters

Each of these three problems can be solved using data mining. These models are chosen from a finite set of predefined models traditional method of forecasting. In data mining, the model is iteratively built as many times as needed in order to extract previously unknown patterns and relationships in data that enhance projections into the future. The number of parameters that are considered in a forecasting model are constrained by the model or the knowledge/imagination of the modeler. However, when forecasting using data mining techniques, the program can detect even minor effects of some parameters, which are almost inconceivable by the human imagination.

DATA MINING: METHODS AND PROCESS

Before we analyze the supply chain and the applications of data mining, a brief overview of data mining concepts, methods and processes is provided.

What Is Data Mining?

Data mining is the process of extracting ideas in data. Data mining can be defined as "a decision support process that tries to discover patterns and relationships, that are beyond the realm of human experience and imagination, in the large database and present them to a knowledgeable user for review and examination" or "as the process of extracting previously **unknown, valid** and **actionable** information from large databases and then using the information to make crucial business decisions" (Groth, 2000).

Data mining is the key to maximizing the data warehouse value. Essentially, data mining discovers patterns and relationships hidden in the data. It is a part of a larger process called knowledge discovery--specifically, the step in which advanced statistical analysis and modeling techniques are applied to the data to find useful patterns and relationships. The knowledge discovery process as a whole is essential for successful data mining because it describes the steps you must take to ensure meaningful results.

Other business intelligence methodologies, such as standard reports, ad hoc queries and on-line analytical processing (OLAP)[1], use a verification-based approach in which the user hypothesizes about specific data relationships and then uses the tools to verify or refute those presumptions. For instance, in OLAP which is user-driven, the analyst generates a hypothesis and uses the OLAP tool to verify the hypothesis. By contrast, data mining uses a discovery-based approach in which pattern matching and other algorithms are employed to determine the key relationships in the data.

For example, an analyst might hypothesize that people with high debt and low incomes are bad credit risks. The analyst would use OLAP in various ways to verify or disprove that hypothesis. A data mining tool, however, would be used to find the risk factors for granting credit. The tool, for example, might discover that people with high debt and low incomes were bad credit risks. In addition, data mining might also discover a pattern that the analyst did not even consider, such as that debt-to-income ratio and age indicate risk.

[1] OLAP is a method of viewing data multidimensionally. It is defined by the OLAP council as "a category of software technology that enables analysts, managers and executives to gain insight into data through fast, consistent, interactive access to a wide variety of possible views of information that has been transformed from raw data to reflect the real dimensionality of the enterprise as understood by the user." Other OLAP tools include ROLAP (Relational OLAP), DOLAP (Desktop OLAP), MOLAP (Multidimensional OLAP) and HOLAP (Hybrid OLAP).

This is where data mining and OLAP complement one another. Before acting on the pattern, the analyst needs to know the financial implications of using the discovered pattern to govern who gets credit. OLAP helps you answer these types of questions. Furthermore, OLAP can enhance the early stages of the knowledge discovery process by helping you understand data by focusing attention on the important variables, identifying exceptions or finding interactions. These operations are important because the better data is understood, the more effective the knowledge discovery process.

DATA MINING METHODS

The various approaches to data mining can be broadly classified into methodologies and technologies. Data mining methodologies consist of cluster analysis, linkage analysis, visualization and categorization analysis. The technologies consist of connectionist models or neural networks, decision trees, genetic algorithms, fuzzy logic, statistical approaches and time series approaches. The two basic categories of data mining methods are statistical models (i.e., correlation, cluster analysis, discriminant analysis, probability distributions and regression) and a branch of artificial intelligence called machine learning/inductive reasoning (i.e., case-based reasoning, decision trees, fuzzy logic, genetic algorithms, neural networks, pattern recognition, rough set and rule induction) (Chen et al., 2000). Data mining is used to build six types of models aimed at solving business problems: classification, regression, time series, clustering, association analysis and sequence discovery. Classification and regression are primarily applied to prediction, while association and sequence discovery are primarily used to describe behavior that is captured in a database. Clustering may be used for either prediction or description.

Classification

In this method, a predictive model is generated based on the historical data. These models are used to assign instances (or membership) to a group or class by calculating the value of a categorical variable. The value of these categorical variables are generally binary in nature, such as, true or false or likely or unlikely responses. It can include multiple but discrete values.

Regression

Regression is similar to classification in the sense that it is also primarily used for prediction of values for categorical variables. However, in this case, the values are continuous, real numbers, i.e., it has values even in decimals. There is no fixed range in which the values of the variables are fitted. Regression uses a series of existing values and their attributes to forecast continuous values since this data can have any value in an interval of real numbers.

Time-Series Forecasting

This method is similar to regression in that it uses a series of existing values and their attributes to forecast future values, except that the values of the categorical variables are dependent on time. Using various data mining tools, the distinctive features of time can be exploited. These features include seasonality, effects of holidays, hierarchy of periods (e.g., number of work days per week or 15-month year), and special considerations such as how much of the past is relevant to the future

Clustering

Clustering is used to segment a database into clusters, with the members of each cluster sharing a number of interesting properties. This is interesting because these classes of clusters are not predefined (as in the case of classification) and hence are not constrained by the limited perception and knowledge of the user. There are generally two basic uses of clustering: one, for summarizing the contents of the target database (by looking at the parameters or characteristics of each cluster) and second, as an input to the other methods, like supervised induction (classification). Clustering differs from other methods in that the objective of this process is less precisely defined as compared to other methods and hence, is subject to occurrence of redundant and irrelevant features.

Association

Association is used to describe behavior that is captured in the database. This method tries to relate the occurrences of various events by identifying patterns or groups of items. Many times related occurrences of events are quite logical and obvious, so much so that they are called related events. For example, the buying of shaving blade and shaving cream are typically considered related events. In such cases, data mining is useful only in the prediction of probability of occurrence. In the shaving example, the relationship is expressed in terms of the likelihood of buying one and the other. Data mining is particularly useful in identifying not so obvious and often interesting associations of events. One such association might be that men who buy red ties often buy cigars.

Sequencing

Sequencing is similar to association analysis except that it also adds a temporal dimension. It identifies items that are likely to occur together on a sequence basis. For example, a set of customers with frequent buying patterns may be analyzed for items bought in sequential order (Weir, 1998). This could help marketers in timing their promotions to correlate with this sequential buying order exhibited by their customers.

DATA MINING PROCESS

Robert Grossman, director of the National Center for Data Mining at the University of Illinois at Chicago, classifies the data mining process into four phases. Each of these phases is described in Table 1 (Grossman, 1998):

Phase 1: Data Warehousing

Data warehousing is the foundation for successfully applying data mining techniques and other analytical and predictive tools. In order to have good results, the data must be accurate and reliable. Users must assess the availability of relevant, clean data to support complex analysis (Fabris, 1998). Data warehousing involves the transfer, conversion and integration of data from legacy systems to a central repository where data is stored and made available to clients. The process involves the conversion of data where it is transformed, normalized and scrubbed to get rid of anomalies, and correctly mapped to the new target database (Grossman, 1998).

The downside of data warehousing is the high cost of implementation and the time it takes to complete the process. Data warehouses can cost in excess of $10 million to build and take anywhere from one to three years to complete (Peacock, 1998). This is a very expensive and time-consuming effort. The Palo Alto Management Group, an industry research firm, estimates that companies will spend $73 billion on hardware, software and services related to sorting out customer data in 2001, up from $10 billion today (Peacock, 1998).

An alternative is the use of a datamart, which is a functional or departmental data repository. A datamart is extracted data from systems that are critical to the unit

Table 1. Four phases of the data mining process

Phase	Name	Description
1	Data Warehousing	System for managing data for decision support. Data is gathered, cleaned and transformed from operational systems and third-party sources to create the data warehouse.
2	Data Mining	Data is extracted from a data warehouse and used to produce a predictive model or rule set. This phase can be automated.
3	Predictive Modeling	One or more predictive models are selected or combined in order to produce an optimal model. The models may be from data mining systems, may be produced by statisticians or modelers or may be purchased from third parties.
4	Predictive Scoring	Predictive models are used to score operational and transactional data.

owning the datamart and from selected external sources. Datamarts can be constructed as individual components. Datamarts usually cost between $10,000 and $1 million to build and can be brought on-line in less than six months. The major drawback of this approach is that the architecture of the datamart often turns out to be inconsistent with the architecture of other datamarts and the data warehouse (Peacock, 1998).

In addition, the data in a data warehouse must be robust enough to support meaningful and effective) analysis and yield hidden patterns and relationships. According to A.J. Brown of Data Mind in California, "Businesses typically lack basic customer information like billing history or call-center information. Too many times they have created the data warehouses or extract files with a limited set of data." To correct this, data may also be enriched with additional attributes. This may be accomplished by adding data extracted from other internal databases or purchased from third-party sources (Asbrand, 1997).

Data mining provides more meaningful data when it uses large databases extracted into data warehouses. Data warehouses are not necessarily needed to support data mining but not using one to support data mining would be analogous to using a bulldozer to landscape a yard. Data mining technology is more commonly used in large consumer-oriented businesses such as banking and the retail industry because of the extremely high cost of implementation. An example of the importance of accurate data in data mining efforts comes from the banking industry, which has used data mining successfully to predict how customers will react to interest rate adjustments, which customers will be most receptive to new product offers, which customers present the highest risk for defaulting on a loan and how to make each customer relationship more profitable.

Banks historically have had separate databases for different areas (i.e., mortgages, auto loans and checking accounts). In order to take advantage of the relationships within and among the data in these areas, an organization needs enterprise-wide access to all customer data. Unfortunately, data fields that appear in more than one database may have different data definitions or data types, thus creating misleading comparisons. These inconsistencies have to be corrected before data mining can begin. This is no simple task and it slows down the work of a data mining group. The Bank of America in San Francisco estimates that about 75% of its time is spent on data validation (Fabris, 1998; Kim, 1998).

Phase 2: Data Mining Tools

Algorithms are applied to the data in order to produce predictive models. Although this step can be automated, the key is the selection of the appropriate techniques. As we see from the examples listed, these are not generic tools that can be applied in all cases. The selection of tools depends on the proper identification of a business problem and analysis to determine the correct technique to use. Some common types of problems and the technique used in data mining are illustrated in Table 2 (META Group, 1997):

The following are high-level definitions of these techniques (Nelson, 1998):

Neural Networks build internal representations of the patterns, attempting to simulate the way the human brain discovers patterns. With this technique, the

Table 2. Problem types and techniques used in data mining

Example	Problem Type	Technique
What are the top three charac- teristics of customers who have switched to my competition?	Classification	Neural Networks Decision Tree
What are the largest buckets within my customer base to which I should be marketing a new service?	Clustering	Neural Networks Decision Tree
What is the likelihood a given individual who opens a bank account will also open an IRA within the next three months?	Association and Sequencing	Statistical Techniques Rule Induction
What will the average exchange rate be over the next three months?	Regression and Forecasting	Neural Networks Statistical Techniques

machine primarily handles the discovery process as the neural network builds its representations. These can best be used when firms have large amounts of data of unknown value.

Induction Techniques (decision trees and rule induction) assign the largest portion of the discovery process to the machine. When patterns are forming, induction techniques are appropriate, but an analyst needs to direct the process to avoid wasting time on spurious relationships.

Statistics incorporate a higher level of user involvement to build the models describing the behavior of the data. Interpreting the results requires a fair amount of expertise.

The key in using these tools is to understand that it requires a team effort between the analysts, the marketing experts and information technology experts. Not only is it very important to understand what approach to use in each case, but also to have an intimate knowledge of the information and the competitive and environmental forces that may have an impact on the final decision (Peacock, 1998).

Phase 3: Predictive Modeling

During this phase, the predictive models are analyzed and combined to produce a single aggregate model. These techniques may be mixed sequentially or in parallel. Sequentially, the user picks a technique to produce a model and then applies another technique to the results. In parallel, the user chooses different techniques and applies them all to the initial dataset.

Phase 4: Predictive Scoring

During this phase, the predictive models are applied to score operational data (Grossman, 1998). For instance, a bank could analyze the attributes and habits of its checking account customers for clues that might reveal an acceptable minimum balance in order to retain profitable customers. The bank can use data mining to develop profiles of customer groups inclusive of members consistently having trouble maintaining minimum balances. The data mining techniques can provide answers to questions like, "How many checks do they draw per month?" "Do they use ATMs or conduct most of their business with tellers?" "What other accounts do they have?" "What products and services do they use?" The answers to these questions can help the bank identify profitable customers and predict the minimum balance needed to retain them. As a result, the percentage of profitable customers can rise by a significant percentage (Fabris, 1998). (Please note: The intent of this chapter is to provide an overview of different data mining methods and not serve as an exhaustive reference.)

APPLICATIONS OF DATA MINING IN SUPPLY CHAIN MANAGEMENT

Manufacturers, airlines, banks, insurance companies, credit card companies and retailers have successfully used data mining technology. For instance, LTV Steel Corporation, the third largest steel maker in the U.S., has managed to reduce defects by 99% using data mining to detect potential quality problems.

Data mining is not the stand-alone solution for the problems of supply chain management. It will work best as a supplement to the existing tools available for supply chain management. It can be used with decision support systems to improve the overall result of the system. For example, data mining tools can be used to provide the most reliable demand forecast to a decision support system (DSS), which then tries to propagate the demand upstream to the supply chain. On the way, data mining tools can be used to provide the most accurate picture of the capacity, maintenance and factory scheduling problems. The DSS can take this information as input to provide the planner with an optimal factory scheduling solution. Further upstream, data mining tools can provide correct prediction of the future suppliers. This information can be propagated forward up the supply chain, helping planners to make correct decisions regarding customer demand.

Figure 1 is a highly simplified and generic view of the supply chain. Under this broad framework of supplier, manufacturer and distributor, the detailed structure of supply chain varies quite a lot depending on the type of industry, e.g., automobile, consumer goods, high technology and so forth. It will be

Figure 2. The supply chain model of the personal computer industry

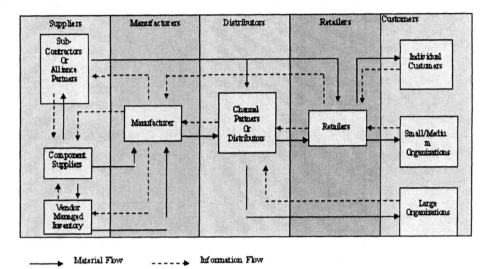

interesting to discuss the application of data mining by focusing on any one particular industry's supply chain in order to control for industry effects. Similar concepts can be applied to other industries. We chose the high-technology industry as the template for this chapter.

The supply chain model of the PC industry is shown in Figure 2.

Next we look at each segment of this supply chain to understand the application of data mining.

Retailers

At this point of the supply chain, retailers receive the forecast from primarily two sources, one directly from the individual customer (this is more of the retailer's own forecast) and the other from small and medium-size organizations. Actual

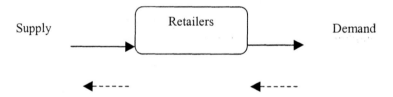

consumption by the individual customers and medium and small organizations is added. The difference between the forecast and the actual consumption is the variation in the demand. On the upstream, retailers send the request to distributors, as well as manufacturers. They respond with the supply from distributors and sub-contractors. The difference between the request and the supply accounts for the variation in the supply.

Data mining can be used at this point in the following ways:

Market Segmentation

This is the first and most obvious use of data mining. One of the first principles of SCM is the segmentation of customers based on service needs of distinct groups and the adaptation of the supply chain to serve these segments profitably. Traditionally, markets were segmented based on certain known parameters. Data mining can help in segmenting the market at a more granular level of detail and also create segments, which until recently were not conceivable by human analysis. This fine-grained segmentation may result in better prediction of customer demand.

Market Basket Analysis

By using the data mining method known as Association, retailers can understand the buying behavior of the customers. For example, the probability that a customer from given market segment (done in the previous step) buys a printer, scanner, other office accessories, when he/she buys a personal computer (PC) may be determined.

Target Promotion

Data mining can help in identifying optimal audience for micro-marketing campaigns. With the use of a computerized approach and an extensive database, retailers can identify the group of people who have switched brands in a given timeframe. They can also determine the reason and pattern associated with brand switching. Thus, the effectiveness of the promotion campaign may be maximized.

Distributors

At this point in the supply chain, distributors receive the forecast from retailers and large organizations. They pair this data with the actual consump-

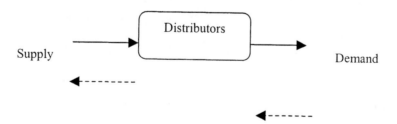

tion by the retailers and large organizations. The difference between the forecast and the actual consumption is the variation in the demand. On the upstream, distributors send the request to manufacturers, in response to which it receives the supply from both manufacturers as well as sub-contractors. The difference between the promise and the actual supply accounts for the variation in the supply. Data mining can be used at this point in the following ways:

Predictions of Supply Uncertainties

Data mining can be used to predict the supply uncertainties at two levels, one at the supplier level (which in this case are manufacturers and sub-contractors) and at the item level. At the supplier level, Classification can be used to classify suppliers based on their past performance in terms of meeting the supply schedule and quantity. At the item level, for each segment of supplier, items can be classified into clusters based on the delivery performance. For every item, predictions can be made about its supply schedule using Regression and Time-Series Forecasting methods.

Predictions of Process Uncertainties

The process involved at the distributor's place is essentially receiving, storing and dispatching. There is not much variation in the process involved at this stage. The only cause of variation during these three sub-processes can be loss and item obsolescence. Rather than using data mining to determine the percentage of losses, the percentage itself should be kept to a minimum by streamlining the business processes.

Predictions of Demand Uncertainties

The first step of predicting demand uncertainties would be to carry out the market segmentation for retailers and big customers based on a multitude of factors such as volume of demand, periodicity, variations, etc. The classification and clustering methods of the data mining tool can be used for this. Then for every segment, probability of variation in demand can be predicted using "Regression" and Time-Series Forecasting.

Stockout Prediction at the Warehouse

This is a direct result of the inaccurate predictions made in the supply, demand and the process. But still there could be some other unknown factors leading to stockouts such as store layout, equipment used for storing and moving goods in the warehouse, human-related issues or other factors. For such applications, data mining can be immensely useful.

Strategic Implications

Bradley (1998) feels that it is no longer sufficient for an organization to focus on cutting costs. Logistics executives must focus on strategies that help create value. Logistics (i.e., the art of moving the goods) needs to become a tool to help accomplish corporate strategic objectives, such as reducing working capital, taking assets off the balance sheet, accelerating cash-to-cash cycles and increasing inventory returns. He identifies three areas that will drive the value of logistics:

- Improving customer value
- Improving company economics
- Improving organizational element.

Data mining can be particularly useful in improving the customer value. Data mining can help in identifying:

- Who are the most valuable customers?
- Who are the customers who are very sensitive to customer service level?
- What supply chain strategies are critical to these customers?

Quinn (1998) gives an example of Polaroid, as to how they designed and implemented an effective supply chain. According to Abbott Weiss, Polaroid's vice president of worldwide logistics, the strategy development effort had to meet the specific performance objectives in three key areas–customer service, inventory turns and operating efficiency. To achieve these objectives they set out four basic strategies:

- Integrate–Design and operate the worldwide logistics network as a single system, coordinated production planning, transportation, distribution, inventory and duty management on global basis.
- Differentiate–Tailor the response of the logistics system to the different needs of customer and product lines in a profitable manner.
- Rationalize–Optimize the work and resource, minimizing the cost of warehousing, freight and duty throughout the system.
- Become flexible or agile–Develop logistic processes that are demand-driven, fast cycle and ready to deal with unexpected customer requirements.

Data mining can be used to accomplish these strategies by differentiating the customers based on their specific needs, identifying the areas in the warehousing and transportation that are cause of the major costs, and accurately predicting the demand patterns.

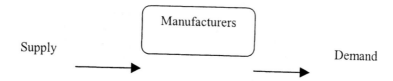

Manufacturers

At this point in the supply chain, manufacturers receive the demand from distributors or directly from retailers. Manufacturers pass on the demand of retailers to alliance partners and try to fulfill only the demand of distributors. The difference between the forecasted demand from distributors and the actual consumption by the distributors is the variation in the demand. On the upstream, manufacturers send the request to alliance partners as well as component suppliers for components. Alliance partners directly send the finished goods to retailers and in some small percentage to distributors. The difference between the promise and the actual supply from component suppliers accounts for the variation in the supply for manufacturers.

Data mining can be used at this point in the following ways:

Predictions of Supply Uncertainties

- Similar to distributors, data mining can be used to predict the supply uncertainties for manufacturers at two levels: the supplier level (which in this case are component suppliers) and the item level.
    - At the supplier level, classification can be used to classify suppliers based on their past performance in terms of meeting the supply schedule and quantity. The classification and resulting prediction in supply can also take into account other known factors such as geography and location of the suppliers, as well as other unknown factors.
    - At the item level, frequent quality-related rejections and late deliveries of items can be related to the nature of the item. There may be certain items with specific manufacturing operations that lead to these quality and delivery problems. There may be other factors such as the material used for manufacturing that item, the manufacturing process used and others. Data mining may be used to group these items using clustering, and then every group-specific case can be related to the problem associated with that group.

Predictions of Process Uncertainties

The uncertainty in the manufacturing process is generally related to the sudden breakdown of the machines, unexplained poor performance of the machines (quality related), worker performance and so forth. The former is related to the maintenance of the machines. Based on the past history of the machine, data mining can be used to predict the timing of the breakdown of the machines, and this can help in carrying out the predictive maintenance of the machines. Data mining can also be used to classify workers based on the best performance time for the worker. Some workers are more efficient in the day shifts, whereas others are in the night. Also, based on the performance and skill sets of the workers and their performance of specific machines, an association can be determined between the machines and the workers, thereby optimally allocating workers to these machines for the best performance of the man and machine.

Predictions of Demand Uncertainties

Data mining can be used to predict uncertainty and the related patterns in demand from distributors based on:

- Type of distributor
- Type of item
- Location of distributor

- Time of the year
- Interaction between multiple items
- Other unknown factors

This prediction can be based either on a single factor or all of the factors (known and unknown). A typical example might be fluctuations in demand for notebooks in a year, based on the type of distributor, its location, the number and type of notebooks, time of the year as well as other factors.

Predicting Future Trends in Demand of the Product

Data mining tools can predict the future with great certainty by discovering trends in the demand of the product. These are particularly useful for high technology industries (e.g., PC), where the product lifecycle is very short, (less than six months) and new technology quickly makes the product obsolete. Under such circumstances, it is of great competitive advantage to the company that can predict future trends based on factors such as technological advances, and changing tastes and preferences of the customers.

Mass Customization

Another area where data mining can be used is in identifying the products for mass customization at the delivery end. Mass customization is a key success factor for the supply chain management of the PC industry. Companies like Hewlett-Packard, Dell and Gateway 2000, among others in the high-tech industry, are trying to follow this strategy. These companies implement mass customization by putting together unique customer orders from a large number of products, while minimizing the inventory of product components. Data mining can be of immense help in identifying these permutations and also in identifying the demand pattern for these permutations. This will greatly help in improving the customer service level.

DATA MINING IMPLEMENTATION ARCHITECTURE

A data mining application can be an effective tool only when implemented along with some existing decision support system, which sits on the top of an enterprise resource planning (ERP) system. The difference between a decision support system (DSS) and data mining application is that unlike data mining applications, DSSs do not perform queries or analysis of data. Instead, they use the data in whatever form is available as an input to a function based on some decision support logic. For example, SCM software would take the customer demand as an input and use it for calculating feasibility of meeting those demands based on some other input such as material and capacity availability. On the other hand, a data mining application would analyze the customer

Figure 3. The data mining implementation architecture

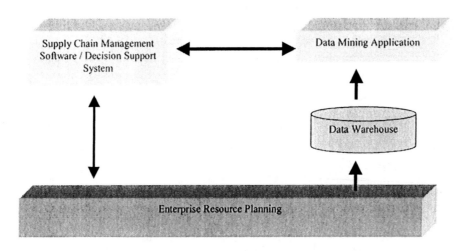

demand and classify these demands based on certain parameters such as recurring demands and seasonal demands. Customer demands, based on these classifications, can be fed into a DSS. If its logic can be built into a DSS to allocate resources (material and capacity) based on this classification, it can result in the optimal utilization of resources to meet customer demand. Figure 3 illustrates the manner in which this marriage between DSS and data mining affects the implementation architecture.

An ERP system integrates processes of an organization. Data related to these processes are scattered throughout the system. This large amount of unorganized data cannot be used as it is for data mining applications. A data warehouse has to be built which organizes ERP data so that it is easily accessible and organized for on-line analysis.

The smooth flow of information from ERP to a data mining tool through a data warehouse will require open metadata integration. Information describing the ERP data, the target data warehouse schema, and the data mappings and transformation rules needs to be stored in an open relational metadata repository and to be easily accessible to the data mining tools used in the architecture. This facilitates changes made to the underlying warehouse. It then passes these changes to the analysis tools and makes available complete information to end-users, such as the source of the data flows and frequency of updates (Coombs, 1999).

Within the data mining implementation architecture, there are a number of specific algorithms or models that may be applied. Each has its own strengths and weaknesses regarding the problem characteristics best addressed, discrimination capabilities, performance and training requirements (Haskett, 2000). Some of the more common implementation issues include results interpretation, data selection and representation, and system scalability considerations.

IMPLICATIONS FOR MANAGEMENT

Data mining creates a fertile ground for the invention of new tools, analytical methods and data management to add value to an organization's most valuable asset—its data. The data in its original form is valuable, but transformations will maximize the information content. Organizations have experienced paybacks of 10 to 70 times their data warehouse investment after data mining components are added (Chen et al., 2000). Data mining can do everything that a statistical querying tool or OLAP can do. But it is not meant to be used for simple querying or reporting purposes, nor complex queries where the parameters are known. Data mining is ideal for cases where only the problem is known, and neither the parameters nor the values of the parameters are known.

In the context of the supply chain management, the decision to use data mining should not start with the data mining tool. Technology is only a partial solution to some of its business problems. It is more important to formulate the business problems and opportunities rather than to start at the technology side. A company should ask the following questions:

1. What are the main business problems and opportunities in the supply chain?
2. What knowledge does a company need to solve these problems or explore opportunities?
3. Can a company use this knowledge to take appropriate action?
4. Does a company have the necessary (historical) data available on demand, supply and process behavior to make an analysis potentially successful?
5. Given a company's knowledge need, what would be the appropriate technique to analyze the available data?

After answering all these questions, a company may decide whether data mining is an appropriate technology. Once data mining has been selected, a company should start by composing a project team, collecting and preparing the right data, performing the analysis by interpreting and deploying models, and monitoring the results. The key to success, however, is to have a thorough understanding of the data and business requirements.

CONCLUSION

A common characteristic shared by the industry users of data mining technology is the data intensive. Data and information play critical roles in achieving organizational goals in these industries.

Now that the benefits of data mining have been sufficiently proven in a wide variety of business sectors, it's time to expand the horizon of the application of data mining to other potential areas such as supply chain management. This chapter makes an initial effort in exploring the possibility of using data mining in supply chain management. There is a huge potential for improvement in supply chain management using the techniques of data mining. The effort required to implement data mining techniques is, by no means, going to be easy given the vastness of the extent and issues in the management of supply chains and the relative infancy of data mining (despite its rapid growth). If small areas can be identified and an incremental approach followed to studying supply chain management, the early adopters of this technology will reap major benefits. As various applications in a wide variety of industries have proven, data mining is increasingly enabling companies to realize the true value of data. Considering the capabilities of today's data mining software, the power of hidden patterns and relations in supply chain data will lead to important differentiating factors in the competitive global business environment.

REFERENCES

Asbrand, D. (1997). Is data mining ready for the masses? *Datamation* 11.

Bradley, P. (1998). The value imperative. *Logistics.* December.

Bucatinsky, J. (1998). Evading regulation gets a little tougher. *Wall Street & Technology*, August, 56-58.

Bernstein, M. and Dresner, H. (1998). *Data Mining Tools for Marketing.*

Callaghan, D. (1998). NBA teams discover power of data mining. *Midrange Systems*, June 15, 53.

Chen, L., Sakaguchi, T. and Frolick, M. N. (2000). Data mining methods, applications, and tools. *Information Systems Management*, Winter, 17(1), 65-70.

Chein, T. W., Chinho, L., Tan, B. and Lee, W. C. (1999). A neural networks-based approach for strategic planning. *Information & Management*, 35, 357-364.

Coombs, J. (1999). A decision support portal for SAP and other ERP applications. *Data Warehousing*, 7.

Davis, B. (1998). Shared vision' makes IT pay off. *Information Week*. September 14, 93-100.

Fabris, P. (1998). Data mining. *CIO Magazine.*

Foley, J. and Russell J. (1998). Mining your own business. *Information Week*, 18-22.

Grossman, R. (1998). Supporting the data mining process with next generation data mining systems. *Enterprise Systems Journal*, 52-56.

Groth, R. (2000). *Data Mining: Building Competitive Advantage.* Prentice Hall, 191-209.

Haskett, M. (2000). An intro to data mining: Analyzing the tools and techniques. *Enterprise Systems Journal*, May, 34-39.

Kim, W. (1998). Data mining: Promises, reality and future. *Journal of Object-Oriented Programming.* 12-14.

Manchur, D. (1998). Mining for fraud. *Canadian Insurance.* September, 24-27.

McGee, M. (1997). Data mine cures common gold. *Information Week.* December 1, 64.

Nelson, S. (1998). Data mining techniques: Solutions or more problems? *Gartner Group Research Report*, T-04-1221

Neyhart, S. (1998). Using data mining to get brand switching. *Medical Marketing & Media*, April, 80-84.

O Brien, J. (1998). ABC Bancorp gets better control of information updates, costs. *Bank Systems and Technology*, September, 56.

Parsaye, K. (1998) Data mining: Bridging the gap. *Database Programming & Design.*

Quinn, F. J. (1998). Building a world class supply chain. *Logistics*, June.

Spangler, W. E., May, J. H. and Vargas, L. G. (1999). Choosing data-mining methods for multiple classification: Representational and performance measurement implications for decision support. *Journal of Management Information Systems*, Summer, 16(1), 37-62.

Thomsen, E. (1998). Smart decision-support systems. *Database Programming Design*, 59-61.

Totty, P. (1998). Data warehousing. *Credit Union Magazine*, November, 58-62.

Weir, J. (1998). Data mining: Exploring the corporate asset. *Information Systems Management*, Fall, 68-71.

Chapter VIII

Accommodating Hierarchies in Relational Databases

Ido Millet
Penn State Erie, USA

INTRODUCTION

Relational databases and the current SQL standard are poorly suited to retrieval of hierarchical data. After demonstrating the problem, this chapter describes how two approaches to data denormalization can facilitate hierarchical data retrieval. Both approaches solve the problem of data retrieval, but as expected, come at the cost of difficult and potentially inconsistent data updates. This chapter then describes how we can address these update-related shortcomings via back-end (triggers) logic. Using a proper combination of denormalized data structure and back-end logic, we can have the best of both worlds: easy data retrieval and simple, consistent data updates.

Figure 1. A typical unit hierarchy

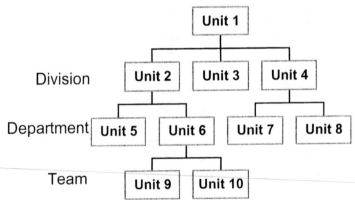

Figure 2. A normalized data model with a unit hierarchy

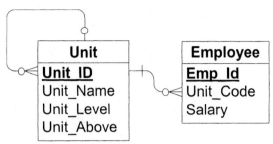

Hierarchies occur in a variety of application areas such as biology, geography, manufacturing, accounting, knowledge management, marketing and human resources. Consider, for example, the organizational unit hierarchy depicted in Figure 1.

Since each unit has at most one parent, we can easily implement this hierarchy via a recursive relationship. This means that each unit record can maintain a foreign key pointing at the unit above it. Figure 2 shows a data model for this situation, including a relationship between Unit and Employee entities.

It should be noted that for many situations involving data hierarchies, flexibility can be gained by adding a lookup table that maintains the domain-specific name for each level. This allows the same data model to serve different needs. For example, some organizations may refer to units at level 2 as Divisions, while others may refer to such units as Departments, Groups, Branches, Stores or Offices. A hierarchy level lookup table allows easy adaptation of the same system to different contexts and different organizations.

To demonstrate the difficulty of hierarchical data retrieval against the normalized data model in Figure 2, consider the following requests:
- Show a list of all units under unit 2
- Show a list of all employees in or under a given division
- Show how many employees work in or under each division
- Show total employee salaries for each division including all units below it

Using SQL, we can easily join each employee with her unit, but we cannot easily identify the division (parent unit at level 2) for each unit. This is because for each unit we know only the immediate parent. This difficulty in locating parent nodes at any given level is at the heart of the problem.

SQL-BASED SOLUTIONS

While hierarchies pose a significant challenge for SQL, complex SQL can solve surprisingly tough problems. For example, the SQL statement in Listing 1 will return all units under division 2. The result set, shown in Figure 3, can then be established as a view and joined with employees to answer more complex queries.

The SQL:1999 standard (ANSI/ISO/IEC 9075-2-1999) pushes the limits of hierarchy data retrieval even further by supporting recursive queries. For example,

Listing 1: Hierarchy Retrieval with UNION Statements

```
SELECT unit_id, unit_name FROM UNIT WHERE unit_above = 2

UNION ALL

SELECT unit_id, unit_name FROM UNIT WHERE unit_above IN
  (SELECT unit_id FROM UNIT WHERE unit_above = 2)

UNION ALL

SELECT unit_id, unit_name FROM UNIT WHERE unit_above IN
  (SELECT unit_id FROM UNIT WHERE unit_above IN
    (SELECT unit_id FROM UNIT WHERE unit_above = 2)) ;
```

the request to show total employee salaries for each division, including all units below it, can be handled using the SQL:1999 query shown in Listing 2.

This query starts by creating a table expression (ORG) populated initially with all unit records as parents of themselves at their own level (path lengths of zero) and appends (UNION) records for all paths of length one from these nodes to the units directly below them. The RECURSIVE option continues the process to build all indirect paths from each unit to all its descendants.

The query then joins the end points of all paths in the ORG result set to the employees of those units. By limiting the start points of these paths to units at level 2 (divisions) and grouping the end result by those divisions, we get the requested information.

It is expected that SQL:1999-compliant versions of popular DBMS implementations will be available by late 2001. As demonstrated above, this would provide powerful tools for hierarchy data retrieval. Still, relying on such complex SQL is beyond the reach of many IT professionals and most end-user reporting tools. Another limitation is that such queries can be rather slow in reporting applications with large hierarchies and frequent queries.

Figure 3. Result set produced by the UNION statement

unit_id	unit_name
5	unit 5
6	unit 6
9	unit 9
10	unit 10

Record: 1 of 4

Listing 2: Recursive Hierarchy Retrieval using SQL:1999

```
WITH RECURSIVE ORG (unit_above, unit_below, top_level,
levels_between) AS
( SELECT unit_id, unit_id, unit_level, 0   FROM UNIT
UNION ALL
SELECT ORG.unit_above, UNIT.unit_id, ORG.top_level,
ORG.levels_between + 1
FROM ORG, UNIT
WHERE ORG.unit_below = UNIT.unit_above )
SELECT ORG.unit_above, sum(EMPLOYEE.salary)
FROM ORG, EMPLOYEE
WHERE ORG.unit_below = EMPLOYEE.unit_code AND ORG.top_level = 2
GROUP BY ORG.unit_above;
```

To address these limitations, the following section describes two data denormalization approaches that can support complex hierarchy data retrieval with simple and intuitive SQL queries. The first approach relies on a path table capturing all ancestor-descendant relations in the hierarchy. The second approach relies on maintaining the complete ancestry information in columns within each node record. Though they simplify and accelerate hierarchy data retrieval, both approaches carry the burden of redundant data and potential update anomalies.

THE PATH TABLE APPROACH

The Path table approach uses a "navigation bridge table" (Kimball et al., 1998) with records enumerating all paths starting from each node to all nodes in the branch above it, including itself. Figure 4 contains a partial view of the 27 records in the path table for the sample hierarchy in Figure 1. For example, Unit 9 has four records in the path table reflecting the paths up to itself, Unit 6, Unit 2, and Unit 1.

To demonstrate how the Path table can simplify data retrieval, consider the challenge of showing total employee salaries for each division including all units below it. By joining the tables as shown in Figure 5, we can easily select all employees that belong to units below each division. Since the Path table includes a zero-length path between each unit and itself, employees that belong directly to the division unit would be included in the result set.

The relatively simple SQL statement in Listing 3 will return the requested information. Other requests for information can use the same approach or variations such as connecting to the unit table via the Unit_Below column in the Path table or adding path length and terminal node information to the Path table (Kimball et al., 1998).

Figure 4. A Path table for the sample hierarchy

Unit_Below	Unit_Above
8	8
8	4
8	1
9	9
9	6
9	2
9	1
10	10
10	

Record: 14 ◄ | of 27

Figure 5. A Path table connects each node with all its parents

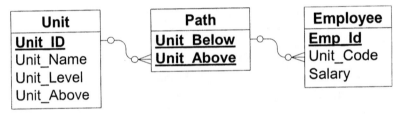

Listing 3. Retrieval via a Path table

```
SELECT unit.unit_name, Sum(Employee.salary) AS SumOfsalary
FROM (unit INNER JOIN Path ON unit.unit_id = Path.Unit_Above)
      INNER JOIN Employee ON Path.Unit_Below = Employee.unit_code
WHERE unit.unit_level = 2
GROUP BY unit.unit_name, unit.unit_level ;
```

One limitation of the Path table approach is that the number of records in the Path table can grow quite large. The following section describes another approach that avoids that problem.

THE DENORMALIZED UNIT TABLE APPROACH

The denormalized unit table approach maintains for each node information about its ancestor nodes at all possible levels of the hierarchy. As demonstrated by Figure 6, if we assume that our unit hierarchy will not exceed six levels, then we need

Figure 6. Using a denormalized unit table

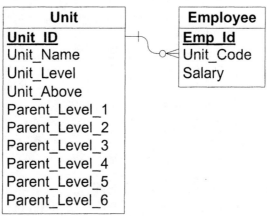

six more columns to maintain this information. Each node will be indicated as its own parent at its own level. For example, unit 6 in Figure 1, would have '1' (the Unit_ID for unit 1) as its Parent_Level_1, '2' as its Parent_Level_2, '6' (itself) as its Parent_Level_3, and Null values for Parent_Level_4, Parent_Level_5 and Parent_Level_6.

To demonstrate how the denormalized unit table can simplify data retrieval, consider again the challenge of showing total employee salaries for each division including all units below it. By joining the tables as shown in Figure 6, we can easily select and group all employees according to the Division (Parent_Level_2) of their unit. Employees that work directly for a unit at the Division level will be included in the result set because each Division is its own parent at level 2. Listing 4 shows that by using this approach, an even simpler SQL statement can generate the requested information.

It should be noted that by adding a join to an aliased copy of the unit table, we can return the unit_name rather than just the unit_id for each division. Such a join would also remove a blank Division row in the result set, since employees in the top unit (unit 1) have a Null in their unit's Parent_Level_2.

Listing 4. Retrieval via a denormalized unit table

```
SELECT unit.Parent_Level_2, Sum(Employee.salary) AS SumOfsalary
FROM unit INNER JOIN Employee ON unit.unit_id = Employee.unit_code
GROUP BY unit.Parent_Level_2;
```

COMPARING THE TWO APPROACHES

As demonstrated above, both the Path table and the denormalized unit table approaches facilitate data retrieval against hierarchies. However, both approaches achieve this at the cost of maintaining redundant data. The redundancy is caused by storing explicit path information from each node to all its ancestor nodes instead of just to its direct parent. While the Path approach is more flexible, the denormalized unit table approach is simpler and easier to maintain.

The Path table approach is more flexible since it does not impose a limit on the number of levels in the hierarchy. In contrast, the denormalized unit table approach limits the number of levels in the hierarchy to the number of Parent_Level_n columns. However, in most application areas one can guard against exceeding the number of levels limitation by assigning several Parent_Level_n columns beyond the maximum expected for the application. For example, if our current organizational structure has five levels, we can design the unit table with 10 Parent_Level_n columns. The chances of exceeding this safety margin are slim.

While the Path table is more flexible, it requires slightly more complex SQL due to the addition of one more table and its associated joins. Another disadvantage of this approach is that for deep hierarchies, the size of the Path table can grow quite large, degrading query performance.

The most important criterion for comparing the two approaches is probably the ease of maintaining the redundant data required by both methods. The following section discusses this issue.

MAINTENANCE OF DENORMALIZED
HIERARCHY DATA

Asking users to maintain the redundant information required by either approach can be a career-limiting move. Users would resist the additional burden, and the chance of incomplete or inconsistent updates would pose significant data quality risk. This section suggests methods that can simplify and automate the maintenance of redundant hierarchy data. The proposed approach and the sample SQL code provide a concrete example of an "incremental evaluation system" for handling recursive SQL queries as advanced by previous literature (Libkin and Wong, 1997; Dong et al., 1999).

An important observation is that the redundant information maintained for each node is a simple extension of the redundant information already maintained for its parent node. Consider a situation where unit 10 in Figure 1 is moved from under unit 6 to under unit 4. Let us review the procedural logic required to update the records in the Path table. We can start by deleting all path records where unit 10 is a child node (10‡6, 10‡2, 10‡1), except the path record of the unit to itself (10‡10). We can then reconstruct the path records going up from unit 10 by simply copying all path records going up from the new parent node (4‡4, 4‡1) and replacing the

Figure 7. Moving unit 10 from parent 6 to parent 4

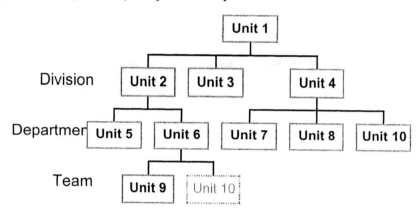

Unit_Below column in these records with the number of the updated unit (10). After this procedure, unit 10 would have three path records going up from it (10Ø10, 10Ø4, 10Ø1) reflecting the correct state of the updated hierarchy, as shown in Figure 7.

Similar and even simpler logic applies to the same situation when using a denormalized unit table. In that case, the Parent_Level_n columns from the new parent node are first copied to the updated unit record (unit 10). We then simply add the unit as its own parent at its own level. Because the denormalized unit table allows for simpler maintenance logic, the remainder of this chapter uses that approach as the assumed data structure.

Using this update logic, users would update the structure of the hierarchy by specifying only the Unit_Above information for each node. The level of the unit can always be established and updated automatically as the level of the parent node plus one. When inserting or updating a unit record to have a null Unit_Above, we can establish the node level as 1. In such cases the node is at the top of the hierarchy and is its own parent at level 1. All other Parent_Level_n columns for such a top node should be set to null.

The main remaining challenge is to handle situations where a whole branch (a node with descendants) is moved in the hierarchy. Consider, for example, moving unit 6 in Figure 7 from under unit 2 to under unit 4. The procedural logic above would update the redundant data for unit 6, but we now need to update the information for all its decendants (unit 9). The most elegant solution is to recursively extend the procedural logic by applying it to all descendant nodes, as if their Unit_Above column was updated as well.

There is one more threat to our hierarchy data integrity that must be addressed by our procedural logic. When the user specifies or updates Unit_Above information for any given unit, we must guard against loops. In other words, the unit_above cannot be a descendant of the current unit. For example, given the hierarchy in Figure 7, the user should be blocked from changing the Unit_Above of unit 2 from unit 1 to unit 6 or unit 9. This test can be implemented by checking that none of the Parent_Level_n columns of the new parent unit is the current unit.

APPLYING THE PROCEDURE THROUGH FRONT-END LOGIC

This procedural logic can be implemented as a front-end function that gets called in application screens each time a user changes the Unit_Above column. The function accepts as arguments a unit_id and its new unit_above. After completing the logic for that unit, the function would use embedded SQL to identify the descendants of the unit and call itself recursively against all these descendants.

One limitation of using such front-end logic to maintain the redundant hierarchy data is that it would require multiple communications between the client and the server. A much more important limitation is that we are dependent on uniform and full compliance by all client applications. The integrity of the hierarchy data can be compromised if some screens or client applications neglect to call or implement the front-end logic appropriately.

APPLYING THE PROCEDURE THROUGH DATABASE TRIGGERS

Moving the procedural logic from front-end functions to back-end triggers removes the threat of multiple points of failure and achieves better performance. We need to implement an Update trigger on the Unit_Above column of the Unit table. We need to also implement an Insert trigger for the unit table. Assuming referential integrity takes care of blocking attempts to delete a unit record if a Unit_Above foreign key is pointing to it from another unit record, we do not need a Delete trigger.

Appendix A and Appendix B provide commented implementations of the Update and Insert triggers. These particular versions are designed for the Sybase *Adaptive Server Anywhere* DBMS. Since triggers are not supported uniformly by all DBMSs, the implementations may differ across DBMSs.

An example of DBMS-specific consideration in the implementation of these triggers is the issue of calling the trigger recursively by re-setting the Unit_Above code of the descendant nodes. *Adaptive Server Anywhere* would not fire an "After Update" trigger if the value in the column has not changed. Hence the "Before Update" declaration of the update trigger.

CONCLUSION

This chapter reviewed the data retrieval and data maintenance problems posed by hierarchical data structures. In most situations the solution is to maintain redundant hierarchy information for the expressed purpose of facilitating data retrieval. The approach of denormalizing the hierarchy node table may be preferred over maintaining a separate hierarchy Path table because it leads to simpler data retrieval as well as simpler hierarchy data maintenance.

The limitation of maintaining redundant hierarchy information is that updates to the hierarchy require special processing logic in order to avoid update anomalies. Since an update to the hierarchy requires specification of a parent node, this chapter describes techniques for selectively refreshing the hierarchy data by exploiting the redundant information already maintained for the specified parent node. The process can then be extended recursively for lower level nodes.

If the necessary trigger options are available for the DBMS in use, it is recommended that the processing logic for maintaining the redundant hierarchy information be implemented as triggers. This removes the burden of hierarchy maintenance from client applications. It also ensures that client applications cannot circumvent the hierarchy maintenance logic.

REFERENCES

ANSI/ISO/IEC 9075-2-1999. ANSI's Electronic Standards Store: http://Webstore.ansi.org

Dong, G., Libkin L., Su J. & Wong L. (1999). Maintaining the transitive closure of graphs in SQL, *International Journal of Information Technology*, 5, 46-78.

Kimball, R., Reeves L., Ross M. and Thornthwaite W. (1998). *The Data Warehouse Lifecycle Toolkit: Expert Methods for Designing, Developing, and Deploying Data Warehouses*. New York: Wiley Computer Publishing.

Libkin, L. and Wong L. (1997). Incremental recomputation of recursive queries with nested sets and aggregate functions. In *Database Programming Languages*. Springer, 222-238.

APPENDIX A: UPDATE TRIGGER FOR UNIT HIERARCHY MAINTENANCE

This trigger completely takes over the task of maintaining:
1. unit_level_code:
   - If unit_above_code is Null then unit_level_code = 1
   - Otherwise, unit_level_code = unit_level_code of parent + 1
2. Parent_Level_n:
   - If unit_above_code is Null then Parent_Level_1 is the unit itself and Parents_Level_n at all levels below are Null
   - Otherwise, the Parents at all levels are the parents of the unit above and the unit is its own parent at its own level

This trigger fires just before the Unit_Above_Code column in the UNIT table gets updated. In order to cascade the updates down the hierarchy branch, this trigger also updates (resets) the Unit_Above_Code of all the unit's children to the same unit_code value. This causes the trigger to fire in those children, and thus a recursive cascade ripples down the branch.

```
CREATE trigger unit_hierarchy before UPDATE of UNIT_ABOVE_CODE
order 3 on "DBA".UNIT
referencing old as old_unit new as new_unit
for each row

BEGIN
 declare v_parent_level integer;
 declare v_p1 integer;
 declare v_p2 integer;
 declare v_p3 integer;
 declare v_p4 integer;
 declare v_p5 integer;
 declare v_p6 integer;
 declare err_illegal_parent exception for sqlstate value '99999';
 declare err_parent_is_child exception for sqlstate value '99998';

 // check that this is not a top node
 IF(new_unit.unit_above_code is not null) THEN

  BEGIN

  SELECT unit.unit_level_code, parent_level_1, parent_level_2,
    parent_level_3, parent_level_4, parent_level_5, parent_level_6 INTO
    v_parent_level, v_p1, v_p2, v_p3, v_p4, v_p5, v_p6 FROM "dba".unit
    WHERE unit.unit_code = new_unit.unit_above_code;

   IF   new_unit.unit_code = v_p1
    or new_unit.unit_code = v_p2
    or new_unit.unit_code = v_p3
    or new_unit.unit_code = v_p4
    or new_unit.unit_code = v_p5
    or new_unit.unit_code = v_p6 THEN
    // call the exception handling specified in the EXCEPTION block
    signal err_parent_is_child
   END IF ;

   IF v_parent_level > 5 THEN
    // call the exception handling specified in the EXCEPTION block
    signal err_illegal_parent
   END IF;
```

```
UPDATE "dba".unit SET
 unit.unit_level_code = v_parent_level + 1,
 unit.parent_level_1 = v_p1,
 unit.parent_level_2 = v_p2,
 unit.parent_level_3 = v_p3,
 unit.parent_level_4 = v_p4,
 unit.parent_level_5 = v_p5,
 unit.parent_level_6 = v_p6
 WHERE unit.unit_code = new_unit.unit_code;

// We must use UPDATE rather than just set the values in new_unit
// because this is BEFORE update and we need the recursive
  // children to have access to the updated property.

 CASE v_parent_level
 when 1 THEN
  UPDATE "dba".unit SET unit.parent_level_2 = new_unit.unit_code
   WHERE unit_code = old_unit.unit_code

 when 2 THEN
  UPDATE "dba".unit SET unit.parent_level_3 = new_unit.unit_code
   WHERE unit_code = old_unit.unit_code

 when 3 THEN
  UPDATE "dba".unit SET unit.parent_level_4 = new_unit.unit_code
   WHERE unit_code = old_unit.unit_code

 when 4 THEN
  UPDATE "dba".unit SET unit.parent_level_5 = new_unit.unit_code
   WHERE unit_code = old_unit.unit_code

 when 5 THEN
  UPDATE "dba".unit SET unit.parent_level_6 = new_unit.unit_code
   WHERE unit_code = old_unit.unit_code

 else
  signal err_illegal_parent
 END CASE;

 // Refresh unit_above of all children to cause recursion
     UPDATE "dba".unit SET
  unit.unit_above_code = new_unit.unit_code
  WHERE unit.unit_above_code = new_unit.unit_code ;
```

```
    EXCEPTION
When err_illegal_parent
        THEN
        message 'Parent Level Is Too Low (below 5)';
        // signal to the outside world to abort
        signal err_illegal_parent

when err_parent_is_child
        THEN
        message 'This unit cannot be a child of its own child!';
        // signal to the outside world to abort
        signal err_parent_is_child

        when others THEN
        // for other exceptions not explicitly handled in the Exception block,
        // simply pass them up to the procedure that caused the Trigger
        resignal
        END
  END IF;
// NULL PARENT (top node handling)
IF (new_unit.unit_above_code is null) THEN
// For top node, set level to 1, parent at level 1 to itself and others to Null
    UPDATE "dba".unit SET
      unit.unit_level_code = 1,
      unit.parent_level_1 = new_unit.unit_code,
      unit.parent_level_2 = null,
      unit.parent_level_3 = null,
      unit.parent_level_4 = null,
      unit.parent_level_5 = null,
      unit.parent_level_6 = null
    WHERE unit.unit_code = new_unit.unit_code ;

  // Refresh unit_above of all children to cause recursion.
   UPDATE "dba".unit SET
    unit.unit_above_code = new_unit.unit_code
    WHERE unit.unit_above_code = new_unit.unit_code ;
  END IF;
END
```

APPENDIX B: INSERT TRIGGER FOR UNIT HIERARCHY MAINTENANCE

This trigger is very similar to the Update trigger, except that there is no need for recursive calls since a newly inserted unit doesn't have descendant nodes. The other change is that instead of attempting to UPDATE the unit information, we just set the values in the columns that are about to be inserted.

```
Create trigger insert_into_hierarchy before insert order 4 on "DBA".UNIT
referencing new as new_unit
for each row
begin
  declare v_parent_level integer;
  declare v_p1 integer;
  declare v_p2 integer;
  declare v_p3 integer;
  declare v_p4 integer;
  declare v_p5 integer;
  declare v_p6 integer;
  declare err_illegal_parent exception for sqlstate value '99999';
  declare err_parent_is_child exception for sqlstate value '99998';

// Unit is not a Top Node
  if(new_unit.unit_above_code is not null) then
begin
select unit.unit_level_code,parent_level_1,parent_level_2,
parent_level_3,parent_level_4,parent_level_5,parent_level_6 into
v_parent_level, v_p1,v_p2,v_p3,v_p4,v_p5,v_p6 from "dba".unit
        where unit.unit_code=new_unit.unit_above_code;

    IF new_unit.unit_code=v_p1
    or new_unit.unit_code=v_p2
    or new_unit.unit_code=v_p3
    or new_unit.unit_code=v_p4
    or new_unit.unit_code=v_p5
    or new_unit.unit_code=v_p6 then
    // call the exception handling specified in the EXCEPTION block
    signal err_parent_is_child
    end if ;

    IF v_parent_level>5 then
```

```
      // call the exception handling specified in the EXCEPTION block
      signal err_illegal_parent
      end if ;



      set new_unit.unit_level_code=v_parent_level+1;
      set new_unit.parent_level_1=v_p1;
      set new_unit.parent_level_2=v_p2;
      set new_unit.parent_level_3=v_p3;
      set new_unit.parent_level_4=v_p4;
      set new_unit.parent_level_5=v_p5;
      set new_unit.parent_level_6=v_p6;

      case v_parent_level
      when 1 then set new_unit.parent_level_2=new_unit.unit_code
      when 2 then set new_unit.parent_level_3=new_unit.unit_code
      when 3 then set new_unit.parent_level_4=new_unit.unit_code
      when 4 then set new_unit.parent_level_5=new_unit.unit_code
      when 5 then set new_unit.parent_level_6=new_unit.unit_code
      else  signal err_illegal_parent
      end case

exception
    when err_illegal_parent
    then
      message 'Parent Level Is Too Low (below 5)';
        signal err_illegal_parent

    when err_parent_is_child
    then
      message 'This unit cannot be a child of its own child!';
      signal err_parent_is_child

    when others then
        resignal
  end
 end if ;

IF(new_unit.unit_above_code is null) then
    // this is a top node: set Level to 1, parent at level 1 to itself and others to
Null.
    set new_unit.unit_level_code=1;
```

```
      set new_unit.parent_level_1=new_unit.unit_code;
      set new_unit.parent_level_2=null;
      set new_unit.parent_level_3=null;
      set new_unit.parent_level_4=null;
      set new_unit.parent_level_5=null;
      set new_unit.parent_level_6=null
    end if

END
```

Chapter IX

Object-Oriented Database Design

Esperanza Marcos and Paloma Cáceres
Rey Juan Carlos University, Spain

INTRODUCTION

In spite of the fact that relational databases still hold the first place in the market, object-oriented databases are becoming, each day, more widely accepted. Relational databases are suitable for traditional applications supporting management tasks such as payroll or library management. Recently, as a result of hardware improvements, more sophisticated applications have emerged. Engineering applications, such as CAD/CAM (Computer Aided Design/ Computer Aided Manufacturing), CASE (Computer Aided Software Engineering) or CIM (Computer Integrating Manufacturing), office automation systems, multimedia systems such as GIS (Geographic Information Systems) or medical information systems, can be characterized as consisting of complex objects related by complex interrelationships. Representing such objects and relationships in the relational model implies that the objects must be decomposed into a large number of tuples. Thus, a considerable number of *joins* is necessary to retrieve an object and, when tables are too deeply nested, performance is dramatically reduced (Bertino and Marcos, 2000).

A new database generation has arisen to solve the above-mentioned problems and it includes both object-relational (Stonebraker and Brown, 1999) and object databases (Bertino and Martino, 1993). Object-relational technology is relational systems extended with new capabilities, such as triggers or object-oriented capabilities allowing us to support complex objects required by new applications. Object databases are well suited for storing and retrieving complex data by allowing one to navigate through the data.

Nonetheless, good technology is not enough to support complex objects and applications. The next step should be to provide appropriate guidelines to get a correct object-oriented database design and not much work has been done in this field.

Some approaches to object-oriented database design are available (Silva and Carlson, 1995; Blaha and Premerlani, 1998; Ullman and Widom, 1997; Kovács and Van Bommel, 1998; Muller, 1999; Bertino and Marcos, 2000). Unfortunately, none of these proposals can be considered as "the method" neither for object-relational nor for object databases. They can be considered just as the first approaches to a standard method, but none of them have been universally accepted by the database community. In addition, despite the fact that some of the mentioned proposals are so recent, they do not take into account the new standards. We can notice that SQL:1999, the standard for object-relational databases, after seven years of discussion and more than four different proposals of the object-relational model, has been approved in 1999 (Eisenberg and Meltón, 1999). On the other hand, latest revision of the ODMG (Object Database Management Group) standard, the standard for object databases, was published January 2000 (Cattell et al., 2000). The main features of the two mentioned standards are shown in a subsequent section.

The main objective of this chapter is to review the state-of-the-art in database design for complex-systems, including both perspectives mentioned above: object-relational and object database technologies. With this aim we sum-up the SQL:1999 and ODMG object models, comparing the main advantages and disadvantages of these two approaches. We also pose, through an example, the main problems of the relational model to represent complex objects and relationships, and we use the same example to explain how these problems can be addressed by the object-relational and object-databases.

In addition to the above-mentioned problems, Web systems each day become more and more important systems. Database integration on the Web involves different problems from traditional databases, that have to be taken into account in the design task. This is the reason, nowadays, that some approaches to Web database design are appearing (Schawe and Rossi, 1995; Atzeni et al.,1998; Fraternali and Paolini, 1998). The last part of the chapter poses the main trends in Web database design.

The remainder of the chapter is organized as follows: the next section provides the needed background summing up object-relational models (SQL:1999 object model) and object database models (ODMG object model); a subsequent section proposes, through an example, some guidelines for object-relational and object database design; then the next section summarizes the new trends in Web database design; the final section finishes with the main conclusions.

BACKGROUND

The application areas covered by relational technology are mainly focused on tasks such as management, invoicing, etc. New database technology, including object-relational and object databases, covers a wide spectrum of application areas ranging from video and graphic management in the multimedia industry to time series analysis problems in the financial market or scientific databases. In addition, Web sites with valuable pieces of information are best served and maintained by object-oriented database technology.

According to Stonebraker and Brown (1999), database applications can be classified in a two-by-two matrix, where each quadrant represents: file systems, relational Database Management Systems (DBMS), object-relational DBMS and object DBMS. In the matrix (see Figure 1) the horizontal axis shows simple data on the left and complex data on the right. The vertical axis differentiates whether the application requires a query capability. Depending on its characteristics, each application fits into at least one of the four quadrants.

Nonetheless, recent advances in object database technology do object DBMS also appropriate for applications with queries. The latest versions of products, such as POET[1] v.6 or Object Store[2] v. 6, provide better support for the Object Query Language (OQL). Therefore, we can conclude that applications with complex data will be supported, in a near future, by either object relational or object databases. Object-relational databases are represented by the SQL:1999 standard whereas object databases are represented by the ODMG standard. The next sections summarize their respective object models.

The SQL: 1999 Standard

The SQL (Structured Query Language) standard is the standard proposed by ISO/IEC[3] and ANSI[4] for relational databases following the relational model proposed by Codd. The latest version, called SQL:1999, supports the object-relational model.

The first SQL standard was approved by ANSI in 1986, and by ISO in 1987. In 1989, ANSI and ISO approved a standard revision, known as Addendum, which incorporated a set of basic features to improve the data integrity. That same year ANSI published another standard about embedded SQL. Three years later a new version, known as SQL-92, was published by ISO and ANSI. SQL-92 improved the

Figure 1. A matrix for classifying DBMS applications (Stonebraker and Brown, 1999)

Query	Relational DBMS	Object-Relational DBMS
No Query	File Systems	Object DBMS
	Simple Data	Complex Data

semantic capability of the relational schema, introduced new operators, improved error handling and incorporated embedded SQL. In this standard, three conformity levels are defined: Entry SQL, Intermediate SQL and Full SQL. Each one subsumes the previous one. This standard has been completed with two new parts, the Call Level Interface and Persistent Stored Modules that make SQL a complete computational language, incorporating control structures, exception handling, etc.

In 1999 a new version called SQL:1999 and *formerly known as SQL3* (Eisenberg and Melton, 1999), was approved. SQL:1999 in addition to new features such as triggers, roles, recursion, etc., incorporates object-relational capabilities by means of the following constructors: User-Defines Types, Structured Types, Type and Table Hierarchies, Typed Tables, Collection Types, etc.

Besides works on a new related standard, SQL/MM (Multimedia) are currently being developed.

In Table 1, the SQL history milestones are presented. This table finishes with the prospective SQL4 which is currently under consideration.

Object-Oriented Extensions

In SQL not everything is an object. Even after the addition of object-oriented capabilities to SQL, this language retains and enhances all these relational capabilities. So, for example, SQL:1999 stores all data in tables, even object data (Melton and Eisenberg, 2000). SQL provides two new sorts of data to support object-oriented extensions: user-defined types and reference types.

There are two sorts of **user-defined types**: the *distinct type*, which merely allows applications to give a new name to SQL's built-in primitive types providing strong typing; and the *structured type*, another variant that relates more closely to object-orientation; SQL's structured type is closest to programming language classes. **Structured types** allow user defining complex data types that can be used

Table 1.- SQL history

1968 - 1970	Born of the relational model
1970 - 1978	Prototypes
1978 -	Products
1986	SQL/ANSI
1987	SQL/ISO
1989	SQL Addendum
1992	SQL-92
1995	SQL/CLI
1996	SQL/PSM
1999	SQL:1999
2000-	SQL/MM, SQL/4

either as column types or as row types (see Figure 2). Structured types as column types allow modeling complex attributes of entities (time series, point, etc.), enhancing the infrastructure for SQL/MM. Structured types as row types allow modeling entities, with relationship and behavior (employees, departments, etc.) enhancing the infrastructure for business objects.

Structured types can be used whenever other predefined data types can be used (type of attributes of other structured types; type of parameters of functions, method and procedures; type of SQL variables; type of domain of columns in tables). They can also be used to define tables, called typed tables, and views. The following SQL statement defines a typed table for *employee:*

CREATE TABLE employees OF employee

Structured types can be a subtype of another user-defined type inheriting structure (attributes) and behavior (methods) from their supertypes. SQL supports only single inheritance and does not currently support any notion of inheritance of interface (see inheritance in ODMG). SQL allows you to specify that a structured type is FINAL, meaning that no subtypes of the type can be defined. It also permits structured types to be declared NON INSTANTIABLE, which means that no values of the type can be created. A NON INSTANTIABLE type is closest to programming language abstract classes. The following SQL statement specifies a subtype of the type employee:

CREATE TYPE manager UNDER employee

Typed tables can also have subtables inheriting columns, constraints, triggers, etc., from the supertable.

CREATE TABLE managers OF manager UNDER employees

Methods are special cases of functions that are associated with a specific structured type by including in the type's definition the specification (signature) of

Figure 2. User-defined structured types as columns and as rows (Mattos, 1999)

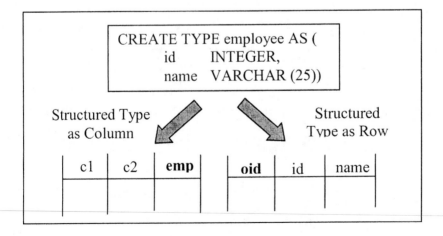

the method. The signature and the body are specified separately. Methods can be original methods (methods attached to the super type) or overriding methods (methods attached to the subtype).

```
CREATE TYPE employee AS (
id              INTEGER,
name                    VARCHAR (25)
base_salary       DECIMAL (9,2)
bonus             DECIMAL (9,2)
INSTANTIABLE NOT FINAL
METHOD salary() RETURNS DECIMAL (9,2));

CREATE METHOD salary() FOR employee
BEGIN
......
END;
```

The second sort of data type provided by SQL to support object-oriented extensions is the **reference type**. As we have already said, structured types can be used to define typed tables. Attributes of the type become columns of the table, and a column to define a REF value for the row (the object identifier) is added. The REF attribute can be user or system generated, or derived from a list of attributes:

```
CREATE TYPE employee AS (
id              INTEGER,
name                    VARCHAR (25)
base_salary       DECIMAL (9,2)
bonus             DECIMAL (9,2));

CREATE TABLE employees OF employee
(REF IS SYSTEM GENERATED)
```

Structured types have a corresponding reference type that can be used whenever other types can be used.

```
CREATE TYPE employee AS (
id              INTEGER,
departmentREF (DepartmentType)
name                    VARCHAR (25)
base_salary       DECIMAL (9,2)
bonus             DECIMAL (9,2));
```

It is important to outline that references do not have the same semantics as referential constraints which specify inclusion dependencies.

SQL's structured types are permitted to contain primitive types, constructed types, other structured types and references to typed tables (that is, tables whose rows are actually values of structured types). A constructed type is a type that must be defined in terms of other types (Melton and Eisenberg, 2000). SQL provides the array and the row constructor types. A row type is like a *structure* in the C language because it allows nesting values within other values. SQL's reference type is also a constructed type, though less structured than array or row types. The following statement shows an example of row type:

```
CREATE TABLE employee (
    Id      INTEGER,
    name    ROW  (first_name  VARCHAR(30),
                  last_name  VARCHAR(30) ));
```

References can be used in path expressions. So, for example, the following SQL statement,

```
SELECT e.name, e.department->address
FROM employee e
WHERE e.department->city="Madrid"
```

retrieves the name of all employees and the address of their department located in Madrid. This query retrieves data of two different tables without using any join expression.

References can be used to invoke methods on the corresponding structured type, as in the following example:

```
SELECT e.name, e.department ()->number_of_employees
FROM employee e
```

References can be also used to obtain the structured value that is being referenced, enabling nested structured types. For example, the following SQL statement retrieves the data of the J. Smith's department:

```
SELECT e.name, DEREF (e.department)
FROM employee e
WHERE e.name="J. Smith"
```

The ODMG Standard

The ODMG standard is the object database standard proposed by the ODMG (Object Data Management Group). Its main goal consists of allowing the ODBMS (Object Database Management Systems) customers to write portable applications. Thus, the data schema, programming language binding, data manipulation language and query language must be portable. As a second goal, the ODMG standard tries to be helpful in allowing interoperability between ODBMS products as well as heterogeneous distributed databases communicating through the OMA (Object Management Architecture) Object Request Broker.

The first version of the standard, release 1.0, came out in 1993. ODMG standard release 1.0 was revised in the releases 1.1 and 1.2. The main improvements of release 1.2 with regard to the previous ones are based on the Object Query Language (OQL). Release 2.0 (Cattell and Barry, 1997), in addition to some improvements like the incorporation of new collection types (as the dictionary type), provides the Java binding which was not included in the previous versions. The current version, release 3.0 (Cattell and Barry, 2000), includes enhancements to the Java language binding and various improvements and corrections throughout the previous releases of the standard. It pays special attention to the broadening of the standard to support object-to-database mappings, which allows objects to be stored in relational databases.

The major components of ODMG release 3.0, currently the latest version, are the following:

- **Object Model**--The object model is based on the core object model proposed by the OMG (Object Management Group). The ODMG object model extends the OMG core model adding components (for example, relationships) to support database needs.
- **Object Specification Languages**--Two specification Languages are supported by the ODMG standard: the Object Definition Language (ODL) and the Object Interchange Format (OIF). ODL is a specification language used to define the object types that conform the ODMG Object Model. It is not a full programming language, but rather an independent definition language for object specifications. The syntax of ODL extends IDL (the Interface Definition Language developed by the OMG). OIF is a specification language used to dump and load the current state of an Object Data Management System (ODMS) to or from a file or set of files.
- **Object Query Language (OQL)**--It is a declarative language for querying and updating ODMS objects. It also provides some constructors to update database objects. Although it is based on the SQL language, their semantics are not always the same. OQL supports, perhaps, more powerful capabilities in regard to the result of a query, allowing it to get in different collection types. Nevertheless, the result of an SQL query is always a table.
- **Language Binding**--The first releases of the ODMG standard defined C++ and Smalltalk language bindings. ODMG 2.0, in addition to these two language bindings, has also incorporated the Java binding that have been improved in ODMG 3.0. These bindings define the mapping between the ODL and the C++, Smalltalk or Java languages. They also include the OML mapping, to write portable codes that manipulate persistent objects using one of the proposed languages. They also include a mechanism to invoke OQL and procedures for operations on databases and transactions. The Java language binding has been submitted to the Java Community Process as a basis for the Java Data Objects Specification.

The ODMG Data Model and its ODL

The basic primitives of ODMG data model are the **object** and the **literal**. Objects have a unique identifier (OID[5]) which should be immutable, and literals have no identifier and are identified by their value.

Objects and literals can be classified into types. A **type** defines the common properties (attributes and relationships) and the behavior (operations) of a set of elements. A type has an external specification and one or more implementations. The external specification is an abstract description of the type, independent of the implementation. ODL provides the following constructs to support the external specification: interface, class and literal.

The **interface** defines just the abstract behavior of an object type. The **class** definition is a specification that, in addition to the abstract behavior, defines the abstract state of an object type. A **literal** definition defines only the abstract state of a literal type. Figure 3, taken from Cattell and Douglas (2000), shows the relationship between interfaces, classes and literals.

An implementation of an object type is a representation and a set of methods. The implementation of an object type has to be carried out by a language binding. A type can have more than one implementation. Classes of programming languages as C++, Smalltalk and Java are implementation classes and should not be confused with ODMG classes (which are definitions without implementation).

Objects are instances of types. An object can be persistent or transient. **Persistent** objects (database objects) are allocated memory and their storage is managed by the ODMS run-time system. They continue to exist after the procedure, or the process, which creates them finishes off. **Transient** objects are allocated memory, managed by the programming language run-time system and they only exist inside the procedure, or the process, that creates them. The lifetime of an object is independent of the type. Some instances of the types can be persistent, while others can be transient.

To illustrate the features of the ODMG data model, we show an interface and a class definition in ODL:

interface person (extent persons)
  { attribute string (30) name;
    attribute short age;
    attribute struct address

class student (extent students
        key name)
  { attribute string (30) name;
    attribute short age;

Figure 3. Type specification in ODMG

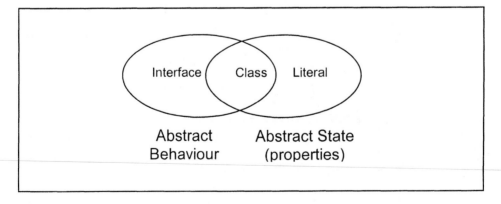

```
{char (20) street,                              relationship course enrolls
  char (15) city };                                     inverse has::course;
    void person ();                         void student ();
    void ~person ();                          void ~student ();
  };                                        };
```

The **extent** of a type is the collection of all the objects (instances) of the type. It is similar to the table in a relational database. Unlike the relational DBMS that maintains an extend for every defined table, the extent definition is optional in the ODMG data model.

A **key** is an attribute, or a set of attributes, that identify each object of a type uniquely. This concept is similar to the candidate key of the relational model. To have a key it is necessary to define an extent, because the unique scope for a key is the extend.

The ODMG data model defines binary **relationships** between types. They are not objects themselves and do not have an object identifier. A relationship consists of two traversal paths, one for each direction of the binary relationship. Thus, in our example, a student is enrolled in a course and the class course should also set a relationship with the student type. A binary relationship may be one-to-one, one-to-many or many-to-many.

A **collection** is a type that has a variable number of elements, all of which must belong to the same type. The ODMG data model supports the traditional collection types (objects or literals), set, bag, list, array as well as the dictionary collection type which is an unordered sequence of key-value pairs with no duplicate keys, and the table collection type. A table type is a collection type defined in the ODMG data model to express SQL tables. It is equivalent to a collection of structures. The following ODL sentence shows an example of a collection type to define a one-to-many relationship between student and course.

```
class course (extent courses)
  { attribute short n_hours;
    attribute string (30) description;
        relationship set<student> has
            inverse enrolls::student;
    void course ();
    void ~course();
  };
```

A **structured** type is a type that has a fixed number of elements that may be of different data types. The ODMG data model supports the following structured types (objects or literals): *date, interval, time* and *timestamp*. In addition to these types, the ODMG data model allows the user to define new structured types.

The ODMG data model supports two different kinds of **inheritance relationships**:

a) The **ISA** relationship (represented by a *colon*) that defines the **inheritance of behavior** between object types, either interfaces or classes. Next, we show an example of an ISA relationship:

interface person (extent persons)
  { attribute string (30) name;
attribute short age;
   attribute struct address
{char (20) street,
char (15) city };
   void person ();
   void ~person ();
  };

class student: person (extent students
key name)
  { attribute string (30) name;
   attribute short age;
  attribute struct address {char (20)
street, char (15) city };
   relationship course enrolls
     inverse has::course;
};

As the ISA relationship defines the inheritance just for the behavior, attributes must be defined in the subtype.

b) The **EXTENDS** relationship (represented by the word *extend*) that refers to the **inheritance of state**. It applies only to object types; thus only classes and no literals may inherit state. Next, we show the same example defined as an EXTEND relationship:

class person (extent persons)
  { attribute string (30) name;
   attribute short age;
   attribute struct address
{char (20) street,
char (15) city };
   void person ();
   void ~person ();
  };

class student **extends** person
(extent students
  key name)
{
   relationship course enrolls
     inverse has:course;
}

The ODMG data model supports simple inheritance and multiple inheritance of object behavior. The EXTENDS relationship is a single inheritance relationship between classes.

The OQL

The Object Query Language (OQL) does not provide explicit update operators. Updates must be completed by invoking operations. The result of a query is always an ODMG data model type. OQL can be invoked from those programming languages for which an ODMG binding is defined and it can also invoke operations programmed in these languages. OQL is very close to SQL with some OO extensions like object identity, complex objects, path expressions, polymorphism, late binding and operation invocation. Queries must be done over the extension.

Joins are allowed, but OQL also supports navigability improving the efficiency of complex queries. In order to illustrate the main features of the OQL, we show some query examples over the schema defined in the previous section (person, student and course):

    select x.age
    from **persons** x
    where x.name="John"

This query returns a literal of the type a bag<short> because there can be several "John" with the same age. Including the key-word *distinct* in the select clause prevents duplicates. Thus,

    select **distinct** x.age
    from persons x
    where x.name="John"

returns a literal of type set<short>.

Selecting different attributes is also allowed. Thus, the following clause,

    select distinct struct (n:x.name, a:x.age)
    from persons x

gets the name and the age of all persons. It returns a literal of type set<struct>.
The select operator can be also used within the select clause,

    select distinct struct (n:x.name, c: (select y
            from x.enrolls y
            where y.description="Databases"))
    from students x

This query returns a literal of type set<struct(n:string, c:bag<course>)>.
The select operator can also be used within the "from" clause. For example, the following query,

    select distinct x.age
    from (select y
            from students
            where y.age>21) x
    where x.name = "John"

retrieves a literal of type set<string> containing the age of all the students named "John."

Queries over the extension, without using the select clause, are also allowed. For example,

    Students

retrieves all the students in the database.

In OQL we can use the path notation ("." or "->"), which enables us to go inside complex object relationships, as well as to follow simple relationships. For example, we want to know the description of the course where a student *s* is enrolled:

    s.enrolls.description

or, we want to know the name of the city where the student *s* lives:

    s.city

Object-Relational *vs.* Object Databases

In conclusion to this section, we can note the main advantages and the main disadvantage of the object-relational technology as well as the object database technology.

Object-relational database advantages:
- Object-relational databases are fully compatible with relational databases, and there are many applications developed using relational technology.
- Object-relational databases, as database technology, are more mature than object database technology.
- As an extension of the relational technology, they are easily accepted by the user.

Object-relational database disadvantages:
- The impedance mismatch with the object model of the programming languages continues to be a problem.
- The integration between the relational and the object model is so *dark,* resulting in a *dirty* model not very intuitive for the user.
- The object-relational model is not really an object model.

Object database advantages:
- This technology provides a single data model for database and programming objects, solving in this way the impedance mismatch problem.
- They increase the expressive power allowing us to represent the complex objects and relationships required by such new applications as CAD/CAM, GIS or Web applications, by means of a pure object model. The object model of these databases is really object-oriented and for this reason is more appropriate for applications that require a true object model.

Object database disadvantages:
- Perhaps the main drawbacks to object-oriented database systems are due to a lack of a common model and an established technology. The former is close to being solved, thanks to the existence of the ODMG standard, which seems to be widely accepted by the community. The latter, in our opinion, is just a matter of time.

MAIN THRUST

Database systems have always provided a selection of built-in data types. They range from types supported by almost every system (either relational or object databases) such as INTEGER, CHARACTER, DATE, TIME to proprietary types defined by individual database system products such as Sysbase's IMAGE type, Oracle's NUMBER type or POET's PtString type. These built-in data types served applications well since database systems were used to manage simple and structured data which were easily represented using number or character strings.

However, nowadays, applications of database systems need new sorts of data types to represent and manage more complex data such as very large text documents, graphics and image data, spatial and geographic information and so forth. These complex types need search operations more complex than equality. The first approach was to support large object types (LOB, Large Object; BLOB, Binary Large Object; and CLOB, Character Large Object). Nonetheless, the database systems don't support the semantics of such data type; they rarely support operations, such as comparison, which have to be handled by the applications (Melton and Simon, 2000).

As a result of customer need, database technology began to explore other approaches to handling the new requirements. Objects and object-relational databases appear a good response to the new user requisites, allowing application builders to define their own specialized data types including code to provide the semantics of those types. In addition to allow defining new complex data types, which permit to support complex objects, new database technology extends their semantics capabilities supporting complex relationships (such as generalization and aggregation). They have also improved their capabilities to query complex objects and relationships.

Earlier we reviewed the object model of the two representative standards for object-relational and object databases, SQL: 1999 and ODMG. We saw how they support user-defined data types, inheritance, OIDs, reference types, etc. The problem now is how to use the new capabilities, taking into account that new functionalities demand a new way to model the system. One of the most relevant differences is, perhaps, the rupture of the 1NF, which constitutes the base of the traditional relational model.

Relational database design techniques and methodologies are not appropriate for design object and object-relational databases. Moreover, we cannot design an object database in the same way as an object-relational one because, as we saw earlier, ODMG's object model differs from SQL:1999's object-relational model. The rest of this section proposes some design guidelines discussing in which manner object-oriented constructors can be represented in ODMG and in SQL:1999, and in which manner object-oriented database design (either object or object–relational) differs from relational design. We also propose the code for some commercial products. As an object-relational product, we have chosen Oracle 8; POET has been chosen as a representative implementation of the ODMG standard. Figure 4 shows the example, in UML (Unified Modeling Language) as the OMG's (Object Management Groups) standard notation.

The Problems

Figure 4 shows a simple example that contains some constructors, which are not directly supported by traditional database systems. Specifically, it shows: a generalization between POLYGON and FIGURE, that represents an Is-a relation-

Figure 4. Example in UML notation

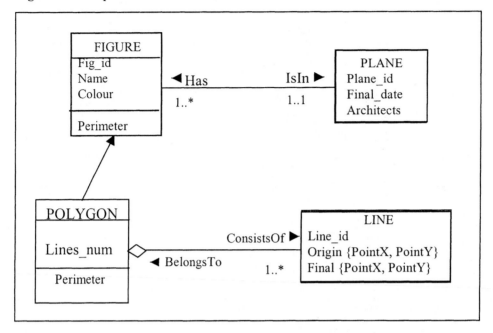

ship; an aggregation between POLYGON and LINE representing that a polygon consists of a set of lines; the *Architects* multi-valued attribute means that a plane can be designed by more than one architect; *Origin* and *Final* are composite attributes that represent the origin and final points of a line.

None of the above-mentioned constructors are directly represented in the relational model. Multi-valued and composite attributes break down with the 1 NF; and the same occurs with the aggregation relationships. The Relational model doesn't support generalization relationships, so inheritance is not supported. As methods cannot be attached to a specific type in relational databases, encapsulation and polymorphism aren't supported either. The example in Figure 4 can be represented in the relational model (using the SQL-92 syntax) as follows:

```
CREATE TABLE Plain (
    Plain_id   INTEGER PRIMARY KEY,
    Final_date  DATE);

CREATE TABLE Architect_Plain  (     /* This table represents the multi-
                              valued attribute Architects
    Plain_id   INTEGER,
    Architect  VARCHAR (30)
    PRIMARY KEY (Plain_id, Architect)
    FOREIGN KEY Plain_id REFERENCES Plain
            ON UPDATE CASCADE
            ON DELETE CASCADE);
```

```
CREATE TABLE Figure (
    Figure_id   INTEGER PRIMARY KEY,
    Name        VARCHAR (25),
    Color       VARCHAR (15),
    Figure_type VARCHAR (10),       /* To implement the IS-A relationships
        IsIn    INTEGER NOT NULL,/* Relationship with Plain (min.
                                    cardinality 1)
    FOREIGN KEY IsIn REFERENCES Plain   /* Relationship with plain
            ON UPDATE CASCADE);


CREATE TABLE Polygon (             /* Generalization is represented by a
                                    Foreign Key,
    Polygon_id INTEGER PRIMARY KEY,    /* as any other relationship
    Lines_num INTEGER,
    FOREIGN KEY Polygon_id REFERENCES Figure
            ON UPDATE CASCADE
            ON DELETE CASCADE);


CREATE TABLE Line (
    Line_id INTEGER PRIMARY KEY,
    OriginX     INTEGER,    /* Composite attributes cannot be represented
    OriginY     INTEGER,
    FinalX  INTEGER,
    FinalY  INTEGER,
    BelognsTo  INTEGER NOT NULL    /* Aggregation is represented by a
                                    Foreign Key,
    FOREIGN KEY BelongsTo REFERENCES Polygon      /* as any other
                                                    relationship

            ON UPDATE CASCADE
            ON DELETE CASCADE);
```

Summing up, we can say that relational database technology is not appropriate to implement complex systems because the relational model provides too many simple structures and data types. To solve this problem a new database generation, based on the object-oriented model, has been born.

An Approach to the Solution

Object-oriented databases, either object-relational or pure object databases, appear as a good alternative to the relational ones when we need to support complex objects and complex relationships. In this section we're going to solve the example of Figure 4 using these two approaches and comparing each one.

Object-relational representation

Next we propose an object-relational database schema representing the same example using the standard SQL:1999 and Oracle 8.

The **multi-valued attribute** architect, represented in the relational schema by a new table, is defined in SQL:1999 as an ARRAY type (VARRAY in Oracle). This is because the 1NF is not mandatory in object-relational models and, due to this fact, an attribute has to take more than one value. Both SQL:1999 and Oracle support only a collection type (the Array); they don't support either set, neither list nor bag types.

The **relationship** between figure and plain is represented by means of a REF attribute that takes, as value, the OID of the referenced attribute. A REF type differs from the foreign key in two ways: on the one hand the REF type doesn't imply an inclusion dependency; on the other hand the REF type allows dangled references. The REF type also allows navigating through the relationships with join tables.

The origin and final **composite attributes** are represented in SQL:1999 through a ROW type, which is similar to the c++ structure type. They are represented as simple attributes in Oracle because ROW type is not supported by Oracle.

With regard to the **generalization**, it is directly supported by SQL:1999 that supports types and tables inheritance. However, inheritance is not yet implemented in Oracle. For this reason, in the Oracle schema inheritance has to be implemented as in the previous relational schema, by means of a foreign key.

Aggregation can be represented in different ways. It depends on the sort of aggregation (physical/logical, navigable/not navigable...). In SQL:1999 we have represented the aggregation between polygon and line, defining in polygon an attribute of the type line. In Oracle it has been represented by means of a nested table, that is to say, the attribute ConsistsOf in polygon, is an object table type.

We can notice as in the object-relational schema, either in SQL:1999 or Oracle, we define types and tables. The first ones correspond to the class concept, whereas the table is the **extension** of the type. In the relational model the definition of a table implied the definition of the type as well as the definition of the extension.

SQL_1999 schema

```
CREATE TYPE Plain AS(
     Plain_id    INTEGER,
     Final_date  DATE,
     Architects  VARCHAR (20) ARRAY [5]);    /* Multi-valued attribute Architects
     /* (break down of 1NF)


CREATE TABLE Plains OF Plain(          /* Plain_type's extent
        Plain_id PRIMARY KEY);
     CREATE TYPE Figure AS(
     Figure_id   INTEGER,
     Name        VARCHAR (25),
     Color       VARCHAR (15),
     IsIn        REF (Plain),          /* Relationship between Plain and Figure
```

```
        INSTANTIABLE NOT FINAL          /* Figure is a instantiable type, with
subtypes
        METHOD Perimeter () RETURNS DECIMAL (4,2));
CREATE TABLE Figures OF Figure(                    /* Figure_type's extent
        Figure_id PRIMARY KEY);


CREATE TYPE Line (
        Line_id     INTEGER,
        Origin      ROW  (PointX INTEGER,      /*Composite attributes
                                               represented by a ROW type
                            PointY INTEGER),
        Final                ROW  (PointX INTEGER,
                             PointY INTEGER));


CREATE TABLE Lines OF Line;                        /* Line_type's extent
                                                   /* Primary Key is not mandatory


CREATE TYPE Polygon UNDER Figure AS(      /* Generalization is directly
                                                       supported

        Lines_num INTEGER,
        ConsistsOf Line                       /* Aggregation
        INSTANTIABLE FINAL                    /* Polygon is an instantiable type,
without subtypes
        OVERRIDED METHOD
        Perimeter () RETURNS decimal (4,2); /* Perimeter is redefined in the Polygon
subtype

CREATE TABLE Polygons OF Polygon          /* Polygons_type's extent
        UNDER Figures;
```

Oracle 8 Schema

```
        CREATE TYPE arch_type AS VARRAY (4) OF VARCHAR (25);

        CREATE  TYPE Plain_type AS OBJECT_TYPE (
            Cod_plain       NUMBER (3),
            Final_Date      DATE
            Architects      ARCH_TYPE,    /* Multi-valued attribute
            )

        CREATE  TABLE Plain_table OF Plain_type ( /* Plain_type's extent
            Palin_id NOT NULL PRIMARY KEY);

        CREATE  TYPE Figure_type AS OBJECT_TYPE (
        Fig_id      NUMBER (4),
            Name    VARCHAR (25),
            Color   VARCHAR (15)
            Fig_typeVARCHAR (10),/* To implement the generalization
        IsIn        REF Plain_type); /* Relationship with plain
```

```
CREATE  TABLE Figure_table OF Figure_type (        /* Figure_type's extent
    Fig_id   NOT NULL PRIMARY KEY,
IsIn         NOT NULL);     /* A figure is in a plain (min. cardinality 1)

CREATE  TYPE Line_type AS OBJECT_TYPE (
Line_id      NUMBER (4),
    OriginX NUMBER (2),    /* Oracle doesn't support ROW type
    OriginY NUMBER (2),
    FinalX  NUMBER (2),
    FinalY  NUMBER (2));

CREATE  TYPE Line_table_type AS TABLE OF Line_type;

CREATE  TYPE Polygon_type AS OBJECT_TYPE (
Fig_id       NUMBER (4),
    ConsistsOf      Line_table_type);/* Aggregation implemented as a nested
table

CREATE  TABLE Polygon_table OF Polygon_type (     /* Polygon_type's extent
Fig_id       NOT NULL PRIMARY KEY
    FOREIGN KEY Fig_id
            REFERENCES Figure_table (Cod_figure)
            ON UPDATE CASCADE /* The foreign key is to implement the
            ON DELETE CASCADE);        generalization not supported by
Oracle 8.
```

Object representation

Next we propose an object database schema representing the same example using the standard ODMG and POET.

The **multi-valued attribute** architect is defined as a collection type. We can also see that 1NF is not mandatory in object models either. ODMG supports list, set, bag, array and dictionary collection types. We have chosen list because the architects can have an order. POET supports cset, lset or hset collection types. All of them are list types and just differ in the way they manage the memory.

The **relationship** between figure and plain is represented in ODMG by means of a relationship. As POET doesn't support relationships, it has to be defined as a pointer attribute that takes, as value, the OID of the referenced attribute. In ODMG relationships are bi-directional (with two transversal paths) whereas in POET we can define one or two paths. If relationship is defined as bi-directional in POET, consistence has to be maintained by the user.

The origin and final **composite attributes** are represented in ODMG through a struct type, which is similar to the C++ structure type. POET doesn't support the struct type, and for this reason, if we want a point type, it has to be defined as any other class.

With regard to the **generalization**, it is directly supported by both ODMG and POET object models. ODMG supports state or behavior inheritance. In our example generalization has been represented using state inheritance (extends) because *polygon* must inherit methods as well as attributes from the class *figure*.

Aggregation has been represented as an attribute of collection types in both ODMG and POET schemata.

We can notice, as in the ODMG schema, we define the **extension** and the class together. However, POET doesn't provide any syntax to define the extension of a class. So, the extension should be defined before querying the class by means of the OQL.

ODMG Schema

```
class Plain (extent Plains
          key Plain_id)
    { attribute short Plain_id ,
    attribute date Final_date
    attribute list <string> Architects,          /* Multi-valued attribute (break
                                                  down of 1NF)


    relationship set <Figure> has     /* Relationship with figure
inverse IsIn::Figure;


    void Plain ();
    void DropPlain ();
    };


class Figure (extent Figures
    key Digure_id)
  { attribute short Figure_id,
    attribute string name,
    attribute string color,


    relationship Plain IsIn    /* Relationship with plain
inverse has::Plain;


void Figure ();
    void DropFigure ();
    float perimeter ();
    };


class Line (extent Lines)    /* Key is not mandatory in the ODMG object
                                        model
  { attribute short Line_id;
    attribute struct points {
        short PointX,
short PointY};
```

```
void Line ();
  void DropLine ();
};
```

```
class Polygon extends Figure        /* Generalization: state inheritance
(extent Polygons)
  { attribute short Line_num,
  attribute set <Line>        /* Aggregation relationship
```

```
void Polygon ();
  void DropPolygon ();
  float perimeter ();
};
```

POET Schema

```
persistent class Plain
    { private:
                  int Plain_id,
              PtDate Final_date,        /* PtString and PtDate are native data
types
              lset <PtString> Architects        /* Multi-valued attribute. Lset
is a native collection type
    public:
              void Plain ();
              void ~Plain ();
    };
```

```
persistent class Figure
  { private:
  int Figure_id,
              PtString name,
              PtString color,
                Plain* IsIn      /* Relationship with plain
    public:
              void Figure ();
              void ~Figure ();
              virtual float perimeter ();
    };
```

```
persistent class Point_type  /* POET doesn't support the C++ type structure
    { private:
  int PointX,
    int PointY
```

```
    public:
    void Point ();
    void ~Point ();
    };

persistent class Line (extent Lines)
  { private:
int Line_id,
    point_type points
    public:
    void Line ();
    void ~Line ();
    };

 persistent class Polygon: public Figure      /* Generalization relationship
 { private:
int Line_num,
    lset <Line*>      /* Aggregation relationship
    public:
    void Polygon ();
    void ~Polygon ();
    float perymeter ();
    };
```

FUTURE TRENDS

Originally the Web appeared as a distributed document access interface. Its success has generalized the use of the Web to diverse fields of knowledge, and it is currently the access platform of many systems. One of the future tendencies that databases will have are these types of Web applications, and for this reason we must work on this to obtain its integration. In the field of database literature, it is also becoming necessary to talk of Web technology (for information treatment and access, see Atzeni et al., 1999.

Web vs. Databases

The appearance of these new systems has given place to the need to take on a new perspective that traditional databases did not account for. Certain characteristics exist that differentiate Web systems from the rest of the systems, such as the fact that the information that they possess is quite heterogeneous. In general, they combine textual information with graphics, audio and video, and the structure of the information contained in these systems is also more complex and less structural than that of traditional databases. Another of the fundamental characteristics that arise in these systems is the flexibility of user-system interaction. This interaction is guided by the user's interest more than by established guidelines, which makes it impossible to predict the operation pattern the user will follow. These new applications are also offered to a large number and variety of users through the Net, a fact that also differentiates them from traditional ones. The Web has introduced a new paradigm for both the distribution and the acquisition of information, which allows easy, flexible and economic access. For this it is necessary to reconsider the development process necessary for this type of system (Atzeni et al., 1999).

Database Necessity

Many Web sites are currently based on files, in other words they store each Web page from the system in a separate file, which means a great maintenance effort. Even though it is never convenient to operate this way, if the Web site is a small system, it is not too difficult to control and maintain the information this way. Nevertheless, if the Web site is a large system, this situation can become chaotic, with serious administration and information management problems (Connolly et al., 1999). Besides, if the information in Web pages is static, it is very difficult to synchronize the information changes both in database and in HyperText Mark-Up Language (HTML) files. Connolly et al. (1999) indicate that it is more appropriate to generate Web pages dynamically, given that this way, the page is generated each time it is accessed through queries that extract the information from the database. In this way the information shown will always be updated. Neither do we have high Web page maintenance costs, something that occurs when they are static. This justifies the need for a dynamic data access interface, apart from a database information organization.

Object-Oriented Design

Schwabe and Rossi (1995) created the Object-Oriented Hypermedia Design Model (OOHDM). This work uses object-oriented abstraction and composition mechanisms to allow a concise description of complex information items, and allows the specification of complex navigation patterns and interface transformations. They propose an object-oriented process model. It is clear they thought an object-oriented paradigm is more adequate for designing Web systems (analysis, database design, navigational design).

The UML presents the deficiency of not being able to represent the necessary requirements that characterize Web applications (Connallen, 1999). The authors of the Unified Process and UML are starting to perform projects that relate object orientation with a possible modeling of Web system requirements.

Atzeni et al. (1999) indicate that if the structure of the Web system information to be developed is regular, and the information is homogeneous, such as in the site of a university (where the different departments have their own professors and courses), it is possible to share some of the techniques of database design for the design of certain parts of the Web system. In this case, Atzeni et al. (1999) propose an object-oriented model to represent the design and navigational structure of the system.

It seems as though the paradigm of the object orientation could be adequate for the design and development of Web applications.

Web System Object-Oriented Design Proposal

This proposal starts with some of the elements necessary to perform Web system object-oriented design. First, it is necessary to indicate three interest aspects or levels of Web sites:

- The information content, which is made up of data. As in databases, we can distinguish between schemas and instances.
- The hypertext structure, which describes how the information content is organized into pages and their links. The hypertext structure can be defined by a hypertext schema, with references to the database schema.
- The presentation, which describes the graphic aspects and the deployment of the content and links within the pages; the definition of presentation can also refer to the hypertext schema.

Atzeni et al. (1999) states that independence exists between levels (information content, hypertext structure, presentation). That is to say that the hypertext structure can be varied without altering the associated database structure. Also the presentation can be modified without modifying the hypertext and database structures.

A design method was suggested based on defining first the content (data) then the hypertext structure and finally the presentation. It seems appropriate to consider that the hypertext design could be the result on one hand of the conceptual database design, because it is necessary to know the information content for designing the hypertext, and on the other, the Web system's own requirements that is to say their characteristics and the needs of the users system. The hypertext structure is obtained of the hypertext design. Figure 5 shows the necessary elements for the design of the hypertext structure of a Web system.

Although the importance and relation between the conceptual data model and the hypertext model design is widely recognized, there are certain differences worth mentioning:

- The conceptual model tries to represent each entity as a class, whereas in the hypertext model, a page can incorporate one or more entity elements.
- In the conceptual model, the relationships between entities are represented in a non-redundant way, whereas in the hypertext, the links are conceived with the ease of navigation, which allows and strengthens redundancies.
- The hypertext model must provide page frameworks and independent links, to help navigation (homepage for instance).

Given that some aspects exist that are necessary to shape in the hypertext model and that are not referenced in the conceptual data-model, Atzeni et al. (1999) propose an intermediate model, termed hypertext conceptual model, where page information organization can be represented conceptually, as well as some necessary auxiliary structures.

Following the definition and justification of all of these aspects necessary for the design of a Web system, the following design method is proposed (see Figure 6):

- Requirements analysis, conceptual design and logical database design phases necessary for any database system.
- Conceptual hypertext design, obtained from the conceptual model and requirements analysis Web system before indicated. This phase represents some links between conceptual model entities, new entities that can indicate the main access structures of the site and new relationships. It is important to represent a hierarchical organization for enabling navigation to page instances.
- Logical hypertext design, which produces the logical hypertext framework from the conceptual. This phase represents the hypertextual structure.
- Presentation design which produces the presentation of each of the page frameworks defined in the logical design.
- Site generation, which refers to the integration of the information and the system navigational structure.

Web System Evolution

Just as in any of the previous technologies that have come up (databases, object orientation), the arrival of methodologies and new tools helps to construct newer systems which are more complete and less efficient, given that they try to cover all the neccessities and weaknesses that at first were not contemplated (Fraternali, 2000). Through this the evolution of any type of system is achieved.

To understand how far determined tools go and what help they provide, it is necessary to know certain characteristics of existing Web applications. Fraternali (2000) states that modern and current Web applications are a hybrid between known information systems and hypermedia applications: as hypermedia, through everything involved with navigatibility and the structure of the user interface information; as information system through the data, as far as its size and persistence in the topic of information distribution.

This mixed nature of a Web system makes its design and development identifiable by a series of requirements, which according to Fraternali (2000) are the following:

Figure 5. Elements needed for hypertext structure design

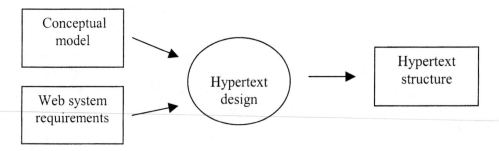

- The need to consider and provide both structural (database registers) and non-structured (multimedia).
- The need to provide navigational interfaces.
- High-quality graphics design.

Along with these requirements, there are a series of considerations to be taken into account in the creation of this type of system such as security, scalability and availability, and the evolution and maintenance of both the information and very system. The study of existing tools made by Fraterneli (2000) takes all these considerations into account.

Web Development Tools

Fraternali (2000) has grouped the different types of existing tools in five categories according to their capacities and Web applications development process coverage.

- **Visual Web site editors and administrator**
  This category covers the simplest tools, meaning those that have evolved directly from HTML editors, and that are not able to support large Web

Figure 6. Method for Web site design

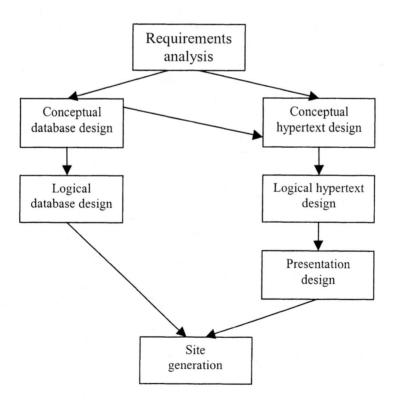

application developments with databases. They are worth mentioning seen as because they were the pioneers and incorporated important concepts such as presentation styles, among others.

They provide the user with the possibility to perform sophisticated HTML design without having to program, and with the possibility to administer the Web site graphically, with tools to review links, repairs, rough notes, etc. Some tools of this type also allow us to generate part of the navigational structure.

The architecture supported by this type of tool is file-based. Database connections are now possible thanks to the arrival of external components with connectivity to databases (Front Page 98 database objects, for example).

- **Web tools from hypermedia**
  These tools appeared with the objective of generating hypermedia applications, even if they have currently evolved to allow Web application development. Most of the commercial products of this sector incorporate database connection and Web development facilities, even though they are not always mutually compatible. All of these products share the following characteristics:
  - Navigational structures, which are generated through scripts, visual programming or assistants.
  - Connectivity to databases with the possibility of being an internal or external database with an ODBC connection or through a DBMS API.
  - The type of Web connectivity can be through a browser or by exporting the hypermedia application to a net language. This connectivity can affect the connectivity to the database, because the exporting of the Web application is allowed to those applications that are not connected to databases.
  - The exporting language can be HTML, Java or a mix of both.

  This type of tool is mainly focused on the generation of long-life hypermedia applications, such as CD catalogues. Due to this fact, they do not provide complete development support, presenting limitations in the modeling, design, tests and maintenance.

  As assistance to the applications that need an additional support, some tools allow us to reconfigure the structure and navigation of system, independent of its content.

- **Web DBPL integrators**
  The main characteristic of this type of tool is the dynamic construction of Web pages with the information from a database. The already-known net languages like JAVA and HTML incorporate DBPl, a database programing language. This is how programmers can jointly carry out Web implementation tasks and database accessing much easier. Due to their nature of generation-code focused tools, they do not assist developers with structure identification, navigation and application presentation.

- **Publication, report composition and Web sheet assistants**
  This tool group's main trait is to present an assistant that allows the prompt

generation of Web applications related to databases. Some of its main functions are:

- Database into exportation: to provide the possibility to export data originating from charts or queries (Microsoft Access 97, for instance).
- Report generators: to allow export reports to the Web (for example, Oracle's Report for the Web).
- Form generators: to allow the construction of consulting forms and information modification. There is a multitude of tools that support this function. Visual Basic 5, Oracle Developer 2000 and Access 97 are some of these.

In any case, these tools do not contemplate a CASE to support the conceptual model, nor the design. They are activities performed independently and later implemented with some of these tools.

- **Web generator applications**

These tools are the most complete of the classification presented here, since they incorporate the highest level of task automatization and life-cycle coverage. A noteworthy tool of this category is Oracle Web Development Suite, which includes Designer 2000. It is a CASE that allows Web application generation based on an entity-relation diagram. This tool's Web generator tool takes the information coming from the repository (designed using Designer), generates PL/SQL code, which is executed in Oracle's Web server to produce HTML pages.

These tools provide the Web application development with all the foundations of software engineering, allowing everything from conceptual level modeling to later code generation.

At the present time, Web technology is still very young and there is not a broad market of tools that are able to cover all the lifecycle necessary for the creation of a Web application. What does exist are a few tools that try to cover these expectations, unnaturally, given that they use processes and models coming from other technologies and contexts (Fraternali, 2000).

CONCLUSIONS

This chapter has briefly considered the main limitations of relational technology to support complex objects and complex relationships, introducing the main benefits of the object-oriented database systems. Object-oriented database technology includes both object-relational and object databases. First the object-relational model of the SQL:1999 standard and the object model of the ODMG standard was summarized. The comparison between relational, object-relational and object models has been made by means of an example. The example has been described in SQL-92 (standard language for relational databases), SQL: 1999 (standard language for object-relational databases) and ODL (standard language of object databases). Moreover, it was also defined for two commercial products: Oracle 8 (compliant with the SQL:1999 standard) and POET 4 (compliant with the ODMG standard). As one of the most relevant applications in the near future of database technology, we have to revise the state-of-the-art of the Web technology.

In the near future, relational technology will continue being the most used technology. Object-relational will be gaining some position on the market for specific applications that require more complex data (image, text, etc.). In the future object-relational technology, in our opinion, will replace the relational one. With regard to the object database technology, it will also continue being used in the market for specific applications for which ones the pure object model is better--we would note distributed and Web applications.

Object-oriented databases seem to be the most appropriate technology to support Web sites. Currently we are studying different products, both object-relational and object database products, in order to conclude which kind of technology is more adequate for Web development.

ACKNOWLEDGMENTS

This work is being carried out in the framework of the MIDAS project partially supported by the CICYT and the European Union (number 2FD97-2163), with the collaboration of INTESYS.

ENDNOTES

1 www.poet.com
2 www.odi.com
3 ISO: International Standards Organization
   IEC: International Electrotechnical Commission
4 ANSI: American National Standard Institute
5 OID: Object IDentifier

REFERENCES

Atzeni, P., Ceri, S., Paraboschi, S. and Torlone, R. (1999). Databases and the World Wide Web. *Database Systems: Concepts, Languages and Architectures*. McGraw-Hill.

Atzeni, Mecca and Merialdo. (1998). Design and maintenance of data-intensive Web sites. *Advances in Database Technology*. Ed. Sheck, Saltor, Ramos, Alonso. (Eds.). *Proceedings of the 6th Conference on Extended Database Technology (EDBT'98)*. Springer Verlag, Valencia.

Bertino, E. and Marcos, E. (2000). Object-oriented database systems. Díaz, O. and Piattini, M. (Eds.). In *Advanced Databases: Technology and Design*, Artech House, London.

Bertino and Martino. (1993). Object-oriented database systems. *Concepts and Architectures*, Addison-Wesley.

Blaha and Premerlani. (1998). *Object-Oriented Modeling and Design for Database Applications*. Prentice Hall.

Cattell, R. G. G. and Barry, D. K. (1997) *The Object Database Standard: ODMG 2.0*. Morgan Kaufmann, San Francisco.

Cattell, R. G. G. and Barry, D. (2000). *The Object Data Standard: ODMG 3.0*. Kaufmann: Morgan, San Francisco, 2000.

Conallen, J. (1999). Modeling Web application architectures with UML. *Communications of the ACM,* October, 42, 63-70.

Connolly, T., Begg, C. and Strachan, A. (1999). Web technology and DBMSs. *Database Systems. A Practical Approach to Design, Implementation and Management.* Second edition. Addison-Wesley.

Eisenberg, A. and Meltón, J. (1999). SQL:1999, formerly known as SQL3. *ACM SIGMOD Record*, March, 28(1), 131-138Fraternali, P. (2000). Tools and Approaches for Developing Data-Intensive Web Applications: A Survey. http://toriisoft.com.

Fraternali and Paolini, (1998). A conceptual model and a tool environment for developing more scalable, dynamic and customizable Web applications. Advances in Database Technology. Sheck, Saltor, Ramos, and Alonso. (Eds.). *Proceedings of the 6th. Conference on Extended Database Technology (EDBT'98)*. Springer Verlag, Valencia.

Heinckiens, P. M. (1998). *Building Scalable Database Applications*, Addison-Wesley.

Kovács, G. and Van Bommel, P. (1998). Conceptual modeling-based design of object-oriented databases, *Information and Software Technology*, 40(1), 1-14.

Mattos, N. M. (1999). SQL:1999, SQL/MM and SQLJ: An overview of the SQL standards. Tutorial, *IBM Database Common Technology*.

Melton, J. and Eisenberg, A. (2000). *Understanding SQL and Java Together. A Guide to SQLJ, JDBC and Related Technologies*. Kaufmann: Morgan, San Francisco.

Muller, R. J. (1999). *Database Design for Smarties*. Kaufmann: Morgan.

Schawe and Rossi. (1995). The object-oriented hypermedia design model. *Communications ACM*, August, 58(8), 45-46.

Silva, M. J. V. and Carlson, C. R. (1995). MOODD, a method for object-oriented database design. *Data & Knowledge Engineering*, 17, 159-181.

Stonebraker, M. and Brown, P. (1999). Object-relational DBMSs. *Tracking the Next Great Wave*. Kauffman: Morgan.

Ullman, J. D. and Widom, J. (1997). *A First Course in Database Systems*. New Jersey: Prentice-Hall.

Chapter X

INTECoM: An Integrated Approach to the Specification and Design of Information Requirements

Clare Atkins
Massey University, New Zealand

INTRODUCTION

An important contributor to the success of any complex database development is the comprehensive and accurate capture and recording of the users' information requirements. Indeed, both the technical and economic success of the system under development is likely to rest largely on the quality of the data structure design and the information requirement analysis on which it is based. The data models, which represent the results of the analysis and design activities necessary to achieve this quality outcome, are therefore critical components of the database development process. Nevertheless, research suggests that this modeling is not always done well and in some cases is not done at all (e.g., Hitchman, 1995). However, implicit in the creation of a database is the design of a data model, and thus the only optional feature is the level of formality that has been followed in its development (Simsion, 1994).

Since the publication of Chen's (1976) original description of an Entity-relationship (E-R) model, a significant amount of academic research into data modeling has concentrated on providing ever richer, more complex and more formal models with which to better represent reality (Hirschheim, Klein & Lyytinen, 1995). In addition, researchers and practitioners have also recognized the importance of data models as a means of communication. However, little attention has been given to examining the appropriateness of various modeling techniques to the very different requirements of the analysis and design activities that they support, although matching tools to activities would seem to be an essential prerequisite for success.

The INTECoM framework, described in this chapter, was developed to emphasize and better serve the differing nature of these activities, and also to improve access for all users to both the process and the outcome of data modeling. The framework was initially instantiated with two widely used data modeling techniques, the NIAM-CSDP (Natural Language Information Analysis-Conceptual Schema Design Procedure) and the Entity-Relationship (E-R) approach. This instantiation was chosen primarily because the two techniques represent significantly different ways of working (Bronts, Brouwer, Martens & Proper, 1995) towards the construction of a relational database. This is not to suggest that other instantiations are not possible or desirable, particularly where the target DBMS is of a different paradigm.

The framework provides a means of using existing techniques to greater advantage, by matching their particular strengths to the specific requirements of analysis and design. It also provides more accessibility through the use of a predictable, formalized subset of natural language and brings an additional benefit through the creation of an effective audit trail from individual user specification to final logical design. It thus encourages not only the production of quality outcomes but also of a quality development process.

BACKGROUND

The ANSI/SPARC report of 1975 (ANSI, 1975) contained proposals that have shaped and guided the development of database applications for the last 25 years. The adoption of the three-level architecture, which the report proposed, implicitly provided a template for a four-stage database design process within which the database designer should:

1. seek to ascertain each user's view of the data, i.e., **analyze** each user's data requirements;
2. amalgamate these views, i.e., **design** the conceptual schema;
3. create physical structures in which to store the relevant data, i.e., **create** the physical database design or internal schema; and
4. reproduce the original views for each individual user; i.e., **create** the external schema.

By implication, the users only needed to describe their view and eventually they would be provided with an interface to the data that accurately matched their initial specification. This rather optimistic view of the user's role in the process was perhaps never a reality and has certainly proved an elusive goal. However, the process, including the distinction between data analysis (step 1) and database design (steps 2 - 4), was formalized by Teorey and Fry (1982) and has remained the general approach to database development ever since.

There were no formal means of representing the conceptual schema until the publication of the E-R Model (Chen, 1976), which offered a relatively simple and intuitive means to fill the gap. The E-R Model was both free of the constraints of physical database structures and, through its diagrammatic means of representing data structures, provided a clearer and more intuitive way of communicating. Within a short time, these E-R diagrams became the most commonly used means of representing the conceptual schema. With the advent of relational database management systems, the use of E-R diagrams spread. As it utilized some constructs that mapped naturally to relational objects, and as no diagrammatic method had been provided for representing the Relational Model, a subset of the E-R notation became the favored way of representing relational schemata. Indeed, Date (1995) suggests that the E-R Model's lasting popularity may be due more to the existence of its diagramming method than to any other factor. The use of relational technology also created a shift in the perception of the internal schema. Database designers and administrators were now buffered from many of the actual physical structures by the DBMS itself, and in many situations technical staff could, like the users, view the database as a collection of tables. As a result, both technical and non-technical users also came to utilize some form of the E-R diagrammatic notation as a useful means of representing the physical database.

These pragmatic adaptations have been largely responsible for the development and widespread use of the E-R/Relational (E-R/R) hybrid (Atkins, 1996). This hybrid uses a subset of the E-R notation to provide a model that is generally characterized, at all three levels of the ANSI/SPARC architecture, by being normalized, having no relationship attributes and resolving all many-to-many relationships.

CURRENT PRACTICE

The ubiquitous use of the E-R/R hybrid has contributed to the creation of a fuzzy distinction between the analysis and design models constructed during database development. Although still commonly described by many texts and presumed by many academic researchers, the development of a Chen-type E-R model is little used by practitioners who prefer to utilize the E-R/R hybrid for both conceptual and design models (e.g., Simsion, 1994), which compounds the difficulties in differentiating them. Often the difference is seen as being one of detail alone, where the conceptual model is considered to be a simplified and highly abstracted view that is accessible to users, while the logical model provides the definitive statement of the users' requirements and needs careful user validation. The inherent contradiction in this position is never properly addressed. Such a conceptual model will not, by definition, contain all the refined detail necessary for rigorous validation, and users will therefore also need to validate the final design model. Yet if the conceptual model is considered to record only the outcome of analysis and the logical model to record the design of an appropriate data structure, a useful distinction can be made.

Analysis is an activity that seeks to determine the elements of something complex and to discover the general principles underlying these elements, while design is the action of creating a plan in accordance with appropriate functional or aesthetic criteria in order to facilitate the construction of an artifact. The benefits of distinguishing between these activities is recognized "because it is advantageous to have a well-defined step that emphasizes an inquiry of what the problem is before diving in to how to create a solution" (Larman, 1998 p.16). Simsion (1994) suggests that there are behavioral differences implicit in the different activities, pointing out that "in analysis, creativity suggests interference with the facts. No honest accountant wants to be called creative. On the other hand, creativity in design is highly valued" (p.7). Analysis requires what Kepner (1996) calls the "rational mode of thinking," where following an auditable, prescriptive method can lead to a conclusion based on observed facts using reason and logic. In other words, analysts are fact-finders and are expected to provide an unambiguous and verifiable statement of their findings.

Conversely, designers are rewarded for providing elegant re-interpretations and combinations of realities, particularly if their designs provide new insights into the problem. It calls on two other modes of thinking, intuitive and creative, which Kepner (1996) describes respectively as, "the thinking that occurs...when an idea simply

Table 1. Analysis and design comparison

Analysis Stage		
Modeler Behavior	**Approach**	**Required Outcome**
a) investigative fact finding b) decomposing complex domain c) accurate reporting of 'what is' or what is perceived to be d) identifying 'problem' e) understanding 'problem'	a) prescriptive, i.e., formal method b) repeatable c) auditable d) non-creative	a) accurate, complete and unambiguous record of users' perceived information requirements b) representation free of most implementation considerations b) representation easily understandable by current and future users
Design Stage		
Modeler Behavior	**Approach**	**Required Outcome**
a) generating alternatives b) creating innovative solutions c) imaginative d) working within specified parameters	a) non-prescriptive b) allow capture of creative thoughts c) allow re-use of previous solutions d) encourage flexible solutions e) provide room for personal judgment and preference	a) detailed design from which an electronic database can be constructed b) representation of the design understandable by technical users

wells up from the unconscious mind in response to the perception of a problem" and "thinking that…puts known elements together to form new ideas and visions"(p.3). The less prescriptive the approach, the more likely it is that innovative solutions can be found.

While individual authors may emphasize different aspects of the data modeling process, common sense would suggest that the database development process must include both requirements elicitation and logical data design, and will therefore require both analysis and design activities. Aspects of both these activities are summarized in Table 1. Considering their diversity, it seems unreasonable to expect one tool to do everything. To work effectively modelers need tools that not only lend themselves to a particular activity but which also produce the required outcomes.

These considerations raise the questions not only of what the analysis and design tasks require, but also the set of behaviors and activities required by different data modeling approaches. Bronts et al. (1995) termed this latter aspect the "way of working," which defines and orders the tasks that are to be performed during the construction of a model and provides guidelines and heuristics on how these tasks should be undertaken. While most modeling approaches use different constructs (e.g. objects, entities, roles, relationships) and thus have different ways of modeling, and through the use of different notations have different ways of communicating, Bronts (1995) suggest that, with the exception of the NIAM-CSDP, most approaches share a common way of working, exemplified by the E-R approach.

Characteristics of the E-R Approach

Most techniques provide methods to translate an E-R diagram to a relational schema, but "do not detail a precise set of rules and heuristics to develop the E-R diagram itself" (Batra & Zanakis, 1994, p.228). Lacking a prescriptive method, novice modelers are directed to identify the important entities and the relationships between them, but beyond a broad definition of what an entity may be, little further direction is given. In general, modelers are left to determine from their own intuition and experience, based on much trial and error, which nouns will make useful entities. This is less straightforward than it may seem as there are literally billions of ways of creating four categories of five items from a set of 20. There is also likely to be more than one workable answer, and part of the modeling task is to identify information structures that are useful to the enterprise. Simsion (1994) summarizes the situation, concluding that "entity identification is essentially a process of classifying data, and there is considerable room for choice and creativity in selecting the most useful classification" (p.82).

If the target implementation is relational, many modelers will view useful entities as partly normalized, candidate relations. Unfortunately, this may move the model away from the language and structure of the user's perception and into the realm of electronic storage. However, in the absence of clear guidelines and encouraged by the construction of an E-R/R hybrid diagram, it must seem safest to equate entities with relations, as Benyon (1997) specifically does, disallow relationships that contain attributes and use normalization to validate the appropriateness of the resulting structures.

The 'way of working' embodied in the E-R approach is thus essentially descriptive and creative. Using a combination of previous experience, trial and error, and personal judgment, a modeler is required to construct useful categories of data that both accurately reflect the user requirement and are potentially implementable. This pattern is extended and refined as the modeler's knowledge of the domain increases, and once a stable pattern begins to emerge, it may be tested for correspondence with the user's view of the enterprise and with the data structure constraints of the target DBMS. However, in the absence of a prescriptive method, there is no mechanism to ensure that this happens, and the quality of both the process and its outcome is dependant on the individual expertise of the modeler.

Characteristics of the NIAM-CSDP Approach

Object-Role Modeling (ORM) views the world as consisting of objects playing roles and expresses all information in terms of elementary facts, constraints and derivation rules (Halpin, 1995). Several methodologies have been developed for creating ORMs, of which NIAM is the best known. While ORM and the E-R Model are capable of expressing a similar level of meaning (Hitchman, 1995), NIAM adopts a very different way of working. The complete NIAM method (NIAM_ISDM) is made up of three stages of which the conceptual schema design (CSDP) is the first.

The CSDP begins with NIAM's "fundamental approach of building a design by *starting with specific examples* and thereafter following a well-defined procedure" (Nijssen & Halpin, 1989, p.31). Initially, information requirements are captured as natural language sentences, termed "facts," sentence patterns or "fact types" are then extracted from these sentences using real examples to validate the facts and assist in identifying the required constraints. On completion of the CSDP, the schema is transformed into a normalized, relational schema by a straightforward published algorithm (Nijssen & Halpin, 1989).

A detailed description of the NIAM-ISDM can be found in the text by Halpin (1995) and will not be discussed in detail here. However, a closer examination of the first step of the CSDP, i.e., the collection of information examples and their transformation into elementary facts and fact types, is useful. This step is the foundation of NIAM's design procedure and is procedurally equivalent to the identification of entities and relationships in the E-R approach.

There are three clear stages in the construction of elementary facts, the first of which is the collection of concrete examples from the system domain. Within NIAM it is considered to be the user's responsibility to provide these examples from their own perspective which, when considered together, should be sufficiently rich to describe all possible relevant facts. The second stage of the process is the expression of these examples in natural language sentences from which qualified elementary facts can be derived. In practice, experienced modelers will often omit the verbalization and move directly from the examples to qualified facts in much the same way as an experienced relational modeler will often instinctively create normalized entities. Qualified elementary facts have a formal structure, and while complex facts may include several objects and roles, in practice most facts are binary and thus include two objects and one role. The final stage is the extraction of the elementary fact types themselves. Noticeable patterns emerge in the derived sentences and the fact types are the expressions of these general patterns.

The NIAM-CSDP way of working is significantly prescriptive in the discovery stage of requirements analysis, and proceeds on the basis that the patterns are not created by the modeler but by the requirements themselves. It is not necessary for the modeler to provide any initial categorization or to use any implementational heuristics to guide the pattern creation. The procedure sets out the steps that must be undertaken in order to specify a formal model. The elementary sentences act as a natural way of expressing a user's requirements, while the examples provide a way of determining the basic constraints and as an aid in minimizing ambiguity. Although the sentences can be represented diagrammatically, it is not usually necessary for the user to view them in graphical form. The model, while directly transformable to a relational schema, does not require any specifically relational constructs and is thus theoretically equally suitable for mapping to any implementation paradigm.

INTECoM: AN INTEGRATED APPROACH

The INTECoM framework has been developed in the belief that viewing the ways of working represented by NIAM and E-R approaches as competing alternatives is less productive than viewing them as complementary. Thus the two ways of working are integrated into the four-step generic framework of database development discussed earlier. While the full framework, covers all four stages in outline, only the first two stages, the activities of which have been the focus of the preceding discussions, are discussed here in any detail. Figure 1 provides an overview of the INTECoM framework and the diagram highlights the inputs from each agent in the process and the outputs produced in each stage. The human agents are largely self-explanatory and represent roles rather than individuals. The data analyst records the information requirements of the users of the proposed system in a form that is acceptable to both the users and the designer. The data designer creates a data structure that both supports the documented requirements and is sufficiently flexible to allow for future changes.

Consequently, the designer must have a thorough understanding of the implementation paradigm of the target DBMS and should also be familiar with corporate data administration issues. The role of the database designer is well described in a number of standard texts (e.g., Date, 1995). Finally, the role of user will be taken by individuals drawn from all sections and levels of the organization, and their main responsibility will lie in describing their own information requirements and providing a full set of relevant examples.

Step 1. The Analysis of User Requirements

As analysis is concerned with determining and describing the components of something complex, when there is a significant element of discovery, or more specifically uncovering, about the activity. When dealing with a specific user, a record of the uncovered information requirements is required that is both comprehensible to, and verifiable by, the user and the analyst. The documented account of the

Figure 1. An integrated conceptual data modeling approach

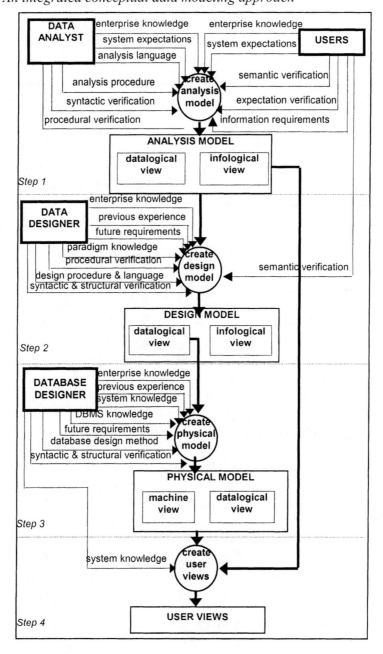

information requirements is the infological analysis model and its primary purpose is one of communication. Ideally, the process followed to discover the user requirements should be predictable and repeatable, i.e., any analyst given the same task should arrive at the same result. In other words, a prescriptive method, which also has the advantage of being auditable, is preferable. In addition, the analysis model needs to be consistent, unambiguous and transformable into a data structuring representation with no loss of validity and, thus, to provide a solid foundation from which to begin design.

The NIAM-CSDP provides a procedure that largely meets these criteria and can act as an exemplar of the kind of technique appropriate to this step. It provides a prescriptive method, which requires the active involvement of the user in providing both the facts and the examples. The direct correspondence between the ORM diagram that is constructed and the formalized natural language example fact types from which it is derived, allow for different representations suitable for either the technical or non-technical user with no information loss. Indeed, non-technical users need never see, or even be aware of, the graphical representation. However, the completed model is transformable, by application of a published algorithm, into a normalized relational design. Most importantly, the requirements can be documented with minimal design decisions having been made, as it is not necessary to decide on the type of construct that will be used to represent an object before the object, or any facts in which it participates, can be recorded.

By recording each user view independently, the CSDP can also be used to explore and document conflicting views and alternative viewpoints. If the requirement specification activity is seen as a precursor to design and not as the design itself, the pressure to resolve any differences in the user's view can be removed. In this way, a discrete record of each user's individual requirement can be preserved which allows for the creation of a detailed audit trail, provides a basis for the construction of the external schemata and ensures that the resolution of conflicts becomes firmly an issue of design rather than analysis.

INTECoM requires the output of this step to be a record of each individual user's data requirements, represented as a set of formalized natural language sentences enhanced with examples and constraint information. A diagrammatic representation of these sentences may also be included as the datalogical version of the model. Each discrete view must also be verified by the appropriate user.

Step 2. The Design of the Logical Model

The design activity is one of creative and innovative construction. It is an attempt to bring together possibly conflicting and disparate elements into a harmonious, and ultimately, useful whole. As such, the activity relies on the individual flair and creativity of the designer, who will almost certainly bring past experience and experimentation to the work. Attempts to constrain this creativity by mechanistic prescription are likely to be counterproductive. However, the designer needs to have clearly defined elements to work with. An understanding of the required data-structuring paradigm is an essential prerequisite, as is a clear idea of what is required. The final output of this step will be a design model of the data, structured in a form that is appropriate to its target DBMS, e.g., a relational model. This output is likely to appear, to the users, to be significantly different from the previous one, and while it is impractical to insist that the method used to create it is auditable, nevertheless there needs to be some means of verifying that the original requirement specifications are still being supported.

The E-R/Relational hybrid approach provides techniques which are appropriate to this kind of design activity, at least where the target DBMS is a relational one. It is an inherently creative technique that encourages the development of alternative data structures, each of which can embody different levels of business rules and constraints (Simsion, 1994). Many of the structures will be those suggested by the patterns identified within the relationships of the data elements themselves, but new patterns can be constructed or existing ones enhanced to provide innovative solutions. Within the design stage the propensity for entities to be equated with relations is no longer problematic, while the need for the designer to make an informed choice of construct for any specific element is no longer dangerous, but should be positively encouraged. The requirement for entities to be strictly typed is also no longer a cause of difficult communication between the user and the analyst/designer. Instead, it can become a positive advantage to the designer who is concerned with identifying entities that can be transformed into their strictly typed counterparts within the relational model. In design, there is no longer any expectation of one correct answer, but instead an expectation of several useful solutions, all of which will demonstrate particular advantages and disadvantages. Likewise, decisions as to which part of the system will handle each business requirement can have a direct bearing on the form of the data model (Simsion, 1994), and belong more properly to the designer rather than to the analyst. After all, understanding the compromises and trade-offs involved in the final choice is part of the designer's skill.

The initial input into the design stage is the output of the analysis phase, described above, which is immediately transformed into a first draft logical design. This will, in fact, be a number of discrete models, representing the individual user views, which will need to be integrated by the designer before further work takes place. There are also likely to be requirements that have not been collected during analysis, such as those which arise from future expectations of the system. An essential ingredient of the design model is the flexibility to adapt to future possibilities, and the designer needs to be aware of, and prepared to incorporate, these. Apart from these unknowns, the designer is able to gain a holistic view of the system's requirements relatively quickly and, if the analysis has been carried out competently, with an assurance that no nasty surprises await discovery at a later stage in the process. Thus the development of alternatives and possibly the creation of exploratory prototypes can begin early in the design phase.

The output of the design stage is a data model conforming to the appropriate paradigm constraints (i.e., normalization) and ready for transformation to a physical database schema. Its form will thus conform to the usual expectation of the E-R/R hybrid approach, that is an E-R/R diagram supported by the usual data dictionary documentation. This final design model may well be unrecognizable to the users who provided the initial specifications, yet it is essential that they are able to judge that, despite the resolution of conflicting requirements and incorporation of future possibilities, their requirements can still be met. Atkins and Patrick (2000) describe NALER, a method for extracting NIAM-type natural language sentences from an E-R/R model, to provide not only an understandable translation of the design specification, but also a means of linking the design model directly back to the original user requirements.

INTECoM-A WORKED EXAMPLE

INTECoM is primarily designed to bring benefits to non-trivial developments involving a number of developers and users. Nevertheless, a small development, in the nature of a worked example, was used to demonstrate its feasibility, its practical application and the validity of the arguments employed in its creation. In addition, it demonstrates the means by which the quality, both of the process and of the models, can be assessed.

The Quality Framework

The INTECoM quality framework illustrated in Figure 2 is based on and extends the work of Lindland et al. (1994) and Krogstie et al. (1995), which viewed a conceptual model as a representation of statements taken from a domain, expressed using some form of formal grammar or language. Each aspect of the framework is clearly defined. **Language** represents the statements that can be made according to the specific modeling syntax, and is constructed using an alphabet (the set of modeling constructs) and a grammar (the rules that govern the use of the constructs). In addition, the language also has semantics, which define the meaning of the constructs and thus enable meaning to be derived from them. The definition of **domain** is close to the relational notion of a pool of allowable values. Thus the framework's domain consists of all the possible statements that would be correct and relevant for solving the problem. The set of statements actually made in the language or which can be derived from such statements, is the **model**, and the **process** is the procedure that is used to create the model. The audience is defined as all those who need to understand the model, and **audience interpretation** is then the set of statements that the audience thinks the model contains, while **participant knowledge** is the collection of all subsets of statements correct and relevant for a particular user or group of users.

The connections between these concepts provide the links which not only create the framework, but which provide the basis for the important quality goals. The **syntax** link relates the model to the modeling language and has as its goal the correct use of the modeling constructs. The **semantics** link represents the meaning conveyed by the use of the modeling language and has two goals, validity and completeness. However Krogstie et al. (1995) consider this to be an unattainable goal and prefer to focus on **perceived semantics**. The goals remain the same but recognize that both the validity and completeness of the model can only ever reflect the participants' knowledge of the domain. The **pragmatics** link relates the model to the audience by considering not only the syntax and semantics, but also how the audience will interpret them. The **procedure** link represents the way in which the model has been constructed and has as its goal proof that the method used was both explicit and followed appropriately. **Social agreement** recognizes the relationship between the different audience interpretations and has the goal of agreement between them. Finally, **structure** describes the way in which the elements of the model have been put together and has the goals of inherent soundness of the model and its fitness for purpose.

The quality goals derived from this framework were used to identify quality measures appropriate to both the analysis and design steps of an INTECoM development using NIAM-CSDP and E-R Modeling, and these are listed in Table 2.

Step 1

The example development was the creation of a database of postgraduate students and began with the creation of an analysis task checklist illustrated in Table 3. The inputs, as identified in the analysis phase of INTECoM, were as follows: both users' and the data analyst's *enterprise knowledge* was extensive and their *system expectations,* captured in a context diagram and a short statement, were realistic and informed. The *analysis procedure* of the NIAM-CSDP and the *analysis language* of

Figure 2. INTECoM Quality Framework

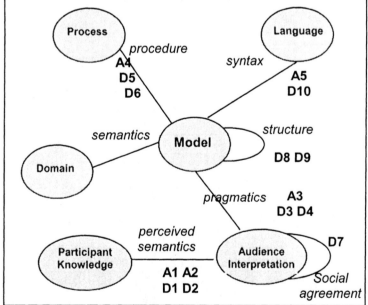

ORM were well understood by the data analyst but not the users. The *information requirements* of the system were considered from four viewpoints, and the requirements were derived from a number of sources, including examination of current documentation and user interviews.

The process followed that laid down by the NIAM-CSDP, adapted to the effective use of a supporting CASE tool. A complete set of fact types, populated with examples, was created independently for each view. At the end of the stage, the fact

Table 2. Quality evaluation of analysis and design models

	Analysis Model	
	Quality Goal	**Means**
A1	Semantic completeness	User confirms view is complete
A2	Semantic correctness	Each fact has complete set of correct & relevant examples
A3	Pragmatic correctness a) understandable b) understood	Confirmation that model is understandable & understood
A4	Procedural correctness	Task checklist in place Task checklist complete
A5	Syntactic correctness	Fact types are well formed and example set is complete. All objects are defined. All constraints are recorded.
	Design Model	
	Quality Goal	**Means**
D1	Semantic completeness	User confirms view, as shown by NaLER sentences, is complete. Confirmation of future requirements
D2	Semantic correctness	Each NaLER sentence has a complete set of correct and relevant examples.
D3	Understandability	Complete set of instantiated NaLER sentences
D4	Understood	Efficient and effective verification User confirmation
D5	Procedural correctness	Task checklist in place and complete
D6	Auditability	All NaLER sentences can be traced to their originating requirement.
D7	Social agreement	Full view integration Complete set of instantiated NaLER sentences
D8	Flexibility	Datalogical model is in BCNF
D9	Simplicity	No redundant relationships, primary keys are minimal, all relations are required
D10	Syntactic correctness	The datalogical model is relationally correct.

types and examples for each user view were *syntactically verified* through the use of the validate function of the supporting CASE tool while s*emantic verification* was provided by each user who was shown only the fact types and examples relevant to their own view. In addition, the modeler provided *procedural verification*.

The outcome of the step was a set of documentation that INTECoM terms the "analysis model," comprising the infological view, i.e., the complete set of verified natural language fact types, object descriptions and examples, and the datalogical view, i.e., the ORM diagrams and repository information.

Step 2

The second stage, the creation of the logical model, also began with the creation of a task checklist for the stage (Table 4), which reflected the main activities required by the use of the E-R/R approach but was augmented with a number of tasks required by INTECoM.

The activities fell into three groups: preparing the first draft design model (Task 1), creating the final design model (Tasks 2-4), and verifying the final design model (Tasks 5-9). The first group of activities required the creation of individual relational representations for each user view and their amalgamation into one model. The second followed the usual design activities required by a relational development and the final group was a mixture of new and traditional validation techniques.

The transformation of the various user views was achieved by the use of the facilities of the CASE tool. For each view, a logical model was generated automatically and a generic SQL schema for each transformation was created. The amalgamation of the views was achieved manually by the application of several heuristics. Firstly, a list showing the primary keys of all entities in all views was created and sorted alphabetically. This allowed the identification of all entities that had the same primary key, and these entities were considered to be equivalent. This heuristic was based on the assumption that entities identified by the same properties would have a

Table 3. Analysis task checklist

No.	Task	Quality Goal
1	Record system expectations	
2	Identify appropriate users	
3	Collect initial sentences	
4	Construct qualified fact types	
5	Confirm qualified fact types	A1, A2
6	Collect examples	
7	Confirm example sentences	A1, A2
8	Verify syntax	A5
9	Confirm expectation met	
10	Confirm sentences are understandable and understood	A3
11	Confirm task checklist fulfilled	A4

high probability of representing the same thing. The remaining entities were combined to form the first draft design model.

This model served as the starting point for the design of the relational data structures, and several alternatives were tested in various areas of concern. In addition, a known future requirement was incorporated and a final draft design model was eventually arrived at. This model was checked for *syntactic* and *structural* errors. A check was also made for *normal form conformity*. This model was then used as the basis for the users' semantic verification.

In order to complete the semantic verification of the model, a complete set of NaLER sentences was created and instantiated with examples taken from the original analysis documents. In order to facilitate the users' verification of the design model and to provide an *audit trail* from analysis to design, a table was constructed to correlate the NaLER sentences of the design model with the original fact types of the analysis model. This provided an opportunity to check that all user requirements had been captured and to ensure that the modeler was familiar with any differences between the original user views and their final relational form. A set of user verification documentation was then assembled for each view. To gain *semantic verification*, the modeler talked through each fact type and corresponding NaLER sentence with the relevant user, using the examples but not the diagrams. Finally, the modeler provided *procedural verification.*

This completed the activities, and the two outputs for this stage. The datalogical model consisted of a standard E-R/R deliverable while the infological model consisted of the set of verified NaLER example sentences derived from the data structure.

Steps 3 and 4

The final steps of creating the physical model and the physical user views followed traditional methods and are not considered here.

INTECoM – SOME OBSERVATIONS

The Collection of Examples

An initial concern had been that the collection of a complete set of examples would not be possible and that this inability would reflect adversely on the outcome of the analysis. Indeed, neither NIAM nor INTECoM can guarantee that a complete list of examples has been gathered. However, in this case the request to provide examples resulted in a very full set and initially did lead to the identification of new fact-types. The disciplined behavior required to collect and document a full set of examples may be an improvement on the more *ad hoc* methods used in the E-R tradition. No problems stemming from an inability to collect sufficient examples were identified. While some fact types were added

Table 4. Design task checklist

No.	Task	Quality Goal
1	Prepare first draft design model	
1.1	Transform analysis models to relational representations	
1.2	Amalgamate logical views	
1.2.1	*List all entities and PKs*	
1.2.2	*Merge entities with same PK*	
1.2.3	*Check for synonyms*	
1.2.4	*Check for similar PKs*	
2	Generate/evaluate alternatives	
3	Incorporate future requirements	
4	Create final draft design	
5	Verify final design	
5.1	Syntax Check	**D10**
5.1.1	***Create 2-way sentences***	
5.1.2	***Check participation constraints***	
5.1.3	***Check PK-FK links***	
5.1.4	***Check normalization***	**D8**
5.2	Simplicity check	**D9**
5.2.1	*Check for minimal primary keys*	
5.2.2	*Check for redundant relationships*	
5.2.3	*Check for trivial relations*	
5.2.4	*Check all relations are required*	
5.3	Semantic check	**D2, D3, D7**
5.3.1	*Create NaLER sentences*	
5.3.2	*Populate NaLER with examples from analysis model*	
5.3.3	*Create cross reference table – analysis facts to NaLER sentences*	
5.3.4	*Check for completeness*	
5.3.5	*Check for consistency*	
6	Audit	D6
6.1	Check source of all NaLER sentences	
7	Peer review	
8	User verification	D1, D4
7.1	Create NaLER user views	
7.2	Correlate NaLER and analysis views	
7.3	Gain user verification	
9	Task checklist complete	D5

during the design phase, they all resulted from legitimate design activities and not from a deficiency in the analysis.

The Use of Examples

The possession of a detailed set of examples was extremely useful in several situations. The amalgamation of views required the identification of synonyms and homonyms, and reference to the values within the relevant example sentences provided a sound basis for such decision-making. In addition, the existence of example sentences allowed the modeler to ensure a significant amount of semantic veracity as the development progressed. At both the end of the analysis phase, and particularly, at the point of creating the NaLER sentences, the existence of the initial example sentences was invaluable. In the latter case it provided a tool to identify whether all the analysis facts had been represented in an appropriate form. The users were enthusiastic in their use of the examples, and it was observed that they were used on several occasions as an aid to understanding.

The Use of Analysis Views

The development demonstrated the benefits of preserving each unique user view throughout the analysis phase. Firstly, the process of amalgamation requires decisions of a design nature to be made. A major element in the justification for the use of INTECoM rests on the principle that design decisions should be avoided in the analysis stage wherever possible. It was also observed that although completeness could not be guaranteed; nevertheless, retaining all aspects of all views throughout the analysis stage minimized the loss of essential facts. In addition, it would seem significantly safer to consciously choose to omit a fact during the design phase than to decide, perhaps early on in analysis, that a fact is either not important or can be accurately captured by an alternative construct in a different user's view.

The Creation of an Audit Trail

The instantiation of the NaLER sentences, with examples taken from the original analysis model, provides an obvious and natural opportunity to identify which NaLER sentences correspond to which analysis fact types. This produces benefits in the later stages of the design phase as it can be used:

- to check that all fact types identified in the analysis have been appropriately incorporated into the design model, and where this is not the case, allow remedial action to be taken before the presentation of the model to the users;
- to re-create the appropriate user views with the NaLER sentences, thus eliminating the need for each user to comprehend the entire design model; and
- to ensure that the modeler can account for all the facts contained in the design model, tracing their individual existence back to either a user requirement, the recognition of a future or functional requirement or the constraints of the database paradigm.

The existence of an audit trail can also provide an improved level of confidence in both user and modeler. If the modeler has already needed to justify the connection between a certain analysis fact type and its equivalent NaLER sentence, it is easier to predict likely questions and prepare clear explanations. In addition, the users can quickly verify the facts that are clearly the same in both models, and concentrate instead on those which appeared to have changed. In the example development, both the modeler and the users felt that this reduced the time necessary for verification and increased their confidence that the verification was accurate.

INTECoM-THE BENEFITS

The most significant effects of the use of INTECoM are likely to result from the clear demarcation between the stages of analysis and design. It is generally accepted in other areas of information systems development that the different stages will require different activities and techniques (Avison & Fitzgerald, 1995). The tacit acceptance of a situation in data modeling that provides a single technique to fulfill the functions of both stages is both widespread and potentially dangerous.

Analysis and Design Demarcation

INTECoM recognizes the differences in analysis and design activities and seeks to match those activities with appropriate techniques and quality goals. In so doing, it also seeks to minimize the amount of design decisions made early in the process by utilizing a technique which defers such decisions until the end of the analysis stage. The use of E-R modeling for recording the results of analysis encourages some fundamental design decisions to be made at the outset, decisions that may never be revisited. During the analysis stage of INTECoM, the focus is very clearly on understanding and recording the data requirements of each user, in a form that is accessible to those users without the need for specific IS skills. As a result, the behavior of the data analysts, and the background and skills that they require, are clearly differentiated from those of the data designers.

Clarification of the Analyst Role

Data analysts using the INTECoM framework could be expected to interact with appropriate users or user representatives, on an individual basis, and be specifically focused on uncovering and recording a complete and accurate view of the users' perceived needs. Using the NIAM-CSDP as an analysis tool, there is no requirement to reconcile those views as they are collected, but only to record each one accurately. The analyst needs to be skillful in assisting the user to identify relevant needs and to provide appropriate examples. Interpersonal skills are likely to be highly valued, and a good understanding of the organization's business is likely to be more useful than a detailed understanding of database theory.

Analysis Consistency

As the NIAM-CSDP provides a significantly more prescriptive approach to analysis than E-R modeling, it should be possible to ensure more consistent results from different analysts. This is an important consideration in cooperative situations, reducing the amount of re-work required in integrating a number of individual models in large applications and reducing the amount of inappropriate creativity which may be introduced by individual categorization at too early a stage. It would, therefore, be reasonable for the analysis to be conducted by a number of different people, even in geographically remote locations, as the resulting fact types, which need to be supported by appropriate examples, will be consolidated and integrated at a later stage.

Clarification of the Designer Role

On the other hand, the second stage of INTECoM would begin with a set of clearly documented, individual user requirements. Although additional requirements may need to be addressed by the designer, in most situations a large part of the analysis work will have been completed. The designer is thus able to focus on creating appropriate data structures to support specific requirements. The skills required by a data designer will thus include a thorough understanding of the database paradigm for which they are designing, together with a flair for innovative problem solving. The primary focus of the designer would not be on interacting with the users but on transforming their documented requirements into appropriate database structures. While designers undoubtedly have a responsibility to the users, it is primarily to their technical colleagues that they should be required to justify their designs and decisions.

User Accessibility

Another benefit is an increase in user accessibility, both to the process and to the models themselves. While expert modelers may use past experience and re-use previous patterns successfully, there is always a danger that a clear focus on the specific information requirements of the users may be lost. This situation runs the risk of only capturing the modeler's view of the requirements. The designers' brief, after all, is to create an optimum solution. However, this behavior requires a considerable degree of faith on the part of the users, to whom it may not be clear whether or not the unfamiliar names and constructs will support their information needs.

The use of the infological models helps to alleviate this alienation and increase the users' level of confidence in the personnel, the process, and the models themselves. The use of a formalized subset of natural language--as, from the users' perspective, the language of analysis and design--improves the chances of accurate validation and releases users from the need to understand technical jargon and techniques. It thus increases the potential for positive user involvement. The conceptual models created during the analysis and design stages provide one of the most important foundations for the development of an information system; errors in them may not be uncovered until much further through the development lifecycle and may be costly to correct. For this reason, if no other, it is essential that user access to them should be as straightforward as possible.

Flexibility

The existence of a distinct analysis stage also provides a much greater degree of flexibility than a process that views analysis and design as a hybrid activity. The INTECoM analysis model should be much less implementation-oriented than its traditional counterpart. If there were to be a significant paradigm shift in database technology, many currently constructed conceptual data models would become obsolete. By avoiding the use of quasi-relational constructs such as entities, the analysis model contains far less implementation bias than its E-R/R counterpart. Such a model would thus be better positioned to become the basis for non-relational database designs.

Quality Control

The use of the INTECoM framework also provides a practical opportunity for quality control, not only of the models themselves but also of the process whereby they are constructed. Conceptual modeling errors can signify errors in database processing, and this is particularly likely to occur if the modelers are unable to account for the use of constructs in their model. The "way of controlling" (Bronts et al., 1995) has not been a central focus here, but INTECoM clearly provides a large number of built-in checks. The existence of individual user requirements, clearly documented in accessible language, together with the expectation that the designer will provide an infological view of the design, combine to offer opportunities to track the means by which specific requirements are being met or conflicts resolved. Thus a two-way audit trail is constructed for every statement of user requirement and every element of the final design, providing a means of accountability that is not possible using traditional methods.

CONCLUSION

Clearly the use of any methods, tools or framework does not substitute for clear logical thinking and conscientious attention to matters of quality. Nevertheless, the use of the INTECoM framework, which by combining the prescriptive, analytical approach of the NIAM-CSDP with the essentially creative elements of E-R/R modeling utilizes the strengths of both approaches while compensating for some of their weaknesses, may well prove beneficial. However, empirical testing of this hypothesis in a medium to large organization is needed and is planned for the future. INTECoM's own strength lies partly in the fact that it does not require the introduction of a large number of new skills, methods or techniques and partly in that it encompasses an already recognized framework for database development. While the use of INTECoM may necessitate a new attitude for the two techniques and how they fit into the overall development cycle, with the exception of NaLER, the techniques themselves are extensively documented and have been widely tested. Although experienced practitioners may find the framework overly constraining, INTECoM offers a number of beneficial implications for less experienced modelers and those organizations that do not currently make sophisticated use of data modeling. Finally, in keeping with the intention of the ANSI/SPARC architecture, users are only required to provide, understand and validate their own view of their information requirements.

REFERENCES

ANSI. (1975). ANSI/X3/SPARC study group on data base management systems: Interim report. *ACM SIGMOD Bulletin,* 7(2).

Atkins, C. F. and Patrick, J. D. (2000). NaLER: A natural language method for interpreting entity-relationship models. *Campus-Wide Information Systems* 17(3), 85-93.

Atkins, C. F. (1996). Prescription or description: Some observations on the conceptual modeling process. Purvis, M. (Ed.). In *Proceedings of Software Engineering: Education and Practice Conference,* University of Otago, Dunedin, New Zealand, 34-41.

Avison, D. E. and Fitzgerald, G. (1995). *Information Systems Development: Methodologies, Techniques and Tools.* Second edition. Maidenhead, UK: McGraw-Hill.

Batra, D. and Zanakis, S.H. (1994). A conceptual database design approach based on rules and heuristics. *European Journal of Information Systems,* 3(3), 228-239.

Benyon, D. (1997). *Information and data modeling.* Second edition. London: McGraw-Hill.

Bronts, G., Brouwer, S. J., Martens, C. L. J. and Proper, H. A. (1995). A unifying object role modeling theory. *Information systems,* 20(3), 213-235.

Chen, P. P. (1976). The entity-relationship model-Toward a unified view of data. *ACM transactions on database systems,* 1(1), 9-36.

Date, C. J. (1995). *An introduction to database systems.* Sixth edition.. Reading, Massachusetts: Addison-Wesley.

Halpin, T. A. (1995). *Conceptual schema and relational database design.* Second edition. Sydney, Australia: Prentice Hall.

Hirschheim, R., Klein, H. K. and Lyytinen, K. (1995). *Information systems development and data modeling: Conceptual and philosophical foundations.* Cambridge, UK: Cambridge University Press.

Hitchman, S. (1995). Practitioner perceptions on the use of some semantic concepts in the entity-relationship model. *European Journal of Information Systems,* 4, 31-40.

Kepner, C. H. (1996). Calling all thinkers. *H R Focus,* 73(10), 3.

Krogstie, J., Lindland O. I. and Sindre, G. (1995). Towards a deeper understanding of quality in requirements engineering. *Proceedings of 7th CAiSE,* Jyvaskyla, Finland.

Lindland, O. I., Sindre, G. and Sølvberg, A. (1994). Understanding quality in conceptual modeling. *IEEE Software,* March, 42-49.

Larman, C. (1998). *Applying UML and Patterns: An Introduction to Object-Oriented Analysis and Design.* Upper Saddle River, NJ: Prentice Hall.

Nijssen, G. M. and Halpin, T. A. (1989). *Conceptual Schema and Relational Database Design.* Sydney, Australia: Prentice Hall.

Simsion, G. (1994). *Data Modeling Essentials: Analysis, Design and Innovation.* Boston: Van Nostrand Reinhold.

Teorey, T. J. and Fry, J. P. (1982). *Design of Database Structures.* Englewood Cliffs, NJ: Prentice-Hall.

Chapter XI

Inclusion Dependencies

Laura C. Rivero
Universidad Nacional del Centro de la
Provincia de Buenos Aires, Argentina
Universidad Nacional de La Plata,
Buenos Aires, Argentina

Jorge H. Doorn and Viviana E. Ferraggine
Universidad Nacional del Centro de la
Provincia de Buenos Aires, Argentina

ABSTRACT

The evaluation of conceptual schemes of actual databases may result in the discovery of inclusion dependencies. An inclusion dependency is defined as the existence of attributes in a table whose values must be a subset of the values of attributes in another table. When the latter set conforms a key for its table, the inclusion dependency is key-based. Key-based inclusion dependencies are fully enforced by most current database systems. On the contrary, if the second set is not the key of the relation, the inclusion dependency is non-key-based. This kind of inclusion dependency is completely disregarded by actual systems, obliging the users to manage them via special-case code or triggers. This implies an excessive effort to maintain integrity and develop applications, among other inconveniences. The chapter goal is to give a heuristics to redesign the conceptual schema. This is based on the identification of hidden business rules and the conversion of non-key inclusion dependencies into key-based ones.

INTRODUCTION

Software engineers seldom have to deal with perfectly conceived software artifacts or with organizational contexts in higher levels of the Capability Maturity Model (Paulk, et. al.). They should be able to deal with poorly controlled processes, facing the challenge of improving them towards well-defined developed environments. The reengineering of available software systems is absolutely necessary in these situations. Software tools, guides, heuristics, etc. could make an important difference in the process of quality improvement. This chapter focuses on these problems in relational database applications.

Frequently the conceptual schema of a relational database becomes obscure and hard to read, since many users do not carefully follow well-defined design methods. This happens no matter how many books, papers and manuals recommend this practice.

In the real-world there are inexperienced and poorly trained database designers building low quality conceptual schemas. However, good training and experience do not ensure a good design. Several other conditions are needed, mainly related to the organizational context.

Malpractices usually lead to a semantically poor database schema restraining the effective utilization of data by the enterprise. Moreover, objects omitted or removed from the physical schema obscure interobject dependencies. However, the schema can be restored since it is always possible to move back to a well-supported process (Figure 1). This chapter is devoted to give support to the reengineering of the actual system.

Conceptual schemas of actual databases holding these design flaws usually contain inclusion dependencies. As can be read in Codd (1990, p. 26), "...Referential integrity is a particular application of an inclusion dependency. Such a constraint requires that the set of distinct values occurring in some specified column, simple or composite, must be a subset of the values occurring in some other specified column (simple or composite, respectively). In the case of referential integrity restrictions (key-based inclusion dependencies), the set of distinct simple foreign key values

Figure 1. The reengineering process

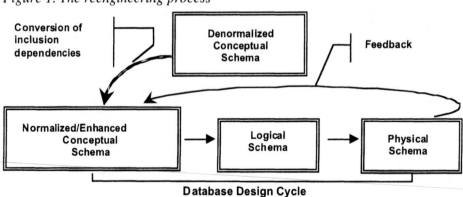

should be a subset of the set of distinct simple primary key values drawn from the same domain. Pure inclusion dependencies, however, may apply between other pairs of attributes also (e.g., non-keys)...." Figure 2 shows the components of an inclusion dependency.

Formally, one inclusion dependency (*id*) is an expression $R_l[X] \subseteq R_r[Z]:(\alpha,\beta,\mu_l, \mu_r)$. R_i and R_j are relation names (possibly the same); $R_l[X]$ and $R_r[Z]$ are named the inclusion dependency's left and right side respectively. X, Z are compatible attributes. α, β, μ_l and μ_r are the referential actions for insertions, deletions and updates over the left and right side respectively. They may be *Cascade, Restricted* or *Set Null*. When Z is the primary key of R_r, the *id* is key-based (also named a referential integrity restriction, *rir*). In this case, X constitutes a FK for R_l. The *rir* is stated as $R_l[FK_l] << R_r[K_r]:(\alpha,\beta,\mu_l,\mu_r)$. From now on *id* is used only for the non-key-based inclusion dependencies and *rir* for the key-based ones. K_i stands for a candidate key over R_i and FK_i represents a foreign key for R_i (Abiteboul, Hull & Vianu, 1995).

Key-based inclusion dependencies are fully (or at least partially) enforced by most current database systems. On the contrary, non-key inclusion dependencies are completely disregarded by actual systems, obliging the users to manage them via special-case code or triggers. Moreover, if a non-key inclusion dependency is present, it is very likely that the schema has other design flaws. The inconvenience created by their presence includes data inconsistency and excessive effort required for the development of application programs and integrity maintenance, among others.

Unfortunately, low quality designs having non-key inclusion dependencies are common, and then it is necessary to have strategies for their correct modeling. The goal is to transform those hard-to-maintain denormalized schemes into schemas with only key-based inclusion dependencies (having the same information content) by using a method as syntactical as possible.

In this proposal, configurations of the inclusion dependencies' left and right sides are considered at first from a syntactic viewpoint. After that, a set of hypotheses related to the presence of non-key inclusion dependencies is developed, highlighting their possible origin from a semantic point of view. With basis on these hypotheses, a heuristics is presented. It will allow the conversion of the conceptual

Figure 2. Components of an inclusion dependency

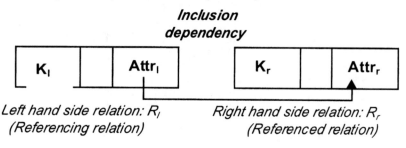

schema into a normalized one, showing omitted objects and hidden relationships. Non-key inclusion dependencies are converted into key-based inclusion dependencies until a point of irreducibility is reached. Next, the context conditions that specify whether the remaining non-key inclusion dependencies can be ignored or maintained are established.

The poor quality problem in conceptual schemas may be also present in object-relational (OR) and object-oriented (OO) databases. The difficulties in understanding these actual physical schemas are similar to those found in relational databases. Although this chapter is concerned primarily with relational design, these ideas are relevant for non-relational systems as well.

With the development of new models, the dependency theory has become in some way out of fashion. Dependency theory analyzes functional, multivalued and inclusion dependencies. However, those concepts are embedded in the more elaborated constructs found in current database models. The knowledge captured in the relational context can be used in such constructs, and the techniques to detect hidden objects, proposed in this chapter, can be used with minor changes to refine obscure designs in OR and OO environments. However, they are easy to understand in the relational paradigm. The concepts developed in this chapter are also of concern in other research areas, such as migration from relational systems to other DBMSs, federated databases, documentation of the meaning of existing databases and legacy systems.

In order to obtain an enhanced conceptual schema, two main activities must be carried out:

a) *Capture of the hidden, poorly specified or confused knowledge recorded in the database.* Particularly, hidden entities and their relationships are detected. A hidden entity is one that has not been made explicit as a relation in the schema, but it conceptually exists.

b) *Enhancement of the metadatabase (relation-schemes and the set of constraints) with the obtained knowledge.*

Figure 3. shows this process. The top box in the "Enrichment of the Metadatabase" frame corresponds to step a) and the following two, to step b).

Figure 3. Enrichment of the metadatabase

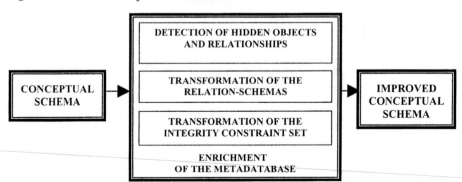

Simple schemes may be treated with a few transformation rules but complex designs involving a large number of tables and attributes need formal methods for the conversion of such schemas.

RELATED WORK

Many research projects are devoted to the development of methodologies and heuristics in order to address the enhancement of the conceptual schema semantic level (i.e., the expressiveness) of the relational systems. Several works on transforming relational database schemas have been published. Relevant to this subject are, for example Johanneson (1994), Castellanos (1993), Markowitz and Makowsky (1990), Rivero and Doorn (1998, 2000), Date (1989), Casanova et al. (1989) and Markowitz (1990).

Markowitz and Makowsky (1990) propose a formal method to capture the structural semantics of information systems. It can be used for analyzing the semantics of existing relational databases and for converting conventional relational schemes into object-oriented database schemas. The method considers functional dependencies and key-based inclusion dependencies.

Castellanos (1993) considers inclusion dependencies under a general viewpoint. They are analyzed according to a set of 25 cases based on the composition of their left- and right-hand sides. This analysis is the basis for a semi-automatic reengineering process that recognizes hidden structures. In this chapter, the problem is studied from a broader point of view. All those cases have been included in this chapter (1, 6, 21, 2, 7, 22, 5, 10 and 25 case numbers).

Johanneson (1994) developed a method that translates a schema in a traditional relational data model into a conceptual schema. His classification of the right term is incomplete since conformations such as "part-of-a-key+secondary-attributes," "key+secondary-attributes" and "part-of-a-key" are not considered.

In Rivero and Doorn (1998, 2000) the treatment of key-based inclusion dependencies is analyzed, extending the results of Markowitz and Makowsky (1990) since two pathological cases are characterized and included in the analysis.

Chapter 4 in Date (1989) can be seen as a foundational analysis of referential integrity focusing only key-based inclusion dependencies in a relational environment, whereas Casanova, et al.(1989) is a seminar paper on the theory of key-based inclusion dependencies. It describes a two-step optimization strategy for relational schemes containing these restrictions, taking into account their corresponding referential actions for insertions and deletions.

OVERVIEW OF DATABASE DESIGN

"...The database design problem can be stated very simply: given some body of data to be represented in a database, how do we decide what objects and relationships among them should exist and what attributes they should have?..."

(Date, 2000, p. 327). Database design is one of the main stages of the lifecycle of the database application. This stage starts only after a complete analysis of the enterprise's requirements has been undertaken. A design methodology consists of phases that guide the designer to manage, control and evaluate database development projects. The design process is divided into three main phases: conceptual, logical and physical design (Connolly, et al. 1999). The main objective of each phase is:

Conceptual database design: to build the conceptual representation of the database. This phase includes the identification of relevant entity and relationship types. The conceptual model is entirely independent of implementation details such as the hardware platform, the target DBMS, the application programs, etc.

Logical database design: to translate the conceptual representation into the logical structure of the database. The model of the enterprise's information is based on a specific data model (OO, OR, relational), but it is independent of a particular DBMS and other physical details. It includes the derivation of relations, the validation of the model using normalization and the definition of integrity constraints.

Physical database design: to allow the designer to decide how the logical structure is to be physically implemented on the target DBMS. The logical data model is a source of information for this stage. In this stage, the designer makes a description of the implementation of the storage structures and the access methods in order to guarantee efficient access to the data. The physical database is tailored to a specified DBMS system.

Database design is an iterative process. Once it has been started, it is a continuous succession of refinements. Notice that the knowledge acquired in one step may change decisions made in a previous step. For instance, some decisions taken during the physical design may affect the structure of the logical data model (Batini, et al. 1992).

Regarding the purpose of this chapter, it should be stressed that a database design strictly adhering to a design methodology only produces key-based inclusion dependencies. However, an ad-hoc refinement of the logical design without concerning the corresponding conceptual design usually leads to the modeling of non-key inclusion dependencies.

REFERENTIAL INTEGRITY IN A RELATIONAL CONTEXT

Referential integrity is one of the most fundamental integrity concepts that arises in practice. The comprehension of semantic issues related to referential integrity is facilitated by the analysis of the involved attributes. One criterion consists in the study of the left and right terms of *id*s, by considering their different placements in relation to the primary key location (Figure 4). Taking into account these dispositions, 25 possible cases of pairs $<R_l[Attr_l], R_r[Attr_r]>$ corresponding to

Figure 4. Placements of the referential constraint's left and right terms

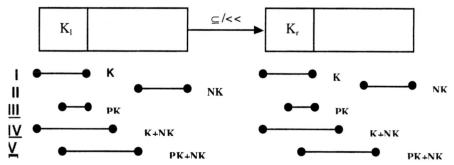

left and right terms can be derived. The five cases holding $R_r[Attr_r]$ as the primary key for R_r (numbered 1 to 5 in Table 1) are the cases of *rir*s described in the next section. The remaining cases stand for *id*s.

Referential Integrity Restrictions

Regarding all possible placements of the foreign key in the left relation, the five different kinds of referential integrity restrictions are: I) $FK_i \int K_i$; II) $FK_i \cap K_i = \emptyset$; III) $FK_i \subset K_i$; IV) $FK_i \supset K_i$; V) $FK_i \cap K_i \neq \emptyset$, $FK_i - K_i \neq \emptyset$ and $K_i - FK_i \neq \emptyset$ (Figure 5). Nevertheless, restrictions of groups IV and V appear as a consequence of an ad-hoc, non-normalized refinement of conceptual designs (Rivero & Doorn, 1998).

KNOWLEDGE ACQUISITION

The purpose of the enrichment process, described in this chapter, is to obtain improved descriptions of an object, inclusive of the semantics supplied by its relationship with the other objects. The basis of this approach is on discovering the constitution of these connections. If a set of attributes is referenced (via a *rir* or an *id*), it may be conjectured that these attributes are the proper identifier of a concerning entity.

As the entities were not properly designed in the schema, the relationships among them and other objects may also be misrepresented. Hence, reflecting on all possible origins of the hidden objects allows for the precise definition of the nature of the connections among them.

Figure 5. Types of referential integrity restrictions

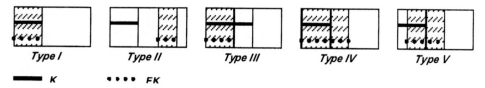

Table 1. Different types of general inclusion dependencies

Left Term Right Term	Key (K)	Part of a Key (PK) (PK + NK)	Part of a Key + Non Key	Key + Non Key (K + NK)	Non Key (NK)
Key (K)	1. K << K	6. K ⊆ PK	11. K ⊆ PK+NK	16. K ⊆ K+NK	21. K ⊆ NK
Part of a Key (PK)	2. PK << K	7. PK ⊆ PK	12. PK ⊆ PK+NK	17. PK ⊆ K+NK	22. PK ⊆ NK
Part of a Key + Non Key (PK + NK)	3. PK+NK << K	8. PK+NK ⊆ PK	13. PK+NK ⊆ PK+NK	18. PK+NK ⊆ K+NK	23. PK+NK ⊆ NK
Key + Non Key (K + NK)	4. K+NK << K	9. K+NK ⊆ PK	14. K+NK ⊆ PK+NK	19. K+NK ⊆ K+NK	24. K+NK ⊆ NK
Non Key (NK)	5. NK << K	10. NK ⊆ PK	15. NK ⊆ PK +NK	20. NK ⊆ K +NK	25. NK ⊆ NK

As a result, the following different origins can be stated:

1. *Intentionally embedded object*: It appears when R_r is the virtual (outer) join of tables through referential integrity restrictions of type I to V (Doorn & Rivero, 1997; Rivero & Doorn, 2000).[1]

2. *Dropped object.* In this case, the subset of referenced attributes also includes an identifier and descriptive attributes, standing for an embedded object. However, its origin is not an intentional virtual join but a poor design.

3. *Intentionally dropped object.* This kind is similar to the previous one, but only its identifiers represent the embedded object.

4. *Duplicated data.* This is a special situation of Case 1. The relation R_r is a view of virtual components obtained via projections, selections and joins through a referential integrity restriction of one of the types I to V (Rivero & Doorn, 1998, 2000).

Cases 2, 3 and 4 are syntactically included in Case 1. However, they are distinguished because they hold semantic differences. As will be seen in next sections, under certain circumstances all cases may represent a *hidden business rule*. In such cases, the subset of referenced attributes symbolizes the definition of a dynamic domain (Alí, 1999; Mullins, 1998).

An obvious question immediately arises at this point: if the problem is related to denormalized schemes, why not just normalize it? In different contexts, this question has different answers depending on how well the schema, is currently understood. In a fully documented, well-designed database schema the best solution is to normalize it, reaching the higher level of normalization allowed by performance and storage considerations.[2] This means that when the user cannot afford the response time required by queries including a join, an option is to denormalize the schema. Now, the query changes as it is applied to only a single table. This modification usually affects the performance of other applications.

In a poorly understood database schema, the heuristics described in the section "Metadatabase Enhancement" ease the discovery of implicit knowledge. Notice that the complete determination of the semantic aspects is required in order to reach decisions related to the schema reengineering process. Even so, the conversion is driven by the syntactic aspects.

In order to transform the actual schema into a normalized one, the following goals should be accomplished:

a) Determination of the type of hidden objects from a semantic/syntactic view-point. Foreign identifiers must be discovered and the objects they identify must be characterized. This is a strongly interactive phase since, from a syntactic perspective, it is not possible to detect the origin of an omitted class of entities. Consider, for example, cases 3 and 5.

b) Inclusion dependency inference. By applying the heuristics given in the section "Metadatabase Enhancement," *id*s types are recognized and these restrictions are reduced or transformed into *rir*s, whenever possible. For the remaining cases, the context conditions for their maintenance can be established.

The restatement of the detected hidden entities permits their removal from those relations containing them. This action improves the normalization level of the system and promotes the generation of new *rir*s. In some situations, business rules masked as irreducible non-key *id*s are discovered. In these situations, the heuristics only clarify the problem but lets the DBA solve the question in a proper way.

*Id*s as a Consequence of Virtual (Outer) Joins

Denormalization speeds up recovery by collapsing two or more tables of non-redundant BCNF (Boyce-Codd normal form) components into a single flat relation. That virtual join is "performed" through the pairs <foreign key, primary key> (Figure 6).

Being $rir_1:R_1[A_1]<<R_2[K_2]$ and $rir_2: R_2[A_2]<<R_3[K_3]$, there is more than one sequence of virtual joins among R_1, R_2 and R_3. When rir_2 is of type IV, and R_2 and R_3 are first joined, rir_1 is always transformed into an *id*. This happens because the virtual join via the *rir* type IV redesigns R_3. If this intermediate relation is R_{23}, the rir_1 is now referencing part of the R_{23}'s key. Tables 2-1 and 2-2 summarize those changes (Cisneros & Fernández, 1998; Doorn & Rivero, 1997).

Figure 6. Path of rir*s*

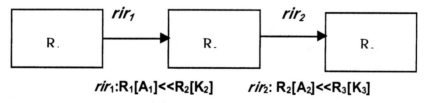

$rir_1:R_1[A_1]<<R_2[K_2]$ $rir_2: R_2[A_2]<<R_3[K_3]$

Right Relation Structure

In this section, the structure of the *id* 's right relation is examined. The possible cases are:

i) *The right term comes from a unification of Type I* (instances 1 to 5 in Table 1; *rir*s are syntactically included in this case):

*Id*s may look like *rir*s but perhaps they are not. Consider the relations (keys are underlined) STUDENT-DATA (<u>Student-id</u>, Student-name, Career, Thesis-Director) and INSTRUCTOR (<u>Student-id</u>, Grade); and the *id* INSTRUCTOR [Student-id] ⊆ STUDENT-DATA [Student-id].

Table 2-1. Transformations of rirs

$(R_1 \rightarrow R_2) \rightarrow R_3$ transforms *rir$_2$* in Type	when original <*rir$_1$*, *rir$_2$*> are
I	<I,I>, <IV,I>
II	<I,II>, <IV,II>, <II,I>, <II,IV>, <II,II>, <II,III>, <II,V>, <III,II>,<V,II>, <V,II>, <V, V>
III	<I,III>, <IV,III>, <III,I>, <III,III>, <V,III>
IV	<I,IV>, <IV,IV>
V	<I,V>, <IV,V>, <III,IV>, <V,I>, <V,IV>, <III,V>, <V,III>, <V,V>

Table 2-2. Transformations of rirs

$R_1 \rightarrow (R_2 \rightarrow R_3)$ transforms *rir$_1$* in Type	when original <*rir$_1$*, *rir$_2$*> are
I	<I,I>, <I,II>, <I,III>, <I,V>
II	<II,I>, <II,II>, <II,III>, <II,V>
III	<III,I>, <III,II>, <III,III>, <III,V>
IV	<IV,I>, <IV,II>, <IV,III>, <IV,V>
V	<V,I>, <V,II>, <V,III>, <V,V>
<u>*id*</u>	**<I,IV>, <II,IV>, <III,IV>, <IV,IV>, <V,IV>**

Suppose that Thesis-Director is an inapplicable attribute, since it is not null only when the student is a postgraduate one. In this case, the correct design is:

STUDENT (<u>Student-id</u>, Student-name, Career), POSTGRADUATE-STUDENT (<u>Student-id</u>, Thesis-Director) and INSTRUCTOR (<u>Student-id</u>, Grade).

Consider the diagrams in Figure 7. Z_1 is the set of referencing attributes and K_r is the R_r's primary key. K_{r1} and K_{r2} are the keys of R_{r1} and R_{r2} respectively. If R_r is considered as the join of R_{r1} and R_{r2}, the relationship between R_1 and R_r through Student-id looks like a *rir*, but it could mask a new constraint. R_r holds two different objects, avoiding any specific reference to one of them. The designer has no choice

Figure 7. Right term of Type I

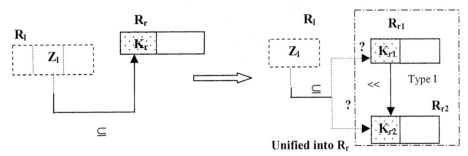

when referencing either a single student or postgraduate students, as the structure only allows a reference to the unified table.

The restriction INSTRUCTOR [Student-id] $\subseteq$ STUDENT-DATA [Student-id] is seen as a *rir* even when "only postgraduate students may become instructors," which is actually an *id*. The only way the designer could preserve the semantics of the data was to introduce an artificial business rule. Thus, if the designer needs to reference any student, the following constraints must be specified:

POSTGRADUATE-STUDENT [Student-id] << STUDENT [Student-id] and INSTRUCTOR [Student-id] << STUDENT [Student-id].

However, if the reference is based on postgraduate students, the correct referential constraints are:

POSTGRADUATE-STUDENT [Student-id] << STUDENT [Student-id] and INSTRUCTOR [Student-id] << POSTGRADUATE-STUDENT [Student-id].

ii) *The right term comes from a unification of Type II* (cases 21 to 25 in Table 1).

Consider the relations (keys are underlined) STUDENT (<u>Student#</u>, Student-name, Career-name, Start-year) and SUBSIDY (<u>Proceeding#</u>, Career-name, Amount); and the *id*

SUBSIDY [Career-name] STUDENT [Career-name]. In this design, the omitted class of entities is CAREER. Consider the Figure 8. Z'_r are secondary attributes in R_r.

In this case, which one was intended by the designer? If he or she wanted to reference CAREER, the hidden object should be directly modeled and the alternative design would result quite naturally. The resulting correct schema is: STUDENT

Figure 8. Right term of Type II

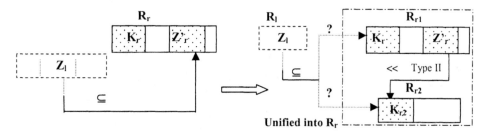

(Student#, Student-name, Career-name, Start-year); SUBSIDY (Proceeding#, Career-name, Amount) and CAREER (Career-name).

Moreover, the set of restrictions is modified replacing the original *id* by: SUBSIDY [Career-name]<<CAREER [Career-name] and STUDENT [Career-name] << CAREER [Career-name].

On the contrary, if the designer wished to reference "only those Careers having Students," the transformation of the set of relations is the same, but the restriction in quotation marks should be represented as the following *id*: CAREER [Career-name] ⊆ STUDENT [Career-name].

This is actually a *hidden business rule* (a domain constraint) since there is nothing in the data structure enforcing that constraint. From the last two restrictions, it follows that STUDENT.Career-name and CAREER.Career-name have always the same values.

iii) *The right term comes from a unification of Type III* (cases 6 to 10 in Table 1).

Consider the relations (keys are underlined) COURSE (Course#, Professor); DELEGATE-STUDENT (Student#) and ATTENDANCE (Course#, Student#, Mark); and the *id*s ATTENDANCE [Course#] << COURSE [Course#] and DELEGATE-STUDENT [Student#] ⊆ ATTENDANCE [Student#].

These *id*s point out that a missing entity of the real-world exists: STUDENT. The following diagrams show this problem. K'_r (K'_{rl}) is a subset of the K_r's (K_{rl}'s) attributes.

Again, two original designs may be possible in relation to the designer intention. If the requirement was just to establish the semantic link among DELEGATE-STUDENT, ATTENDANCE and STUDENT, then the references should have been the following:

DELEGATE-STUDENT [Student#] << STUDENT [Student#];
ATTENDANCE [Student#] << STUDENT [Student#] and
ATTENDANCE [Course#] << COURSE [Course#].

On the other hand, if the designer actually wanted to specify a constraint such as "only those students with a mark in at least a course may be delegates," the following reference should be added: STUDENT [Student#] ⊆ ATTENDANCE [Student#].

Figure 9. Right term of Type III

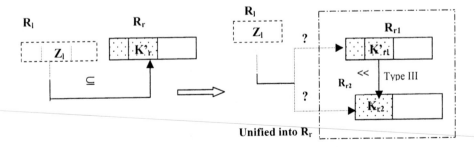

Again, the expression in quotation marks is a *hidden business rule*.

iv) *The right term comes from a unification of Type IV* (cases 16 to 20 in Table 1) or *the right term comes from a unification of Type V* (cases 11 to 15 in Table 1).

Again, it is impossible to know which relation the designer wanted to reference. If the designer's intention was to reference R_{r2}, the proper set of relations and restrictions should be reformulated in an analogous way similar to the previous case. On the other hand, if the restriction "R_l references just only those instances in $K_{r1}+Z_r$ ($K'_{r1}+Z_r$, respectively)" has to be maintained, it must be specified via an inverse *id*, similar to the previous case.

Notice that through the analysis of the possible origin of the R_r, the normalized design can be figured out. However, it is insufficient because the designer's intention must be guessed. Furthermore, notice that some of the suggested schemas seem to require the modeling of an *id* in order to maintain the equality of two sets of attributes.

Embedded Object Semantics

Considering the possible origin of R_r, many different situations may be imagined. Even so, they can be summarized as follows:

1. If the class of embedded objects in R_r is completely defined (i.e., it has identifiers and descriptive attributes), and it also appears independently modeled in the schema, it may be conjectured that this class contains *intentionally embedded objects*. If it does not appear independently modeled, the objects of this class are considered as *dropped objects*.

Figure 10. Right term of Type IV

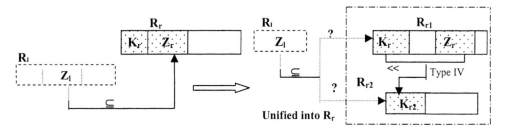

Figure 11. Right term of Type V

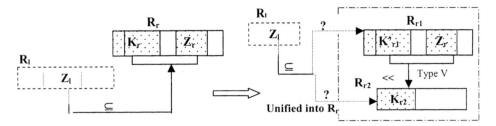

2. If the class of embedded entities in R_r is partially defined (i.e., it contains identifiers and some descriptive attributes), this case corresponds to duplicated data.
3. If the class of embedded objects in R_r is defined just by the presence of the identifiers, and it also appears independently modeled in the schema, it represents a *hidden business rule*. If it does not appear independently modeled, this case corresponds to *intentionally dropped objects*.

Case 1i. can be considered a rare one since it could be a signal of an extremely bad design. Cases 1ii., 2i. and 2ii. are frequently observed in real systems. Finally, cases 3i and 3ii are the result of common practice. The first one might occur when the objective is to restrict the reference definition domain; the second, when the object is not perceived as an object but as an attribute at design time. The situations in which the set of entities is also modeled in another part of the schema could represent the following: a mistake (the isolated entity should be referenced) or the modeling of domain restrictions. When just the identifiers represent an object, habitually they are not modeled as isolated entities.

METADATABASE ENHANCEMENT

In this section, a set of heuristics to convert the real schema into an enhanced one is presented. Let the original relational schema be $R=<R,D>$, being $R=\{R_1, R_2, ..., R_m\}$ and $D=\{FD, ID, NR\}$ the set of relations and the set of constraints respectively. **FD, ID** and **NR** are the sets of functional dependencies, inclusion dependencies and null restrictions respectively. A functional dependency held in R_i is expressed as: $R_i:X \rightarrow Y$. If X is the key of R_i, the functional dependency is a primary one. Otherwise, it is a secondary one. Particularly $FD = \{..., R_i:K_i \rightarrow Z_i; R_r:K_r \rightarrow Z_r, Z'_r; R_r:Z'_r \rightarrow Z''_r; ...\}$. The last one is a secondary functional dependency. Z_i, Z_r, Z'_r and Z''_r are sets of non-prime attributes in R_i and R_r respectively. Z'_r may be empty. $ID = \{ ...; R_i[X] \subseteq R_r[Z'_r]; ...\}$. Let the enhanced schema be defined as $R^e=<R^e,D^e>$ with its components similarly expressed. Once the missing entities have been detected and their classes identified, the following steps permit the schema reengineering:

1. For each missing entity detected, a new relation (NEW) must be created. Its identifier K_{NEW} is formed by the right term of the *id*. All descriptive attributes for the hidden object (detected by means of the secondary functional dependency) must be considered as descriptive attributes in NEW. They must be dropped from R_r.
2. All *id*s whose left term is the set of attributes identifying the missing object must be relocated in NEW (i.e., $R_{ij}[X] \subseteq R_r[Z'_r] \rightarrow\rightarrow R_{ij}[X] << NEW[K_{NEW}]$, $j = 1, 2, ...$)
3. A new *rir*, $R_r[Z'_r] << NEW[K_{NEW}]$ must be included in ID^e.
4. A reverse *id* $NEW[K_{NEW}] \subseteq R_r[Z'_r]$ must be added to ID^e only when this constraint is a *hidden business rule*.

Then: $\mathbf{R}^e = \mathbf{R} \cup \{NEW\}$; $\mathbf{ID}^e = \mathbf{ID} \cup \{R_r[Z'_r] << NEW[K_{NEW}]$; $R_{ij}[X] <<$ $NEW[K_{NEW}];...\} - \{R_j[X] \tilde{O} R_r[Z'_r]\}$ $j=1,2,....$ For the case pointed in 4., $\mathbf{R}^e = \mathbf{R} \cup \{NEW; R'_r\} - \{R_r\}$, being R'_r the old R_r projected over the attributes K_r, Z_r and Z'_r.

$\mathbf{ID}^e = \mathbf{ID} \cup \{R_r[Z'_r] << NEW[K_{NEW}]$; $R_{ij}[X] << NEW[K_{NEW}]$; $...$; $NEW[K_{NEW}]$ $\subseteq R_r[Z'_r]\} - \{R_{ij}[X] \subseteq R_r[Z'_r]\}$ $j=1,2,...$ and $\mathbf{FD} = \mathbf{F} \cup \{NEW:K_{NEW} \rightarrow Z"_r\} - \{R_r:Z'_r \rightarrow Z"_r\}$.

Example: In order to make clearer the examples informally developed in the section Right Relation Structure, the third example is reconsidered. The relations are COURSE (Course#, Professor); DELEGATE-STUDENT (Student#) and ATTENDANCE (Course#, Student#, Mark). The restrictions are: ATTENDANCE [Course#] << COURSE [Course#] and

DELEGATE-STUDENT [Student#] $\subseteq$ ATTENDANCE [Student#].

Step 1) Those *id*s indicate STUDENT as the real-world missing entity (NEW), then

$\mathbf{R}^e$ = {ATTENDANCE, STUDENT, DELEGATE-STUDENT, COURSE}.

Step 2) The *id* must be reformulated as the following *rir*:
DELEGATE-STUDENT [Student#] << STUDENT [Student#]

Step 3) The following *rir* must be added to $\mathbf{ID}^e$:
ATTENDANCE [Student#] << STUDENT [Student#]

Step 4) At this point, two scenarios may be possible. If the requirement is just to establish the semantic link among DELEGATE-STUDENT, ATTENDANCE and STUDENT, then the reengineering process is done. In contrast, if the designer actually wants to specify a constraint such as "only those students with a mark in at least a course may be delegates," the next (irreducible) *id* must be included into $\mathbf{ID}^e$:
STUDENT[Student#]$\subseteq$ATTENDANCE[Student#].

About the Reverse *id*

The expression in quotation marks "only those students with a mark in at least a course may be delegates" is just a particular case of a business rule: a domain constraint. This restriction controls the values of one attribute in a relation against the elements of a set defined by intension. Update operations may change this set. A truly conceptual implementation should calculate the permissible values before using them, although performance reasons naturally suggest that a better solution should be to build this set incrementally. It is a pragmatically wise approach if the designer does not give the status of a table in the system to this set. Moreover, if this set is held in the schema in the same way as the relations, everybody should remember that it is a calculated table having the same status as any other table obtained via project operations. If the designer persists in taking such a table into account, the following referential actions must be implemented:

Insertions: an insertion over R_r provokes an insertion in the table NEW (insertions with Cascade as the referential action) if and only if the value of the concerning attribute is a new one. Insertions over the table NEW are prohibited in other cases.

Deletions: when the deleted tuple of R_r contains a last instance of the referred attribute, it must provoke the deletion of the tuple containing the same value in the table NEW. Deletions over NEW are prohibited in other cases.

It must be stressed again that the table NEW cannot be modified by direct operations.

REFERENTIAL INTEGRITY IN OO AND OR DATABASES

As it was mentioned in the introduction, low quality in conceptual schemas may also be present in OR and OO databases. A brief background on these models is provided, showing how the relational inclusion dependency problem is seen in these models.

The current research trend is on models that generalize the relational one, especially by loosening the first normal form constraint. OO languages and semantic models have been the basis for this trend. These issues and many others have been considered in the last years by researchers and practitioners. As a result, next generation database systems have emerged. Today, however, the relational market is huge while the OO market is about a hundredth of it. It is expected that the size of the OR market will be 50% larger than the relational market in the next five or 10 years (Stonebraker, 1996).

ORDBMSs integrate the relational data model and SQL query languages with features coming from the OO world, namely inheritance, methods, and late binding. A true OR system is a relational system that supports the relational domain concept. OO literature typically uses the term relationship to mean relationships supported by foreign keys in a relational system (Date, 2000). This implementation, which is the only one available in a traditional SQL-92 system, may be used in an ORDBMS. On the other hand, OR systems provide the references as a natural substitute for primary key-foreign key relationships. In these systems, a column in a table may contain a value that is a reference to an instance of a type stored in another table. Conceptually this data type is a pointer to a record of a specific type in the table. This implementation is supported by the unique object identifier (OID), which all rows in a table have. In this case, each value stored in the referencing column is an OID. Whenever available, a pointer implementation (reference via an OID) is preferable because an OID is guaranteed to be unique and never changed, while the foreign key value is not necessarily time invariant.

Triggers are very useful in supporting data integrity in a database, especially to deal with those restrictions that cannot be expressed declaratively. Relational systems provide some support for rules using triggers, but OR and OODBMSs demand a much more flexible system.

Missing objects and the need to express some relationships having the relational non-key inclusion dependency semantics exist in these models too. Therefore, this notion comes back to the center of the scenario again, usually in the form of an artificial business rule.

Business rules respond to application needs: they model the reaction to events, which occur in the real-world, with tangible side effects on the database content.

Triggers for referential integrity are an alternative to the use of foreign key constraints in commercial SQL92-relational products. Even so, foreign key constraints are normally preferable to explicit triggers because they are declarative and then easier to manage.

CONCLUSIONS AND FUTURE WORK

The work presented in this chapter extends known studies by considering basic concepts of the relational model, mainly *id*s whose right sides are denormalized tables, i.e., particular views.

The possible origins of embedded objects are highlighted and a heuristics for the complete reengineering of the schema is detailed. When an irreducible *id* must remain, the contextual conditions for its maintenance are established, leading to the definition of a specific business rule.

The heuristic method presented is similar to the ones developed in Castellanos (1993) and Johanneson (1994), but three aspects have been improved: i) denormalized tables in the right side are considered, then the first step promotes the normalization by transferring the descriptive attributes to NEW; ii) despite the fact that the right term may be one of five structures, the heuristics is the same for all of them; and iii) special cases of masked business rules have been completely analyzed, and a new conceptual perspective of its need was given.

Although with the current development of OO or OR models the theory of dependencies has become a bit out-of-date, the concepts developed in this chapter remain useful and portable to other areas such as federated databases, database migration, reengineering of legacy systems, etc.

This work could be extended studying the inference of the referential actions of the initial *id*s into the final ones. With basis on the heuristics, the design and implementation of an interactive computerized tool to assist the designer to obtain a better quality schema could be faced.

REFERENCES

Abiteboul, S., Hull, H. and Vianu V. (1995). *Foundations on databases*. Addison Wesley Publishing Company.

Alí, A.V. (1999). *Dependencias de Inclusión: Un Estudio Sistemático*. Unpublished manuscript, System Engineering Thesis. Universidad Nacional del Centro de la Provincia de Buenos Aires, Argentina.

Batini, C., Ceri, S. and Navathe, S. (1992). *Conceptual Database Design: An Entity-Relationship Approach*. Addison Wesley Publishing Company.

Casanova, M., Tucherman, L., Furtado, A. and Braga, A. (1989). Optimization of relational schemes containing inclusion dependencies. *Proceedings of 15 VLDB Conference*. Amsterdam. 317-325.

Castellanos, M.G. (1993). A methodology for semantically enriching interoperable databases. In *Proceedings of 11th British National Conference on Databases*, Keele.

Cisneros, C. and Fernández, N. (1998). *Generalización de Dependencias y Operaciones en Relaciones No Normalizadas*. Unpublished manuscript, System Engineering Thesis. Universidad Nacional del Centro de la Provincia de Buenos Aires, Argentina.

Codd, E. (1990). *The Relational Model for Database Management*. Version 2. Addison Wesley Publishing Company.

Connolly, T., Begg, C. and Strachan, A. (1999). *Database Systems: A Practical Approach to Design, Implementation and Management*. 2nd Edition. Addison Wesley.

Date, C. (1989). *Relational Databases, Selected Writings*. Addison Wesley. Reprinted with corrections.

Date, C. (2000). *An Introduction to Database Systems*. Addison Wesley.

Doorn, J. and Rivero, L. (1997). Normalization of non-BCNF relations integrity constraints. *Proceedings of the XII International Conference of Systems Engineering, ICSE-97*, Coventry UK. 217-222.

Johanneson, P. (1994). A method for transforming relational schemas into conceptual schemas. *IEEE Transactions on Software Engineering*, 190-201.

Markowitz, V. and Makowsky, J. (1990) Identifying extended entity-relationship object structures in relational schemas. *IEEE Trans. on Software Engineering*. 16(8), 777-790.

Markowitz, V. (1990). Referential integrity revisited: An object-oriented perspective. In *Proceedings of the 16th VLDB Conference*. Brisbane. Australia.

Mullins, C. S. (1998). *Using check constraints to simulate domains*. [On-line] Available: http://www.tdan.com/i007ht02.htm.

Paulk, M.C., Curtis, B., Chrissis, M.B. and Weber, C.V. (1993). The capability maturity model for software. Version 1.1, *IEEE Trans. on Software Engineering*, July, 18-27.

Rivero L. and Doorn J. (1998). Integridad referencial y actualizaciones en relaciones desnormalizadas. In *Proceedings of XIV Conferencia Latinoamericana de Informática - CLEI Panel 98*. Quito, Ecuador. 911-921.

Rivero L. and Doorn J. (2000). Managing referential integrity and non key-based dependencies in a denormalized context. In *Proceedings of 2000 IRMA International Conference*. Anchorage, Alaska. 883-886.

Stonebraker, M. (1996). *Object-Relational DBMSs. The Next Great Wave*. Morgan Kauffman Publishers.

ENDNOTES

1 As was detailed in the chapter, the presence of a referential constraint of Type IV produces non-key *id*s. The same happens when two or more tables linked by a many-many relationship are joined (if one or more of those tables is a referenced one).

2 Even more, it replicates the values of the attributes involved in the join, thus causing a serious integrity danger. If an update is performed, all copies must be updated, so the cost of this manipulation may grow significantly.

Chapter XII

Semantically Modeled Databases in Integrated Enterprise Information Systems

Cheryl L. Dunn
Florida State University, USA

Severin V. Grabski
Michigan State University, USA

INTRODUCTION

In the past several years, huge investments have been made in enterprise resource planning (ERP) systems and related applications. While the integrated database and data warehouse in such systems provides value, more value could be realized if the databases could more semantically reflect the underlying reality of the organization. Inter-enterprise commerce can be facilitated with the use of ontologically based systems with common semantics (Geerts and McCarthy, 2000; Haugen and McCarthy, 2000) instead of reliance on electronic data interchange (EDI) standards. This chapter presents a normative semantic model for enterprise information systems that has its roots in transaction processing information systems. Empirical research on semantically modeled information systems is reviewed and an example company's semantic model is provided as a proof of concept. This model is used as the basis for a discussion of its application to ERP systems and to inter-organizational systems. Future trends and research directions are also discussed.

Semantically modeled databases require their component objects to correspond closely to real-world phenomena and preclude the use of artifacts as system primitives (Dunn and McCarthy, 1997). Semantically modeled enterprise information systems allow for full integration of all system components centered on a single integrated database and facilitate the joint use of information by decision-makers. Researchers have advocated semantically designed information systems because they provide benefits to individual decision-makers (Dunn and Grabski, 1998, 2000) and because they facilitate organizational productivity and inter-organizational communication (Cherrington et al., 1996; David, 1995; Geerts and McCarthy, 2000).

Many organizations have invested immense sums of money in enterprise resource planning (ERP) systems and associated "bolt-on," applications such as customer relationship management (CRM) and advanced planning systems (APS). Much of the value of these ERP systems is in the integrated database and the associated data warehouse that is implemented. Unfortunately, a significant portion of the value is lost if the database is not a semantic representation of the organization. This value is lost because relevant information needed to reflect the underlying reality of the organization's activities is either not stored in the system at all, or it is stored in such a way that the underlying reality is hidden or disguised and therefore can't be interpreted.

Ontologically based systems with common semantics are regarded as a necessity to facilitate inter-organizational information systems (Geerts and McCarthy, 2000). This is critical, as business-to-business e-commerce becomes a major component of the economy. Presently, most inter-organizational data is sent via EDI (which requires very strict specifications as to how the data are sequenced and requires some investment by adopting organizations). The same requirement holds true for Web-based systems. There is no or very limited knowledge inherent in those systems. Alternatively, if trading partners implement systems based on the same underlying semantic model, many of the current problems can be eliminated.

This chapter first presents a normative semantic model for enterprise information systems that has its roots in transaction processing information systems. We use this model because the majority of information processed and tracked by information systems is transactional in nature. We review empirical research on semantically modeled information systems and then provide an example company's semantic model as a proof of concept. Then, we discuss how this model can be applied to ERP systems and to inter-organizational systems. We present issues and controversies associated with the model and discuss how the single company model can be extended into an inter-organizational system. Finally, we present future trends and research directions associated with this model and with inter-organizational systems in general, and provide concluding comments.

SEMANTIC MODEL DEVELOPMENT

In this chapter, similar to David et al. (1999), we are interested in an information system that captures, stores, manipulates and presents data about an organization's value-adding activities to aid decision-makers in planning, monitoring and controlling the organization. This definition is also consistent with much of the research on ERP systems. Also similar to David et al. (1999), we recommend that the normative Resources-Events-Agents (REA) semantic model (McCarthy, 1982) be used as the core foundation of enterprise information systems due to the model's robust nature, which we will discuss throughout this chapter. The basic REA model is presented in Figure 1 using entity-relationship notation, however, it has also been implemented in NIAM (Geerts and McCarthy, 1991) and in object notation; (Nakamura and Johnson, 1998). The REA model for any particular transaction cycle consists of the following components. These components are presented in list form for the sake of brevity. Readers are encouraged to read McCarthy (1982) for more detail.

- Two *economic events* that represent alternative sides of an economic exchange (one increment event and one decrement event).
- Two *resources* that represent what is received and given up in the economic exchange.
- Two *internal agents* that represent the company's personnel that are responsible for each of the economic events (one agent for each event).
- One *external agent* that represents the person or company with whom the company is engaging at arms' length in the exchange.
- *Duality* relationship between the increment and decrement economic events.

Figure 1. The original REA model (McCarthy, 1982)

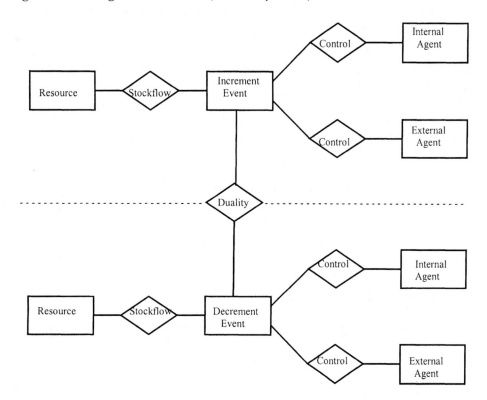

- *Stock-flow* relationships between the events and the associated resources, representing the inflows or outflows of the resources resulting from the events.
- *Responsibility* relationships between the events and the internal agents.
- *Participation* relationships between the events and the external agents.

The original model was described at only the operational level. Since 1982, the REA model has been extended to an inter-organizational database systems ontology that incorporates both the operational and knowledge levels and includes the following additional features and components, again presented in list form (see Geerts and McCarthy, 2000 for more detail).

- Integration of process (cycle) level models into a value-chain level model.
- Expansion of process (cycle) level models into workflow or task level models.
- Separation of components into *continuants* (enduring objects with stable attributes that allow them to be recognized on different occasions throughout a period of time) and *occurrents* (processes or events that are in a state of flux).
- *Type images* that represent category level abstractions of similar components.
- *Commitment images* that represent agreements to engage in future economic events.
- *Assignment* relationships between agents that represent the designation of an agent category to work with another agent category (e.g., salesperson assigned to customer).
- *Custody* relationships between agents and resources that represent the agents that are accountable for various resources.
- *Commits To* relationships between commitment images and the resulting economic events.
- *Partner* relationships between commitment images and the participating agents.
- *Reserved* relationships between commitment images and the resources that are the proposed subject of the future exchange, e.g., reducing the inventory available to promise.
- *Typification description* relationships between continuant components and the categories to which they belong, e.g., resource-resource type relationships and agent-agent type relationships.
- *Characterization* description relationships between continuant type images, e.g., agent type-agent type relationships and agent type-resource type relationships.
- *Typification history* relationships between physical occurrents and their types, indicating that the occurrents share the same script, e.g., event-event type.
- *Scenario history* relationships between abstract occurrents and other abstractions, e.g., event type-resource type.
- *Business Process* as a description of the interaction between resources, agents and dual events.
- *Partnering* as the purpose of the interaction between resources, agents and commitments.
- *Segmentation* as a description of the grouping of physical categories into abstract continuant categories.

- *Policy or Standard* as a description of the expression of knowledge level rules between abstract types (e.g., scripts and scenarios).
- *Plan* as a description of the application of a script to physical occurrents.
- *Strategy* as a description of rules for the execution of a Business Process or Partnering.

The semantics contained within the expanded REA model facilitate the information exchange between trading partners and likely provide a needed core foundation for ERP systems. Limited research supports this view. For example, research reported by Andros et al. (1992) and Cherrington et al. (1996) found that IBM was able to obtain significant benefits from a semantically modeled system based on the REA model. Eighteen separate systems were originally used for employee expense reimbursement, each with its own edit and audit routines. This resulted in labor-intensive and costly error correction and reconciliation processes within each of the 18 systems. Reported benefits of the new system included a significant reduction in the time to process employee reimbursements, significant cost reductions and a generally high level of employee satisfaction with the new system due to reduced reimbursement time and a simplified reimbursement process. These two studies demonstrated how the semantic models were used as the basis for systems design, and then how the resultant systems were perceived by the end-users, thereby completing the research loop from design to end-user. These studies also quantified the benefits associated with the new system and presented foregone opportunities due to other factors within the organization.

Satoshi (1999) reported on a financial data warehouse project in IBM Japan. The data warehouse project was prompted by the problems typically encountered by large organizations in the management of their data. In particular, the various systems were connected by stand-alone and batch programs, individual applications had overlapping functions, no standardized data definitions existed, data duplication and inconsistency existed, error correction was difficult and time consuming, and difficulties existed in providing accurate data in real time (Yasuhiro, 1995). The new system was based on the REA-L model (Denna et al., 1993). The new financial data warehouse system was not implemented due to the time and development cost, but even more so because the organization changed to purchased software rather than writing software at each national site to allow for worldwide coordination of all systems. A commercially available enterprise resource planning software package was implemented and that software was perceived as having the same philosophy as the original data warehouse project.

Weber (1986) empirically evaluated the REA semantic model. His objective was to determine whether software practitioners had both identified and solved the same problems as identified by academicians. The rationale was to look to practice, to determine whether the issues identified by academic researchers were real problems, whether the practicing community had already solved the problems, or if they had identified the same problems but had not arrived at a solution, in which case the semantically modeled systems could be used to identify where users would encounter deficiencies in the software. Order entry modules of 12 wholesale distribution software packages were examined. He looked at both the infological and datalogical format. Specifically, Weber determined whether the semantics in the software adhered to the normative prescriptions of semantically modeled systems. He also examined at a detailed level, whether the packages were designed based on a common underlying semantic model. Finally, he examined whether the record structures of the software adhered to the principles of normalization.

Weber found that the REA model fulfilled its objective as a generalized model and that it was a good predictor of the high-level semantics found in all 12 packages. He believed that the REA model excluded certain types of events such as contracts and suggested extensions (many of which have been subsequently incorporated into the model). He reported that important differences in the low-level semantics existed across all packages, and that these seem to reflect the relative complexity of the different packages. Nonetheless, the clustering of the low-level semantics of the packages according to the REA model allowed for the identification of similarities and differences among the packages, and the likely strengths and limitations of the package become apparent. On a datalogical level, Weber found few violations of normal form given the number of fields in the packages. He concluded that theory was a good predictor of design practice and that the empirical evidence supports normalization theory.

David (1995) developed a metric to classify organizations' accounting systems characteristics (ASC) along a continuum between traditional general ledger-based accounting systems and REA systems. The ASC metric was developed based upon characteristics that were identified in theoretical research as critical for REA systems including: the lack of a chart of accounts; support for critical events; maintenance and storage of detailed data about resources, events and agents; and store non-financial data about resources, events and agents. David visited eight companies in the pulp and paper industry and conducted structured interviews and used the ASC metric to determine each system's position on the continuum. Data was also gathered as to the companies' productivity, efficiency and the company executives' perceptions of competitive advantage. REA-like systems were found to be associated with productivity and administrative efficiencies.

O'Leary (1999) compared the REA semantic model with an enterprise resource software package. He compared information about SAP from various sources and determined that SAP is consistent with the REA model in its database, semantic and structure orientations. However, SAP was also found to contain implementation compromises in the structuring and semantic orientation, based in part on accounting artifacts.

Research has demonstrated that organizations are able to obtain significant benefits from a semantically modeled system based on the REA framework (Andros et al., 1992; Cherrington et al., 1996). However, even semantically modeled systems are not sufficient to ensure success. Rather, success is dependent upon a variety of factors including top management support and corporate philosophy, in addition to the benefits inherent in the semantically modeled system (Satoshi, 1999). The REA model is sufficient as a generalized model (Weber, 1986; O'Leary, 1999). The more

REA-like a system is, the more it is associated with productivity and administrative efficiencies (David, 1995).

We next present, in some detail, an REA model of a prototypical retail firm that sells, leases and repairs products. This example will serve as further proof of concept and allow the reader to verify that the semantic data model accurately represents the reality of the described organization, and that there is an application of the REA template with consistent patterns. First, we will provide a narrative for the firm and describe in detail the sales and acquisition cycles. Then we will describe the components of a REA model (in entity-relationship notation using guidelines set forth by Batini, et al., 1992) that captures the reality. Finally, we will discuss the benefits of the REA model that occur independent of the entity-relationship notation. Our example is for a company called Robert Scott Woodwinds (RSW), a retail organization that sells supplies, leases and also repairs woodwind instruments. This particular organization setting encompasses many of the activities performed by most business organizations. While the semantics of the model we present are specific to RSW's environment, the model provides a generic template for a retail organization's semantic model; it also provides a template for leasing organizations, and it has significant commonalities with manufacturing firms in the repair aspects of the business.

REA Semantic Model Example

For the scenario presented below, the events, resources and agents are captured in REA diagrams (in entity-relationship form) in Figures 2 through 9. RSW sells, repairs and leases musical woodwind instruments, as indicated in the diagrams in Figures 2 through 6. At the present time a single store exists; however, market research has determined there exists a need in the area for at least two more stores to meet anticipated customer demand. The business caters to professional musicians, casual musicians and children who are involved in school music programs. Consequently, while RSW clearly needs to have a Web presence at least to inform potential customers, it anticipates only a minor portion of its revenues from Web sales (primarily for consumables such as reeds, sheet music and so forth). Professional musicians want to play and get a feel for the particular instrument that they are interested in purchasing and will always come into the store. Further, they are very particular about who will repair their instrument, and the personal touch is critical. For repairs, the instrument must be brought or sent to the store. School sales are a direct result of sales staff calling on the band directors at the various schools and gaining permission to be the supplier for that school (Usually this means that the children will rent from RSW, not that the school will purchase the instruments from RSW; however, there is some variation depending on school districts). Again, the personal contact is critical in obtaining these sales. Following is detailed information about RSW's revenue (including sales, sales returns, repairs and leases) and acquisition (including inventory, general and administrative supplies, and purchase returns) cycles.

Revenue Cycle

RSW generates revenue in three ways. The first is through sales of instruments to retail customers; the second is through rental of instruments to customers; and the third is through the repair of instruments. In the retail instrument business, renting instruments so that customers can try before they buy is a great way of generating sales. This is particularly true in the school marketplace. Parents are reluctant to buy expensive instruments for their children without knowing if their children have any interest (or talent). Thus, what RSW will do is send salespeople (who also have music teacher training) into the schools to host "music talent exploration" sessions for the children. When a child has been identified as having talent for (and some interest in) a specific instrument, the parents will be offered the opportunity to rent that instrument for 3 months in order to see if the child continues to be interested. At the end of the three-month trial period, the parents may purchase that instrument (or a different instrument), and the sale price they pay will reflect a discount equal to the amount of rent paid. For example, if the normal selling price of a student clarinet is $585, and the customer had rented a student clarinet for three months for $58.50, the sale price offered to that customer would be $526.50. When an instrument is rented out, it is transferred from "Inventory for Sale" to "Inventory for Rent." If it is later sold, the "Inventory for Rent" category will be decreased.

RSW's salespeople fill out sales invoices and rental invoices for customers. The customer may purchase (rent) multiple instruments on a single sales (rental) invoice.

Figure 2. RSW sales revenue expanded REA data model

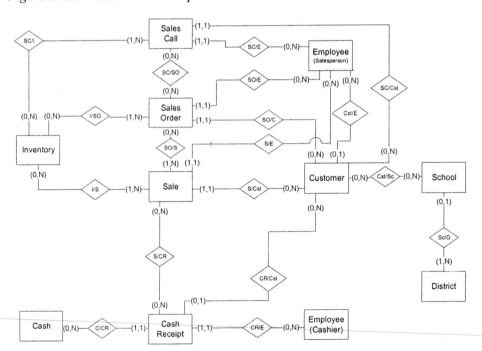

Instruments are either delivered to the customer at the school during the salesperson's next sales call, or the customer may pick up the instruments at the store. Cash receipts are processed by cashiers and are deposited into the company's main bank account each day. The semantic data models for sales and for leases are presented in Figures 2 and 3, respectively.

As can be seen in the sales revenue data model (Figure 2), the original REA template has been applied. The resource (inventory) is associated with an economic decrement event (sale) via a stockflow relationship. The sale event is associated with the internal agent (salesperson) and the external agent (customer) via control relationships. There is a duality relationship between the economic decrement event (sales) and the economic increment event (cash receipt). Cash receipt is associated with the resource (cash) via a stockflow relationship and to the internal agent (cashier) and the external agent (customer) via control relationships. Note that the cardinalities between sale and cash receipt disclose that a sale does not require the immediate receipt of cash. Rather, a sale may be paid for at one later point in time, in installments over a period of time or not paid for at all (because of a sale return or bad debt). Newer aspects of the REA ontology have also been included in this model. The sales order event is a commitment image and is related to the resulting economic event (sales) via a CommitsTo relationship. It is also related to salesperson via a Control relationship, to customer via a Partnering relationship, and to inventory via a Reserved relationship. In addition, there is an Assignment relationship established between salesperson and customer. Sales personnel can be assigned to many different

Figure 3. RSW rental revenue cycle expanded REA data model

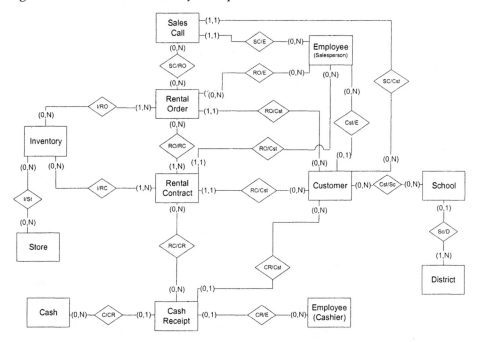

customers, and a customer has, at most, one sales person assigned to them. The REA ontology allows for the inclusion of additional entities that managers need information about for planning, controlling and evaluating individual and organizational performance. These additions do not change the underlying REA template; they simply add to it. For example, the sales call event that leads to the sales order event is modeled, and is linked to the associated resource and agents. Further, the external agent set has been expanded to include school and district. A customer does not need to be associated with a school, and a school may be listed even if no customers from that school have begun to trade with RSW. A school does not need to belong to a school district (i.e., it is a private school); however, if it belongs to a school district, it can only belong to one school district. A school district has at least one school.

The information presented in the semantic model is a representation of the reality of the world of RSW. The cardinalities contain the business rules that are followed by the entities in their relationships. A similar analysis can be performed for the lease revenue data model (Figure 3), and in fact, the only differences between the two are the events of rental order and rental contract in place of sales order and sale. The observation of such commonalities allows for the development of common business practices for all revenue activities and facilitates reengineering at the task level.

In a similar manner to the sales and leases, a semantic model of sales returns, and lease returns can also be created. The sale return data model (Figure 4) has the economic decrement sale event associated with the economic increment event sale

Figure 4. RSW sales returns expanded REA data model

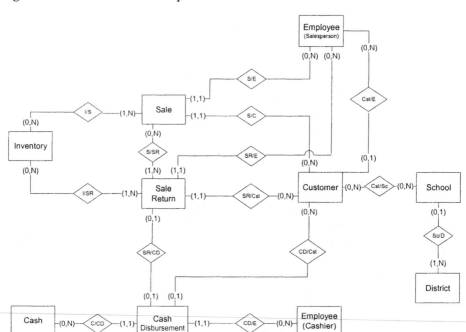

return, and the sale return is associated with the subsequent economic decrement event cash disbursement. (The sale return might not result in a cash disbursement if no cash was received at the time of the sale; this is represented by the 0 min cardinality on the sale return.) The rental returns data model (Figure 5) can be analyzed in a similar manner. The REA pattern centered on the duality relationship between economic events and including stockflow and control relationships is maintained.

The third form of revenue generated by RSW is through instrument repair services. RSW offers a variety of repair service types. Complete overhauls are available for many instruments. For example, a complete overhaul of a woodwind instrument involves the buffing and cleaning of the body and all plated parts, the replating of keys, repair of all mechanical problems, replacement of all pads and corks, and replacement of springs and screws as needed. Prices of these overhauls vary by instrument type. Repad overhauls are also available for each instrument type. For a wind instrument, this type of overhaul involves the cleaning of the body and all plated parts (no buffing) and replacement of all pads and key corks. These are less expensive than complete overhauls; price varies by instrument type. Customers may have individual keys replated at a fixed cost per key. Crack repairs will be judged as minor or major and will be priced accordingly. Other repairs are also available. The semantic model for repair revenue is presented in Figure 6.

In the repair service REA model, more of the features of the newer REA ontology are introduced. Typification is used, with an event-event type relationship

Figure 5. RSW rental returns expanded REA data model

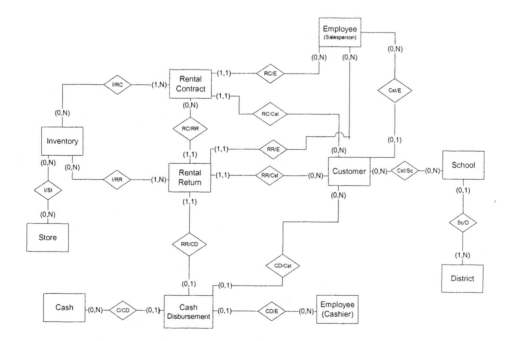

between repair service and service type and also a commitment-commitment type relationship between repair service order and service type. The service type entity represents the details of the various repair service types RSW can provide (e.g., complete overhauls, repad, etc.). This serves as the bill of materials for the service and allows storage of information about the categories to which the repair services belong. Another internal agent is also included, that of repair person. This allows RSW to track the person responsible for a given repair. This is similar to any type of job shop or organization that must track employee time (e.g., consulting firms).

Acquisition Cycle

RSW purchases merchandise inventory and general and administrative (G&A) services from various vendors. Buyers place orders (purchase orders or G&A orders) for the needed items. Cash disbursements are made to vendors according to the G&A Service amount on the G&A order or according to the purchase amount as per the match between the receiving report and purchase order (unit price on purchase order is multiplied by the actual quantity received on the receiving report to get the purchase amount). RSW will sometimes pay for more than one G&A order or for more than one purchase with one cash disbursement. Other times, RSW may pay for a G&A order or for a purchase in installments. Figures 7, 8 and 9 present the data models for the acquisition of merchandise, for the acquisition of G&A services and for purchase returns, respectively.

Figure 6. RSW repair service revenue expanded REA data model

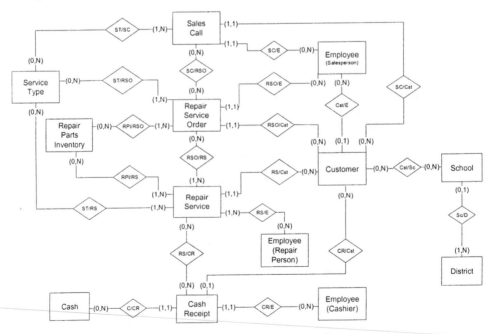

The analysis of these models is similar to that for the revenue cycle, and as such we do not present it in detail here. Further, for simplicity and in the interest of brevity, we do not present the payroll or financing cycles. The payroll cycle would be similar to the acquisition cycle except that services are acquired from employees (hence employees act as external agents) instead of from vendors or suppliers. The financing model is also similar to the acquisition process except that the resource acquired and consumed is cash. Each of these models is again centered on an economic exchange, represented with a duality link between an economic increment event and an economic decrement event. Each event is related to one or more resources via a stockflow relationship. Sometimes the flow of the resource may not be measurable, for example, in the payroll cycle the resource acquired is employee labor. This is an intangible resource that may be difficult, if not impossible to measure in terms of stockflow. The REA ontology requires that such things be considered and only left out of the model if they are impossible to implement.

The REA ontology can be implemented using alternative notations, including object notation, UML and others. We have chosen to represent it with entity-relationship notation because of its simplicity and widespread use. The benefit of the REA ontology is not found in the notation itself, but in the repeated application of the pattern to all of the various business cycles. Consistent use of the template gives users an ability to understand the reality being represented, and it also provides system reusability and extendibility. Dunn and McCarthy (2000) describe the following four benefits of the REA model. First, the standardized use and definition of information

Figure 7. RSW acquisition cycle expanded REA data model

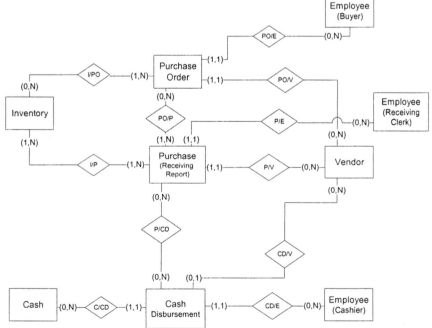

Figure 8. RSW general and administrative supplies acquisition cycle expanded REA data model

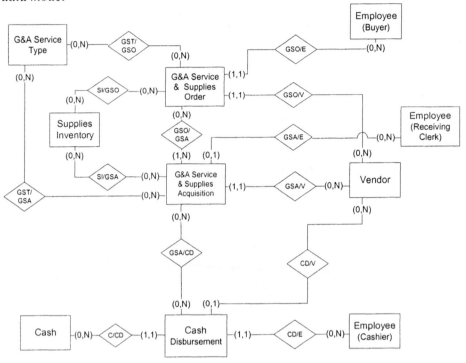

Figure 9. RSW purchase returns expanded REA data model

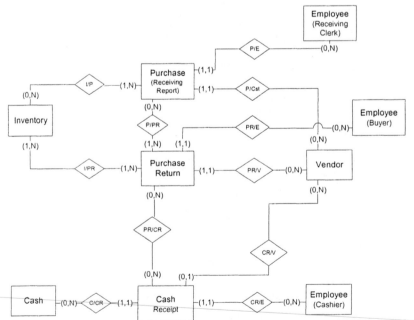

structures across organizational boundaries facilitates electronic commerce, by enabling the retrieval, sending and integration of data among business partners or research sources. Second, intellectual complexity is made manageable by the use of natural primitives that abstract to generalized descriptions of structures, which in turn cover many thousands of cases with as few exceptions as possible. Third, consistent use of the REA pattern can enable system-based reasoning and learning. Fourth, use of system primitives that closely mirror the underlying phenomena enables system adaptability.

It is important to note that the REA ontology and other semantic modeling approaches have been studied at the individual decision-making level, both for system designers and users. Dunn and Grabski (2000b) provided an extensive literature review of individual-level semantic models research. Overall conclusions of their review were as follows. Accounting systems based on the REA model are perceived as more semantically expressive by end-users than are accounting systems based on the traditional debit-credit-account model. Also, accounting systems perceived as semantically expressive result in greater accuracy and satisfaction by end-users than do non-semantically expressive accounting systems (Dunn and Grabski, 2000a). Conceptual modeling formalisms are superior to logical modeling formalisms for design accuracy (Sinha and Vessey, 1999; Kim and March, 1995). The ability to dissembled the essential objects and relationships between the objects in complex surroundings depends on a cognitive personality trait, field independence and leads to more accurate conceptual model design (at least for undergraduate students) (Dunn and Grabski, 1998). The focus on increment and decrement resources and events, along with the associated agents to those events, is consistent with database designers' thought processes. Additionally, knowledge structures consistent with the REA template's structuring orientation are associated with more accurate conceptual accounting database design (controlling for knowledge content, ability and experience level) (Gerard, 1998). The lack of mandatory properties with entities is not critical (Bodart and Weber, 1997), perhaps because of the semantics inherent in the modeled system. System designers distinguish between entities and relationships, with entities being primary (Weber, 1996). Data and process methodologies are easier for novices than the object methodology, and resulted in less unresolved difficulties during problem-solving processes (Vessey and Conger, 1994), and there is a more pronounced effect for process-oriented tasks (Agarwal, Sinha and Tanniru, 1996a). Experience in process modeling matters, regardless of whether the modeling tool (process versus object-oriented) is consistent with the experience (Agarwal, Sinha and Tanniru, 1996b).

SEMANTIC MODELS, ERP SYSTEMS AND INTER-ORGANIZATIONAL SYSTEMS

The American Production and Inventory Control Society (APICS, 1998) defined an ERP system as "an accounting-oriented information system for identifying and planning the enterprise-wide resources needed to take, make, ship and account for orders." David et al. (1999) proposed using REA as a basis for comparison among systems and ERP packages. This was based, in part, on Weber's (1984) analysis of 12 wholesale distribution software packages that disclosed that a comparison at the level of symbol sets made semantic similarities and differences apparent. Additionally, O'Leary (1999) compared SAP to the REA model and determined that SAP is REA-compliant; however, SAP has significant implementation compromises based on accounting artifacts. No other ERP packages have been compared to the REA model. Consistent with David et al. and based upon the APICS definition of ERP systems, we believe that REA is a robust candidate to which ERP systems may be compared because of its strong semantic, microeconomic and accounting heritage. More importantly, we believe that semantic models must be used as a basis for the information system because of the information contained within the semantics.[1]

Watson and Schneider (1999) also emphasized the importance of ERP systems in providing the process-centered modeling perspective necessary for successful organizations. They emphasized understanding the underlying process model inherent in ERP systems. That is, the underlying semantics of the system. Further, the SAP R/3 business blueprint provides four enterprise views: process, information, function and organization. It is in the organization view that the semantic relationships among organizational units are represented. As most ERP implementations will require some modifications to meet the specific business needs, the analysts, designers and users need to understand the changes and their subsequent planned and unplanned impact. A semantically based model will facilitate this understanding.

The REA framework as an enterprise ontology provides a high-level definition and categorization of business concepts and rules, enterprise logic and accounting conventions of independent and related organizations (Geerts and McCarthy, 2000). The REA ontology includes three levels: the value chain level, the process level and the task level. The value chain level models an enterprise's "script" for doing business. That is, it identifies the high-level business processes or cycles[2] (e.g., revenue, acquisition, conversion, financing, etc.) in the enterprise's value chain and the resource flows between those processes. The process level represents the semantic components of each business process. An earlier example depicted the process level of the REA ontology for RSW. The task (or workflow) level of the REA ontology is the most detailed level, and includes a breakdown of all steps necessary for the enterprise to accomplish the business events that were included at the process level. The task level can vary from company to company without affecting the integration of processes or inter-organizational systems; therefore we do not present an elaboration of this level. (It is also the level at which most reengineering occurs.) An illustration of the value chain level for RSW is presented in Figure 10.

The value chain level describes how the business processes within the company fit together and what resources flow between them. In RSW, financing is obtained, and as a result, cash is distributed as needed to the various acquisition processes. Some of that cash is used to acquire labor, which is then in turn distributed to each of the other business processes. Some of the cash is used to acquire instruments and supplies (both supplies for sale and also supplies used in the repair services). Some of the cash is used to acquire G&A services. The instruments, supplies, G&A services and labor are received by the three revenue processes and are combined in various ways to generate revenue. The resulting cash is then distributed to the financing process where it is used to repay financing (including distribution of earnings to stockholders if this were a corporation) or to re-distribute cash to the other business processes. The value chain level demonstrates integration opportunities for the enterprise-wide information system. Resources that flow from one business process to another can be modeled in the database one time and accessed by the appropriate business processes. Then as the separate business processes have their events linked to those resources, the entire system is integrated and can be examined at a level of abstraction higher than the individual business process level.

For inter-organizational system modeling, a fourth level could be added to the REA ontology–the value system level. This enables an integration that spans the conceptual models of each organization to recognize that many business activities and phenomena, such as electronic commerce and supply chain management, involve multiple organizations. A company's value system consists of its relationships with all other entities with which the company makes exchanges. For example, a company engages in exchanges with its employees, its suppliers, its customers and its creditors. An enterprise system model at this level would represent the resource flows between the various types of organizations in the enterprise's value system. For example, for RSW, the value system model is depicted in Figure 11. Partnering organizations that

Figure 10. RSW value chain level model

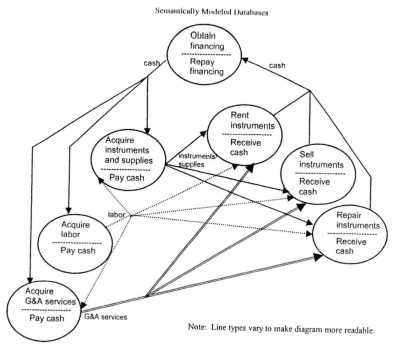

Semantically Modeled Databases

Note: Line types vary to make diagram more readable.

build their enterprise databases on the REA ontology will be better able to integrate their databases. Note that this does not require them to use exactly the same names for their resources, events, agents, etc., nor do they need to use the same business process practices. Each company can use its own practices and its own terminology as long as the system includes a specification as to what each component with a set of synonyms and homonyms to facilitate integration (Rockwell and McCarthy, 1999). This will probably be best accomplished using object technology and artificial intelligence concepts such as automated intensional reasoning (Geerts and McCarthy, 1999) and automated intelligent agents. Automated intensional reasoning systems make inferences based on database table intensions, and require completely consistent use of any underlying pattern such as REA.

Although REA is being used by some consultants and software developers, as indicated in the earlier literature review, there are various other approaches to integrating systems within and across organizations. Approaches to integrating systems within organizations have primarily been ERP software-driven. Approaches to integrating systems across organizations have primarily focused on document exchange, although ERP vendors are working toward inter-organizational integration. We will first discuss the document-centered approaches and then review the ERP software approaches. Wakayama et al. (1998) state that "rethinking the role of documents is central to (re)engineering enterprises in the context of information and process integration" because documents "are a common thread linking integration

Figure 11. RSW Value System Level Model

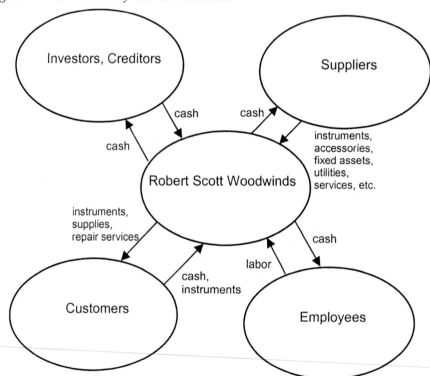

issues." Electronic data interchange is certainly document-oriented, with standards developed for issues such as which field on an electronic purchase order transmitted between companies represents the quantity ordered. More recent advances for Web-based transmission of documents, such as various mark-up languages, have also focused on identifying fields that exist on these documents.

We believe it is not the documents themselves that provide the common thread among company's business processes. Rather it is the similar nature of the underlying transactions and information needs associated with managing these transactions that are depicted within the organization's semantic model. Although organizations can have very different scripts for doing business, the core of the scripts is often the same. Therefore, rather than taking a document-oriented approach to inter-organizational system integration, we believe it is more important to apply an enterprise ontology approach such as REA.

Vendors of enterprise resource planning systems recognize the need for inter-organization integration and supply chain management. This integration issue has not been easily resolved. "Bolt-on" applications are typically used, tying the systems together with what is often referred to as "spaghetti code." It is possible that some of the difficulties in integrating systems across organizations with ERP systems are due to the requirement of many ERP packages that organizations conform to the software (in the form of best practices) at the task level. REA encourages conformance to a core pattern at the business process level (or at least to a core set of pattern components), but allows considerable variation at the task level. We suggest that the integration of organizations' information systems does not need to occur at the task level; it can occur at the value system and process levels where the core pattern components can easily be standardized. (However, as noted above, the systems need to include task level specifications of homonyms and synonyms to facilitate integration.) As Swagerman, Dogger and Maatman (2000) note, standardization of patterns of behavior ensure the semantic context is clear to every user. We believe the standardization of patterns and pattern components, along with the development of appropriate artificial intelligence tools, will allow system integration without imposing formal structures on the social domain.

Limited research has been conducted as to the similarities of the semantic models underlying the current ERP packages. Nonetheless, these models do exist and many organizations reengineer themselves to become consistent with the best practices embodied within these models. Unfortunately, this is often at the task level, and the benefits of the underlying semantics are lost. This is very apparent when organizations seek to extend their value chains up and down their supply chain. If the underlying semantics were preserved, along with the standardization of semantic patterns, then automated intentional reasoning and other knowledge-based tools would be able to facilitate the inter-organizational trading. Semantically modeled enterprise information systems will provide many benefits, from the individual decision-maker level to the inter-organizational level. The critical issue is to ensure that the semantics are not lost upon the implementation of the system and obscured by the task level mechanics. When this occurs, all subsequent benefits are lost and we are faced with the task of integrating disparate systems that are conceptually identical.

FUTURE TRENDS IN SEMANTICALLY MODELED SYSTEMS

Gualtieri (1996) defines electronic commerce as "a way of conducting business where information and communication technologies act as a conduit between trading partners to create greater value from business relationships." The most common current use of information and communication technologies (i.e., information systems) for electronic commerce is to transmit data back and forth between companies in rigidly structured formats. In business-to-consumer electronic commerce, businesses create Web sites from which they display their product offerings to potential customers. Customers fill out on-line order forms that transmit the data in the company's chosen format. Most business-to-business electronic commerce utilizes electronic data interchange with its rigid standards. Information systems structured in these ways meet the definition of conduits–they are pipes through which the data flows (and how well the data flows depends on the size and layout of the pipes). Whether they meet the definition of creating greater value is not as clear. Certainly they add value beyond not having Internet sites or EDI or any other alternative. However, we must consider whether they can add even more value and whether they can be facilitators rather than simple conduits. We believe that the use of an ontological modeling approach, such as the REA ontology discussed in the previous sections, has the potential to enhance electronic commerce, particularly in the business-to-business environment.

The issues related to supply chain management are similar to e-commerce. In fact, when examining inter-organizational systems from a supply chain perspective, the same set of issues apply as found in business-to-business e-commerce. Consequently, our recommendations and expectations are the same, and these have been presented in the prior sections. The use of an ontological system like the REA ontology is a necessary but not sufficient condition to facilitate effective and efficient inter-organizational systems. Again, intelligent agents and automated intensional reasoning is also required for this to occur. Further, the semantics of the systems must not be obscured by subsequent implementation artifacts.

Another area that would receive benefit from semantically modeled systems is the data warehouse. At the present time, data warehouses and data marts are required because of the limitations of hardware and software. It is not physically possible to store all of the data for all events on a single system for both current transaction processing and all queries to that system and still obtain sufficient performance. However, on a conceptual level, if a system were designed based on the REA ontology as presented here, there would be no need for a separate data warehouse. Information in data warehouses is simply a set of views of the operational data that are prepared for specific functions. These views could be produced directly from the operational database and manipulated by users. Only technological speed and capacity limit the feasibility of discarding the data warehouse.

There are many issues that still need to be resolved, and as such these present many research opportunities. One issue focuses on the scalability of the systems based on the REA ontology. The system presented in this chapter is for a relatively small organization. How this translates into a system for a large multinational firm needs to be explored. Also, while research has been conducted on automated intensional reasoning (Rockwell and McCarthy, 1999), much more is needed. Further, this needs to be extended to the use of intelligent agents and to object-based environments.

Another issue is that of preserving the semantics at an operational level, beyond the level of the database itself. This would allow decision-makers additional insight into the problems and the information available to address the issues that they face. Again, object-based systems seem to provide the most benefit, but additional research is needed.

Regardless of what the research demonstrates, organizations will need to be convinced that they should change the relatively new ERP systems that they have acquired. These systems required an immense investment, and in some cases, these systems are still not functioning in an acceptable manner. It is most likely that change will need to be driven by the ERP vendors themselves. They would have a vested interest in selling upgrades to their systems as long as they can demonstrate some type of advantage for the consumer. This has occurred with a great deal of regularity in the PC market. A significant number of organizations would need to make the change in order for the benefits discussed in this chapter to occur. The first fax machine sold did not provide as much value as the one millionth fax machine sold; the more fax machines are sold, the greater are the opportunities for sending and receiving information on the first fax machine. Similarly, the value of the first REA based system for inter-organizational use will be limited (although it will facilitate intra-organization needs), but the more companies that realize the value of these systems and build them, the more value will accrue to the first such system.

CONCLUSIONS

In this chapter we presented a normative semantic model for designing integrated databases for enterprise information systems. This model was developed by McCarthy (1982), and its expanded form has been proposed as an enterprise ontology by Geerts and McCarthy (2000). This ontology is intended to serve as a foundation for integrated enterprise-wide and inter-organizational systems. To take full advantage of the semantically rich ontological patterns and templates, the REA ontology must be implemented with current advances in artificial intelligence technology and object-oriented database technology. Many of the current problems faced by companies who attempt to install ERP systems and integration tools such as EDI can be minimized by use of common semantic patterns that can be reasoned about by intelligent systems. Companies may integrate their systems, without using identical business practices.

Non-accounting researchers have conducted most of the existing research on semantic models, both at the individual level and at the organization level. Because REA originated in an accounting domain, non-accounting researchers have not embraced it (perhaps because of their lack of awareness of the REA ontology). We hope that by making information about this enterprise ontology more available to non-accounting researchers who are interested in semantically modeled information systems we will encourage more interest and participation in REA research.

REFERENCES

Agarwal, R., Sinha, A. P. and Tanniru, M. (1996a). Cognitive fit in requirements modeling: A study of object and process methodologies. *Journal of Management Information Systems*. Fall. 13(2), 137-162.

Agarwal, R., Sinha, A. P. and Tanniru, M. (1996b). The role of prior experience and task characteristics in object-oriented modeling: An empirical study. *International Journal of Human-Computer Studies*. 45, 639-667.

Andros, D., Cherrington, J. O. and Denna, E. L. (1992). Reengineer your accounting the IBM way. *The Financial Executive*. July/August, 28-31.

APICS. (1998). Defining enterprise resource planning. http://www.apics.org/OtherServices/articles/defining.htm.

Batini, C., Ceri, S. and Navathe, S. B. (1992). *Conceptual Database Design: An Entity Approach*. Redwood City, CA: Benjamin Cummings.

Bodart, F. and Weber, R. (1997). *Optional Properties Versus Subtyping in Conceptual Modeling: A Theory and Empirical Test*. Working paper. April.

Cherrington, J. O., Denna, E. L. and Andros, D. P. (1996). Developing an event-based system: The case of IBM's national employee disbursement system. *Journal of Information Systems*. 10(1), 51-69.

Curran, T.A. and Ladd, A. (2000). *SAP R/3 Business Blueprint: Understanding Enterprise Supply Chain Management*. Prentice Hall.

David, J. S. (1995). *An Empirical Analysis of REA Accounting Systems, Productivity and Perceptions of Competitive Advantage*. Unpublished doctoral dissertation, Michigan State University.

David, J. S. (1997). Three "events" that define an REA methodology for systems analysis, design and implementation. Working paper. Arizona State University.

David, J. S., Dunn. C. L. and McCarthy, W. E. (1999). *Enterprise Resource Planning Systems Research: The Necessity of Explicating and Examining Patterns in Symbolic Form*.

Dunn C. L. and Grabski, S. V. (1998). The effect of field independence on conceptual modeling performance. *Advances in Accounting Information Systems*. 6, 65-77.

Dunn, C. L. and Grabski, S. V. (2000a). Perceived semantic expressiveness of accounting systems and task accuracy effects. *International Journal of Accounting Information Systems*.

Dunn, C. L. and Grabski, S. V. (2000b). Empirical research on semantically modeled accounting systems. Research monograph published by *The American Accounting Association's Information Systems*.

Dunn, C. L. and McCarthy, W. E. (1997). The REA accounting model: Intellectual heritage and prospects for progress. *Journal of Information Systems.* 11(1), 31- 51.

Geerts, G. L. and McCarthy, W. E. (1991). Database accounting systems. Williams, B. C. and Spaul, B. J. (Eds.). *IT and Accounting: The Impact of Information Technology.* London: Chapman & Hall, 159-183.

Geerts, G. L. and McCarthy, W. E. (1998). Accounting as romance: patterns of unrequited love and incomplete exchanges in life and in business software. Working paper. Presented at the *Arizona State University REA Roundtable Workshop.* Tempe, AZ.

Geerts, G. L. and McCarthy, W. E. (2000). An ontological analysis of the primitives of the extended-REA enterprise information architecture. *International Journal of Accounting Information Systems.*

Gerard, G. (1998). REA Knowledge Acquisition and Related Conceptual Database Design Performance. Unpublished doctoral dissertation. Michigan State University.

Hollander, A., Denna, E. and Cherrington, O. (1996). *Accounting, Information Technology and Business Solutions.* Chicago, Irwin.

Kim, Y. K. and March, S. T. (1995). Comparing data modeling formalisms. *Communications of the ACM.* June, 38(6), 103-115.

McCarthy, W. E. (1982). The REA accounting model: A generalized framework for accounting systems in a shared data environment. *The Accounting Review.* 57(3), 554-578.

Nakamura, H. and Johnson R. E. (1998). Adaptive Framework for the REA Accounting Model, *Proceedings of the OOPSLA'98 Business Object Workshop IV.* http://jeffsutherland.com/oopsla98/nakamura.html.

O'Leary, D. E. (1999). On the relationship between REAL and SAP. Working paper. Presented at the *1999 American Accounting Association Annual Meeting.* San Diego, CA.

Rockwell, S. R. and McCarthy, W. E. (1999). REACH: Automated database design integrating first-order theories, reconstructive expertise, and implementation heuristics for accounting information systems. *International Journal of Intelligent Systems in Accounting, Finance & Management.* 8(3), 181-197.

Satoshi, H. (1999). The contents of interviews with the project manager of FDWH in IBM Japan. *Proceedings of the 1999 SMAP Workshop.* San Diego, CA.

Scheer, A-W. (1998) . *Business Process Engineering: Reference Models for Industrial Enterprises.* Springer-Verlag.

Sinha, A. P. and Vessey, I. (1999). An empirical investigation of entity-based and object-oriented data modeling. De, P. and DeGross, J. (Eds.). *Proceedings of the Twentieth International Conference on Information Systems.* Charlotte, NC. 229-244.

Swagerman, D.M., Dogger, N. and Maatman, S. (2000). Electronic markets from a semiotic perspective. *Electronic Journal of Organizational Virtualness.* 2(2), 22-42.

Vessey, I. and Conger, S. A. (1994). Requirements specification: Learning object, process and data methodologies. *Communications of the ACM.* May, 37(5), 102-113.

Wakayama, T., Kannapan, S., Khoong, C. M., Navathe, S. and Yates, J. (1998). *Information and process integration in enterprises: Rethinking documents.* Kluwer Academic Publishers.

Watson, E. E. and Schneider, H. (1999). Using ERP systems in education. *Communications of the Association for Information Systems.* 1(9).

Weber, R. (1986). Data models research in accounting: An evaluation of wholesale distribution software. *The Accounting Review.* 61(3), 498-518.

Weber, R. (1996). Are attributes entities? A study of database designers' memory structures. *Information Systems Research*. June, 7(2), 137-162.

Yasuhiro, A. (1995). The new concepts of accounting systems in IBM Japan. *IBM Professional VISION*. 5, 88-93.

ENDNOTES

1 An alternative semantic model has been presented by Scheer (1998). Additional research is needed comparing these two semantic models with subsequent evaluations of commercially available ERP packages.

2 The REA framework uses the term business process to mean a set of related business events and other activities that are intended to accomplish a strategic objective of an organization. In this view, business processes represent a high level of abstraction. Some non-REA views define business processes as singular activities that are performed within a business. For example, some views consider "process sale order" to be a business process. The REA view considers "sale order" to be a business event that is made up of specific tasks, and it interacts with other business events within the "Sales-Collection" business process.

Chapter XIII

Set Comparison Queries in SQL

Mohammad Dadashzadeh
Wichita State University, USA

INTRODUCTION

One of the most important promises of the relational data model has been that it frees the decision maker, the manager, from the necessity of resorting to an intermediary, the programmer, in retrieving information from the organization's database in response to unanticipated needs. That promise is founded on the availability of very high-level relational query languages such as SQL. Unfortunately, the current specification of the SQL standard fails to support users adequately in formulating complex queries involving set comparison that tend to arise in on-line analytical processing (OLAP) situations. As pointed out by Rao et al. (1996): "SQL's syntax is too restricted to express quantified queries. While SQL allows subqueries to form sets, the relationships that can be expressed over sets are limited, and must be written in awkward and complicated ways." This chapter presents a systematic approach for teaching users how to formulate in SQL complex set comparison queries encountered in ad-hoc decision-making scenarios.

BACKGROUND AND MOTIVATION

Consider the following relational database about suppliers and parts. (The primary key of each relation is underlined.)

SUPPLIER(S#, Supplier_Name, Supplier_City)
PART(P#, Part_Name, Part_Color)
SHIPMENT(S#, P#)
SUPPLY(S#, P#)

The relation SHIPMENT records information on what parts are *currently* shipped by each supplier, while the relation SUPPLY indicates what parts can be supplied, *in the future*, by each supplier. An instance of the relations SHIPMENT and SUPPLY is depicted below.

CURRENT *SHIPMENT*		FUTURE *SUPPLY*	
S1	P1	S1	P1
S1	P2	S1	P2
S1	P3	S1	P3
S1	P5	S1	P4
		S1	P5
S2	P1	S2	P1
S2	P2	S2	P2
S2	P3		
S3	P1	S3	P2
S4	P1	S4	P1
S4	P2	S4	P2
S5	P5		
		S6	P5
		S6	P6

Now, consider the following queries:

Q1: Which suppliers are shipping *at least one* red part?

Q2: Which suppliers are shipping *no* red parts?

Q3: Which suppliers are shipping *only* red parts?

Q4: Which suppliers are shipping *every* red part?

Q5: Which suppliers are shipping *exactly* the red parts?

Q6: Which suppliers are shipping *no* part that they will supply in the future?

Q7: Which suppliers will not continue to supply the same parts that they are currently shipping?

Of the queries listed, Q2-Q7 are considered *set comparison queries* since their result sets (i.e., the desired supplier numbers) can only be determined by comparing two sets (e.g., the set of part numbers shipped by each supplier against the set of part numbers for red parts). In contrast, the result set for Q1 can be obtained by merely matching (i.e., joining) the part number from a SHIPMENT row with that of a red PART row as shown below:

Q1: Which suppliers are shipping *at least one* red part?

```
SELECT   DISTINCT S#
FROM     SHIPMENT, PART
WHERE    (SHIPMENT.P# = PART.P#) AND (PART_COLOR = 'RED');
```

Despite their innocuous appearances, queries involving set comparison are very difficult to formulate in relational query languages (Blanning, 1993; Celko, 1997;

Dadashzadeh, 1989, 1992). To fix ideas, consider the following equivalent, yet markedly different, SQL formulations for Q2:

Q2 Version 1: Which suppliers are shipping *no* red parts?

```
SELECT    DISTINCT S#
FROM      SHIPMENT
WHERE     S# NOT IN    (SELECT    S#
                       FROM      SHIPMENT, PART
                       WHERE     (SHIPMENT.P# = PART.P#) AND
                                 (PART_COLOR = 'RED'));
```

Q2 Version 2: Which suppliers are shipping *no* red parts?

```
SELECT    DISTINCT S#
FROM      SHIPMENT X
WHERE     NOT EXISTS
          (SELECT         *
          FROM            SHIPMENT
          WHERE(S# = X.S#) AND
               P# IN
               (SELECT P# FROM PART WHERE
               PART_COLOR='RED'));
```

At first glance, it might appear that the second formulation of Q2 is more difficult than the first. However, it, in fact, represents a *general* approach to formulation of set comparison queries involving ***disjointness*** (e.g., the set of parts supplied being disjoint from, that is, having an empty intersection with, the set of red parts). This *general* approach to be presented in the next section makes it a simple matter to formulate complex set comparison queries such as Q6 shown below, where a simpler formulation is, indeed, quite hard to come by.

Q6: Which suppliers are shipping *no* part that they will supply in the future?

```
SELECT    DISTINCT S#
FROM      SHIPMENT X
WHERE     NOT EXISTS
          (SELECT         *
          FROM            SHIPMENT
          WHERE           (S# = X.S#) AND
                          P# IN
                          (SELECT P# FROM SUPPLY WHERE S# = X.S#));
```

A GENERALIZED APPROACH TO SET COMPARISON QUERIES IN SQL

A general set comparison query can be modeled in the following ***intermediate*** SQL-like representation:

```
SELECT    desired-columns
FROM      desired-table(s)
WHERE     ( desired-non-set-comparisons )
```

AND
((desired source set of values subquery)
set-comparison-operator
(target set of values subquery));

where *(desired source set of values subquery)* is a **correlated** subquery while *(target set of values subquery)* may or may not be correlated.

For example, consider the following **intermediate** representation:

SELECT   DISTINCT S#, Supplier_Name
FROM   Supplier X
WHERE   (Supplier_City = 'LONDON')
         AND
         {(SELECT   P#
         FROM   SHIPMENT
         WHERES# = X.S#)
         CONTAINS
         (SELECT   P#

desired-columns	S#, Supplier_Name
Desired-table(s)	Supplier X
(desired-non-set-comparisons)	(Supplier_City = 'LONDON')
(desired source set of values subquery) *correlated* subquery	(SELECT P# FROM SHIPMENT WHERE S# = X.S#)
Set-comparison-operator	CONTAINS
(target set of values subquery) *non-correlated subquery*	(SELECT P# FROM PART WHERE Part_Color = 'RED')

FROM   PART
WHEREPart-Color = 'RED')}

This query is intended to list S# and Supplier_Name for those suppliers located in London whose set of part shipments contains *every* red part. Here, the following correspondence with the general template can be established:

Converting the **intermediate** SQL-like representation to standard SQL is guided by a series of transformation rules depicted in Figures 1-9. Specifically, given an SQL-like query in the format shown in Figure 1, Figures 2-9 give the equivalent standard SQL representations when the set-comparison-operator is, respectively, CONTAINS, DOES NOT CONTAIN, IS (CONTAINED) IN, IS NOT (CONTAINED) IN, IS DISJOINT FROM (i.e., having an empty intersection), IS NOT DISJOINT FROM, IS EQUAL TO and IS NOT EQUAL TO.

Applying the transformation rule from Figure 2 to our example query above, we get the final equivalent SQL representation:

SELECT   DISTINCT S#, Supplier_Name
FROM   Supplier X

```
WHERE      (Supplier_City = 'LONDON')
           AND
           NOT EXISTS
           (SELECT      P#
           FROM         PART
           WHERE        (Part-Color = 'RED')
                        AND
                        P# NOT IN
                        (SELECT      P#
                        FROM         SHIPMENT
```

Figure 1. The general form of the intermediate SQL-like representation

```
SELECT           desired-columns
FROM             desired-table(s)
WHERE( desired-non-set-comparisons )
            AND
            (        (SELECT        select-column-1
                     FROM           from-list-1
                     WHERE          where-list-1)
                     set-comparison-operator
                     (SELECT        select-column-2
                     FROM           from-list-2
                     WHERE          where-list-2)      );
```

Figure 2. The equivalent standard SQL representation of Figure 1
when set-comparison-operator is CONTAINS

```
SELECT       desired-columns
FROM         desired-table(s)
WHERE        ( desired-non-set-comparisons )
             AND
             NOT EXISTS
             (SELECT      select-column-2
             FROM         from-list-2
             WHERE        where-list-2
                          AND
                          select-column-2
                          NOT IN
                          (SELECT      select-column-1
                          FROM         from-list-1
                          WHERE        where-list-1));
```

Figure 3. The equivalent standard SQL representation of Figure 1 when set-comparison-operator is DOES NOT CONTAIN

SELECT	desired-columns
FROM	desired-table(s)
WHERE	(desired-non-set-comparisons)
	AND
	EXISTS
	(SELECT select-column-2
	FROM from-list-2
	WHERE where-list-2
	AND
	select-column-2
	NOT IN
	(SELECT select-column-1
	FROM from-list-1
	WHERE where-list-1));

Figure 4. The equivalent standard SQL representation of Figure 1 when set-comparison-operator is IS (CONTAINED) IN

SELECT	desired-columns
FROM	desired-table(s)
WHERE	(desired-non-set-comparisons)
	AND
	NOT EXISTS
	(SELECT select-column-1
	FROM from-list-1
	WHERE where-list-1
	AND
	select-column-1
	NOT IN
	(SELECT select-column-2
	FROM from-list-2
	WHERE where-list-2));

WHERE	S# = X.S#));

Figures 10-14 depict, respectively, the final SQL representation of queries Q3-Q7, derived by applying the appropriate transformation rules to the ***intermediate*** representation of these queries.

Figure 5. The equivalent standard SQL representation of Figure 1 when set-comparison-operator is IS NOT (CONTAINED) IN

```
SELECT        desired-columns
FROM          desired-table(s)
WHERE         ( desired-non-set-comparisons )
              AND
              EXISTS
              (SELECT        select-column-1
              FROM           from-list-1
              WHERE          where-list-1
                             AND
                             select-column-1
                             NOT IN
                             (SELECT        select-column-2
                             FROM           from-list-2
                             WHERE          where-list-2));
```

Figure 6. The equivalent standard SQL representation of Figure 1 when set-comparison-operator is IS DISJOINT FROM

```
SELECT        desired-columns
FROM          desired-table(s)
WHERE         ( desired-non-set-comparisons )
              AND
              NOT EXISTS
              (SELECT        select-column-1
              FROM           from-list-1
              WHERE          where-list-1
                             AND
                             select-column-1
                             IN
                             (SELECT        select-column-2
                             FROM           from-list-2
                             WHERE          where-list-2));
```

CONCLUDING REMARKS

Set comparison queries comprise those queries against a relational database whose result sets can only be determined by comparing two sets of values for inclusion, exclusion or disjointness. Although queries directly employing the common set operations of union, intersection and difference fit this definition, the majority of interesting set comparison queries do not lend themselves to a straightforward formulation via union, intersection or set difference. This chapter has presented a generalized approach to formulating such queries in SQL.

Figure 7. The equivalent standard SQL representation of Figure 1 when set-comparison-operator is IS NOT DISJOINT FROM

```
SELECT      desired-columns
FROM        desired-table(s)
WHERE       ( desired-non-set-comparisons )
            AND
            EXISTS
            (SELECT     select-column-1
            FROM        from-list-1
            WHERE       where-list-1
                        AND
                        select-column-1
                        IN
                        (SELECT     select-column-2
                        FROM        from-list-2
                        WHERE       where-list-2));
```

Figure 8. The equivalent standard SQL representation of Figure 1 when set-comparison-operator is IS EQUAL TO

```
SELECT      desired-columns
FROM        desired-table(s)
WHERE       ( desired-non-set-comparisons )
            AND
            NOT EXISTS
            (SELECT     select-column-1
            FROM        from-list-1
            WHERE       where-list-1
                        AND
                        select-column-1
                        NOT IN
                        (SELECT     select-column-2
                        FROM        from-list-2
                        WHERE       where-list-2))
            AND
            NOT EXISTS
            (SELECT     select-column-2
            FROM        from-list-2
            WHERE       where-list-2
                        AND
                        select-column-2
                        NOT IN
                        (SELECT     select-column-1
                        FROM        from-list-1
                        WHERE       where-list-1));
```

Figure 9. The equivalent standard SQL representation of Figure 1 when set-comparison-operator is IS NOT EQUAL TO

```
SELECT        desired-columns
FROM          desired-table(s)
WHERE         ( desired-non-set-comparisons )
              AND
              (EXISTS
              (SELECT       select-column-1
              FROM          from-list-1
              WHERE         where-list-1
                            AND
                            select-column-1
                            NOT IN
                            (SELECT       select-column-2
                            FROM          from-list-2
                            WHERE         where-list-2))
              OR
              EXISTS
              (SELECT       select-column-2
              FROM          from-list-2
              WHERE         where-list-2
                            AND
                            select-column-2
                            NOT IN
                            (SELECT       select-column-1
                            FROM          from-list-1
                            WHERE         where-list-1)));
```

Figure 10. The equivalent standard SQL representation of Q3

Q3: Which suppliers are shipping *only* red parts?
Intermediate SQL-Like Representation:

```
SELECT      DISTINCT S#
FROM        SHIPMENT X
WHERE       (SELECT      P#
            FROM        SHIPMENT
            WHERE       S# = X.S#)
            IS CONTAINED IN
            (SELECT      P#
            FROM        PART
            WHERE       PART_COLOR = 'RED');
```

SQL Transformation (via Figure 4):

```
SELECT      DISTINCT S#
FROM        SHIPMENT X
WHERE       NOT EXISTS
            (SELECT      P#
            FROM        SHIPMENT
            WHERE       S# = X.S#
            AND
            P#
            NOT IN
            (SELECT      P#
            FROM        PART
            WHERE       PART_COLOR = 'RED'));
```

From a practical perspective, the generalized approach presented in this chapter can be used to teach advanced users how to formulate complex set comparison queries in on-line analytical processing scenarios. Arguably, it also provides the most appropriate context for teaching the role of correlated subqueries and NOT EXISTS construct in SQL.

From a technical perspective, the transformation rules presented in this chapter can be implemented in an SQL pre-processor, allowing users to formulate complex set comparison queries in the intermediate SQL-like representation put forth in this chapter. Such SQL pre-processing can be readily imagined as a standard feature in tomorrow's syntax-aware SQL editors.

Finally, from a technological perspective, as data warehousing and OLAP capabilities become standard features of relational database management systems based on the SQL standard, it may be wisest to re-introduce direct support of set comparison operators (such as CONTAINS and EQUALS) to the SQL standard.

Figure 11. The equivalent standard SQL representation of Q4

Q4: Which suppliers are shipping *every* red part?
Intermediate SQL-Like Representation:
```
SELECT      DISTINCT S#
FROM        SHIPMENT X
WHERE       (SELECT      P#
            FROM         SHIPMENT
            WHERE        S# = X.S#)
            CONTAINS
            (SELECT      P#
            FROM         PART
            WHERE        PART_COLOR = 'RED');
```

SQL Transformation (via Figure 2):
```
SELECT      DISTINCT S#
FROM        SHIPMENT X
WHERE       NOT EXISTS
            (SELECT      P#
            FROM         PART
            WHERE        PART_COLOR = 'RED'
            AND
            P#
            NOT IN
            (SELECT      P#
            FROM         SHIPMENT
            WHERE        S# = X.S#));
```

Figure 12. The equivalent standard SQL representation of Q5

Q5: Which suppliers are shipping *exactly* the red parts?
Intermediate SQL-Like Representation:
```
SELECT      DISTINCT S#
FROM        SHIPMENT X
WHERE       (SELECT      P#
            FROM         SHIPMENT
            WHERE        S# = X.S#)
            IS EQUAL TO
            (SELECT      P#
            FROM         PART
            WHERE        PART_COLOR = 'RED');
```

SQL Transformation (via Figure 8):
```
SELECT      DISTINCT S#
FROM        SHIPMENT X
WHERE       NOT EXISTS
            (SELECT      P#
```

```
FROM          SHIPMENT
WHERE         S# = X.S#
              AND P# NOT IN
              (SELECT      P#
              FROM         PART
              WHERE        PART_COLOR = 'RED'))
AND
NOT EXISTS
(SELECT       P#
FROM          PART
WHERE         PART_COLOR = 'RED'
              AND P# NOT IN
              (SELECT      P#
              FROM         SHIPMENT
              WHERE        S# = X.S#));
```

Figure 13. The equivalent standard SQL representation of Q6

Q6: Which suppliers are shipping *no* part that they will supply in the future?
Intermediate SQL-Like Representation:

```
SELECT        DISTINCT S#
FROM          SHIPMENT X
WHERE         (SELECT      P#
              FROM         SHIPMENT
              WHERE        S# = X.S#)
              IS DISJOINT FROM
              (SELECT      P#
              FROM         SUPPLY
              WHERE        S# =X.S#);
```

SQL Transformation (via Figure 6):

```
SELECT        DISTINCT S#
FROM          SHIPMENT X
WHERE         NOT EXISTS
              (SELECT      P#
              FROM         SHIPMENT
              WHERE        S# = X.S#
              AND
              P#
              IN
              (SELECT      P#
              FROM         SUPPLY
              WHERE        S# = X.S#));
```

Figure 14. The equivalent standard SQL representation of Q7

Q7: Which suppliers will not continue to supply the same parts that they are currently shipping?

Intermediate SQL-Like Representation:

```
SELECT      DISTINCT S#
FROM        SHIPMENT X
WHERE       (SELECT      P#
            FROM        SHIPMENT
            WHERE       S# = X.S#)
            IS NOT CONTAINED IN
            (SELECT      P#
            FROM        SUPPLY
            WHERE       S# = X.S#);
```

SQL Transformation (via Figure 5):

```
SELECT      DISTINCT S#
FROM        SHIPMENT X
WHERE       EXISTS
            (SELECT      P#
            FROM        SHIPMENT
            WHERE       S# = X.S#
                        AND
                        P#
                        NOT IN
                        (SELECT      P#
                        FROM        SUPPLY
                        WHERE       S# = X.S#));
```

REFERENCES

Blanning, R. W. (1993). Relational division in information management. *Decision Support Systems,* 9(4), 313-324.

Celko, J. (1997). *Joe Celko's SQL Puzzles & Answers.* San Francisco: Morgan Kaufmann Publishers.

Dadashzadeh, M. (1992). A proposed change to the SQL standard. Tinnirello, P. C. (Ed.) In *Handbook of Systems Management: Development and Support.* Boston, MA: Auerbach Publications. 465-472.

Dadashzadeh, M. (1989). An improved division operator for relational algebra. *Information Systems,* 14(5), 431-437.

Rao, S. G., Badia, A. and Van Gucht, D. (1996). Providing better support for a class of decision support queries. In *Proceedings of the 1996 SIGMOD International Conference on Management of Data,* 217-227. New York, NY: Association for Computing Machinery.

Chapter XIV

Toward a Framework for Advanced Query Processing

Suk-Chung Yoon
Widener University, USA

INTRODUCTION

Traditionally, database systems have accepted queries specified with precise search expressions directly based on primitive data stored in databases and have returned a set of database instances (extensional answers) based on primitive data as answer sets. As the size and complexity of databases with the advance in storage technologies have been increased, we believe we need much more sophisticated query-formulation and answer-finding schemes in database systems in order to satisfy the needs of a truly intelligent information system, and to serve more new applications such as e-commerce and Web-based information systems well. In certain queries, users may prefer to express queries with more general and abstract information instead of primitive terms directly based on the data stored in a database. This type of query is referred to as *flexible query*. With flexible queries, users who may not formulate precise query conditions ask general queries involving meaningful abstract terms that do not directly come from information stored in a database. For example, a manager may wish to query, "What are the *expensive digital* products which are purchased by *young* on-line shoppers in the *Midwest* area?" The query uses abstract terms, "*expensive*," "*digital*," "*young*" and "*Midwest*" which are not stored explicitly in the database. A flexible query can be expressed in terms of predefined abstract terms such as *expensive, digital, young,* and *Midwest* that can be derived from primitive information in a database. We believe flexible queries provide users with the flexibility of expressing query conditions at a relatively high-level concept, which relaxes the requirement of the preciseness of query conditions and allows them to ask more general questions to a database.

In certain queries, users may be interested in extracting the conditions and/or the characteristics that justify extensional answers or summarize the general features of extensional answers. This type of query is referred to as intensional query. For example, a user may wish to ask a conventional query such as "Retrieve all of the customers who bought Ford Escorts in 1999" or a flexible query such as "Retrieve all of the customers who bought *compact car.*" The constant *Compact Car* is a high-level concept. In the example, simple retrieval of the names of the customers who bought Ford Escorts or compact cars is an extensional answer, whereas the answer such as "young and single people with a middle income" is an intensional answer, which describes general characteristics of the extensional answer.

The answers for the intensional queries provide a more compact, intuitive and informative form than extensional answers could ever do. Giving us exactly what conditions must be fulfilled to get a certain extensional answer, an intensional answer can be considered as a kind of interpretation or explanation of the extensional answer. A conventional query to request intensional answers is called an intensional and conventional query, while a flexible query which requests intensional answers is called an intensional and flexible query. Both types of a conventional query and a flexible query can be intensional queries. That is, both types of queries can be answered extensionally or intensionally. In our approach, queries are classified into four types: extensional and conventional query (ECQ), intensional and conventional query (ICQ), extensional and flexible query (EFQ), and intensional and flexible query (IFQ).

The current database systems support only ECQ types of queries. We believe there will be more database applications where it is important to be able to pose and answer queries flexibly rather than with expressions directly based on primitive data. In recent years, there has been an emerging area, called data mining or knowledge discovery, that addresses the problems in finding implicit, previously unknown and potentially useful patterns from large databases (Frawley, 1991). Data mining or knowledge discovery has been the subject of intense research and development. Most of the data mining technologies have been applied in the areas of decision support and market strategies. In addition to those applications, there are other applications that would benefit from the use of the data mining techniques. This motivates the development of mechanisms for processing two basic categories of query answering: flexible query answering and intensional query answering using data mining techniques.

In this chapter, we introduce a method for flexible query answering, which is a mechanism to answer queries specified with general and abstract terms quickly and intelligently. In addition, we introduce a partially automated method for generating intensional answers to represent answer-set abstractly for a conventional query and a flexible query in the database systems.

Our approach consists of two phases: preprocessing, and execution. In the preprocessing phase, we build a set of concept hierarchies (Han et al., 1993) constructed by generalization of data in attributes defined in a database schema, and a set of virtual hierarchies to provide a global view of relationships among high-level concepts defined in concept hierarchies. We create summary tables by preprocessing primitive data in frequently referenced relations and store previously processed meaningful patterns in the related summary tables.

In the execution phase, we receive a user's query, process the query and generate answers intelligently according to its type in a form that can be understood and analyzed easily. For intensional queries, we collect an extensional answer, select a set of relevant attributes to be generalized in the extensional answer and characterize the features of those relevant attributes in the extensional answer with the concept hierarchies and the virtual hierarchies by using data mining methods, especially the inductive and attribute-oriented method introduced in Han, et. al.

The contribution of our approach is that we develop a framework for processing and answering queries flexibly by applying data mining techniques. In addition, we suggest strategies to reduce the computational complexity of the advanced query answer generation process. We believe that our approach enhances user-machine interfaces significantly to conventional databases with additional features.

This chapter is structured as follows. The next section introduces motivating examples to show the advantages of advanced query processing. Following that we survey related works on intelligent query processing. Then we present our approach to process different types of queries using data mining techniques. The final section discusses our conclusions and possible extensions of our work for future research.

MOTIVATING EXAMPLES

The following examples illustrate the advantages of advanced query processing.

Example 1: Suppose we have a *sales database*. For example, a marketing manager at the company who is interested in the sale patterns of various types of customers may formulate a query asking, "What kinds of products are preferred by *young* and single customers with a *high income* who live in *Midwest* areas?" which contains abstract terms such as *"young," "high income"* and *"Midwest."* Even though the answer can provide very meaningful information to the manager, current databases cannot answer the query because those terms are not actual values stored in the database. That is, there is no place in the database where those terms are explicitly mentioned. If a database system can process flexible queries involving abstract terms, the system helps non-expert users make ad-hoc queries easily and find useful and meaningful answers. As the above example shows, the capability of flexible query answering enhances the usefulness and flexibility of a database and provides an interface for users to specify their interested set of data easily. Furthermore, answers for flexible queries may be a valuable resource used for a competitive advantage in promotion and marketing. We believe that many new applications are well served by flexible queries.

Example 2: Suppose there is a customer database in an automobile company. Now, a vice president may have a query asking, "Who are typical buyers of sports cars?" The query may be answered with an extensional answer that might be a long list of people who bought sports cars like $t_1, t_2, ..., t_n$ where each t_i, $1 \leq i \leq n$, represents a person who bought a sports car. Such an extensional answer may be meaningless to the vice president. If a database system can support intensional query answering, an intensional answer may be represented as follows: "typical buyers of sports cars are young people with a high income who live in urban areas," which is more informative and meaningful to the vice president.

As the above example shows, extensional answers would only provide a list of all the objects that satisfy queries, whereas intensional answers provide more insight into the nature of extensional answers. Thus, intensional answers can be more informative than extensional ones. In addition, intensional answers may be used in many ways. For example, the intensional answer in Example 2 may be a valuable resource used for a competitive advantage in decision support and market strategy to the vice president.

Example 3: Suppose that there is a database in a large retailer company. Let us assume that the *customer* relation is a frequently referenced relation and that there have been many query patterns related to the combinations of different types of items and different groups of customers in the relation. We can preprocess information about customers and construct summary tables to include general and abstract information based on different types of items and different groups of customers from the customer relation. Now, we have a query asking, "What are the popular *digital* items of *young* customers?" If we can answer the query with the summary table that includes the general term *young*, it will be efficient and effective because we do not need to access the actual database.

In this chapter, we show how to process a flexible query and an intensional query with the help of the concept hierarchies, virtual hierarchies and the summary tables.

RELATED WORKS

In this section, we survey the area of intelligent query answering which is related to our work. Recently, there have been several research works aimed at improving conventional query answering in various data models (Cholvy and Demolombe, 1986; Imielinski, 1987; Motro 1989, 1994; Motro and Yuan, 1990; Pascual and Cholvy, 1988; Pirotte and Roelants, 1989; Pirotte, et al., 1991; Yoon and Henschen, 1996). Two major areas are intensional query answering and cooperative query answering.

Intensional query answering generates intensional answers, which are conditions and characteristics that justify or explain extensional answers. An overview of the various intensional query answering techniques is given in Motro (1994). These works share a common goal--to generate answers in a more abstract form. Their works consider integrity constraints and/or deduction rules to generate intensional answers.

Our approach takes a fundamentally different approach from those discussed so far. To provide intensional answers, our approach considers extensional answers, whereas their approaches consider integrity constraints and/or deduction rules. That is, we generate intensional answers, which are dependent on extensional answers. In that sense, our approach is a data-driven approach while other approaches are integrity constraints and/or rule-driven ones.

Cooperative query answering answers queries cooperatively by analyzing the intent of queries. Cuppens and Demolombe (1991) have shown methods to provide cooperative answers by rewriting queries with additional variables or additional entities satisfying less-restrictive conditions, which carry relevant information for users. Chu and Chen (1992) have explored a method for generalizing queries in order to provide generalized and associated information, which is relevant to the queries. Chu and Chen start with a query, generalize the conditions in the query and then generate a cooperative answer. The major difference between cooperative answering and flexible query answering is that the former approach provides additional information that is not explicitly requested by queries, while the latter approach starts with queries specified with abstract terms and refines the terms in the queries to more specific conditions to find answers. Flexible query answering is a process to provide answers to imprecisely specified queries with some general terms. In that sense, the latter approach is top-down, whereas the former approach is bottom-up.

Our approach uses concept hierarchies that are introduced by Han (1993). In Han's work, the attribute domains were defined in the given concept hierarchies and, in turn, used to generalize the attribute values in a table. He used the hierarchies as a method for mining characteristics and discriminate rules in relational databases. However, our approach uses the hierarchies as background knowledge for formulating and answering queries. We apply and extend their approach developed for data mining in relational databases to the advanced query processing. In addition, we use virtual hierarchies, summary tables and previously processed meaningful patterns. We also suggest strategies to reduce the computational complexity of the answer generation process.

OUR APPROACH

In this section, we present our approach to process advanced queries. We divide our approach into two phases: preprocessing and execution. The preprocessing phase is done statically once, while the execution phase has to be performed at run time. The preprocessing phase is independent of queries posed to a database and hence is computed once, prior to the processing of any query. We now consider each phase in detail.

Preprocessing Phase

In this phase, we perform three steps. First, for each attribute defined in a database schema, we build a concept hierarchy to define generalized relationships for the values in the attribute. The concept hierarchy forms a taxonomy of concepts in a set of different layers from most specific value to most general concept. In each layer except bottom layer, there are nodes labeled by concepts. The nodes in different layers contain concepts at different levels of abstraction. A node in a higher layer stores general information extracted from nodes in lower layers. That is, a node in a high layer represents a more general concept and covers more cases than a node in a lower layer. The concept in a node is subsumed by the concept of its parent node. The bottom levels of the hierarchy are the specific values of an attribute stored in a database. It may not be possible to build concept hierarchy for every attribute. Especially if an attribute satisfies one of the following two cases we can not build a concept hierarchy for the attribute.

Case 1: There is a large set of distinct non-numeric values of an attribute, but any meaningful high-level concepts for those values are non-existent.

Case 2: There is a large set of distinct numerical values, but a finite number of meaningful intervals (a range of values) based on the distribution of the attribute values are non-existent.

Example 4: Suppose that there is a customer relation in a database. In the database, we have an attribute, *customer-name*. We cannot find any high-level concepts for the values in the attribute, there is no concept hierarchy for the attribute. On the other hand, we can easily build a concept hierarchy of the attribute type-of-product as shown in Figure 1.

Second, we build a set of virtual hierarchies to provide a global view of relationships among multiple high-level concepts from concept hierarchies. The relationships might be meaningful and interesting to users. The node in the virtual hierarchy can be formed by joining two or more high-level concepts from concept hierarchies.

Figure 1. Concept hierarchy for the attribute type-of-product

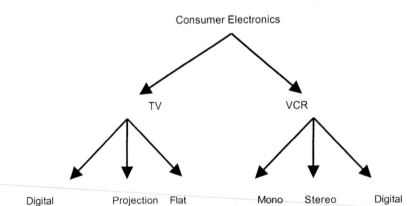

Example 5: Suppose that there is a database of students in a university and there exists a concept hierarchy for the attribute Class and a concept hierarchy for the attribute GPA. We can build a virtual hierarchy to show interesting relationships between high-level concepts in those two concept hierarchies. For example, we can define a node whose label is *Honor Student* by combining the concept *Undergraduate* in the Class concept hierarchy and the concept *Excellent* in the GPA concept hierarchy. The node says that a honor student is a undergraduate student whose GPA is excellent. Similarly, we can define another node *Teaching Assistant* in the virtual hierarchy by combining the concept *Graduate* in the Class concept hierarchy and the concept *Excellent* in the GPA concept hierarchy.

In our approach, the concept hierarchies and the virtual hierarchies have necessary background knowledge, which is used to direct the advanced query processing. That is, the concepts in concept hierarchies and virtual hierarchies can be used to formulate complicated expressions quickly in flexible queries and to perform generalization process with extensional answers in intensional queries.

Third, we construct a set of summary tables by preprocessing and generalizing primitive data in frequently referenced relations. Specifically, we remove some attributes and replace the values of attributes by abstract terms defined in concept hierarchies or results of aggregation functions on the values. During this process, we merge identical tuples in the relation and store the total count of such merged tuples. The challenge is how to perform generalization selectively because a large number of combinations of different sets of attributes are possible. It is unrealistic to store all of the possible summary tables because a large number of combinations of different sets of attributes are possible. So we need to perform generalization selectively. We apply the following heuristic guideline when we construct the summary tables.

Step 1: Select frequently referenced relations from previous database usage patterns.

For each selected relation, repeat steps 2-5:

Step 2: Remove rarely used attributes but retain frequently referenced ones by considering past query patterns.

Step 3: Select a frequently referenced attribute as a generalization criterion.

Let us assume that the relation *Customer* (name, type-of-product, age, income, address) is a frequently referenced relation in a sales database and that there have been many query patterns related to type-of-product. In this case, the generalization criterion is the attribute type-of-product.

Step 4: Keep the attributes that have meaningful correlations with the generalized criterion and remove attributes that do not have any correlations.

For example, the attributes age and income may be correlated to the attribute type-of-product, while there is little chance that attributes customer's name and type-of-product are related. Knowledge relating type-of-product and age is more useful than knowledge relating type-of-product and name.

Step 5: Cluster data retained in the relation according to the generalization criterion, generalize the values in the criterion in multiple layers and create a summary table for each layer.

For example, the relation customer is partitioned according to the values in the attribute type-of-product. That is, all the customers who purchased TVs are stored in one partition; all the customers who purchased VCRs are stored in a second partition and so on. During this process, different products can be merged into a general product. For example, Flat TV and Projection TV can be merged into a general product type TV. Different product types can be merged into a more general product type. For example, TV, VCR and camcorder can be merged into a more general product type, consumer electronics. That is, the values in the attribute type-of-product can be generalized into several layers. We may construct a generalized customer table for each layer. A user or an expert may specify explicitly a designated concept as the starting concept or a desirable concept. We create generalized summary tables with the designated concept. The group by operation may be used to cluster data.

Step 6: Generalize the values of the retained attributes, except the attribute used as the criterion in each generalized summary table with the concept hierarchies of those attributes, and store the generalized information in the table.

For example, assume that there is meaningful relationship between type-of-product and age in the relation customer. Then we generalize the values of the attribute age in each generalized customer relation and store general characteristic information for each generalized type-of-product in terms of age in each generalized customer relation.

Step 7: If there are previously processed interesting patterns about the criterion used for generating summary tables, we can add those patterns to the related summary tables.

All generalized summary tables include more general and abstract information extracted from their corresponding original relations stored in the database. The generalized summary tables are also much smaller than their original relations in the database and provide a global view of their original relations in the database. For efficiency of access, we can create an index for general terms and the names of the generalized summary tables including those terms.

This phase is independent of queries posed to a database and hence is computed once prior to the processing of any query. Our approach tries to minimize the number of operations performed at run time.

Execution Phase

In this phase, we receive a user's query and process the query according to the type of a query. Queries are divided into four basic categories: extensional and conventional query (ECQ), intensional and conventional query (ICQ), extensional and flexible query (EFQ), and intensional and flexible query (IFQ). Current database systems support ECQ. So, we explain our approach to process ICQ, EFQ and IFQ in the following subsections in details.

Intensional and conventional query (ICQ) processing

To process an intensional and conventional query, we perform six steps. First, collect the extensional answer for the query. The extensional answer consists of a set of tuples that satisfy specific conditions in the query. When we process a query, we use available query optimization techniques in databases. Thus, this step can be done efficiently.

Second, we identify attributes that are not relevant to our task in the extensional answer and then eliminate those attributes. We apply the following strategy to find those attributes removed:

Strategy: If an attribute contained in an extensional answer does not have its corresponding concept hierarchy, we eliminate the attribute from the extensional answer. We believe the attribute does not play a role in forming intensional answers because the attribute does not provide any additional information over extensional answers. For example, if a key attribute is included in extensional answers, it should be removed. Our purpose of this step is to eliminate meaningless attributes in forming intensional answers.

Third, if the extensional answer still contains many attributes, we select a set of the relevant attributes to be generalized among those attributes. The selection can be based on a user's preference or some selection standards as follow:

Strategy 1: Choose attributes that have meaningful correlations. For example, when we form an intensional answer, the information showing relationship between experience and salary is more useful than the information showing relationship between name and sex.

Strategy 2: Choose attributes that have occurred frequently in the past queries. We believe that the values in those attributes could play a key role in forming intensional answers.

Strategy 3: Choose infrequently updated attributes. We believe intensional answers derived from those attributes are valid for a longer period of time.

The extensional answer in which non-relevant attributes are eliminated is passed to the next phase for deriving intensional answers.

Fourth, we generalize each specific value in each relevant attribute into its corresponding higher-level concept by ascension of the concept hierarchy one level at a time. Replace the value by its corresponding concept. Then, generalize the high-level concept into much higher-level concept. In this step, a user can provide a threshold value to control the number of distinct concepts in each relevant attribute. Thus, we repeat the substitution process until we find the maximal concept that subsumes all values in the attribute or the number of distinct concepts is not greater than the threshold value. That is, for each relevant attribute contained in extensional answers, we repeatedly substitute the lower-level concept with its corresponding high-level concept until we find a common concept that is satisfied by those values in the attribute or the number of distinct concepts is less than or equal to the threshold value. This step transforms a less generalized concept into a more generalized concept. The concept hierarchies assist in generalizing lower level concepts to higher level concepts. The attribute values are replaced by the concept in which they belong. If there are identical tuples, then merge them into one tuple and store the total count of such merged tuples. The count can be used to calculate the number of the tuples in an extensional answer, which are contained in the intensional answer versus the number of tuples in the extensional answer, if necessary.

Fifth, we generate an intensional answer. If there is only one tuple in the final result, the intensional answer is represented as the conjunction of maximal concepts in the tuple. Otherwise, each tuple is transformed into a conjunction of maximal concepts in the tuple. Then, each conjunction is combined into a disjunction, which represents the intensional answer. The intensional answer subsumes extensional answers and summarizes the general characteristics of extensional answers. An intensional answer can be represented using a certain language such as logical formulas in the first-order logic and the intensional answer is presented to a user.

Sixth, if the user is not satisfied with the answer, the user can adjust the level of the answer to find more interesting answers. That is, the user can get another intensional answer at different abstraction levels. Our approach can derive those intensional answers as follow:

Case 1: If a user requests more general and abstract intensional answers, check if there are any concepts in the virtual hierarchies that match to conjunctions of maximal concepts in the normal intensional answer. If any, we replace those maximal concepts by the concepts found in the virtual hierarchies and generate an intensional answer to include the concepts.

Case 2: If a user requests less general and more specific intensional answers, we perform back substitution which replaces maximal concepts in the normal intensional answer by their corresponding specific conditions that define those concepts.

Our approach can generate intensional answers at different abstraction levels, which allows users to find interesting answers according to their needs. We believe that the generation of intensional answers at multiple abstraction levels helps users find relatively interesting answers.

Extensional and flexible query (EFQ) processing

Upon receiving an extensional and flexible query, we need to figure out what constitutes a query. Our main goal in this type of query is to find an equivalent rewriting Q', which can be processed by current database systems, for a given extensional and flexible query Q. Q' is expressed with the set of precise conditions of data in a database. In this case, we perform a specialization process, which finds the set of precise conditions directly based on primitive data. After identifying abstract terms contained in the query, appropriate mappings are performed to transform the abstract terms into the set of the conditions based on the primitive data. That is, we specialize each abstract term by descending its concept hierarchy or its virtual hierarchy one level at a time from the level including the abstract term until we reach the bottom level of the hierarchy in order to find all precise conditions for the abstract term. Often, the abstract term includes more than one less generalized concept. That is, a higher level concept corresponds to multiple lower level concepts. In this case, we need to find a set of conditions from each less generalized concept path in the hierarchy. If an abstract term has more than one descendant at a lower level, we perform specialization process for each descendant. Then, we need to combine the conditions from each less generalized concept path into a set of all conditions for the abstract term. We repeat the specialization process until we find all the conditions, which the abstract term subsumes. That is, we repeatedly substitute each abstract term with its corresponding lower level concept(s) until we find specific conditions based on data stored in the database. This step transforms a more generalized concept into a less generalized concept. To reduce searching time for an appropriate level in a concept hierarchy, a user or an expert may specify explicitly a concept level as the desirable starting level. After transforming the extensional and flexible query into its equivalent query that is expressed in terms of conditions on primitive data, we process the query to collect answers by using available query optimization techniques. To process this type of query, the main steps are to map the abstract terms referred to in a query into appropriate levels in concept hierarchies or virtual hierarchies and to move downward along the concept hierarchies to transform the abstract terms into the set of precise conditions.

Intensional and flexible query (IFQ) processing

IFQ queries can be divided into three types according to the types of conditions in the queries: simple IFQ query, complex IFQ query and mixed IFQ query. Each type has its appropriate query-processing scheme.

In the simple intensional and flexible query type, a query can be processed directly by accessing only the generalized summary tables. In this case, we map the query conditions into appropriate generalized tables and process the conditions with those tables without accessing the database. A query in this type inquires about general characteristics or summary information of a particular portion of data in a database. Since the generalized summary tables are usually much smaller than the original database, the query processing is expected to be more efficient. If we use the index on abstract terms, we can avoid retrieving any generalized summary tables but the required one. A certain query may involve a join operation of two or more generalized summary tables. In this case, we can perform the operation if they can be joined with equality conditions on attributes that are either keys or foreign keys in a way that guarantees that no spurious tuples are generated. If a user needs a less general answer, we may perform back substitution, which is a process of replacing high-level concepts in the answer by their corresponding specific conditions that define those concepts.

In the complex intensional and flexible query type, queries cannot be answered directly by searching only the generalized summary tables. In this case, we perform the specialization process mentioned earlier to transform the abstract terms into the set of precise conditions based on the primitive data, get the extensional answer and then perform the generalization process to get the intensional answer.

In the mixed intensional and flexible query type, the conditions in queries are a combination of complex intensional and flexible query type conditions and simple intensional and flexible query type conditions. We divide the conditions referred to in queries into two groups: conditions which should be transformed into a set of conditions based on primitive data with concept hierarchies and virtual hierarchies, and conditions which can be answered with the generalized summary tables. For the conditions in the first group, we apply the techniques which are used in the complex intensional and flexible query processing. For the conditions in the second group, we apply the techniques which are used in the simple intensional and flexible query processing.

CONCLUSION

When a user needs to retrieve information in current databases, the user provides a precise search expression that identifies the information to be retrieved. Conventional queries and conventional answers for the queries, expressed with precise conditions directly based on data stored in databases, are not always the best means of efficient and effective communications between users and database systems. We often need to express queries and get answers, involving concepts at different levels of abstraction. Current databases cannot answer and process queries involving concepts at any level higher than the level of the actual values.

In this chapter, we have presented a method for advanced query processing, including flexible query processing and intensional query processing. Flexible queries may allow users to ask more useful and meaningful questions than current queries could ever do. In addition, users can outline requests that may be hard or impossible to describe with a standard SQL query, which enhances the man-machine interface to databases. We believe many new applications, such as market databases, which do require ad-hoc querying, are well served by flexible query processing scheme that can use more high-level concepts and relax the requirements of queries in current databases. An intensional query characterizes an extensional answer and can provide more insight into the nature of the extensional answer. The intensional answers may be used in many applications, including promotion and marketing.

Our approach provides a simple and reasonable way of incorporating users' needs and preferences into query processing. It may be interesting to use different computational methodologies to process queries flexibly. Our approach can be applied with some modifications to other data models, including object-oriented and deductive ones.

REFERENCES

Agrawal, R., et al. (1993). Mining association rules between sets of items in large databases. *Proceedings of ACM SIGMOD*, 207-216.

Bancilhon, F., et.al. (1992). *Building an Object-Oriented Database System*, Morgan Kaufmann Publishers.

Cholvy, L. and Demolombe, R. (1986). Querying a rule base. *Proceedings of the First International Conference on Expert Database Systems*, 365-371.

Chu, W. and Chen, Q. (1992). Neighborhood and associative query answering. *Journal of Intelligent Information Systems*, 1, 355-382.

Cuppens, F. and Demolombe, R. (1991). Extending answers to neighbor entities in a cooperative answering context. *Decision Support Systems*, 1-11.

Dhar, V. and Tuzhilin, A. (1993). Abstract-driven pattern discovery in databases. *IEEE Transactions on Knowledge and Data Engineering*, 5(6), 926-938.

Frawley, W.J., et al. (1991). Knowledge discovery in databases: An overview. Piatetsky-Shapiro, G. and Frawley, W. J. (Eds.). *Knowledge Discovery in Databases*, AAAI/MIT Press, 1-27.

Freytag, J., et al. *(1994). Query Processing For Advanced Database Systems*, Morgan Kaufmann Publishers.

Gallaire, H., et al. (1984). Logic and databases: A deductive approach. *Computing Survey* 16(2), 153-185.

Han, J., et al. (1993). Data-driven discovery of quantitative rules in relational databases. *IEEE Transactions on Knowledge and Data Engineering*, 5(1), 29-40.

Imielinski, T. (1987). Intelligent query answering in rule based systems. *Journal of Logic Programming*, 4(3), 229-258.

Kim, W. (1990). *Introduction to Object-Oriented Databases*, MIT Press.

Motro, A. (1989). Using integrity constraints to provide intensional answers to relational queries. *Proceedings of 15th VLDB Conference*, 237-246.

Motro, A., and Yuan, Q. (1990). Querying database knowledge. *Proceedings of the International Conference on Management of Data*, 173-183.

Motro, A. (1994). Intensional answers to database queries. *IEEE Transactions on Knowledge and Data Engineering*, 6(3), 444-454.

Park, J. S., et al. (1995). An effective hash-based algorithm for mining association rules. *Proceedings of ACM SIGMOD*, 175-186.

Pascual, E. and Cholvy, L. (1988). Answering queries addressed to the rule base of a deductive database. *Proceedings of the Second International Conference on Uncertainty in Knowledge-based Systems*, 138-145.

Piatetsky-Shapiro, G. and Frawley, W. J. (Eds.). (1991). *Knowledge Discovery in Databases*, AAAI/MIT Press.

Piatetsky-Shapiro, G. (1991). Discovery, analysis and presentation of strong rules. *Knowledge Discovery in Databases*, AAAI/MIT Press, 229-248.

Pirotte, A. and Roelants, D. (1989). Constraints for improving the generation of intensional answers in a deductive database. *Proceedings of 5th International Conference on Data Engineering*, 652-659.

Pirotte, A., et al. (1991). Controlled generation of intensional answers. *IEEE Transactions on Knowledge and Data Engineering,* 3(2), 221-236.

Siegel, M. D. (1991). Automatic rule derivation for semantic query optimization. *Knowledge Discovery in Databases*, AAAI/MIT Press, 411-427.

Silberschatz, A., et al. (1991). Database systems: Achievement and opportunities. *Communications ACM*, 34, 94-109.

Song, I. Y. and Kim, H. J. (1991). Design and implementation of a three-step intensional query processing scheme. *Journal of Data Administration*, 2(2), 23-25.

Stonebraker, M. (Ed.). (1994). *Readings in Database Systems*, 2nd Edition, Morgan Kaufmann Publishers.

Ullman, J. (1988). *Principles of Database and Knowledge-Base Systems* 1-2, Computer Science Press.

Yoon, S. C. and Song, I. Y. (1994). A general method for generating intensional answers in an intelligent information system. *Proceedings of the 1994 ISCA International Conference on Computers and Their Applications*, 94-98.

Yoon, S. C., et al. (1994). Intelligent query answering in deductive and object-oriented databases. *Proceedings of the Third ACM International Conference on Information and Knowledge Management*, 244-251.

Yoon, S. C., et al. (1995). Semantic query processing in deductive object-oriented databases. *Proceedings of the Fourth ACM International Conference on Information and Knowledge Management*, 150-157.

Yoon, S. C. and Henschen, L. J. (1996). Mining knowledge in object-oriented frameworks for semantic query optimization. *SIGMOD Workshop on Data Mining and Knowledge Discovery*, 109-116.

Chapter XV

Security in Database Systems: State of the Art

Eduardo Fernández-Medina Paton and Mario G. Piattini
Universidad de Castilla-La Mancha. Spain

INTRODUCTION

Rapid technological advances in communications, transport, banking, manufacturing, medicine and other fields are demanding more sophisticated information requirements in organizations worldwide. As a result, large quantities of data must be handled, while a high level of security must be maintained in order to ensure information needs are met. The alarming growth in electronic crime is forcing organizations to take a look at how information systems can maintain security while meeting the technological needs of real-time systems in a global market. It is important therefore, that in information systems analysis and design, security requirements are taken into account.

Security is an important quality characteristic as described in the ISO/IEC (International Organization for Standardization/International Electrotechnical Commission) (1999). According to this standard, the main components of internal and external quality are reliability, efficiency, usability, functionality, maintainability and portability. All of these quality factors have several quality sub-factors, viewing security as a quality sub-factor of functionality. This standard defines security in the following way:

"Security is the capacity of the software product to protect data and information so that unauthorized persons or systems cannot read or modify them and so that access is not denied to authorized personnel."

Currently, a technical report is being created (ISO/IEC, 1997), which is dedicated exclusively to managing information system security. The proposed guideline establishes security concepts and models, manages security planning and establishes techniques to choose safeguards appropriate for each case, especially for systems with external connections. This means that organizations for standardization consider security as an important factor of the information system quality and that they are working hard to establish guidelines so that the software companies build more secure information systems.

Quite frequently, information systems are comprised of information that can be considered sensitive and to which access must be restricted. Often they contain personal information about individuals, which must be specially protected, such as social security numbers, addresses, phone numbers, religious affiliation, sexual preferences and medical data, among others. If this information is used without certain security precautions, individual rights may be violated. The information systems that manage this type of information must be provided with security techniques in order to guarantee that personal rights are not infringed upon.

The use of information technologies is regulated by law, serving mainly to ensure that citizen's rights are upheld. To this end, most countries have established data protection laws, especially when this data is of a personal nature. For instance, in Spain there is the *Personal Data Protection Law* (Ley Orgánica, 1999) and security rules (Real Decreto, 1999), which dictate the security actions that organizations must carry out in order to comply with the law. Information systems that do not guarantee data security will not only be facing fines and penal sanctions for violating laws, but also the negative impact of security breaches (Peso and Ramos, 1998).

As a consequence of the technological changes that are occurring at an ever-increasing pace, there is a great need for security support. Technology has produced the evolution of several fields with special characteristics from a security point of view, requiring important changes in the traditional ways of handling security. Some of these fields are:

a) The progress that the Internet has experienced, and especially the access to databases via the Web, requires secure communications. Information must be safely transmitted.

b) Electronic business, given its dynamic nature, demands the fulfillment of new data security requirements. It is of vital importance to guarantee the security of e-business in order to convert it into another secure and reliable way to do business.

c) The arrival of data warehousing has brought about the necessity to establish new security techniques, owing to architectural problems, of inference, administration and auditing. Also, the use of data recuperation techniques like data mining can lead to privacy problems, provoking new security requirements (Thuraisingham et al., 1997).

All of these factors, including legislative, regulative and technological factors, justify the importance of security in information technologies. In addition, there is the economic perspective of ensuring long-term growth and stability in this technologically driven environment. For instance, Baskerville (1993) confirms that one-fifth of U.S. organizations suffer one or more physical or logical information system disruptions within a three-year time period. The study also concludes that 12% of the U.S. companies were electronic fraud victims, with the average fraud amounting to

$75,000 per company.

Database security is concerned mainly with the following aspects: confidentiality integrity and availability. Respectively, these refer to problems associated with the discovery of confidential information by unauthorized persons, the alteration of information by unauthorized personnel and unavailability of information when it is needed (Castano et al., 1994). The range of possible threats that affect each one of the security factors is so broad that they cannot be attacked as a group, but each threat must be addressed individually. In this chapter, we present a state-of-the-art of database security focusing on confidentiality.

The chapter provides an overview of the history of the methodologies of system development together with security design techniques. Then the techniques of access control that have been most widely used in recent years are analyzed. Finally, we show the Semantic Data Model for Security (SDMS) to model the security requirements, and Multilevel Object Modeling Technique (MOMT) as an object-oriented methodology for designing multi-level secure database applications.

INFORMATION SYSTEM SECURITY DESIGN

In this section, we are going to look at the evolution that has occurred in the methods of analysis and design in information system security, focusing mainly on the methodologies for security system development. This evolution is shown considering three generations of security methods (Baskerville, 1993) which allows us to compare security system methods.

Methods of security development should form an integral part of the methodologies of software development, actively participating in all methodology phases and viewing security as another objective of software quality.

First Generation: Method of Checklists

The main objective of this first generation of system design is the selection of one solution among many.

Checklists as a Method of System Development

The first approaches of the use of checklists were often not methodological. They used narrative languages to describe systems and user requirements. Essentially, designers choose their items from a checklist with all the available options.

This type of method has various drawbacks, the main one being that it needs to avail of a wide range of possible solutions to be able to choose the appropriate one in each case. Furthermore, the checklist does not show the benefits of the choice of one alternative over the rest of the possibilities. Therefore, the designers need some economical way to differentiate between the elements on the checklist that are necessary from those that are not; in other words, a cost-benefit analysis is necessary.

Checklists as a method of security development.

In this method, the analyst chooses the best control from the possible controls that are available for each security problem that is handled.

With this philosophy, quality is lost in problem solving, given that what is proposed is what can be done, and not what we need to be done. In this way security checklist methods do not start from the point of the risks that affect the case that is being treated, but start their design with an analysis of existing risks and controls.

The following checklists are the most important that have been used in this paradigm: *SAFE Checklist Organization, Computer Security Handbook Checklist Organization* and *AFIPS Checklist Organization.* The three are different as far as item organization and terminology are concerned, but all of them share many aspects, such as communication encrypting, backups, physical security, etc.

Checklists became the center of the first generation of security development methods to specify security controls, but they needed a formal cost-benefit model to help the designers eliminate those controls that were inadequate for a specific situation. Risks analysis is an attractive way for analysts to be able to justify their decisions in the choice of a security control.

The positive aspects of this method of security development are that it is low-cost, needs little experience and training, and there are a wide variety of tools that admit it. On the other hand, it simplifies security aspects too much which are continually increasing with new systems. Moreover, the very same security controls can be used for different security problems of varying importance. Another disadvantage is that checklists are dependent on risk analysis techniques.

Second Generation: Engineering Methods

The second generation is oriented to dividing the problem into various components, solving each one, and later integrating the solutions of the subproblems to solve the original problem with a systematic approach; in other words, using sequential phases established by a methodology.

Engineering as system development methods

Engineering methods are distributed throughout a sequential lifecycle, typically known as waterfall or bottom-up, that indicates a series of steps or product transformations before you finally obtain the product in the last stage just as in the case of checklists, second-generation methods do not have adequate mechanisms to estimate the benefit obtained by the organization upon building an information system, and because of this the cost-benefit analysis also plays an important part.

Engineering as a security development method

This type of method is clearly differentiated from those of the first generation, given that they are oriented towards the analysis of new system security requirements, and are not centered in the technology that is available.

As in the engineering techniques used for the development of information systems, the methods for the development of security in information systems are similarly based on the lifecycle formed by various sequential stages. Various lifecycle models exist, such as Fisher (1984) and Parker (1981), but all of them approximately coincide in the following stages:
- identification and evaluation of system assets;
- identification and evaluation of possible threats;
- identification of possible safeguards or controls;
- risks analysis;
- the establishing of priorities for control implementation;
- implementation and maintain and enhancement of controls;

This kind of method can be implemented via a software system. Some widely used tools in this generation that mainly admit risk analysis and security management are *CRAMM*, *RISKPAC* and *DBSS*.

Although this system is comprehensive, organizes and details documentation well, reduces maintenance costs and is useful for many systems, it does also have some drawbacks, such as requiring a high level of training, having a high cost and maintaining a barrier between security design and system design.

Third Generation: Logic Transformation Methods

The approach applied in this third generation is to consider different abstractions of the problem and of the solution, modeling essential aspects of the problem. This generation is different from the other two in that it proposes successive system abstractions, beginning with a close-up view of the problem and finishing with a close-up view of the machine, where it can be implemented.

Logic transformation as a method to develop systems

Systems that have to be built in this generation have become more complex, and cannot be taken on without a technique that achieves a deep understanding of the essential aspects of these. The abstract modeling helps us to understand the essential parts of the information system that are to be built, in such a way that it becomes a strong link between definition of requirements and the design stage. In this generation the cost-benefit analysis loses importance, given that the abstract model provides a faithful representation of the resulting system.

Some examples of methodologies that belong to this generation are the structured techniques of software engineering defined by Yourdon and Constantine (1978), the analysis and structured design by DeMarco (1978) or Gane and Sarson (1979), and the later object-oriented design methods from Booch (1993), Rumbaugh et al., (1991) or Jacobson (1994) among others.

Logic Transformation as a security development method

If we take the concepts of third-generation systems development methodologies and apply them to security development, we find that what is intended is to design adequate security types for each specific case, more than implement security correctly. Also, risk analysis loses importance once abstract models are used. This generation of security design methods is not all that consolidated, given that there are not many examples. One of these is *SSADM-CRAMM*, which uses an extension of one *CRAMM* (security design method of second generation) which operates throughout all *SSADM* stages, and which is a method of structured analysis and design of the third generation. Another example is *logical controls design*,w hich is a method oriented to security design but getting away from hardware.

There is not much experience by which to judge this generation of security design techniques, but it shows promise, judging by the success this generation has had for software development.

Secure Database Technology: Access Control Techniques

In this section, an aspect of great importance to information system security will be looked at. The access control to information system resources. In the following lines basic concepts relating to access control are described, and in the following sections a selection of the most important access control techniques are analyzed, such as discretionary, mandatory, task-based and role-based access control.

Access control is a mechanism through which we ensure or try to ensure that resources can only be accessed by authorized personnel, and that these personnel can only perform authorized activities.

Usually, access control to resources is done using authorization rules, which are signified by **<s,o,a>** which indicate that the subject **s** can access an object **o** performing action **a**. The three concepts that play an important part in authorization rules are:

- The *subjects* are the entities to which access to the objects can be authorized. Although these are usually individual users, they can also be user groups, roles, or even processes that are performed in the name of users.
- The *objects* are elements whose access we want to control. In relational database systems, the objects can have different granularity; in other words, both complete relations, views and individual attributes can be accessed.
- The *actions* are the possible operations that can be performed, and in relational databases are usually *select*, *insert*, *delete* and *update*.

Discretionary Access Control

This strategy to manage access control is the oldest, and is based on the idea that the subjects access the objects according to their identity and some rules of authorization. These authorization rules indicate to the subject the actions that can be performed on each system object. With this strategy, if a user wants to perform an operation on an object, a search is carried out in the system for an authorization rule that gives them permission to perform that operation on that object, and if one is not found, access is denied.

As indicated in Ferrari and Thuraisingham (2000), this access mechanism has the following variants which are not mutually exclusive:

- *Positive* and *negative authorization.* According to positive authorization, the existence of an authorization rule indicates that access can be conceded, while its absence prohibits access. However, in negative authorization, access is only granted when a negative authorization rule does not exist, while the existence of a rule prohibits access. The main difference is that in the case of positive authorization, if a subject does not have authorization, in a given moment a privilege propagation may occur in such a way that another subject cedes their access to the first, in which case they would be infringing the access control. This cannot happen with the negative authorization mechanism.

- *Strong* and *weak authorization.* With strong authorization, neither positive nor negative authorizations can be invalidated, whereas weak ones can be invalidated by other strong or weak authorizations, according to some specific rules.

- *Explicit* and *implicit authorization.* Implicit authorizations are automatically derived by the system from the body of explicit authorizations, following a set of rules. The implicit authorizations can be derived using two mechanisms: a set of propagation rules, based on a hierarchy supported by the model; or by using a set of derived rules defined by the user, allowing the concession of an authorization conditioned by the presence (or lack of) another authorization. For instance, a derived rule can be used to express that a subject can access a given object only if another subject has access explicitly denied.

  Different authorization propagation policies exist depending, among other things, on the type of subject in question. For example, in the case of roles that form a hierarchy, once a positive authorization is granted, it would be propagated towards all the superior roles in the hierarchy, and if the authorization is negative, it would propagate downwards. On the other hand, if groups are studied, the most common approach consists of authorization propagation, positive or negative, to all elements of the groups.

- *Content-based authorizations.* These condition the access to an object given the content of one or more of its components, for instance, to restrict the access to data of people who earn more than $500,000 a year. This access control policy has also been applied to object-oriented databases. For this paradigm, different authorization variables have appeared, such as the inherited variable, where a user that has access to one class is allowed access at the same time to all corresponding sub-classes and the inherited attributes of the class; the class access variable, where the access to a complete class implies the access to the attributes defined in the class as well as those inherited by the superclasses; and the visibility variable, where an attribute defined in a subclass is not accessible from any of its superclasses.

This access control policy has been widely used, but authorization of each access attempt depends exclusively on the existence (or not) of an authorization rule, without explicitly taking into account the confidentiality level of the data, or the level that each subject can access. There also exists a mechanism that grants authorization that allows the possibility of granting access to certain data to a user who did not have it before, thus violating data confidentiality. These reasons lead to the conclusion that discretional access control is inadequate for current database systems, which usually give data its own entity, independent of the subjects that want to access them.

Mandatory Access Control

This access control policy is based on the model designed by Bell and LaPadula for operating systems, and it consists of the classification of both the subjects and the data in different levels of security that can be unclassified, confidential, secret and top secret.

The two basic rules that define the way to access data using this policy, adapted to the paradigm of databases, indicate that a subject has reading access to an object if the subject security level dominates the object, and that a subject has writing access to an object if the security level of the subject is that of the object, in other words, a subject can modify objects of its level.

The main characteristic of this access control policy is that access is authorized if a certain relation exists between the subject security level and the object security level that is wished to be accessed. Also, the data has proper security levels, without taking into account who wants to access it.

To support this access control policy, it is necessary to use special databases that classify the data by levels. These are known as multi-level databases, and they support mandatory access control through different security levels in the data and different accreditation levels for users. Each security level has hierarchical components like those previously mentioned (top secret, secret, confidential, unclassified). Each level can also have non-hierarchical categories such as finances, sales, research, etc.

In the case of relational database systems, there is not too much consensus on the size of the data classified at diverse security levels. Objects can be classified by security levels in a relational database management system according to their size or granularity, which could be whole databases; relations or tables; tuples or rows, or even simple data elements or attributes.

If we classify files in different security levels, the following could occur: Suppose that we have a relation with the attributes Code Used, Name, Last Names, Post and Salary. Suppose also that a file is considered in the top secret security level when the subject has a salary greater than $120,000. We could have a top secret file with this data (123, Peter, Berry, Director, 200,000). If someone classified as secret (without access to this information) tried to insert this new tuple (123, Peter, Berry, Director, 50,000), the system would produce an error indicating that a file already exists with that code and data. The information that the system is giving a secret classified person would be providing them top secret knowledge, given that it would be indicating that the person that has that data receives a salary greater than $120,000 given that from their classification level, they cannot see that information. We would be losing security.

To solve the previous problem, caused by the possibility to be able to classify entities in different security levels, it is necessary to use a technique called "polyinstantiation" which consists of the possibility of having various versions of the same entity. At first, this could seen wrong, seeing as how the primary key would be repeated and this would result in a violation of integrity. This is solved by making a new primary key, with the old code and security level, in such a way that when an entity is repeated various times, it will always be different. In this way, if the previous case occurs, the problem would be solved by accepting the insertion of the new file and that way we would not have an integrity violation given that for the first file, the primary key would be (123, Top Secret) and for the second it would be (123, Secret). An in-depth analysis of polyinstantiation can be found in Jajodia et al. (1995) and in Castano et al. (1994).

Over the last few years, a series of structures for supporting multi-level database access control have appeared. These are characterized among other things by the amount of confidence in security measures given by the operating system, in order to be able to delegate greater security aspects to the database management system. The main structures considered are the following: a) *simple kernel architecture*, where the operating system is in charge of security management; b) *distributed architecture*, according to which some machines are available where the data is classified according to its security level--there are two varieties, partitioned and replicated; c) *trusted subject architecture*, where the database management system is in charge of carrying out all security activities instead of the operating system; d) *integrity lock architecture*, which involves a machine where the data is, another machine that acts as an interface with the user and a filter which is in charge of safe encryption and transmission; e*) extended kernel architecture*, in which both the operating system and the database management system perform security control (Ferrari and Thuraisingham, 2000).

Both SeaView and Lock Data View are prototypes of multi-level relational data models. Over the last few years, multi-level object-oriented database models have appeared, such as SODA, SORION, Millen-Lunt, Jajoia-Kogan, Mogenstern, UFOS, etc. All of these offer some solution to the problem of protection in object-oriented database systems. Nevertheless, each one only handles some of the problems, leaving many questions unanswered.

Task-Based Access Control

This is a paradigm for access control and management of authorizations that are different from usual, known as *Task-based authorization control (TBAC)*, which is appropriate for distributed computation and for information processing activities with multiple access control points. An in-depth review of this technique is shown in Tomas and Sandhu (1997).

This model deals with activities or tasks to represent authorizations, modeling them as time periods during which an authorization remains valid. The main idea is to grant the correct amount of permission at the right time, and only those which are strictly necessary, as well as retract permission once unnecessary. Therefore, what is shown is a method where the access control permits are granted and revoked in line with a mechanism of control validity of the authorizations, also without the necessity of manual management.

In TBAC, access control is seen as a tuple with five elements: *"Subject* **X** *Object* **X** *Action* **X** *Usage and validity counts* **X** *Authorization-step,"* where each authorization-step represents an abstraction where permissions are grouped and trustees are in charge of administrating these permissions, activating and deactivating them opportunely. Therefore, each authorization step maintains its proper state of protection. A usage counter is associated with a permit, and when this counter reaches its limit, the associated permit is deactivated and the corresponding action is no longer allowed.

This access control technique differs from passive models oriented to the subject in many ways, mainly in the following:

- There is a notion of protection states, representing active permissions that are maintained throughout each stage of authorization;
- TBAC recognizes the lifecycle notion and processing stages associated with each authorization;
- TBAC dynamically manages permissions as authorizations in progress.

Role-Based Access Control

Role based access control (RBAC) is an alternative to traditional, discretional and mandatory access control methods. Traditionally, security management requires low-level controls, and normally some access control lists need a considerable maintenance effort.

In RBAC, permissions are associated with roles, and users are made members of the roles. This is the way that users obtain permissions, which greatly simplifies permit management. The roles represent each functional group of organizations, grouping in each one users with similar functions and responsibilities. Through this mechanism it is very easy to carry out certain actions, such as change users from one role to another, as well as add or eliminate from the roles certain permissions as required.

For instance, the roles in a bank could be clerk and accountant, where each one of these has a unit of privileges. Some of these, as in this case, are hierarchical and shared. This access control technique has been widely published. Updates and new utilities constantly come up, like Sandhu and Bhamidipati (1997) and Ferraiolo, et al. (1999).

SECURE DATABASE DESIGN

Database design, due to its great complexity, is an activity that requires a methodological approach. Although most software development organizations have accepted this fact, it is not usual for the models and techniques to take security aspects into consideration.

Normal database development methodologies usually consist of the following three phases (Connolly et al., 1998; Batini et al., 1992).

- *Conceptual modeling.* In this stage an analysis of requirements is made and a good representation of the information that makes up the universe of discourse is obtained. Usually an entity-relationship scheme is obtained.
- *Logical design.* The objective of this phase is to adapt the conceptual scheme obtained in the previous stage to the data model on which the desired database management system is based.
- *Physical design.* In this stage the objective is to install as efficiently as possible the logical scheme.

These methodologies should be complemented by adding various models or extending the existing ones. In the initial stages it would be necessary to identify and model the security requirements (if they exist) and determine the security policies and access control necessary for each particular case. In the more advanced stages, it is necessary to design multi-level databases and access control policies respecting the requirement identified in the previous stages.

Secure Conceptual Database Models

An important aspect of the design of secure databases is the modeling of security requirements. It is necessary to use a model which allows both designers and users to mould their security requirements in-depth, just as is done with other semantical aspects like integrity in the universe of discourse.

There are a few proposals for secure database modeling. One of these proposals was SAMS (Semantic Data Model for Security) (Smith, 1990, 1991), which consists of the extension of the conceptual models used in database design.

The use of a model like SAMS helps the designer in the identification of inference problems (the ability to use data from a certain level of sensitivity to deduce data from another superior level), aggregation problems (if the aggregation of some data with a security level must have a higher security level), and overclassification (if a higher than necessary level is assigned to the data).

In the SAMS, secret restrictions are identified, such as:

- *Semantic restrictions*: these specify the level of classification that data and its associations receive;
- *Access control restrictions*: These specify the authorized users to access groups or data elements.

Secret semantic restrictions are described in the model using objects, attributes and associations, and they are represented using diagrams similar to entity-relationship, highlighting the figures corresponding to those that are attached to the classification level (unclassified, secret, confidential, etc., see Figure 1).

A concept worth mentioning is the identifier which is an object attribute which from the perspective of security allows object identification. This concept does not completely coincide with the candidate key of the relational model, seeing as there are

Figure 1. SDMS (Smith, 1990)

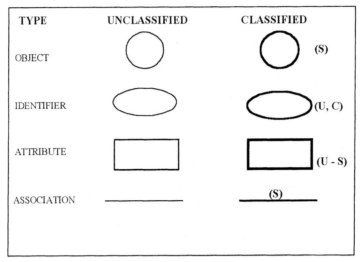

almost unique attributes that even though they can be repeated (thus voiding them as candidate keys), they must be considered identifiers. In this sense the identifiers are said to be quasi-keys.

As far as classification level is concerned, it can be specified as one value (S, for example) a set of values (U,C) or a range (U-S).

Just as what happens with semantic models, in addition to these elements a unit of restrictions is described. These are:

- Inherent, which can be divided into:
  - uniform classification, if all the objects instances that the restriction applies to are classified at the same level;
  - value-dependent classification, if the objects, attributes or associations are classified according to their values, for example with salary greater than $200,000 are classified as "S," while the others are "U";
  - explicit, which are those that cannot be directly represented in the data model, like associations among attributes of different objects.
- Implicit, with two important restrictions:
  - the result of associating any data with a classified attribute is classified with a level that is at least as much as the attribute;
  - if two classified attributes are associated, the resulting classification is the higher of the attribute classification and the direct association classification.

In Figure 2 an example of a scheme designed according to the SDMS model is shown, where object security requirements are shown, along with attributes, identifiers and associations.

Associated with the graphic, the model includes a language to express security restrictions, based on an extension of the language ALICE (Assertion Language for Integrity Constraint Expression), which essentially results in the ability to represent

Figure 2. Example of modeling using SDMS

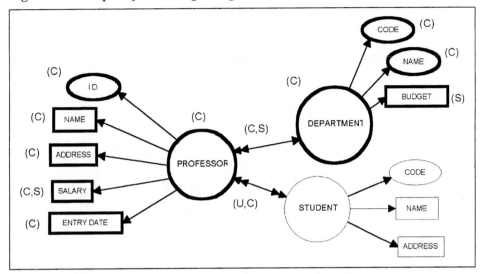

explicit restrictions. An example of this language's syntax is the following, in which employees' salaries are specifically classified with level C, for all professors whose salaries are $1,000.

FOR
ALL P in Professor
(WHERE p.Salary > 1000
(CLASSIFICATION OF p.Salary IS C);

The language has an underlying logical representation which facilitates the analysis of the application requirements in terms of security.

Secure Database Logical Models

In the '80s and early '90s some prototypes of secure database logical models appeared, and some of the most important are the following:

- *SeaView*. It is based on a viewing concept, in such a way that a subject with security level L can only view relations that are classified at level L or below. It comprises two models--the MAC (mandatory access control) and the TBC (trusted computing base). The first defines the mandatory security policy, and the second defines multilevel relations and formalizes the discretional security policy.
- *LOCK data views*. In this prototype the language for consultation SQL is improved with declarations that allow the management of the security levels of the elements classified in the databases. It is composed of both compulsory and discretional security policies.
- *The Jadodia and Sandhu model*. This model extends the standard relational model to consider the classification levels. Therefore a multi-level relation consists of a scheme of a multi-level relation and a collection of requests of the

relation. This model defines a series of properties so that the principles of the mandatory security policy are complied with.

Many models have appeared for modeling and implementing secure object-oriented databases. These models differ in many aspects, above all because each one focuses on different aspects of the problem of security. In Oliver and Von (1994), a taxonomy of these models is presented in which the differences between these models are analyzed. The following are examples of these models.

- *The SODA model.* It is a very simple model for secure databases based on a general object-oriented model. The objects or instances are assigned an accreditation. According to these security levels, and in accordance with the properties defined by Bell and Lapadula, a subject is allowed to carry out the method of an object, or messages are sent between the objects.
- *The SORION model.* Each entity of the system--subjects; objects; variables; messages, etc.--is assigned a security level. A list of rules is proposed in order to ensure that none of the operations violate the security policies established.
- *The Millen-Lunt model.* It is based on an architecture by layers. The security kernel that provides the mandatory access control is found in the lowest level. In the next layer the object system that implements the object-oriented services is located. Rules for managing the layers adequately are defined in the model.

A Methodology For Security Databases Design

In the following paragraphs a methodology based on OMT (Rumbaugh et al., 1991) is analyzed. This methodology is MOMT (Marks et al., 1996), formulated to design secure applications based on multi-level databases.

Multilevel design

MOMT is an extension of OMT incorporating semantic characteristics in order to be able to design multi-level databases. Therefore each element of data will be assigned an appropriate and independent security level.

Stages of methodology

Just like OMT, MOMT is made up of three principal stages.

- *The analysis phase* is the principal stage of methodology and consists of three models: the multi-level object model; the dynamic multi-level model; and the functional multilevel model, each representing in turn the static, dynamic and transformational characteristics of the system.
- *The system design phase*, in which the high level structure of the system is defined.
- *The design object phase*, where a detailed base is drawn up to implement the objects.

Models of the Methodology

The most important phase in the development of databases is analysis, because more effort should be made at this stage since diverse abstractions of the problem can be obtained, as well as help in understanding clearly what exactly it is that the system should do. In this part we describe the most important aspects of the analysis stage in MOMT, focusing on the three models that the methodologies consider: the object model; the dynamic model; and the functional model. A highly detailed study of this method can be found in Marks et al. (1996).

Not all databases require the same level of security. It depends on the type of data they are going to deal with, the environment for which they are designed to be used in, etc. In this stage of methodology, the designer evaluates the required level of security for the design he is working on.

- *The multi-level object model*

The object model captures the static aspects of the applications. All the different parts of the system and all the associations between those parts are represented in this model, considering the desired level of security for each entity and association.

In the object model, each object will be associated with a level of security of such a form that it will be unseen in inferior levels of security. The different objects are grouped into classes through which the properties that they will subsequently inherit are defined. It seems logical that a group of objects should also be associated with a level of security. Just as in the case of each individual object, each class will be unseen in levels of security inferior to its own, and be visible in equal or superior levels. A relationship exists between a class and the instantiated objects relative to the particular security level of each one, which is as follows: if an object (OB1) belongs to a class (CL1), and the security level of the object is LevelOB1 and that of class LevelCL1, then LevelOB1 must be greater or equal to LevelCL1. In other words, an object with a security level lower than the level of the class to which it belongs cannot exist, since otherwise it could not inherit the class properties.

Each class can have a range of associated security levels. The lowest level in the range indicates the level of the class. The range of levels of a class specify the required levels of security in the class. In other words, the level of an instance of a class has to be included in the range of levels of the class.

In terms of attributes, a class can have different levels, but the level of an attribute has to be greater than the level of the class. Furthermore, the security level of the attribute with the role of identifier has to be the same as that of its class. The value of an attribute can have a range of associated levels, since the values applied to attributes will have to have a security level within this range.

The methods which are the medium through which the operations are implemented also have to have an associated level of security and have to fulfill a specified relationship with that of their class. The security level of the methods has to be dominant over the level of the classes. In other words it has to be greater or equal to the level of the class.

The associations will also have a level of protection. The level of security demanded by each of the associations always has to be equal or superior to the classes to which it relates. In the same way, an instance of an association, in other words a link, will have a greater or equal level than that of the association, and that of the related object.

The mechanism of generalization permits us to refine the classes (superclasses) into more specific groups which inherit the properties of the first groups (subclasses). The considered rule for the relationships of generalization is that the security level of the subclasses has to be dominant or more restrictive than the security level of the superclass, in such a way that makes it impossible for a person class with a confidential level to inherit properties from a countable class with a non-classified level. In this case security would be violated since a subclass would be able to access the properties of the superclass that should effectively remain inaccessible.

- *The dynamic multilevel model*
The dynamic model represents aspects related to time and changes in the objects. An event is a stimulus provoked by an object that has a certain effect on another object, changing the value of its properties, in other words, changing its state. Since an interaction happens between objects, and given that these can have distinct security levels, it will be necessary to adapt the model so that no security violations of the system occur.

The key information used in this model will give rise to all the graphic representations used as diagrams of the plan of events, events diagrams, etc. These are the events produced and the order or sequence in which these are produced.

The aim of a dynamic multilevel model (in terms of security) is to analyze each stage and determine the security problems which can arise, resolve them if possible and if not, negotiate with the client to reach an agreement in terms of the modifications necessary to the security requisites and assume the detected security risks.

The objects can be classified as active or passive. The objects that cannot produce events (passive objects) will only have the security level which is assigned to them during the construction of the object model, while the objects that can generate events (active objects) will be assigned two security levels; one which is the inherent level of the object, and another level (operational level) in which the object can operate and which will never be superior to the level of the object.

The security-related actions that will have to be carried out will firstly determine which are active objects and which are passive, and subsequently assign an operational level to each active object (the inherent level of the object, either passive or active, has now been assigned to construct a multi-level object model).

Once all the types of objects and events have been identified, it is then necessary to carry out an event analysis to check that no security problems have arisen.

Finally a diagram of states has to be drawn up for each one of the classes, which show the possible states that the objects are able to carry, depending on the received events and showing, as such, the behavior of the objects.

- *The multilevel functional model*

This model helps to construct the class methods, determining not only their security levels but also the levels of execution for each method. For the construction of this model, when or how the functions will be executed is not taken into account. This will be supported by flow charts showing the data, and specification techniques or processes like pseudocode.

The level of execution of a method has dominance over the security level of the class with which it is associated. The level of execution of the functions will vary in each stage, depending on the level of the object which triggers the event and provokes the execution of the method, taking into account that the level of execution has to be greater or the same as the object with which it is associated.

FUTURE TRENDS

Security in databases is a subject which currently has many lines of investigation open, including those relating to new access control techniques, new models for the management of multi-level database systems, security in Web-oriented databases, security in data warehouses, etc. Our investigation is centered mainly on the following three fields: a) the adaptation of the development methodology for MOMT secure multilevel databases to the unified language; b) the amplification of the query language SQL:1999 so that it would be possible to consult multilevel databases; c) given the importance of establishing satisfactorily security requirements, we aim to design a formal language for the specification of security requirements.

CONCLUSIONS

The field of security is an incredibly open concept which embraces everything from the organizational politics of security to the encryption of a piece of data being transmitted through a network and passing through an infinity of intermediate levels. In this chapter we have justified the repercussions which a lack of security can have on society, and we have drawn up a synthesis of the principal aspects that affect confidentiality in the design of databases: the control of access; the modeling of security requirements; and a retrospective view of the important generations of methodology for the development of security techniques. Finally we have introduced a methodology through which multi-level databases can be designed, considering the desired confidentiality requisites, and establishing techniques to detect this principal risk focus, evaluating these risks and, if (financially) possible, establishing opportune methods that reduce or eliminate these risks.

REFERENCES

Baskerville, R. (1993). Information systems security design methods: Implications for information systems development. *ACM Computing Surveys*. December, 25, 375-415.

Batini, C., Ceri, S. and Navathe, S. (1992). *Diseño conceptual de bases de datos.* Addison-Diaz de Santos: Wesley.

Booch, G. (1993). *Object-oriented Analysis and Design with Applications*, 2nd edition. Benjamin Cummings, Redwood City.

Castano, S., Fugini, M., Martella, G. and Samarati, P. (1994) *Database Security.* Addison-Wesley.

Connolly, T., Begg, C. and Strachan, A. (1998). *Database Systems.* Addison-Wesley.

DeMarco, T. (1978). *Structured Analysis and System Specifications*, Yourdon Press.

Ferraiolo, D., Barkley, J. and Kuhn, R. (1999). A role-based access control model and reference implementation within a corporate intranet. *ACM Transactions on Information and Systems Security,* February, 2, 34-64.

Ferrari, E. and Thuraisingham, B. (2000). *Advanced Databases: Technology Design.* Secure database systems. Piattini, M. and Díaz, O. (Eds.). Londres: Artech House.

Fisher, R. (1984). *Information Systems Security.* NJ: Englewood Cliffs, Prentice-Hall.

Gane, C. and Sarson, T. (1979). *Structured Systems Analysis: Tools and Techniques.* Prentice Hall.

ISO/IEC 9126-1 (1999). *Information Technology- Software Product Quality - Part 1: Quality Model.*

ISO/IEC TR 13335. (1997). *Information Technology- Guidelines for the Management of IT Security.*

Jacobson, I. (1994). *Object-Oriented Software Engineering.* Addison-Wesley Publishing Company.

Jajodia, S., Sandhu, R. and Blaustein, B. (1995). Solutions to the polyinstantiation problem. *Information Security, An Integrated Collection of Essays.* Abrams, M., Jajodia, S. and Podell, H. (Eds.). IEEE Computer Society. California.

Ley Orgánica. (1999). *de Protección de Datos de Carácter Personal.* BOE, 298

Marks, D., Sell, P. and Thuraisingham, B. (1996). MOMT: A multilevel object modeling technique for designing secure database applications. *Journal of Object-Oriented Programming.* 9(4), 22-29.

Oliver, M. and Von S. (1994). A taxonomy for secure object-oriented databases. *ACM Transactions on Database Systems,* March, 19(1), 3-46.

Parker, D. (1981). *Computer Security Management.* Reston, Reston: Mass.

Peso, E. and Ramos, M. A. (1998). *LORTAD, Análisis de la Ley.* Diaz de Santos. Madrid.

Real Decreto. (1999). *del Ministerio de Justicia.* BOE, 151.

Rumbaugh, J., Blaha, M, Premerlani, W., Eddy, F. and Lorensen, W. (1991) *Object-Oriented Modeling and Design.* Englewood Cliffs: Prentice Hall.

Sandhu, R. and Bhamidipati, V. (1997). The URA97 model for role-based user-role assignment, in *Database Security XI: Status and Prospects.* T.Y. Lin and S. Qian. (Eds.). London: Chapman and Hall, 262-275.

Smith, G. W. (1990). The semantic data model for security: Representing the security semantics of an application. *Proceedings of the Sixth International Conference Data Engineering, IEEE,* 322-329.

Smith, G. W. (1991). Modeling security-relevant data semantics. *Proceedings of the IEEE Trans. On Software Engineering,* November, 17(11), 1195-1203.

Thuraisingham, B., Schlipper, L., Samarati, P., Lin, Jajodia, S. and Clifton, C. (1997). Security issues in data warehousing and data mining: Panel discussion, T.Y. Lin and S. Qian. (Eds.). In *Database Security XI: Status and Prospects.* Chapman and Hall, London, 3-16.

Tomas, R. and Sandhu, R. (1997). Task-based authorization controls (TBAC): A family of models for active and enterprise-oriented authorization management, T.Y. Lin and S. Qian. (Eds.). In *Database Security XI: Status and Prospects*. Chapman and Hall, London, 166-181.

Yourdon, E. and Constantine, L. (1975). *Structured Design*. Englewood Cliffs: Prentice-Hall.

Chapter XVI

A Case Study of the Military Utility of Telemedicine

David J. Paper
Utah State University, USA

James A. Rodger
Indiana University of Pennsylvania, USA

Parag C. Pendharkar
Penn State Harrisburg, USA

INTRODUCTION

In order to meet the medical management challenges presented by increasing global crises, the U.S. military must find ways to more effectively manage manpower and time. In response, Joint Medical Operations–Telemedicine (JMO-T) has been developed by the Department of Defense (DOD) to collect and transmit near-real-time, far-forward medical data and to assess how this improved capability enhances medical management of the battlespace. JMO-T has been successful in resolving uncertain organizational and technological military deficiencies and in improving medical communications and information management. Deployable, mobile telemedicine teams are the centerpieces of JMO-T. These teams have the capability of inserting essential networking and communications capabilities into austere theaters and establishing an immediate means for enhancing health protection, collaborative planning, situational awareness and strategic decision-making. One objective of this chapter is to relate the rationale used by the DOD to determine the military utility of the Joint Medical Operations–Telemedicine Advanced Concept Technology Demonstration (JMO-T ACTD) or ACTD for short. ACTD is a JMO-T initiative developed for the purpose of improving joint medical planning capabilities, access and timeliness of medical care, and integration of medical situational awareness. The chapter discusses in detail the complexities involved in the ACTD initiative. A second objective of the chapter is to articulate the development of Critical Operational Issues (COIS) and Measures of Effectiveness (MOE) as methodologies for investigating the military utility of telemedicine.

BACKGROUND

In November 1997, several town hall meetings were held between the Army, Navy and Air Force to discuss the feasibility and practicality of telemedicine. These meetings served to identify customer requirements and service positions on the delivery of health care to combatants in future military operations. The goal was to reach a balance between technology push and requirements pull. In other words, do we let the technology or the requirements drive the reengineering project? Can there be a happy medium between the two?

In December 1997, a meeting was held at Camp Smith, Hawaii. At this meeting an understanding of the Commander in Chiefs (CINCS) operational requirements and the beginnings of a Concept of Operations (CONOPS) was developed. Every branch of the military must have a CONOPS before they undertake an exercise. CONOPS is somewhat analogous to a strategic plan with step-by-step documentation of what will occur along the process path. From the meeting emerged a proposal to the Deputy Secretary of Defense presented on January 15, 1998. The proposal articulated four critical issues for early planning in the ACTD.

1. *Enhance force medical protection through early, far-forward (future planning) diagnosis and treatment.* The ACTD initiative is charged with evaluating the utility of early and far-forward detection and mitigation of diseases and injuries to minimize their operational impacts.

2. *Enhance capability to keep combatants on station whenever possible.* The ACTD is charged with evaluating emerging capabilities in order to minimize evacuation and the resulting need for personnel replacements and personnel movements.

3. *Enhance medical capabilities to employ the minimum assets required to meet operational needs.* The ACTD is charged with evaluating novel modeling capabilities for tailoring medical support to a variety of battlespace situations. A Joint Operational Scenario was established to enhance medical capability. From this scenario, it was determined that smaller, more mobile, flexible medical units better support tactical operations.

4. *Enhance deployment planning and realization of telemedicine capabilities in tactical operations.* The ACTD is charged with evaluating emerging Army, Navy and Air Force concepts that provide enhanced organizational capabilities to the tactical operations of telemedicine.

These critical issues are all well grounded in terms of enhanced force medical protection and within the vision of the armed forces (for more detailed information, please consult: www.actd.tatrc.org and www.odusa-or.army.mil/TEMA/ref.htm). The initial CONOPS is also detailed in this proposal, and assumes that this ACTD includes the employment of a tailored Joint Task Force (JTF) to accomplish their missions.

In April 1998, the ACTD team met for a second time at Camp Smith, Hawaii. The purpose of this meeting was to develop a CONOPS and form a team to oversee the integration of the project. This team was called the Performance Integrated Concept Team (PICT). At the conclusion of the meeting, a list of objectives and issues developed by PICT concerning redesign of telemedicine deployment for the entire military was presented to the full ACTD team. The mission of the ACTD was to provide the CINC and JTF commander with the capability to defeat time and distance obstacles, and to cost effectively maintain joint health support in austere and non-linear operations.

The supporting objectives from this meeting were listed as:
• Improve joint medical planning capabilities
• Improve access and timeliness of medical care far forward
• Enhance integrated medical situational awareness
• Sustain joint medical operations using joint forces and resources

The Training and Evaluation Integrated Product Team (T&E IPT) met in June 1998 at the Naval Health Research Center in San Diego, California, with representatives from the Army, the Navy and the Air Force. The purpose of the meeting was to develop Critical Operational Issues (COIS) and Measures of Evaluation (MOE) that could become the approved evaluation guide for the ACTD. The T&E IPT also studied the proposed timelines for the next few months in order to assign tasks to responsible organizations and persons for completion. Five COIS were agreed upon. COIS, by definition, are those key operational concerns expressed as questions that, when answered completely and affirmatively, signify that a system or material change is operationally ready to transition to full production. There are four key components of a properly structured critical operational issue statement:

1. *The interrogative.* An interrogative word demanding a "yes" or "no" answer (i.e., "Does," "Can" or "Is").
2. *The system.* Identification of the system of concerns (i.e., system "X" or a platoon equipped with system "X").
3. *The capability.* A capability of concerns (i.e., robust voice and data communication or effective aerial reconnaissance).
4. *The conditions.* A set of applicable operational conditions (i.e., "during combat operations" or "as employed by Special Operations Forces").

Measures of Effectiveness (MOE) are quantifiable measures used in comparing systems or concepts, or estimating the contribution of a system or concept to the effectiveness of a military force. It expresses the extent to which a combat system accomplishes or supports a military mission.

Measures of Performance (MOP) are quantifiable measures used in comparing systems or concepts, or estimating the contribution of a system or concept to the effectiveness of a military force. It expresses the extent to which a combat system accomplishes a specific performance function. In general, higher-level MOP are themselves composed of either lower-level MOP or data requirements.

A data requirement (DR) is a quantitative or qualitative piece of information relevant to the determination or categorization of one or more MOP. A DR can consist of specific test measures such as start time, velocity, position, type or target. It can also consist of arithmetically combined measures from tests such as elapsed time, calculated distance between points a and b, or number of rounds fired. A data requirement does not generally involve summary or descriptive statistics such as mean, median or percent. These are usually considered lower-level MOP.

The mission of the ACTD is translated into COIS in the following manner. The translation process is handled through a decomposition of the operational issues. This decomposition is analogous to a dendritic process. A dendritic process is like the branching of a tree or dendrites on a nerve cell. The COIS lead to several MOE that lead to several MOP that finally lead to data elements. During this process, factors and conditions are integrated, and necessary event dendritics are developed to both improve and structure test and evaluation planning. This is basically the process that was used by the T&E IPT. When revising the COI document at hand, all references used in developing the ACTD, in understanding the technologies nominated to be a part of the ACTD and in deciding which candidates for the software will be fielded for the ACTD telemedicine teams, are taken into account.

The military's systematic methodology for planning and executing the vast ACTD telemedicine demonstration is supported in the literature. During the last decade, the military has progressively developed telemedicine applications and tested them in real and simulated civilian disaster emergencies (Garshnek & Burkle, 1998). Projects such as AKAMAI are congressionally mandated, Department of Defense (DOD) medical research and development programs. AKAMAI is a project sponsored by the Tripler Army Medical Center (TAMC) in Hawaii. It is aimed at applying and assessing the value of telemedicine technologies (Floro et al., 1998). Likewise, the Theater Telemedicine Prototype Project (T2P2) initiated by the Pacific Medical Network (PACMEDNET) focuses on providing support for telemedicine clinical workflow in the Pacific (Rasberry, 1998).

Advanced information technology and improved information infrastructure have made telemedicine an increasingly viable health care delivery alternative to U.S. civilians as well as the military. Its success has been measured in clinical, technical and economic terms (Olivia et al., 1999). Success has also been measured in terms of quality. In recent studies, research is beginning to focus on quality guidelines and organizational factors that impact quality in relation to the potential of technology (Burzynski, 1998; Corey et al., 1996; Cykana et al., 1997). The use of information technology to deliver health care from one location to another has the potential to increase the quality and access to health care at lower costs (Paul et al., 1999).

The adoption of this technology is not unique to the United States. France, Hong Kong and many other countries have also adopted telemedicine initiatives (Dardelet, 1998; Au et al., 1996). It is clear that despite the geographical location, telemedicine enhances efficiency-oriented organizational networks and enables creation of expertise-oriented professional networks (Tanriverdi & Venkatraman, 1998).

Sheng et al. (1999) suggest that the success of telemedicine efforts demands systematic analysis and effective technology management to be successful. One of the most critical features involved with technological change in an organization is that the technology must be implemented as a strategic intent. Telemedicine, and the changes that it brings, must be deliberate, championed and strongly led from the top, not from within a single department or functional area (Bangert et al., 1998). Rodger and Pendharkar (2000) argue that enterprise-wide telemedicine implementation requires systematic planning and coordinated execution to integrate disparate technologies across vast geographic boundaries. Paul et al. (1999) agree that systematic planning is critical to success, but report that technological barriers are negatively impacting the use of telemedicine as a viable decision-making tool. The largest technological barriers include end-user and technical training, and the mismatch between the sophistication of the technology and end-user requirements. Sheng et al. (1999) add that a paradigmatic shift is needed to surmount the inertia generated by years of compartmentalized decision-making, technology management and people management. According to Rodger and Pendharker (2000), the military's ACTD initiative employs a systematic methodology for planning and execution of its telemedicine efforts. In addition, there is a paradigmatic shift because the military is treating the ACTD initiative as an enterprise-wide effort and is supporting it with tremendous resources in terms of capital, personnel, technology and time.

MAIN THRUST OF THE CHAPTER

It is well known that organizations need information in order to compete (Ives & Jarvenpaa, 1993). In the aggregate, the Armed Forces are seeking to "lighten up the heavy forces" and to "heavy up the capabilities of the light forces." In other words, make them both mobile and hard-hitting, that is, to get the best of both worlds. The major problem the military faces is how to deploy and coordinate thousands of troops worldwide in a timely, efficient and effective manner. To realistically address this problem, the military understands that technology must be leveraged to its fullest potential. From mission receipt through deployment, to operations and transition, the Armed Forces execute their responsibilities through a deliberate set of patterns of operation. These patterns are:

- Project the Force
- Protect the Force
- Shape the Battlespace
- Decisive Operations
- Sustain the Force
- Gain Information Dominance

The vastness of the military in terms of logistics problems, geographic dispersion, military emphasis and telemedicine issues makes it a unique organization. Multinational organizations may be faced with enterprise-wide technology issues, but they do not have to be concerned with military fatalities, wartime medical

Figure 1. Deliberate pattern of operation

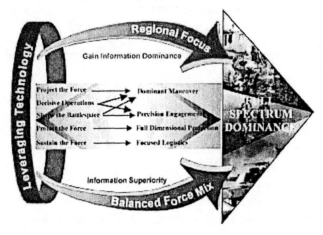

situations, strict chains of command, mobile medical station management, expedient evacuation requirements and life-threatening espionage. Figure 1 illustrates the deliberate pattern of operation model the military follows to integrate technology across its various organizations. The basic idea of the model is to leverage technology to facilitate robust information sharing between military people in the field and officers in the major command centers.

"Project the force" means that people in the field have information tools they can use to get the information they need when they need it. "Protect the force" means that people in areas of danger can obtain the information they need to either evacuate or solve the problem in the field. "Shape the battlespace" means that every part of the battlespace is connected by information technology. The battlespace is therefore no longer hard to reach from any command center. Also, people can be informed instantaneously of any movements in troops or patients. Technology helps commanders make better and more decisive decisions about operations because they have better information about the battlespace. Leveraging technology helps the military sustain its forces in the field by being able to move resources where they are best needed, based on the intelligence gathered via the information systems in the field. The goal is to leverage the power of technology to bring together people from all over the battlespace and command centers.

These patterns are all aligned with the Joint Vision 2010 concepts of Dominant Maneuver, Precision Engagement, Focused Logistics and Full Dimensional Protection. Vision 2010 is a joint vision for the armed forces that states where they want to be in the year 2010. The technology initiatives utilize dedicated, small mobile teams, with a sophisticated IT infrastructure, to provide telemedicine capabilities wherever they are needed in the medical battlespace (Mann, 1997). This IT infrastructure includes novel Medical Equipment Sets (MESS) with digital capture devices such as digital cameras, digital scopes, digital blood and urine laboratories, physiological monitors, advanced digital radiography and digital ultrasound (Perednia & Allen, 1995). This ACTD has charged itself with operating within the concept of Focused

Logistics and Full Dimensional Protection. Focused Logistics provides logistical support for the telemedicine, equipment and personnel resources. Full Dimensional Protection provides protection from all threats including nuclear, germ and conventional warfare. It is, therefore, pertinent to understand just how this ACTD can accomplish its missions/objectives and meet the operational concepts of JV2010.

One technology that is mentioned in the document that applies to this ACTD is the use of "advanced soldier technologies." It is necessary for this ACTD to fit within this concept and provide the warfighter with information that identifies, early on, those countermeasures that can be used to defeat medical threats. It is also important to recognize other action that may be used to defeat enemy deployment of weapons of mass destruction (WMD), especially biological agent dispersal.

The concept of Focused Logistics mentions telemedicine. Focused Logistics is the fusion of logistics and information technologies. It uses flexible and agile combat service support organizations, and new doctrinal support concepts to provide rapid crisis response to deliver precisely tailored logistics packages directly to each level of military operation. Medical support for Focused Logistics can be applied to Internet triage and telemedicine in order to enhance the survivability of the joint force (Zajtchuk, 1995). This ACTD will best support this concept by demonstrating the ability to:

- capture the data,
- see the data,
- use the data,
- use decision tools to plan and prioritize,
- model and simulate, and
- utilize the Global Communications Support Systems (GCSS) strategy to accomplish the above.

The GCSS strategy is used to develop the hardware, software, database and network solutions that impact the computer-based patient record, medical threat

Figure 2. The GCSS strategy model

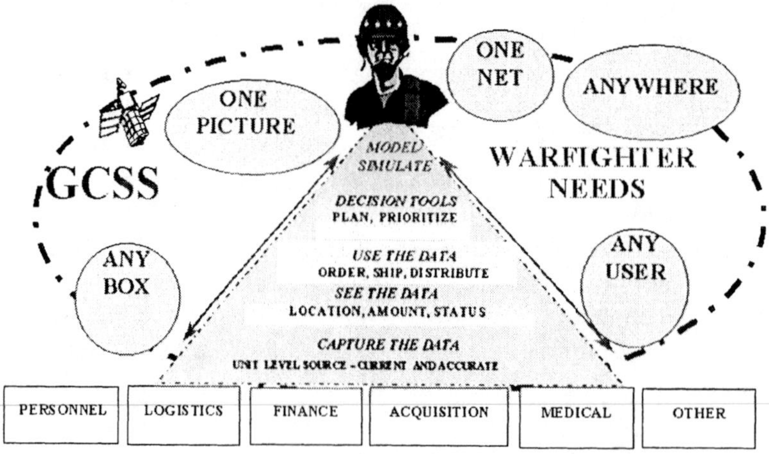

identification, and command and control of medical units. As depicted in Figure 2, the overall strategy is to move toward complete technology integration. The premise of the model is that every system user must have the capability to transmit and receive information with the same quality picture to and from any other location in the battlespace or any command center. The model infers that the system crosses every critical functional area in a seamless manner that is transparent to the user. Implementation of the strategy will be accomplished through management of information and information technologies, deployed throughout the battlespace. Most logisticians consider medical under their purview. Therefore, logistics organizations are to be streamlined and right-sized to allow the delivery of service in a balance between just-in-time and just-in-case being equal to just enough. The operatives utilize Focused Logistics to develop reduced footprint and tailoring on the fly units. These units provide rapid crisis response that requires tracking and shifting of assets while en route, and the delivery of tailored logistics packages and sustainment directly at the operational and tactical levels of operation. The JMO-T ACTD further tailors forces using novel modeling and simulation packages.

The most important facet of JV2010 is that the enablers and technologies will empower soldiers not to replace them. The enablers listed for Focused Logistics are germane to this ACTD as well. These are:

- Integrated Maneuver & Combat Service Support Systems Command and Control
- Total Asset Visibility
- Modular Organization
- Movement Tracking System
- Wireless Information Management Systems

JV2010 provides the overall strategic roadmap to facilitate implementation of a telemedicine system in the field. To be viable, the system must provide telemedicine capabilities when and where they are needed in the medical battlespace. JMO-T ACTD is the entity in charge of the telemedicine system. JMO-T ACTD uses COI and MOE to systematically test the viability of the system in the field. The GCSS strategy provides the technical infrastructure for the system. It provides the technical roadmap that enables the system to effectively capture, view, use and model the data for decision support purposes. CONOPS provide the step-by-step operation strategy for telemedicine deployment. PICT teams oversee the overall integration of the system in accordance with the CONOPS plans. T&E IPT develop COI within the context of the existing legacy system changes required, budgeted resources, the GCSS strategy and the CONOPS. Each COI set leads to several MOE. MOE sets provide a paper trail that shows the general effectiveness of the telemedicine system in operations. MOP sets are components of each MOE that show a quantifiable contribution of the telemedicine system to a military mission. MOP sets are broken down into DR sets. DR sets represent the actual data and information pertinent to the MOP.

The complexity involved in JV2010 is immense because it represents the overall roadmap used for telemedicine across all operations in each branch of the military. The complexity is also necessary because the system must have a very low failure rate. Keep in mind that lives are at stake in the battlespace. Every second the system is down or performing below expectations can mean the difference between the life and death of a wounded soldier. ACTD was created to oversee the development of JV2010 and its complex implementation in the field. The telemedicine system is meant to be a central repository of critical medical information that can be accessed quickly and effectively from multiple users in the battlespace under adverse conditions. As such, an effective telemedicine system has the potential to facilitate battlefield supremacy in terms of management of information. The end result of the JV2010 vision is therefore to defeat time, distance and space with the aid of state-of-the-art telemedicine technology. The military believes that this is possible only through integrated collaboration provided by the complexities of the JV2010 vision as presented. The proposed telemedicine system, by following the edicts of this massive proposal, will eventually replace antiquated processes such as medical evacuations and field hospitals.

So far, we have concentrated mainly on the business infrastructure surrounding the telemedicine system. We now turn to actual pieces of the system. A suite of software, databases and architecture standards has been adapted by the armed forces to provide deployable medical information management. The suite includes an enterprise database system, workstations, expert systems and portable computers.

The Theater Medical Core Services (TMCS) is a database that stores data locally and is capable of sending encrypted e-mail to several redundant database servers via store-and-forward. The database servers aggregate information and store it in databases for distribution. Web servers supply data to medical personnel as customized encrypted reports.

The Medical Workstation (MeWS) is a network-based workstation equipped with portable medical devices, clinical support capabilities, medical information support and a graphical user interface. The MeWS will support multi-patient monitoring, interface with the patient's clinical record and provide access to a searchable database. It will also provide full Personal Information Carrier (PIC) read and write implementation. The PIC card is worn around the soldiers' necks who are stationed at the front line in battalion aid stations. Medical personnel now have the ability to use the PIC card to enter information into the MeWS directly from the field of operations. The MeWS collects, stores and forwards medical device data and images into database tables that can be accessed by commanders at major military centers to aid decision-making. By utilizing a Global Positioning System (GPS), MeWS has the capability to enter the patient's geographical location. The various software components of the MeWS help to facilitate clinical data entry, acquisition and retrieval. MeWS enables the generation of medical facility status reports, the monitoring of disease surveillance, the updating of supplies and the tracking of evacuation requirements.

The Field Medical Surveillance System (FMSS) is an expert system that systematically detects and monitors epidemiological trends and profiles patient populations. FMSS integrates patient information into the Global Infectious Disease and Epidemiology Network (GIDEON) knowledge base. Demographic and symptomatic information is used to arrive at a presumptive diagnosis or classify the patient using discriminate analysis. FMSS is also capable of providing incidence and prevalence trends for infectious diseases.

The Libretto is a commercial-off-the-shelf (COTS) hand-held computer, manufactured by Toshiba. It has the capability to automate field medic PIC card software by reading a service member's demographic information from the PIC into the software. It can also write GPS medical encounter information to the PIC and store the information as a pre-formatted message for transmission.

Tactical medical communications require updating of the existing IT infrastructure. TMCS, MeWS, PIC, FMSS, GIDEON and COTS were implemented in order to enable this change and facilitate the transmission of medical-unique information over the existing communications hardware and command, control, communication, computers, intelligence, surveillance and reconnaissance (C4ISR) networks. However, telecommunications from the operational area of responsibility (AOR) to the medical sustaining base uses the existing Defense Information Systems Network (DISN).

The technologies described above have been assembled into an exportable capability that is specifically tailored to meet the medical information management (IM) and information technology (IT) needs of the unit they are supporting. This assemblage of technologies is referred to as the capability package. Figure 3 presents a conceptual picture of the purpose of the capability package in general terms. The capability package must work in concert with the unit's infrastructure, communications, tactical situation and logistical constraints if the military is to realize its full

Figure 3. The capability package

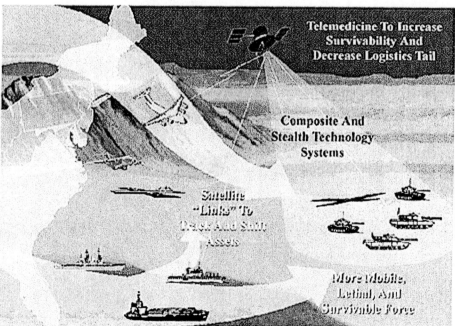

potential in meeting today's global crises. This is why upfront planning and documentation included in JV2010 and its associated documents is necessary. The Capability Package pulls together the entire suite of hardware and software used by the military to make real-time telemedicine a reality.

SOLUTIONS AND RECOMMENDATIONS

The present crisis in Kosovo has provided an opportunity to test the telemedicine system. Many U.S. troops man remote military outposts in Bosnia that are inaccessible due to poor road infrastructure, bad weather or numerous land mines. Despite this isolation, medics are well equipped to treat the soldiers stationed there. The suite of telemedicine gear that is available links them to medical specialists worldwide. For example, a spider bite resulted in a rash on a Bosnian peacekeeper's arm. The soldier's vital signs were transmitted, via the telemedicine suite infrastructure, to a specialist at Walter Reed Hospital in Washington DC. The specialist confirmed the medic's diagnosis and recommended treatment. The condition cleared up within a few days.

In another application of JMO-T technology, a medic performed a minor operation for a sinus infection under the guidance of a remote specialist. In northern Bosnia, a physician's assistant experienced a rapid heartbeat that may have deteriorated into a life-threatening arrhythmia. EKG images sent over the telemedicine link allowed a higher echelon cardiologist in Tuzla to direct the onsite administration of medication that slowed the heart rate. All of these conditions could have resulted in a costly and dangerous medical evacuation, had the situation not been remedied in the far-forward remote location.

Telemedicine in Bosnia has many advantages for the troops deployed there. First, it establishes a real-time automated patient record-keeping system. Second, it keeps evacuations to a minimum and maximizes return to duty. Third, it provides a rapid response to trauma. Fourth, it guarantees high quality health care to soldiers, independent of their geographic location. Finally, it provides the big picture for medical decision-makers, enabling them to implement concurrent medical support.

Training in the use of JMO-T capability package is essential. In Bosnia, medical personnel receive intensive training on the applications of telemedicine. The Medical Advanced Technology Management Office (MATMO) provides training. Manuals and handouts are periodically updated to ensure that the forward medical units in Bosnia are provided with the most recent advances in telemedicine. Troubleshooting is also an important aspect in the smooth operation and maintenance of the capability package.

There is a strong likelihood that the hostilities in Bosnia will continue at some level, and it is fortunate for our military that the telemedicine capability packages are in place. Lives are being saved and costly medical evacuations curtailed by the application of the JMO-T suite of gear. JMO-T has enabled a paradigm shift in battlefield medicine, and it has the capability of leveraging the scarce resources of Bosnian peacekeepers.

The JMO-T capability package is constantly being tested and evaluated (T&E) to improve effectiveness and efficiency. Kernel Blitz, a seven-day exercise off the California coast, provided a T&E opportunity to gather data ranging from the number of records sent and received to top-level perceptions of the success of the JMO-T effort. T&E data was gathered from the Patriot Medstar exercise in Idaho and California, and from Pacific Warrior in Hawaii. The capstone exercise, Cobra Gold, was conducted in Thailand in May of 2000.

In summary, telemedicine effectively minimizes the military forward footprint during times of war by utilizing distributed computing power, human expertise and connectivity to provide medical care throughout the world. During peace, telemedicine is critical in maintaining the health and readiness of the U.S. military forces, so that they can provide real-time responses to disasters. Telemedicine is helping the joint armed forces meet global crises at the speed of thought.

The first objective of the ACTD for telemedicine was to determine its utility in action. The military live tested the telemedicine suite in Bosnia and found it to be tremendously effective in terms of expedient medical diagnosis independent of geographic location. More data needs to be collected from different sites around the world, but the Bosnian tests were extremely applicable because the battlespace was a true war environment. Troops were under live fire, and war casualties were experienced.

The second objective was to explore the effectiveness of COI and MOE as systematic and effective methods for testing system effectiveness. The military believes that these methodologies work as they are used for all large-scale information systems deployment. However, the military continues to compare COI and MOE developed for this ACTD, with the results from Bosnia and other live tests. The military views its methodology as one that needs constant refinement over time.

Lessons were learned and are still being learned from the JMO-T ACTD for determining the military utility of telemedicine. Improved consistency, reliability and cost effectiveness have been demonstrated in several field exercises. Underestimating the military utility of telemedicine could lead to increased costs of medical evacuations, increased costs for logistical support and increased costs in terms of human lives. Furthermore, the utility of telemedicine cannot be measured solely in terms of war. Telemedicine also has utility during peacetime. Armed forces that lack adequate preventative and primary care have lower morale and lack a sense of family well-being. In turn, these attitudes could have an effect on military preparedness. The military utility of telemedicine helps the Department of Defense to avoid these undesirable consequences.

We were able to develop a few general lessons that other organizations involved in integrating disparate technologies might learn from. The lessons are as follows:

Lesson 1 – The database is only one critical piece of the telemedicine puzzle.

Careful strategic and IT infrastructure planning is a must when the system must serve a myriad of people spread across many geographical locations. In addition, the locations are always changing, which means that the system must be mobile and portable.

Lesson 2 – An overall vision is necessary to get all the players on the same page and focused in the right direction with common goals.

Lesson 3 – Since the military is immense with established processes and standards, it cannot completely reinvent itself to accommodate a new system, no matter how important it might be. Therefore, the vision, IT infrastructure plan and associated tactical plans must be made within the context of the existing organization.

Lesson 4 – The complexity and interrelationships between the objectives are related to the complexity and size of the telemedicine project. The acronyms used for the organizations, teams, measures and strategies are a result of these complexities. Keep in mind that the telemedicine system is intended as a real-time information-sharing vehicle for all military personnel involved in medical activities in the battlespace.

Lesson 5 – The purpose of technology is to empower people to make better decisions, enhance local and global communication, integrate processes and increase organizational effectiveness. It is not meant to replace people.

Lesson 6 – A paradigm shift in the way an enterprise operates requires a systematic plan of action. With ACTD, COI and MOE were the cornerstones of the methodology for determining enterprise-wide operational issues and Measures of Effectiveness. The military would never venture into an enterprise-wide telemedicine deployment without a systematic plan of action. The costs associated are astronomical, the logistics are extremely complex and lives are at stake.

FUTURE TRENDS

To insure that the information system architecture closely fits the operational architecture, the JMOT-ACTD continues to be tested and evaluated. In the testing and evaluation, system statistics are compared to existing benchmarks and standards. According to the results of the various exercises, the JMO-T has successfully fulfilled the requirements of the ACTD. The results of the Pacific Warrior exercise, conducted in Hawaii, suggest that the JMO-T data can be transmitted consistently and reliably. Signal quality, system availability, software and hardware reliability and sustainability of each JMO-T system was assessed and found to meet or exceed standards set prior to the exercise. For example, there were no failure rates in message transmission by node. In other words, 100% of messages sent by the far-forward mobile units were received at their destination.

No failures were reported for the application servers, Netscape Communicators, Oracle Databases, Libretto Computers or Smartcard readers within the network. Signal quality was reflected by the results of software tests between the WavePoint and a remote unit taken to various spaces in the facility. The data reflected adequate signal strength for approximately 450 feet in all directions. More than 100 MB of data was successfully moved between the two servers. One specific file transfer test sent a single file of 244,736 bytes to every client in the network. Server uptime was 4,871 out of 4,905 minutes, for 99.3% availability for one server and 4,905 minutes for the other server (100%). The Libretto sub-notebook hardware was operational 99.7% of the time over the course of the exercise. The Smartcard software was successfully read 96.2% of the time. The Web server was highly reliable and processed 17,863 requests, with only four requests trapped as errors.

Testing and evaluation of the JMO-T ACTD has produced tangible evidence for the military utility of telemedicine. Exercise results from Pacific Warrior-99 (PW-99) indicate that the essential data transport requirements of JMO-T can be met consistently, reliably and cost effectively. Cost parameters are gathered for each candidate system and presented in a matrix to serve as the basis for cost tradeoff analysis for operational managers. Specific technologies are examined relative to each other for specific operational requirements of data throughput, transmission distance, time-to-setup, time-to-train and actual costs to acquire, maintain and dispose. These architectural elements selected for PW-99 reflect a first iteration of the cost parameter matrix. The data collected at PW-99 on ease of use, performance, reliability, and consistency contribute to the cost parameter matrix and assist in determining the relative costs of systems. It must be noted that the cost associated with this criterion is based solely on the costs of transmitting data and does not include the cost of communication assets, JMO-T ACTD systems infrastructure, time, the value of providing care to a patient or the value of a person.

Several parameters could not be measured directly by the field exercise at PW-99. These parameters will be determined through the use of laboratory testing and evaluation methods. For example, analysis is still not complete on the availability of high frequency and very high frequency radios, the overall reliability of the Toughbook laptops, the software reliability of several of the communication modules and the sustainability of several of the software, hardware, networks and databases used in the exercise. As new data becomes available through laboratory testing, a more complete picture of the military utility of telemedicine will evolve.

Testing of the ACTD telemedicine effort has shown that the exercise is very valuable to the military. The future of telemedicine in the military is secure and will continue to grow. However, rigorous testing on effectiveness is a priority and will continue to be. Testing not only shows that the benefits exceed the costs, it can uncover ways to better deploy the telemedicine suite for increased performance. Keep in mind that the military obtains funding from the government and therefore must carefully justify expenditures.

CONCLUSION

The first objective, to relate the rationale used by the DOD to determine the military utility of the JMO-T ACTD demonstration, is currently in the testing phase.

The Bosnian case exhibits the potential of the telemedicine suite to greatly increase diagnostic capabilities, save lives and decrease evacuation statistics. Winning a war quickly with the fewest possible casualties is the goal of the military. The military is committed to the use of telemedicine technologies to keep soldiers mentally and physically healthy with less cost and greater efficiency. One case is not enough to prove the utility of the ACTD, that is why several future tests are scheduled. In addition, testing in peacetime circumstances also needs to be explored.

The second objective, to articulate the development of COI and MOE as methodologies for investigating the military utility of telemedicine, is also in the testing phase. The military uses COI and MOE for all large project planning. Therefore, the same methodology is used to systematically plan and test the utility of the ACTD initiative. Many organizations tend to consider information systems at a tactical or operational level. However, the trend exhibited by world-class organizations places information systems integration at a strategic level. By considering the implementation of telemedicine at a strategic level, the military is moving toward the status of a world-class organization. The military is leading the world with the telemedicine efforts of ACTD. With budgets for the military deteriorating, it seems prudent to leverage technology to improve effectiveness at lower costs.

REFERENCES

Au, G., Higa, K., Kwok, C. and Cheng, Y. (1996). The development of telemedicine in Hong Kong. *Journal of Organizational Computing and Electronic Commerce,* 6(4), 365-383.

Bangert, D., Doktor, R. and Warren, J. (1998). Introducing telemedicine as a strategic intent. *Proceedings of the 31st Hawaii International Conference on System Sciences (HICSS-31)*, Maui, Hawaii.

Burzynski, T. (1998). Establishing the environment for implementation of a data quality management culture in the military health system. *Massachusetts Institute of Technology Conference on Information Quality*, 18-46.

Corey, D. J., Cobler, L, Longsdale, T. and Haynes, K. (1996). Data quality assurance activities in the military health services system. *Massachusetts Institute of Technology Conference on Information Quality*, 127-153.

Cykana, P., Paul, A. and Stern, M. (1997). DOD guidelines on data quality management. *Massachusetts Institute of Technology Conference on Information Quality*, 154-171.

Dardelet, B. (1998). Breaking the wall: The rise of telemedicine as the new collaborative interface. *Proceedings of the 31st Hawaii International Conference on System Sciences (HICSS-31)*, Maui, Hawaii.

Floro, F. C., Nelson, R. and Garshnek, V. (1998). An overview of the AKAMAI telemedicine project: A Pacific perspective. *Proceedings of the 31st Hawaii International Conference on System Sciences (HICSS-31)*, Maui, Hawaii.

Garshnek, V, and Burkle, F. M. (1998) Telemedicine applied to disaster medicine and humanitarian response: History and future. *Proceedings of the 31st Hawaii International Conference on System Sciences (HICSS-31)*, Maui, Hawaii.

Institute of Medicine. (1996). *Telemedicine: A Guide to Assessing Telecommunications in Health Care.* Washington, DC: National Academy Press.

Ives, B, and Jarvenpaa, S. L. (1993). Competing with information: Empowering knowledge networks with information technology. *The Knowledge Economy Institute for Information Studies*, 53-87.

Mann, S. (1997). Wearable computing. *Computer,* 30(2), 25-32.

Sheng, O. R. L., Hu, P. J. H., Wei, C. P. and Ma, P. C. (1999). Organizational management of telemedicine technology: Conquering time and space boundaries in health care services. *IEEE Transactions on Engineering Management*, 46(3), 279-288.

Paul, D. L., Pearlson, K. E. and McDaniel, R. R. (1999). Assessing technological barriers to telemedicine: Technology-management implications. *IEEE Transactions on Engineering Management*, 46(3), 279-288.

Perednia, D. A. and Allen A. (1995). Telemedicine technology and clinical applications. *Journal of the American Medical Association*, 273(6), 383-388.

Rasberry, M. S. (1998). The theater telemedicine prototype project: Multimedia e-mail in the Pacific. *Proceedings of the 31st Hawaii International Conference on System Sciences (HICSS-31)*, Maui, Hawaii.

Rodger, J. and Pendharkar, P. (2000). Using telemedicine in the Department of Defense. *Communications of the ACM*, 43(3), 19-20.

Tanriverdi, H. and Venkatraman, N. (1998). Creation of professional networks: An emergent model using telemedicine as a case. *Proceedings of the 31st Hawaii International Conference on System Sciences (HICSS-31)*, Maui, Hawaii.

URL: www.actd.tatrc.org.

URL: www.odusa-or.army.mil/TEMA/ref.htm).

Zajtchuk, R.S. (1995). Battlefield trauma care. *Military Medicine*, 160, 1-7.

ENDNOTE

The views expressed in this chapter are those of the authors and do not reflect the official policy or position of the Department of the Army, Department of the Navy, Department of Defense or the U.S. Government.

About the Authors

EDITOR

Dr. Shirley A. Becker received her MBA from St. Cloud State University and an MS and PhD in information systems from the University of Maryland at College Park. Dr. Becker is a professor of computer science at Florida Institute of Technology, Melbourne, Florida, and co-director of its Software Engineering Research Center. Dr. Becker's funded research includes Web usability and testing, Web-enabling tools and technologies, e-commerce systems development, and database systems. She has edited several books and published numerous articles and book chapters in these areas. Dr. Becker recently served as editor of the *Journal of Database Management*, and serves on several editorial review boards. She is a member of IEEE, ACM, and AWC.

CONTRIBUTORS

Firas Alljalad is a PhD student and currently working for a major financial firm as a senior Java architect and technical specialist. His research interests concern distributed components, Java and Web development.

Clare Atkins is a senior lecturer in the Department of Information Systems at Massey University in New Zealand. Her research and teaching interests are mainly in the area of relational database design, particularly in requirements acquisition and conceptual modeling where she considers that full user involvement is essential. She also leads the EBIS Collaboration, an international network of researchers investigating the application of evidence-based practice to information systems. Before emigrating to New Zealand, Ms. Atkins spent a number of years working in the IT industry in the UK and spent several years as the Data Manager for the Statistics Division of the Inland Revenue.

Anirban Bhaumik is a graduate student in the Department of Computer and Information Science at the New Jersey Institute of Technology, Newark, New Jersey. He has a bachelor's of Engineering in Chemical Engineering from the Regional Engineering College, Durgapur, India and a master's of Science in Chemical Engineering from the New Jersey Institute of Technology. Mr. Bhaumik is employed at Concero, an Austin, Texas-based software consulting company. When not working or studying, Anirban likes to kayak on the Delaware.

Michael Bieber is associate professor of Information Systems in the Computer and Information Science Department at the New Jersey Institute of Technology, where he also teaches in the distance learning program. He co-directs NJIT's Collaborative Hypermedia Research Laboratory. Dr. Bieber is affiliated with the New Jersey Center for Multimedia Research and the National Center for Transportation and Industrial Productivity. He holds a PhD in Decision Sciences from the University of Pennsylvania. Dr. Bieber has been performing hypermedia research since 1987, when he embarked on a research path in automating hypermedia support for analytical information systems. He is active in the hypertext community, co-organizing conference minitracks and co-editing special journal issues about hypermedia topics. He has published many articles in this and other areas.

Paloma Cáceres teachs Software Engineering in the Department of Experimental Sciences and Engineering at King Juan Carlos University, Madrid, Spain. She has 10 years of professional experience in projects management, consulting and analysis and design of applications in private enterprise. She has published several articles. Her research interests include methodologies for software engineering research, specially for designing and developing Web applications. Her e-mail address is: pcaceres@escet.urjc.es.

Coral Calero has an MSc in Computer Science (University of Sevilla). Professor Calero is an assistant professor at the Escuela Superior de Informática of the Castilla-La Mancha University in Ciudad Real. She is a member of the Alarcos Research Group, in the same university, specializing in information systems, databases and software Engineering. She is a PhD candidate on Metrics for Advanced Databases, and author of articles and papers in national and international conferences on this subject. She belongs to the ATI association and is a member of its Quality Group . Her e-mail address is: ccalero@inf-cr.uclm.es.

Dr. Mohammad Dadashzadeh is a graduate of M.I.T. (BSc in Electrical Engineering; MSc in Computer Science) and the University of Massachusetts (PhD in Computer and Information Science). He has been affiliated with the University of Detroit and is currently the W. Frank Barton endowed chair in MIS at Wichita State University. Dr. Dadashzadeh has served as the editor-in-chief of the *Journal of Database Management* (formerly *Journal of Database Administration*) and as a member of the Advisory Board for the Information Resources Management Association.

Deepti Dixit has an MS in Mechanical Engineering from Maulana Azad College of Technology, Bhopal, India, and a post-graduate course in Foreign Trade from the Indian Institution of Foreign Trade, New Delhi. She has extensive work experience in the field of materials management. She is completing her master's in Computer Science at the New Jersey Insitute of Technology.

Jorge H. Doorn is full professor in the Computer Science Department at the Universidad Nacional del Centro (UNCPBA), Argentina, since 1989. He has wide experience in actual industrial applications. He has been project leader in several projects, and currently he is the leader of the database research team at the Computer Science and Systems Department. His research interests include compilers design and database systems.

Cheryl Dunn is an assistant professor of accounting information systems at Florida State University. She earned her PhD in accounting at the Eli Broad Graduate School of Management at Michigan State University in 1994. Her research interests include behavioral, cognitive and memory issues involved with enterprise-wide information systems and particularly with the Resources-Events-Agents accounting model. Her research appears in *Journal of Information Systems, Advances in Accounting Information Systems,* and in the *International Journal of Accounting Information Systems*.

Viviana E. Ferraggine has received her BS degree in Systems Engineering from the Universidad Nacional del Centro (UNCPBA), Argentina, in 1997. She is currently an auxiliary assistant with the Department of Computer Science and Systems, and a master student in Computer Science at the Universidad Nacional de La Plata. Her research interests include database systems and data structures.

Roberto Galnares received his bachelor's degree from Universidad la Salle, A.C., Mexico. He has worked in the the computer and information systems field since 1980. He was awarded a Fulbright Scholarship for PhD studies in Computer and Information Sciences in 1995. Currently he is conducting research on hypermedia, Web technologies and Web engineering.

Marcela Genero is an assistant professor in the Department of Computer Science at the University of Comahue, Neuquén, Argentina. She received her MS degree in Computer Science from the National University of South Argentina in 1989. She is a PhD student at the University of Castilla-La Mancha, in Ciudad Real, Spain. Her research interests are: advanced databases design, software metrics, object-oriented metrics, conceptual data models quality and database quality. Her e-mail address is: mgenero@inf-cr.uclm.es.

Severin V. Grabski is an associate professor of Accounting Information Systems at the Eli Broad Graduate School of Management at Michigan State University. His research interests include behavioral and cognitive issues associated with the design and use of enterprise information systems, and the impact of information systems, in particular, enterprise systems on firm performance. His research has appeared in *MIS Quarterly, Information Technology & People, Journal of Information Systems, Cornell Quarterly, Journal of Applied Social Psychology, Advances in Accounting Information Systems,* and in the *International Journal of Accounting Information Systems*.

John A. Hoxmeier is an associate professor at Colorado State University. He received his PhD from the University of Colorado-Boulder, where his research included collaborative and group support systems. Prior to joining CSU in 1995, he was an executive VP and CIO at The Fuller Brush Company, where he was actively involved in a major IT reengineering effort and corporate acquisition. Dr. Hoxmeier's research includes data modeling, database design, information quality and E business system response time. He has published in many IT journals, including *Journal of Management Information Systems, Journal of End User Computing, Journal of Business* and *Management, Software Quality Journal and Journal of Applied Management Studies.* Dr. Hoxmeier has more than 20 years of database design, implementation and administration experience, is an active speaker, consultant and educator in the areas of IT strategy, database quality, performance and information management.

Aparna Kishna has a Master's of Science in Computer and Information Science from the New Jersey Institute of Technology, Newark, New Jersey and a Bachelor's of Technology in Computer Science and Engineering from the Jawaharlal Nehru Technological University, Hyderabad, India. Aparna is employed at Lucent Technologies, Holmdel, New Jersey.

Qiang Lu is a professor in the Computer Science Department at Suzhou University in the People's Republic of China. He currently is visiting at the New Jersey Institute of Technology.

Dr. Ronald Maier, born in 1968 in Linz, Austria, received his Master from the Johannes-Kepler-University of Linz, Austria in 1992 with High Honors. He received his PhD from the Koblenz School of Corporate Management-Otto Beisheim Graduate School of Management (WHU). His dissertation was on "Quality of Data Models". In 1998/1999 he spent a year as Visiting Assistant Professor at the University of Georgia in Athens, GA (USA), Terry College of Business, Department of Management Information Systems. Currently he works towards his habilitation about "Knowledge Management Systems - Concepts for the Application in Organizations" at the Department of Business Informatics at the University of Regensburg, Germany. His experience in data base design is based on a three-year period as software engineer and data base designer in a software house and numerous projects during his academic career. He published several articles about data management in journals and conference proceedings.

Esperanza Marcos is an associate professor in the *Department of Experimental Sciences and Engineering* at *King Juan Carlos University,* Madrid, Spain. She teaches Advanced Data Bases and Data Base Design and Information Security. She also teaches master's courses on software engineering. She received a PhD in Computer Sciences from the *Politechnical University of Madrid,* Spain, in 1997, and has been visiting scholar at the Telecom University, Paris, France. Professor Marcos is co-author of a book and has published several articles and book chapters. Her research interests include object-oriented database design, conceptual modelling and methodologies for software engineering research. Her e-mail address is: cuca@escet.urjc.es.

Eduardo Fernández-Medina Paton earned his MSc in Computer Science at the University of Sevilla. He is Assistant Professor at the Facultad de Ciencias Jurídicas y Sociales of the University of Castilla-La Mancha at Toledo. He has been a researcher and assistant professor for two years at the Universidad Antonio de Nebrija. He is a member of the ALARCOS Research Group, specializing in software engineering, database and information systems. He is a PhD candidate in secure database and personal data protection. He has an additional research line focused on methods of effort estimation for object-oriented systems. He is author of several articles and papers in national and international conferences on these two subjects. He belongs to the ATI association and collaborates with some working groups (Security Group and Software Engineering Group in AENOR). His e-mail address is: efmedina@jur-to.uclm.es.

Ido Millet is an associate professor of Management Information Systems at Penn State Erie. He received a BS in Industrial Engineering and Management from the Technion-Israel Institute of Technology, an MBA from Tel-Aviv University and a PhD in Information Systems from the Wharton School, University of Pennsylvania. His industrial experience includes systems analysis and project management for large-scale information systems, consulting and development of information systems. His research interests include management reporting systems, issue management systems and the analytic hierarchy process. His e-mail address is: ixm7@psu.edu.

Vincent Oria received his Diplôme d'Ingénieur in 1989 from the Institut National Polytechnique, Yamoussoukro, Côte d'Ivoire (Ivory Coast), a DEA in 1990 from Université Pierre et Marie Curie, Paris, France, and a PhD in 1994 in Computer Science from the Ecole Nationale Supérieure des Télécommunications (ENST), Paris, France. He worked as a research scientist at the ENST Paris from 1994 to 1996 before joining the Department of Computing Science of the University of Alberta, Canada, as a post-doctorate from 1996 to 1999. He is currently an assistant professor in the Department of Computer and Information Science at the New Jersey Institute of Technology. His current research interests include multimedia databases, geographical information systems, data management issues in e-commerce and e-learning.

Mehdi Owrang is currently a professor of Computer Science in the Department of Computer Science and Information Systems at American University in Washington, DC. Dr. Owrang received his BA degree in Economics in 1975 from the College of Economics and Social Sciences, Babolsar Iran, and his MS and PhD degrees in Computer Science from the University of Oklahoma in 1980 and 1986, respectively. He has authored or co-authored 40 papers in computer journals and conferences. His current research interests include rule-based expert systems development, automatic knowledge acquisitions, database modeling, distributed databases, intelligent databases, knowledge discovery in databases, optimization and validation in knowledge discovery. Dr. Owrang has been a program committee member of several ACM, IEEE, ISCA and IASTED conferences. He is a member of the ACM, IEEE and ISMM; editorial board member of the database journal, and the associate editor of the *Software and Information Engineering* of the ISCA Journal.

David Paper is an associate professor at Utah State University in the Business Information Systems Department. He received his PhD in MIS from Southern Illinois University. He has several refereed publications appearing in journals such as *Journal of Technology Cases and Applications, Journal of Systems and Information Technology, Long Range Planning, Knowledge and Process Management, Creativity and Innovation, Accounting Management and Information Technologies* and *Journal of Computer Information Systems*. He has also spent time in industry working for Texas Instruments, DLS, Inc., the Phoenix Small Business Administration and Wides Village Real Estate Company. His teaching and research interests include global electronic commerce, business process reengineering and database management.

Parag C. Pendharkar is assistant professor of Information Systems at Penn State Harrisburg. His research interests are in artificial intelligence and expert systems. His work has appeared in the *Annals of Operations Research, Communications of ACM, Decision Sciences* and several other publications. He is a member of INFORMS, APUBEF and DSI.

Mario Piattini is an MSc and a PhD in Computer Science from the Poltechnical University of Madrid, is a Certified Information System Auditor by ISACA (Information System Audit and Control Association), associate professor at the Escuela Superior de Informática of the Castilla-La Mancha University, and author of several books and papers on databases, software engineering and information systems. He leads the ALARCOS research group of the Department of Computer Science at the University of Castilla-La Mancha, in Ciudad Real, Spain. His research interests include: advanced database design, database quality, software metrics, object-oriented metrics and software maintenance. His e-mail address: is mpiattin@inf-cr.uclm.es.

Mahesh S. Raisinghani is the founder and CEO of Raisinghani and Associates, a diversified global firm with interests in software consulting and technology options trading. As a faculty member at the Graduate School of Management, University of Dallas, he teaches MBA courses in information systems and e-commerce, and serves as the director of research for the Center for Applied Information Technology. As a global thought leader on e-business and global information systems, he has been invited to serve as the local chair of the World Conference on Global Information Technology Management and the track chair for E-Commerce Technologies at the Information Resources Management Association.He has published in numerous leading scholarly and practitioner journals, presented at leading world-level scholarly conferences and has recently published his book *E-Commerce: Opportunities and Challenges*. He has been invited to serve as the editor of the special issue of the *Journal of Electronic Commerce Research on Intelligent Agents in E-Commerce*. Dr. Raisinghani was also selected by the National Science Foundation after a nationwide search to serve as a panelist on the Information Technology Research Panel and the E-Commerce Research Panel for Small Business Innovation. He serves on the editorial review board for leading information systems publications and is included in the millennium edition of *Who's Who in the World, Who's Who Among America's Teachers* and *Who's Who in Information*

Technology. He can be reached at: mraising@gsm.udallas.edu.

Laura Rivero received her BS degree in Systems Analysis from the Universidad Nacional del Centro (UNCPBA), Argentina, in 1979. She is a professor in the Department of Computer Science and Systems of the UNCPBA and a doctoral student in Computer Science at the Universidad Nacional de La Plata. Her lecturing and research activities concentrate on data structures and database design and integrity.

James A. Rodger is an associate professor of Management Information Systems at Indiana University of Pennsylvania (IUP). He received his Doctorate in MIS from Southern Illinois University at Carbondale in 1997. Dr. Rodger teaches network administration, system architecture, microcomputer applications and Intro to MIS, at IUP. He has worked as an installation coordinator for Sunquest Information Systems, and presently does consulting work on telemedicine connectivity for the Department of Defense and Management Technology Services Inc. Dr. Rodger has published several journal articles related to these subjects. His most recent article, "Telemedicine and the Department of Defense" was published in *Communications of the ACM.*

Manoj K. Singh is a senior consultant with i2 Technologies Inc., a leader in intelligent e-business solutions and supply chain optimization software. He has extensive experience in architecting and deploying e-business solutions. As part of his job, he has been working with leading players in the high-technology industry sector, like PC manufacturers, semiconductor and telecommunications, and helping them in defining the B2B strategy and solutions for procurement and collaboration with their partners. He has an article on manufacturing optimization in the *International Journal of Production Research.* He holds a BS in Mechanical Engineering and an MS in Industrial Engineering, and is currently pursuing an MBA in Information Technology. His e-mail address is: manoj_singh@i2.com.

Manolis Tzagarakis holds a Diploma in Computer Engineering and Informatics from the University of Patras, Greece, where he currently is pursuing his PhD. He is collaborating with Research Unit II of the Computer Technology Institute (CTI), Greece, working on hypertext and database systems. His research interests include open hypermedia systems, hypermedia models, structural computing and database management systems.

Michalis Vaitis holds a Diploma in Computer Engineering and Informatics from the University of Patras, Greece, where he also is studying for his PhD. He is collaborating with Research Unit II of the Computer Technology Institute (CTI), Greece, working on hypertext and database systems. His research interests include hypermedia models and services, structural computing and databases interoperability. He is a student member of the ACM.

Suk-Chung Yoon received MA and PhD degrees in Computer Science from Northwestern University, Evanston, Illinois, in 1988 and 1991, respectively. He is currently an associate professor in the Department of Computer Science at Widener University, Chester, Pennsylvania. His main research interests include data mining, data warehousing and Web-based systems. He has published more than 20 papers in journals and international conferences, and has served on program committees for dozens of international conferences and workshops.

Li Zhang received her Bachelor's degree in Biomedical Engineering from Xi'an Jiaotong University, China. She holds a master's in Electrical Engineering from Southeast University, China. Currently she is pursuing her PhD in Computer Science at the New Jersey Institute of Technology.

Index